Through a Black Veil

Through a Black Veil

Readings in French Caribbean Poetry

E. Anthony Hurley

Africa World Press, Inc.

P.O. Box 1892
Trenton, NJ 08607

P.O. Box 48
Asmara, ERITREA

Africa World Press, Inc.

P.O. Box 1892
Trenton, NJ 08607

P.O. Box 48
Asmara, ERITREA

Cover design: Jonathan Gullery

Library of Congress Cataloging-in-Publication Data

Hurley, E. Anthony.
    Through a black viel : readings in French Caribbean poetry / by E. Anthony Hurley.
       p.   cm.
    In English, with some text in French.
    Includes bibliographical references and index.
    ISBN 0-86543-595-2. -- ISBN 0-86543-596-0 (pbk.)
    1. Caribbean poetry (French) -- History and criticism. I. Title.
PQ3942.H87   1998
840.9'9729--dc21

98-19102
CIP

PQ3942
.H87
1998

To Dorothy,

my first reader, best friend, and soul mate

my undying love and appreciation.

Contents

Acknowledgements

The author and publisher would like to thank the following for permission to reprint their material:

Editions Gallimard — extracts from *Un champ d'île*, *La terre inquiète*, and *Les Indes* in *Poèmes complètes* by Edouard Glissant © Gallimard, 1994.

Editions du Seuil — extracts from *Cadastre* by Aimé Césaire © Editions du Seuil, 1961.

Présence Africaine — extracts from *Pigments* by L.-G. Damas © Présence Africaine, 1962, from *Névralgies* by L.-G. Damas © Présence Africaine, 1970, and from *Balles d'or* by Guy Tirolien © Présence Africaine, 1961.

L'Harmattan — extracts from *Martinique debout* by Joseph Polius © L'Harmattan, 1977.

Imprimerie Bené — extracts from *Clins d'œil* by Gilette Bazile ©
Imprimerie Bené, 1988.

Joseph Polius — extracts from *Bonheur de Poche* and *Martinique debout*.

Yves Padoly — extracts from *Le Missel noir*.

Yolande Marie-Magdeleine — Marie-Magdeleine Carbet's poems.

Preface

I am not sure what were the first poetic voices I heard. I have more or less confused early childhood memories of the rhythms of folk songs and religious songs sung by my mother, grandmother, great-grandmother, and aunts, of calypsos sung by my uncles, of the iambic pentameters of English poets recited by my father. I cannot remember making any distinction of quality or importance among these voices. For me they grew to constitute access to a realm of experience, knowledge, joy, and beauty beyond the too many frustrations of daily life. Later, I somehow gained the impression that there were hierarchies in poetic expression, that the productions of the Greeks, Romans, British, and French were inevitably superior, intellectually, morally, and aesthetically, to the productions of people like myself from the Caribbean. So while I continued to be viscerally more attracted to certain musical and poetic voices, particularly African American and Caribbean, I was at the same time aware that this attraction was an indication of the baseness of my nature and of my lack of real civilization. Consequently I pursued my studies of French literature (which, I had become convinced, was by any standards at the top of the literary hierarchy) with compulsive enthusiasm, knowing that my mastery of this field gave me entitlement to a truly superior level of civilization. In my undergraduate program I became part of an elite group of Special Honours French students who made an intensive and extensive study of French language and literature. After graduating top of my class with the rare distinction of First Class Honours, I proceeded to London where I continued for four years my study of French literature. At the end of that period I felt confident of my expertise in my chosen field and was offered and accepted a position at the University of the West Indies in Jamaica as a nineteenth-century specialist. It was then that a West Indian colleague introduced me to Aimé Césaire's *Cahier d'un retour au pays natal/Return to My Native Land*. It was a shock and a revelation. I felt shocked and even ashamed that in the many years up to that point that I had studied French literature I had never become aware of writings in French by black people from the Caribbean. Césaire's book was a revelation in its power, the conspicuously high quality of the writing, and in its personal relevance to me as a black West Indian. But it was also difficult to read, not only because of a self-consciously opaque and often erudite vocabulary, but because of its apparently deliberate transgression of what I had been trained to accept as the traditions of good French poetry. Even though I immediately loved it, I also felt that my attraction had to be secret, like my childhood attraction to prohibited "banjo" music, to calypso, and to writers from the English-speaking Caribbean like George Lamming, Samuel Selvon, and Edgar Mittelholzer. It was this experience that started me on my journey to discover more and more about French Antillean writing, and it was just two or three years later that my colleagues and I started teaching courses in French Caribbean and French African literature at the University of the West Indies.

The original impetus for the present volume came from the need my Caribbean colleagues and I felt even then for texts that provided a mixture of general historical background and critical commentary on a body of written material for readers whose access to such information was severely limited. Since then much has changed, both in the critical treatment of French Caribbean literature and in my own professional career. There is a difference, I have noticed, between teaching such literature to mainly Caribbean students in the Caribbean in the 1970s and teaching it in the United States in the 1990s. The main difference, I have found, is that in the Caribbean, then and now, it is unnecessary for West Indians to have to explain who and what they are as the source of their critical perspective to a student or to a colleague; whereas, in the US, I have consistently felt pressured by some colleagues and students to justify my right as a black person to teach or read from my own perspective. This new concern has had an impact on the critical and ideological stances I adopt in this study. I will explain later in the Introduction the critical climate that has contributed most to the shaping of these stances.

Introduction

U ndertaking an examination of a body of literature designated as "French Caribbean" requires a discussion of certain questions that impinge on such a designation: questions of definition and of the historical and literary contexts within which such a literature must be situated. A convenient starting point is the problem of defining what constitutes the French Caribbean. Within the geopolitical area known as the Caribbean, there are four main territories with long-term cultural and political links to France: Haiti (sharing part of the large Antillean island previously called Hispaniola with the Dominican Republic), the islands of Martinique and Guadeloupe, and Guyane on the northern coast of South America. To these comparatively larger territories may be added the small island dependencies of Les Saintes, Marie-Galante, La Désirade, and Saint-Barthélemy, and the northern half of Saint-Martin. While the cultural impact of France remains strong in Haiti, and French is the language of choice for the upper classes as well as for many intellectuals and writers, yet that country has been independent since 1804 and cannot be considered as "French." The political status of the territories of Martinique,

Guadeloupe, and Guyane, however, is totally different. They are all overseas departments of France and hence definitely "French."

According to Caribbean historian Hilary Beckles (1990), the populations occupying the Caribbean islands in the fifteenth and sixteenth centuries when the waves of European attempts at conquest in the Americas gained momentum were communities of what are now called Saladoid-Barrancoid people (Galibis, Arawaks, Caribs) who had migrated from the Orinoco region of the South American mainland to the islands and traded among themselves (6). Some of them may have spoken a language similar to what became known as Arawakan (2). The Spaniards had apparently tried to take possession of Guadeloupe when Columbus landed there for the second time in 1496 (the first time having been in 1493), but met with fierce resistance from the indigenous communities of Caribs or Kalinagos. Three successive attempts were made to conquer Guadeloupe, first in 1515, again in 1520, and it was only in 1523 that the English and Spaniards were finally able to take possession of the island. Beckles reports that "[d]uring the second half of the sixteenth century, Amerindians in the Lesser Antilles, referred to by Europeans as Caribs, managed to organize a military force in the Windwards — St. Lucia, St. Vincent, Grenada and Dominica — which held up the pace and undermined the effectiveness of European colonisation" (6). Thus the history of the region is marked by unsuccessful but repeated attempts by local groups to repel the European intruders and to resist being dominated by them.

The French presence in the Caribbean goes back to 1625[1], when the French landed on the island they named Saint-Christophe, now St. Kitts. It is reported that the French entered into alliances with the Amerindian population of Caribs they found in these islands (who had been resisting the Spanish conquistadors since the end of the fifteenth century) to combat a common enemy, the Spaniards. The French then turned on the Caribs to gain possession of the islands of Guadeloupe, Martinique, Marie-Galante, and Saint Lucia. Within 40 years the Caribs were almost totally wiped out by disease and treachery. In 1626 France, represented by Pierre d'Esnambuc, gained official possession of Guadeloupe and by 1635 had occupied both Guadeloupe and Martinique. From 1635, with the slave trade already established, France started to colonize Martinique and Guadeloupe and around 1680 began a massive importation of Africans to replace a labor force of indentured whites who were succumbing to the combined effects of climate and hard labor. The French colony of Cayenne was founded in 1643 and became officially French in 1677. In 1685 the infamous Code Noir [Black Code] was published, establishing a legal basis for the slave trade. This Code legitimized plantation society, formalized the rights and responsibilities of slave owners, specified forms of punishments for slaves guilty of resistance (including whipping, chaining, mutilation, and amputation), forbade among other things sexual relations between blacks and whites, and condemned the children of unions between masters and slaves — as well as their mothers — to perpetual enslavement. In 1794 the Cayenne colony became French Guyana and was used primarily for interning convicts. In 1852 the famous prison was built and was not closed until 1947. When gold was discovered in Guyane in the mid 1850s that territory saw the invasion of tens of thousands of adventurers of different sorts, both from the Caribbean and from Europe.

Slavery was temporarily abolished in the colonies by the Revolutionary Convention government in France in 1794 but was reimposed forcibly by Napoleon Bonaparte, who sent military expeditions to the Caribbean to ensure that this be done. There was fierce resistance throughout the Caribbean. In 1802 in Guadeloupe, for instance, the Martinican Louis Delgrès and the Guadeloupean Ignace, officers in the French army, fought valiantly against the attempt to reimpose slavery. The group of resistance fighters was finally surrounded by a French expeditionary force under Richepanse and they opted to blow themselves up at Matouba in Guadeloupe rather than surrender. Meanwhile in Santo Domingo slaves led by Toussaint Louverture defeated the Napoleonic forces and declared the country's independence in 1804 under the Amerindian name of Haiti. The decree for the abolition was eventually published in 1848. In the 1850s East Indians and Chinese were recruited as indentured laborers to replace the newly liberated blacks on the sugar plantations. Syrian immigrants started to arrive in the 1870s.

Even after the abolition of slavery, resistance to European domination continued. 1870 witnessed a revolt in the south of Martinique by a group trying to wrest political and economic power from the hands of the local whites. The revolt was crushed. Martinique, Guadeloupe, and Guyane became overseas departments in 1946 — effectively part of France — by a law proposed by Aimé Césaire, but this did not put an end to resistance to French domination. In 1967 there were riots in Guadeloupe, supported by the Groupement de l'Organization nationaliste Guadeloupéenne, when a European set his dog on a black shoemaker. Forty Guadeloupeans were killed and several others were arrested and tried. Jean-Paul Sartre and Aimé Césaire pleaded on their behalf and they were acquitted. The year 1974 witnessed the massacre of several agricultural workers on a banana plantation in Martinique by metropolitan anti-riot police. A regional council was set up in 1983 for these territories, suggesting a greater level of administrative autonomy. Even in the 1990s, however, resistance to what is seen by many as French cultural and economic imperialism still continues.

This brief historical survey underlines the fact that the whole notion of a history of the French Caribbean is fraught with obscurity and ambiguity. The French Caribbean is in any case a European invention, so that even professional Caribbean historians experience difficulty in drawing lines of distinction between the history (the stories and perspectives) of the Caribbean people and that of Europeans (their stories and perspectives) in the Caribbean. Moreover, despite the present political status of Caribbean territories, even those that are independent states, it is difficult to refrain from imposing the dates of significant European events (landings, letters patent, emancipation decrees, etc.) as the focal points of Caribbean history. There are, in fact, at least two parallel and often conflicting histories always at play in the Caribbean: that of the non-white Caribbean masses and that of whites, local and overseas. There is an additional conflict of histories between all locals (including whites) and the metropole. This situation prompts the question: Whose history is the authentic history? The answer is that all of them are, since all these groups can rightfully claim a form of "authorship" of the disputed sociopolitical, cultural, and geographical space.

The designation of a body of literature as "French Caribbean" presents a similar problem, since the French Caribbean does not exist as an independent national unit. This fact provokes the following question: Is it possible to draw lines of demarcation between French Caribbean literature and French literature, when it is a political fact that the French Caribbean is part of France and participates in the French cultural traditions? The ambiguous relationship between France and the French Caribbean is reflected in the problem of determining who may be considered to be a French Caribbean writer. There is no *de iure* French Caribbean official identity, therefore the following possibilities need to be considered as legitimate claimants: a person born of French Caribbean parents and brought up in the French Caribbean; a person born and brought up in the French Caribbean but with only one French Caribbean parent; a person born and brought up in the French Caribbean but whose parents are not French Caribbean; a person born of French Caribbean parents but brought up elsewhere; a person born and brought up somewhere else, but who has a French Caribbean parent; a person brought up in the French Caribbean, but who was not born there and neither of whose parents is French Caribbean[2]. This indicates that there is a large measure of individual choice in claiming or privileging a French Caribbean identity.

The identity of the literature we designate as French Caribbean needs also to be related to the literary tradition or traditions within which it is located. Antillean author-critics, particularly Maryse Condé, Marie-Magdeleine Carbet, Willy Alante-Lima, Edouard Glissant, Patrick Chamoiseau, and Raphaël

Confiant, have drawn surprisingly unconflicting, interconnected, and mutually complementary pictures of the history of this literature. The variations that exist in their analyses result more from differences in perspective than from any fundamental contradictions.

The Guadeloupean Maryse Condé (1977) relates the history of French Caribbean poetry to social evolutionary developments within a framework of vaguely chronological but sometimes overlapping movements. The first movement identified by Condé represents the productions of the white minority, who alone had access to formal education. Some of these writers, like Poirié de Saint-Aurèle and Nicolas-Germain Léonard, celebrated the superiority of the white race and opposed the liberation or social rehabilitation of blacks. Others (like Vincent Campenon, Pinel Dumanoir, and Auguste Lacour) produced nostalgic poetry that ignored social problems and focused on the beauty of the tropical landscape and plantation society. In an attempt to justify this slave society, these writers produced stereotypical representations of blacks. Condé even cites a poet of color, Privat d'Anglement, who displayed no interest in people of color or even in his native island. Condé recognizes a second movement, corresponding to the end of the nineteenth and the beginning of the twentieth century, that was dominated by exoticism. Within this movement Condé places poets like Fernand and Daniel Thaly, René Chalupt, and Emmanuel-Flavia Léopold, who focused on descriptions of the Caribbean décor. According to Condé, this strain of literary production has persisted throughout the twentieth century, as some of the work of André Thomarel, Jean-Louis Baghio'o, and Marie-Magdeleine Carbet would attest. Condé identifies a third movement of regionalist poetry, in which poets like Gilbert de Chambertrand, Gilbert Gratiant, and Florette Morand focus more on the social situation of people of color. Marie-Magdeleine Carbet (1985) agrees in part with Condé but claims that it was the abolition of slavery that generated the birth of a regionalist literature colored with exoticism, following the Romantic current then popular in

Europe. Carbet cites as representatives of this current the white René Bonneville, Victor Duquesnay, Augustin Ferréol (b. 1892 who used the pen-names of Marcel Achard and Jean Foyal), Virgile Savane (who wrote under the name of Salavina), and Drasta Houel. According to Condé, a fourth strain appears with the Negritude movement, with adherents from all over the Caribbean, principally Léon Damas, Serge Patient, Christian Rollé, and Elie Stephenson from Guyane, Aimé Césaire and Georges Desportes from Martinique, and Guy Tirolien from Guadeloupe. This has been followed by Glissant's movement of "Antillanité," supported by poets such as Henri Corbin and Gérard Delisle. Other recent movements have manifested a renewed focus on Creole, most notably by Sonny Rupaire and Hector Poullet and a host of other young writers. Condé points out that there had always been literature written in Creole either by Antilleans or by French residents.

No account of French Caribbean literature can ignore the importance of the three principal literary and sociocultural "movements" of the twentieth century French Caribbean — Negritude, Antilleanity, and Creolity —which have stimulated tremendous creative energy and have been at the root of much of the literary production, particularly of male writers. It must be cautioned, however, that there is a substantial body of literature, written both by women and men, that does not fit neatly into any of the ideological or theoretical patterns implicit in those perspectives.

The story of the rise and fall of Negritude has been so well documented (Kesteloot 1963; Irele 1981; Gérard 1986) that a detailed recapitulation would be redundant. Within the French Caribbean context, Negritude is inextricably linked to the Martinican Aimé Césaire, who was the first to use the term in a literary work. When Césaire arrived in Paris in the early 1930s, he came to what was effectively the cultural center of a Europe that was experiencing a variety of influences, not all of them welcome. Germany was a lit fuse and Russian Communism was proving uncomfortably attractive to many workers. Du Bois's *Souls of Black*

Folk had been translated into French and was available. Paris had been host to DuBois's First Pan-African Congress in 1919, a conference that may be regarded as a continuation of the movement initiated by the Trinidadian lawyer, Henry Sylvester Williams, who had organized a Pan-African conference in London in 1900. This Pan-African movement was the first step toward the common identity that was later to be expressed through Negritude. Marcus Garvey is reported as speaking at another conference in Europe around 1920-21 about African citizenship and an African "nationhood," attached more or less automatically to racial identity. The works of the Harlem Renaissance writers, particularly the writings of Langston Hughes, were available in translation. Hughes's manifesto, published in the journal *Fire* in 1926, stated: "We, the makers of the new black generation, want to express our black personality shamelessly and fearlessly. If White people appreciate, we are delighted. If they do not, we do not care...." This manifesto attracted attention among black intellectuals in Paris. Issues of the Black American periodicals *Crisis* and *Opportunity* were also available in translation and were read by Caribbean and African students and intellectuals in Paris. Césaire himself was to prepare a thesis on the theme of the South in Black American Literature in the US. The Haitian ethnographer, Dr. Jean Price-Mars, had published *Ainsi parla l'Oncle* in 1928, in which he insisted that Haitians were not colored French people, but a people of a double heritage born under specific historical conditions. Price-Mars also suggested that if Haitians wanted to be themselves they could not reject any part of their ancestral heritage — which was, for the most part, a gift from Africa. A Martinican woman, Jeanne Nardal, had started calling herself an Afro-Latin and, in 1930, in collaboration with the Haitian Dr. Sajous, launched the periodical *La Revue du Monde Noir/Review of the Black World*, a truly bilingual French/English publication, with every article translated. Its expressed aims were to provide the intellectual elite of the Black Race and their friends with an organ in which they could publish their artistic, literary, and scientific works; to study and publish everything related to Negro Civilization and the natural riches of Africa, the sacred motherland of the Black Race; and to create an intellectual and moral link between Blacks the world over (J. Nardal 1932: *Foreword*). Césaire himself a couple of years later took over the direction of another student journal, changing its title from *The Martinican Student* and renaming it *The Black Student*. It was here, according to Martin Steins (1986), that the Senegalese Léopold Sédar Senghor first posits an "âme nègre," a black soul, as the inspiration of an African civilization, and envisioned "a cultural movement that has the black man as its aim, western reason and the black soul as instruments of research" (*L'Etudiant Noir*, March 1935). But whereas Senghor came to the conclusion that biculturalism was the solution for the future, Césaire, basing his approach on the physical blackness of Africans, established a firm link between "race" and civilization and developed the idea of his participation in a racial culture with African origins.

Negritude has sometimes been dismissed as the manifestation of a French Caribbean sensibility, as the literary and ideological movement of a few French-speaking black intellectuals. Such a narrow interpretation carries the implication that the applicability of Negritude beyond this narrow circle of adherents is severely limited. In fact, it is clear that in the early decades of this century blacks from different geographical locations were struggling with and articulating similar concerns, in relation to an awareness of solidarity among themselves as black people.

The Guyanese Léon-Gontran Damas was the first of the Negritude triumvirate (comprising Damas, Césaire, and Senghor) to publish a literary text that owed its inspiration to "negritude," even though the term is not explicitly mentioned in the body of the text. In 1937 Damas published a slim volume of poems bearing the significant title *Pigments*. In its dedication it bore a quotation from Claude MacKay, "Be not deceived, for every deed you do I could match, outmatch: Am I not Africa's son. Black of that black land where black deeds are done." This collection exhibited a clear awareness of the significance and responsibility of biological and cultural blackness. The first time the word "negritude" appears in a literary text is in Césaire's *Cahier d'un retour au pays natal* [*Return To My Native Land*], first published in 1939 in an obscure journal, *Volontés*. The term is first used at a point in the poem when the poet is trying to define what is his, what belongs to him, and to delineate those elements that form part of his geographical, historical, and cultural identity. Included in the list of his possessions is "Haiti where negritude first stood up and said it believed in its humanity" (Césaire 1971:67; this and all subsequent translations mine unless otherwise indicated). Negritude is clearly associated here with a group of black people existing in a problematic relationship to a "white" world that resists accepting the humanity of blacks. Negritude in this context implies self-awareness, but also self-affirming action — independent of the actions, expectations, and opposition of whites. Another reference to negritude in the text occurs when the poet-protagonist, as he moves towards full acceptance of himself as a black man, recounts his encounter with a black "bum" in a trolley (103). Here negritude refers specifically to the man's pigmentation, to his biological blackness. But the incident enables the poet to become more lucid, more honest, to get in touch with his own cowardice, his desire to distance himself publicly from his unfortunate brother-in-negritude. The most often cited reference to negritude is this often misunderstood or misinterpreted passage that occurs toward the end of the poem, when the poet reaches the stage of ecstatic pride in all aspects of his negritude, paying tribute to:

> those who invented neither gunpowder nor compass
> those who never vanquished steam nor electricity
> those who explored neither seas nor sky
> but those without whom the earth would not be the earth
> ....

my negritude is not a stone, its deafness hurled against
the clamor of the day
my negritude is not a speck of dead water on the dead eye of the earth
my negritude is neither a tower nor a cathedral
it plunges into the red flesh of the earth
it plunges into the ardent flesh of the sky
it perforates opaque dejection with its upright patience
Eïa for the royal *Kaïlcedrat*!
Eïa for those who never invented anything
who never explored anything
who never conquered anything
but who abandon themselves to the essence of all things
ignorant of surfaces, caught by the motion of all things
indifferent to conquering but playing the game of the world
truly the eldest sons of the world
porous to all the breath of the world (115-119)

Césaire, unlike Senghor, never devoted much effort to articulating a comprehensive definition of negritude. For him negritude was "the simple recognition of the fact of being black, and the acceptance of this fact, of our destiny as blacks, of our history and of our culture," arising out of the awareness of the dangers of depending on European criteria for judgements of humanity.

The term "Antillanité" [Antilleanity], more acceptable to many Caribbean intellectuals than "Negritude" (which tended to privilege African roots to the exclusion of other cultural influences), was first used by Glissant in the mid-1950s and analyzed in his theoretical writings and published interviews to connote the specificity of the Caribbean islands. (For a full discussion of the term, see Roget 1975: 155-234). Unlike Negritude or Creolity, Antilleanity is not inscribed specifically in any one text, although Glissant's *L'Intention poétique* provides an intensive elaboration of the concept. Antilleanity as proposed by Glissant presents itself as a coherent "prise de position" that does not necessitate minimizing the cultural importance of Africa but privileges the consideration of historical and geographical factors. It suggests that all Caribbean people (of color) have more in common among themselves even across differences of language than with Europeans speaking the same language. "*Antillanité*" as conceived by Glissant includes an acceptance of the significant difference of the Antillean islands as islands from continents, even from Africa:

> La terre immense en Afrique ouvre sur l'irrué: le monde y est tentation gigantesque de l'Autre. Nous ne connaissons pas, insulaires, ce vertige allé de la terre.... Notre champ est de mer, qui limite et qui ouvre. L'île appelle d'autres îles. Des Antilles.... (Glissant 1969: 158)

> [The immense land in Africa opens on to the untrodden: the world there is a gigantic temptation of the Other. We, islanders, do not know about this vast vertigo of land.... Our field is sea, which both limits and opens. An island calls other islands. Antilles....]

Antillanité also includes an acceptance of the variety of cultural influences that contribute to the specificity of the Antilles. The undeniable and characteristic feature of this Antillean cultural identity is its composite nature, which Glissant designates as "le métissage" [racial mixing]:

> [C]ette communauté dépérit d'accepter sa honte (le métissage), faute de promouvoir en valeur le

composite (qui n'est pas ici le disparate). Ni le mot
ni sa réalité signifiée ne sont à rejeter. La Relation
porte l'univers au fécond métissage. (219)

[By not accepting its shame (racial mixing), this
community is dying, because it does not promote
the value of the composite (which in this case is
not disparate). Neither the word nor the reality it
signifies should be rejected. Relationship carries
the universe to a fruitful crossbreeding.]

In *Poétique de la relation [Poetics of Relation]*, Glissant (1990)
discusses   two   variants   of   identity,   "l'identité-racine"
[identity-as-root] and "l'identité-relation" [identity-as-relation] (219).
According   to   Glissant,   it   is   within   the   framework   of
identity-as-relation that the specificity of the Caribbean's culture
becomes validated:

Ainsi les littératures de la Caraïbe, qu'elles soient
de langue anglaise, espagnole ou française ....
ne peuvent plus être estimées des appendices
exotiques aux corps littéraires français, anglais ou
espagnols; ... elles entrent soudain, avec la force
d'une tradition qu'elles se sont elles-mêmes forgée,
dans la relation des cultures. (85)

[Thus the literatures of the Caribbean, whether
they be English, Spanish or French ... can no
longer be considered exotic appendices to the
French, English or Spanish literary bodies; ... they
suddenly enter, with the force of a tradition that
they have forged themselves, into the relation of
cultures.]

The most recent attempt by Caribbean writers to define a cultural identity has resulted in the adoption of "Creolity" in a published manifesto (Bernabé et al. 1989). It must be remembered, however, that this term, like Negritude, is grounded in a long-standing tradition within the French Caribbean intellectual tradition. Before the term "negritude" was first used by Césaire in the *Cahier*, French Caribbean writers in Paris had been experimenting with other designations for what they perceived as their true identity. Some were attracted by the notion of sharing in a "pan-nègre" [pan-negro] identity, under the influence of ideas trickling in from the conferences organized by both Du Bois and Marcus Garvey. It is of some significance that women were at the forefront of this search in Paris for an appropriate cultural designator. The Martinican Jeanne Nardal, for example, felt it was impossible to deny any aspect of the two major components of her cultural identity and, as I indicated earlier, referred to herself as an "Afro-Latin." In the April 1932 issue of *The Review of the Black World*, Jeanne's sister, Paulette Nardal, published an article entitled "Awakening of Race Consciousness" that signified her interest in cultivating a specific cultural identity. Nardal noted the fact that certain Antilleans had already been stirred to race consciousness as a result of having left their small native islands: "The uprooting and the ensuing estrangement they felt in the metropolis, where Negroes have not always been so favourably received as they seem to be since the Colonial Exhibition, had given them a real Negro soul, in spite of their Latin education" (P. Nardal 1932: 25). What is significant about the *Review* is that women rather than men provided its driving force. In fact, it was the only periodical we know of, particularly from the period that was to produce Negritude, that had women at the helm, and it made the claim that it was women students in Paris who were in the forefront of the race consciousness and racial solidarity movement among blacks.

Willy Alante-Lima (1985), like other French Caribbean literary historians, notes that the poets of the nineteenth and early twentieth century were for the most part related to the plantocracy:

Poirier de Saint-Aurèle, Nicolas-Germain Léonard, Vincent Campenon, Pinel Dumanoir, Auguste Lacour, and Privat d'Anglemont (*sic*). She further observes that there existed, even in the nineteenth century and at the beginning of the twentieth, poets who favored Creole poetry — most notably, around 1860 Paul Baudot (known as Fondoc), later Gilbert de Chambertrand, and during the first World War the veterinarian Rémy Nainsouta, who actually founded a Creole Academy. Two of the principal proponents of Creolity, Patrick Chamoiseau and Raphaël Confiant (1991), in a study of Creole elements in Caribbean letters, allude to the emergence, at the very end of the nineteenth century, of a mulatto intelligentsia greedy to capture a culture that promised to transform half-beasts into full men (88). Like Condé, Chamoiseau and Confiant present this group as practitioners of regionalist and doudouist poetry. Chamoiseau and Confiant, however, provide the additional insight that this group started to develop political consciousness and the feeling of belonging to a specificity. They place in this group: Daniel Thaly (1879-1950), who, born in Dominica of Martinican parents and brought up in Martinique, studied medicine in Toulouse, and remained torn between Dominica, Martinique, and France; Victor Duquesnay (1870-1920), a light-skinned Martinican; the Guadeloupean Eugène Agricole (1834-1901); the Martinican Marraud de Sigalony (b. 1890); Salavina (b. 1865); Maurice Boyer (1974-1938); and Fernand Thaly (1882-1947). According to Chamoiseau and Confiant, the early twentieth century witnessed a double movement: the assimilation of the Caribbean elites into metropolitan cultural models and the increasing rootedness of the colored middle class into popular creole culture. Chamoiseau and Confiant (1991) note further that light-skinned, economically privileged French Caribbean writers like Gilbert Chambertrand (1895-1985) and Marie-Thérèse Lung-fou (1909-1980) in Martinique, and in Guadeloupe Rémy Nainsouta and Gilbert de Chambertrand (b. 1890) (who, Chamoiseau and Confiant point out, was a local white assimilated into colored society because his marriage infringed the endogamous rules of his caste), started to stake a claim for Creole language and culture (105-6).

It is incumbent at this juncture to examine more closely a notion (Creolity) that, we shall see, is fraught with more ambiguity than either Negritude or Antilleanity. Ambiguity arises as soon as we try to answer the question: What in fact is a Creole? The Petit Larousse dictionary gives as its definition of a Creole: a white race person born in the former colonies (particularly the Antilles and Guyane). For the Creole language it gives: a language coming from a speech constituted of borrowings from several languages (particularly based on French, English, or Spanish) and become the maternal language of a linguistic community (as in the Antilles, Haiti, Reunion, etc.). The American Webster's (1971 ed.), citing the etymology of French créole, from the Spanish *criolla*, from the Portuguese *crioulo*, meaning a white person born in the colonies, gives the following "modern" applications: 1. a person of native birth but of European descent — used especially in the West Indies and Spanish America; 2. a white person descended from early French or Spanish settlers of the US Gulf states and preserving their speech and culture; 3. a person of mixed French or Spanish and Negro descent speaking a dialect of French or Spanish; and 4. the French spoken by many Negroes in southern Louisiana. It is worthy of note that in both the French and the Euro-American dictionaries the primary referent for both the language and the individual is Europe. This conflicts with the opinion of some Caribbean linguists who believe that the referent ought to be African, since the one factor that all so-called Creole languages have in common is their African base. Hubert Devonish (1986) suggests that "while African languages brought to the region presented a partial picture of diversity, particularly in their vocabulary and superficial syntactic features, they shared a lot in common in the area of phonology, semantics and underlying syntactic features" (41). He states further:

> The fact that Caribbean Creole languages owe their
> existence to the continuity of African language

features under some degree of influence from European languages, has encouraged Alleyne (1980) to consider that the term 'Creole' is a misnomer, and that these languages should be more correctly referred to as 'Afro-American.' (42)

"Creole" therefore is a term that conceals or disguises the African association and this may partly explain why the use of the Creole language in the context of French Caribbean literature was for a long time to a large extent folkloric and decorative. There tends in any case to be some confusion between Creole as a linguistic phenomenon and as a sociocultural identity. Naturally, there is an area of overlap, particularly when the language is associated with a cultural specificity or a politico-ideological position as a vector of culture or of nationalist opinion. This overlap has acquired currency in the recent struggles — particularly in Guadeloupe — for greater autonomy, where Creole has been and is being used deliberately in the political arena and in trade union activities, as a means of signifying nationalist aspirations. Particularly since the 1970s, leaders of peasant groups like the Agricultural Workers Union/UTA (Union des travailleurs agricoles), and the Guadeloupe Liberation Union/ULPG (Union pour la libération de la Guadeloupe), have been agitating for the exclusive use of Creole in their union meetings, political meetings, and even in artistic creations (patriotic songs, popular poetry, and theatre). The Guadeloupean poet Sonny Rupaire (1941-1991) took the lead in a nationalist movement, introducing the notion of political commitment in Creole poetry.

With reference to Creole as a cultural designator, Jean Bernabé, in a 1992-93 article that examines the evolution from Negritude to Creolity, supports the dictionary contention that the adjective, creole, in colonial terminology designated only individuals of European origin who were born in the colonies. Bernabé notes, however, that acceptance of the term was later extended to include both blacks (mixed or not) and fauna and flora that were, so to speak, "born" in the colony and thus effectively part of the local culture. Bernabé attempts a clarification of the significance of "Creole" by comparing it to the two other terms used in Creole, each of which corresponds to the three spatio-anthropological points of reference (Europe-Africa-America) that are at issue in the Caribbean: "Vyé Blan," "Bossale," and "Créole." According to Bernabé, "Vyé Blan" came to represent whites born in Europe, "Bossale" blacks born in Africa, while "Creole" referred specifically to the Antillean/American land.

The shift that has taken place in the signification of "Creole" from indicating white as opposed to black colonists, to white and light-skinned (mixed-race) as opposed to black ("pure" African), and now to blacks and whites (locals) as opposed to metropolitans, is a phenomenon of undoubted interest. Even more intriguing, however, is an underlying element that has not changed. What has remained intact is the perception of difference between the (ex-) colonies and the metropole (Europe), and the perception of an exposure (cultural, racial, geographical) that results in a permanent change (including the stereotypical marks of the native: darkening of the skin and of the morals).

The claiming of an identity designated specifically by Caribbean people of color as "Creole" is not new, not even in the twentieth century. Maître Jean-Louis contributed an article to the October 1931 issue of the *Review of the Black World* on "The Creole Race." This article was intended as an "Introduction to a Study on Creole Art and Literature." Jean-Louis saw as a most important consequence of European colonization "the creation of entirely new races" (8). These new races he considered as European creations: "In Canada, Louisiana and in both the West and the East Indies, France gave birth to the Creole race" (9). Jean-Louis described the Creole in the following terms:

> The traits of the Creole character are defined by its turbulent temperament, independent and bellicose, on the one side, and its refined spirit which placed above all a cultivated mind, on the other. If we

> add to this the contribution of the African race, just
> as tumultuous, and moreover, mystic, one will see
> that it was because of their similarity that these two
> racial elements completing one the other, have
> blended perfectly to form the Creole race. (10)

This document is an interesting antecedent to the manifesto published by Bernabé, Chamoiseau, and Confiant (English translation "In Praise of Creoleness," 1990), in which they declared bluntly: "Neither Europeans, nor Africans, nor Asians, we proclaim ourselves Creoles" (886). Their new identity rests on the perception that they are "at once Europe, Africa, and enriched by Asian contributions, ... [and] are also Levantine, Indians, as well as pre-Columbian Americans, in some respects" (892). Evidently this choice of terminology was predicated by a desire to avoid a designation that drew reference explicitly to skin color and to transcend the preoccupation with skin shade and its relation to race and class fragmentation that has become at the end of the twentieth century endemic to the Caribbean. As the Creolists put it, "[i]n multiracial societies, such as ours, it seems urgent to quit using the traditional raciological distinctions and to start again designating the people of our countries, regardless of their complexion, by the only suitable word: *Creole*" (893). They also place Creolity within the context of the history of Caribbean writing, which in its early periods exhibited a form of exteriority characterized by "mimetic expression, both in the French language and in the Creole language" (887). They note, however, that even among this writing that imitated metropolitan models, there was some writing that bore a "local cultural coloration" but that was incorrectly read as regional, doudouist, and therefore thin. Gilbert Gratiant's *Fab Compè Zicaque* of 1958 is cited as an example of a misjudged but historic Creole work. Creolity is thus associated with the practice of writers who understand the interior reality of the Caribbean and communicate through local cultural color.

The Creolists' attitude to Negritude is ambivalent. They give credit to Césaire's Negritude for providing, through its emphasis on Africa, a much-needed antidote to the superficiality of previous doudouist writing (888) but criticized it because in their view it manifested itself in forms of exteriority that denied local cultural specificity on which any "authentic" identity must be based: "*the exteriority of aspirations* (to mother Africa, mythical Africa, impossible Africa) and *the exteriority of self-assertion* (we are Africans)" (889). Thus Negritude is rejected for having "replaced the illusion of Europe by an African illusion" (889). Jean Bernabé explains more fully in his later (1992-93) article the root of his objection as a Creolist to Negritude. He places Negritude within the historical context of the *Code Noir [Black Code]* of 1685, which not merely formally forbade interracial unions, but institutionalized the black-white, master-slave dichotomy while effectively obliterating the African and creating the "nègre" [negro]. Thus for Bernabé Negritude has two faces: on the one hand it may be considered as a creation of whites, who invented the Negro by robbing Africans of their humanity; on the other it is a recuperation by blacks who need to find Africa again and reintroduce it into the Americas. Creolity, in Bernabé's view, fulfills the Negritude program better than Negritude itself did, both in the area of the construction of poetic language and in the area of the exploration of the imaginary (23).

Thus the authors of the Creolity manifesto, while acknowledging the seminal importance of Césairean Negritude to the development of new ways of thinking and writing for people of color in so-called postcolonial situations, regarded Negritude as a trap, and cast doubt on its efficacy to solve the aesthetic problems that confront the French Caribbean writer. Other critics of Negritude have alluded to the "essentialism" implicit in Césaire's and Senghor's articulation of Negritude, and to the limitations of a concept that projected a mythical and false image of "Africa" and proposed an untenable solidarity among "blacks." Still other critics have noted the exclusion of women from the movement, the contradiction between Césaire's words and his political choices, and the unconscious dependence on European philosophical traditions. Some blacks have found it impossible to reconcile Negritude with the shortcomings of other blacks and have rejected any notion of solidarity with other blacks that act as exploiters or murderers. For the new Creolists, Glissant's Antilleanity is attractive since it requires an apprehension of Caribbean civilization in its American space and encourages a turning away from "the fetishist claim of a universality ruled by Western values in order to begin the minute exploration of ourselves" (890). The Creolists consider Antilleanity limited, since it is in their view essentially a geopolitical concept (890). Creolity, in contrast, they contend, is not a geographic concept and is not limited to the American continent (893). Antilleanity could therefore be considered in many respects as a transition towards Creolity.

It is impossible to deny the importance of this Creolity, since the quality of the writing that has been generated by its proponents and particularly the breadth and beauty of the novels of Chamoiseau and Confiant attest to the creative power that has been released by such a "prise de conscience." But the claims of the Creolists should not be accepted uncritically. Creolity seems on the surface far more attractive than Negritude, particularly since the implications of "blackness" are very difficult for both whites and non-whites of "white"-dominated societies to embrace, in a so-called postcolonial world in which the same forces of capitalist expansion contradictorily welcome market diversity but resist full acceptance of cultural and racial diversity. It must be remembered that when Europeans created the Caribbean, they also created plantation society. As a consequence of this fact, it is impossible to conceive of the Caribbean except in relation to the construction of the often antipathetic identities by which plantation society is characterized: White/Black, European/Other, Master/Slave. It is also beyond dispute that a Creole exists directly as a result of colonialism, as a result of white European contact with — and of what was perceived by Europeans as "contamination" by — black Africa in the

Americas. The Creole occupies an assigned space in the actual and conceptual hierarchy established within the plantation system: Metropolitan Whites → Creoles → Blacks. Blackness and Africanness have always been sources of discomfort for both blacks and whites in the colonial world, and this discomfort has persisted in the so-called postcolonial world. The ideology of colonialism has always exhibited a tendency to want to take the African out of everything, even out of Africans. Creolity may in some respects, therefore, be considered a new form of assimilation, since it seeks, as colonialism did, to efface Africa as a positive presence.

It would of course be highly presumptuous to suggest what designation or name others should accept for themselves. What seems to me to be highly significant is that Negritude represented the only moment in the history of French Caribbean literature when the association with Africa was proclaimed and inscribed in the literary production. Antilleanity or Caribbeanness still exercises a powerful hold on the imagination of many Caribbean people. It emphasizes their geopolitical connectedness and helps to underline their difference in relation both to Europe and to Africa. In so doing, however, it blocks full identification with Africa. Because of the realities of economic and cultural power in the Caribbean, Antilleanity unwittingly gives more weight to European and Euro-American components. Some critics of Antilleanity caution that the underlying notion is illusory since the term itself ("Antillanité" [Antilleanity]) only perpetuates the illusion created by Europeans four centuries ago in ascribing a common denominator to a group of territories that had never perceived of themselves as unified. Creolity has an even more powerful effect of erasing distinctions of geography and of color, and hence erasing or at best minimizing the African cultural element. It is difficult not to see it as a form of assimilation — an appropriation of attitudes, of designations, and of barely concealed lactifying aspirations that serve to reinforce the colonialist agenda.

The attempts on the part of French Caribbean writers to define their sociocultural identity, however limited or inadequate these attempts may be, serve as a reminder that we are dealing with a highly self-conscious society and literature, engaged in an evolutionary struggle to carve out and appropriate their own creative space. The contradictions and ambiguities that characterize the French Caribbean in relation to its history, geography, and language will necessarily be reflected in the literature and will have an impact on critical approaches and reading strategies. It is particularly relevant, in my view, to refer to an emerging tradition within the French Caribbean, rather than to any European tradition of literary theory or critical practice, to construct a framework within which critical approaches may be situated. In the following pages, therefore, I will examine some of the key texts (essays) produced by three of the primary critical thinkers from the French Caribbean (Aimé Césaire, Frantz Fanon, and Edouard Glissant) in order to draw attention to major issues that have an impact on a critical approach to this literature.

As I indicated earlier, the complexities of French Caribbean society can be traced directly to the long and painful experience of colonialism and it is in this context that literary production must be situated. In other words, literature in the French Caribbean cannot be divorced from the need to develop strategies of self-affirmation in the face of the negating pressure of colonialism and neocolonialism. The primacy of this need should also be acknowledged in developing critical approaches to this literature that are free from colonizing or recolonizing biases. Césaire's recognition that it was important to tell the truth about the colonial enterprise led to his bitter denunciation of colonialism in his 1955 *Discours sur le colonialisme [Discourse on Colonialism]*. In this essay Césaire alludes to the function and purpose of literary creation in a colonized society. The equation he establishes, "*colonisation = chosification*" [colonization = thingification] (22), implies that colonization has the dehumanizing effect of stifling creativity. Césaire also explains the way in which past African civilizations may be used as an inspiration for creative activity:

Once again, I make a systematic defense of our old negro civilizations: they were courtly civilizations.

Then, I will be told, the real problem is going back to them. No, I say again. We are not "either this or that" people. For us, the problem is not one of a utopian and sterile attempt at reduplication, but one of getting ahead. We do not want to bring a dead society back to life. We leave that to the exoticism lovers. Neither do we want to prolong the present colonial society, the toughest bit of meat that ever rotted under the sun. What we have to do, with the help of all our slave brothers, is create a new society, rich with all modern productive power, warm with all ancient fraternity. (34)

Césaire thus implicitly posits a profoundly anticolonialist function for the literature of the Caribbean.

In an article on African American poetry, entitled "Introduction à la poésie nègre américaine" [Introduction to Negro American Poetry], published in *Tropiques* in July 1941, Césaire (1941 c) identified what he called "intolerance" as the emotive driving force of these black poets who fascinated him and with whom he empathized: "The dominant feeling of the black poet is a feeling of malaise, or rather of intolerance. Intolerance of reality because it is sordid; of the world because it is caged in; of life because it has been diverted from the highway of the sun" (17). Césaire well knew that many blacks share the perception that there is something not quite right, not quite acceptable, about their life, and that creative activity is often generated by the emotional impact of this perception. He could therefore establish a link between such a "malaise" and the sociocultural climate of the Caribbean that militates against creative activity on the part of the Antillean people: "The most important component of the Antillean malaise is the fact that there exists in these islands a homogeneous bloc, a *people* who for three centuries has been seeking to *express itself* and to *create*" (Césaire 1944:7). Implicit in Césaire's statement is the recognition of the cultural and historical unity of the Caribbean people, who share both a common historical experience and a common aspiration, which he sees as consisting of two interrelated desires: the desire to make themselves understood ("expression") and the desire to bring something new into existence ("creation"). Césaire returned to these two characteristics in a presentation to the Second Congress of Black Writers and Artists, held in Rome, March 26 – April 1, 1959, where he articulated his conception of the situation and responsibility of the black writer:

> I will never say, like a Romantic, that poets or writers are creators of nations or of national values. It is a question of something simpler, which is this: that the man of culture is one who, through creation, expresses and gives form. And this *expression* itself, by the very fact that it is *expression*, hence brought up to date, creates or recreates — dialectically — in his own image the feeling of which he is, all things considered, merely the emanation. (Césaire 1959:117)

Thus, for Césaire, the source of the creative act is the community, and this act manifests itself as the representation by an individual of the ideas of the community to which the writer belongs. Although he rejects the Romantic myth of the writer as a spokesman for national values, Césaire's own poetic practice, particularly in his earlier writings, indicates a tendency to play that role. Implicit, however, in Césaire's statement is the notion that the poetic voice is more than that of an individual trying to find his or her "self." The implication is that this voice emerges from and becomes the expression of a communal identity.

Later in the same speech, Césaire (1959) expressed his conviction of the sacred nature of the task of artistic production within the context of the colonial and neocolonial situation: "In our situation, the greatest ambition of our literature must be to try to become *sacred literature*" (121). The term "sacred" as used by Césaire is not invested with religious connotations, but refers to the quality and function of an art dedicated to the service of the awakening of the spiritual and creative potential of a people, in opposition to the profanation and desecration of humanity associated with colonialism, toward a full participation in the creative experience of life:

> By raising the particular situation of our peoples to the universal plane, by linking them to history, by hoisting them up to a level which is precisely one of becoming, and hence of the negation of stagnation, artistic creation must through its force mobilize virgin emotional forces, and then we see rising up at its call unsuspected psychic resources that contribute toward the restoration of the social body whose capacity for resistance and whose vocation for enterprise have been shattered by the impact of colonialism. (121-22)

Césaire's allusion to "virgin emotional forces" is an indication of his desire to tap sources of creative expression that have been untouched by white colonizers. His aim, therefore, is to foster and produce writing which will be necessarily different from that of the white colonial world.

In a lecture delivered at Laval University in Quebec in 1972, Césaire sketched the situation of the Caribbean individual, whose specificity as an "Antillais" or "West Indian" is officially and unofficially denied: "The Caribbean man is crushed and denied because he is lost in a vast undifferentiated totality in which his specificity is not recognized and even less institutionalized" (Césaire

1973:11). Césaire argues that this lack of recognition which typifies the West Indian's relationship with the Other affects negatively the cultural activity as well as the psychology of the West Indian: "The feeling that characterizes this psychology is the poignant feeling of a lack, of a non-actualization of self, in a word, of an immense frustration" (14). In the same lecture, Césaire introduced the notions of the validity and self-justification of Caribbean literature, which he linked to the issue of the recovery of an identity: "Caribbean literature, for it to be valid, or rather, for it to be justified, can only be an act of prospecting for and salvaging one's being" (18). Furthermore, he emphasized the importance of the linkages between the Caribbean writer and his native land: "Caribbean literature is going to be thorough study, research, the study of a communion and the restoration of man in his fundamental belonging to and relationships with his land, his country, and his people" (19).

Césaire's analysis is that of a Caribbean "man of culture" — with all that this term connotes — who has been frustrated by contact with the self-affirming, "superior" Other. While some Antilleans of Césaire's generation and of more recent times shared the intensity of his reaction (for example, Etienne Léro, Aristide Maugée, René Ménil, and Frantz Fanon), others such as Gilbert de Chambertrand, Gilbert Gratiant, and Marie-Magdeleine Carbet did not. Yet it is out of this "lack," out of this cultural and psychological limbo, that the French Caribbean poet attempts to forge a voice that is uniquely Caribbean, and to undertake the communal project of breaking through the fragmentation, lack, and frustration by which French Caribbean culture is defined.

Frantz Fanon, the Martinican psychiatrist and political theoretician and activist, in his clinical (psychological) study of French Antilleans, presented his perception of the difficulty Antilleans experienced in identifying themselves as black or as African: "The Antillean does not think of himself as black; he thinks of himself as Antillean. The Negro lives in Africa. Subjectively, intellectually, the Antillean behaves like a white man"

(Fanon 1952:140). In fact, Fanon went on to assert that "up to 1940 no Antillean could think of himself as a Negro" (144). While there have been, particularly since the 1960s, throughout the African diaspora, including the Caribbean territories, popular movements that have stressed the importance of African cultural linkages and have contributed to an increased appreciation of expressions of African cultures, explicit identification with Africa is still problematical for the large majority of descendants of African slaves throughout the Caribbean. In other words, Fanon's assertion remains largely true half a century after he made it.

Fanon saw this kind of identity conflict as an inevitable consequence of the experience of colonization. He established a causal link between the suppression of local creative activity by colonizers and the resulting inferiority complex experienced by the colonized people. This inferiority complex, Fanon (1952) suggests, is manifested in the attitude of the colonized people toward metropolitan language and culture:

> Every colonized people — that is, every people within whom a complex of inferiority has developed, as a result of the entombment of the local cultural originality — takes up a position in relation to the language of the civilizing nation, that is, of the metropolitan culture. (34)

French Caribbean literature, for Fanon, is necessarily affected by this inferiority-superiority dialectic, to the extent that, as he suggests, the use of French poses a major problem psychologically for the black Antillean:

> The more the Antillean Black makes the French language his, the whiter he will be, that is, the closer he will be to being a true man.... A man who has mastered the language has also, as an

indirect consequence, mastered the world
expressed and implied by that language. (144)

Fanon was also sensitive to the danger of Euro-centered critical
approaches to Caribbean literature and reacted particularly harshly
to Jean-Paul Sartre's (1948) attempt, as a French intellectual, to
identify with and explain the literary and cultural phenomenon of
"Négritude." Fanon (1952) perceived that Sartre's intellectualization
of Négritude within the framework of European philosophical and
literary traditions served only to deny the validity and authenticity
of the black experience and to threaten the very creativity of blacks:
"*Black Orpheus* is a key date in the intellectualization of black
existence. Sartre's mistake was not only to want to go to the source
of the source, but in some way to dry up that source"(128). Fanon
realizes that the resistance of the Other is an inevitable aspect of the
reality of the existence of blacks in a colonial situation. He suggests
that one way out of this cultural and identity dilemma would be the
search for meaning and direction through a process of rigorous
self-examination: "Man liberated from the springboard formed of
the resistance of others and digging deep into his own flesh to find
some meaning for himself" (27). Fanon is thus clearly positing an
essentially Antillean mode of self-expression and critical analysis
for the peoples of color of the French Caribbean.

Edouard Glissant is the foremost literary theorist of the
French and English-speaking Caribbean. Over a period of more
than twenty years he has shared his ideas on a poetics of the
Caribbean and has explored the problematic of the Caribbean writer
in essays published in three separate collections: *L'Intention
poétique* (1969), *Le discours antillais* (1981), and *Poétique de la
relation* (1990). Particularly in the first two of these collections he
attempted an accurate delineation of the convergence of personal,
communal, and historical associations by which writer and work
create an authentic identity. In his characteristically "opaque" style,
which for him is a manifestation of the complexity of his situation

as an Antillean,[3] Glissant describes, in *L'Intention poétique*, the significant dimensions of the creative work:

> There are three ways in which the (literary) work concerns us: as community, in that it is the thrust of a group of people; as intention, in that it is linked to the will of an individual; as relation, in that it is human work and drama still continuing here. The land of the group, the language of this man, the duration for humanity: these are the elements of the poetic, played out from one to the other. (1969:24)

Glissant is particularly sensitive to the importance of geography as a crucial component of the identity of the Caribbean writer and stresses the special link between the writer and the land: "The poet appeals to his land, but the poem lays claim to it. For the land is the final argument of the poet; but it is the secret generator of the poem"(150). This notion of the creative interdependence of poet and land is at the heart of Glissant's aesthetic. Glissant suggests, with evident truth, that, as far as literary production is concerned, the Caribbean lacks the continuity of traditional linkages on which every new literature depends:

> In the history of literatures, written texts are first produced *in continuity* with traditional oral productions. Whenever a national literary corpus appears, there has always been an intervention by one writer or several, to collect the oral texts and work from that material. The tradition of writing develops out of such work and gradually becomes more and more independent of the oral sources. In the production of written texts in Martinique, there is no continuity with the popular tradition, but with fashions imported from France, in an outdated,

passive, and most often backward way" (1981:181).

While there have been attempts to collect and transcribe French Caribbean folk tales (Césaire and Laurent 1976; Césaire 1942b), it is clear that there is some hiatus in direct continuity with an oral tradition, which in turn forms part of the difficulty confronting the Caribbean writer and is therefore an important contributor to the manifestation of problems in relation to the communal voice. All Caribbean literature is in some way a response to this problem.

Glissant's reference to the need for interdependence between writers and their natural community in the creation of an authentic voice complements the notion of "malaise" articulated by Césaire, and Glissant's perception of a lack of continuity in the oral tradition is closely related to the Césairian perception of a "lack" from which the poetic voice emerges. Glissant also meets Césaire in asserting that the problematical situation of the Caribbean writer imposes special responsibilities:

> Here we are a few of us, alone at the exasperated
> forefront of the word. Trembling at the enormous
> privilege of our limited knowledge. We are calling
> to the future nation, and already we cannot breathe
> without it.... We are stifling. We are shouting for
> those who have no voice; but it is their word that
> sustains us. Glissant 1969: 51)

Glissant's personal theoretical solution to the problems facing the Caribbean writer was, as we have indicated earlier, the theory of "Antilleanity," a theory which situates Martinican specificity within a larger Afro-Caribbean cultural context where the various searches for rootedness converge: "That is what I have called the theory of Antilleanity. Its ambition is to continue enlarging both the African dimension, which is changed here as it rediscovers itself, and the language root, which gains in strength as it multiplies (1981: 182).

Glissant's concept of Antilleanity leads him to view the production of autonomous Caribbean texts as an urgent necessity in the process of liberation (161) and even to suggest that African or Caribbean commentators should be the primary arbiters in judging the relative greatness of Caribbean writers (327).

Glissant's ideas have been further refined in *Poétique de la relation*, where he examines the sources of Caribbean writing and challenges European philosophical assumptions that hinder the acceptance of diversity. In the very first footnote to the first essay he stresses the link between Caribbean writing and the experience of slavery: "On the slave ship the only writing is in the account book, that dealt with the exchange value of the slaves. Within the area of the boat, the cry of the deportees is stifled, as it will be in the universe of the Plantations" (1990:17). Glissant's comment hints at the significance that the act of writing perforce has for the descendants of those slaves who still live within the universe created by slavers and controlled by their descendants. The comment also suggests that all Caribbean literature is a continuation of the suppressed voice. Glissant insists on the different motivation of metropolitan French literature which in his view combines two conditions: "a culture that has projected on to the world (with the aim of dominating it); a language presented as universal (with the aim of legitimizing the attempt at domination)" (40). Glissant develops his poetics by examining the notions of a (European) Center and peripheries. He conceives of literary history within the Francophone orbit in terms of three trajectories: the first, from Center to peripheries (citing as examples writers like Victor Ségalen, Blaise Cendrars, André Malraux, and others); the second, from the peripheries to the Center (e.g., Jules Supervielle, Saint-John Perse, and Georges Schéhadé); and the third, in which each periphery is constituted as a center or in which the very notion of center or periphery is abolished (citing Kateb Yacine, Cheik Anta Diop, and Léon Gontran Damas as examples) (41). For Glissant such writers have the distinction of creating new expressions in the same language. As he puts it, "Maghrebine, Antillean, and African poets are not going towards an elsewhere in a projecting movement, nor are they returning toward a Center. They are setting their works up as metropolises, thereby accompanying the springing up of their peoples" (43). One implication of Glissant's theory is that no (European) philosophy or critical opinion should be considered as the "Center" on which new literatures should be focused or in relation to which new texts should be read or judged.

With reference to the Caribbean, Glissant (1990:82-87) relates the literature to the context of the plantation societies that were established in the region. He distinguishes three "moments," three phases and functions in Caribbean literary production: first as an act of survival, secondly as a form of snare, and thirdly as an effort of memory (82). In the first phase, literature is a form of "marronnage" or escape for the slave, who has to find a means within a system that censures expression to express what is forbidden.[4] Glissant suggests that resistance often took an oral form: storytelling, proverbs, sayings, and songs. This accords with the view of Patrick Chamoiseau and Raphaël Confiant, who have analyzed the role of Creole orality and of the Creole storyteller (1991:56-64). They represent the function of the storyteller as threefold: to preserve communal memories, to entertain, and to verbalize resistance. The Creolists, therefore, interpret the use of Creole as resistance against colonial edicts, against slave law, and against white writing.

Glissant identifies a second form of expression produced by colonists, planters, and visitors who felt the need to justify and legitimize the plantation system. This was an elitist, written literature, in opposition to the survival tendency of the popular oral literature of the slaves. This form of literature focuses on the physical beauty of the Caribbean scenery, thereby effacing the turbulent realities of plantation life. This phase, according to Glissant, is characterized also by erotic representations of slave women, and by references to the animality of Africans (1990:84-85).

As a third phase, Glissant identifies the literature produced after the breakdown of the plantation system. This literature, in Glissant's view, manifests and tries to supplement the hiatus in memory occasioned by the rupture in the oral tradition, and represents the land as a speaking character implicated in a history (1990:85). It is linked to the first phase in its application of a form of "marronnage." Indeed, the defining characteristic of French Caribbean literature becomes for Glissant what he calls "creative marronnage" (85): the practice of escaping European enslavement. This insistence on the appropriation of a different — Caribbean, non-European — way of thinking, writing, and even reading, is one of the fundamental implications of Glissant's philosophy and practice. His recommendations for reading strategies include an acceptance of textual opacity, since in his view the literary text is necessarily a producer of opacity (129): "Working on a literary text thus involves an opposition between two opacities: the irreducible opacity of the text, even if it the most innocuous of sonnets, and the ever-moving opacity of the author or reader" (129). He insists, above all, that the specificity of new literatures (like those of the French Caribbean) and their separation from the metropole must be acknowledged: "these literatures can no longer be considered as exotic appendages to the French, English, or Spanish literary bodies" (85).

What inferences should be drawn from this review of some of the critical perspectives advanced by these three French Caribbean writers on issues affecting their literature and what relation does all of this bear to my own critical approach? All these writers accept by implication that writing has a different function for a French Caribbean writer of color than for a European. They all appear to intimate that the sociological, psychological, philosophical, and cultural effects of European colonization present a new matrix and a new role for creative activity. I have noticed over the years that critical perspective is often determined by such factors as national, racial, and cultural affiliation, although this fact tends to be ignored, minimized, or denied. Is it conceivable that the national, racial, and cultural affiliations of Althusser, Barthes, Derrida, Spivak, Said, Gates, Kristeva, Foucault, De Man, Bakhtin, Cixous etc. be of no or little account? I know that my own critical perspective is profoundly influenced by my personal history and by my chosen sociocultural affiliations. I have had to undergo the process of lucid self-examination suggested and practiced among others by Césaire, Fanon, and Glissant. I have to accept that I have been trained first within a European (British and French) critical tradition of practical criticism and *explication de texte* (traditional stylistic and rhetorical analysis) and later in structuralist, poststructuralist, Marxist, psychoanalytical, feminist, even Africanist approaches and methodologies. It would be impossible for this training not to have left its mark. I am also conscious, however, that no European or Euro-American theory that I have ever been exposed to operates, whether intentionally or not, to the ultimate benefit of black people or has been developed with the best interests of blacks in mind. Consequently, I have had to be cautious in my appropriation of any European approach when applied to the activities of blacks. I have therefore turned to the black critical tradition to find alternative approaches, recognizing all the while that all black critics, myself included, whether trained in North America, continental Africa, the Caribbean, Europe, or elsewhere, bear traces of the experience of colonization and that these traces manifest themselves in a need to acknowledge the presence of the colonizer and in a consciousness of participation in the colonizer's world. My approach to reading French Caribbean literature has been informed specifically by the debates among the French Caribbean literary tradition, including the "movements" of Negritude, Antilleanity, and Creolity already discussed, as well as those among African, Caribbean, and African American scholar-critics.

African American critics, both women and men, have supported my own awareness of the importance of "race" even in relation to critical discourses. Evelyn Brooks Higginbotham (1993) points to the connections among race as a social construct, difference, and power:

> Like gender and class, then, race must be seen as a social construction predicated upon the recognition of difference and signifying the simultaneous distinguishing and positioning of groups vis-à-vis one another. More than this, race is a highly contested representation of relations of power between social categories by which individuals are identified and identify themselves. (93)

Vèvè A. Clark (1993) reminds me that "the notion of race as a natural and homogeneous category suppresses the richness and heterogeneity within black experience itself" (5) while Houston A. Baker, Jr. (1988) expresses with commendable directness an observation that supports my own experience:

> Somehow, I cannot persuade myself that a black person in America, or South Africa, or the Caribbean, or anywhere else in today's world is anything other than a *black* person -- a person preeminently and indisputably governed, in his life choices and expectations, by a long-standing and pervasive discourse called *race*. (109)

Henry Louis Gates, Jr. (1985, 1986) joins Baker in posing the question that lies at the heart of all "black" critical approaches: "What importance does 'race' have as a meaningful category in the study of literature and the shaping of critical theory? (2)" Gates notes: "In much of the thinking about the proper study of literature in this century, race has been an invisible quantity, a persistent yet implicit presence" (2). He also alludes to a critical problem that exists for the black writer in the context of the space occupied by blackness within the language: "how can the black subject posit a full and sufficient self in a language in which blackness is a sign of absence?" (12). Gates proposes further a stance black and other Third World critics should take in relation to European critical theory:

> ... the concern of the Third World critic should properly be to understand the ideological subtext which any critical theory reflects and embodies, and the relation which this subtext bears to the production of meaning. No critical theory — be it Marxist, feminist, post-structuralist, Kwame Nkrumah's "consciencism," or whatever — escapes the specificity of value and ideology, no matter how mediated these may be. To attempt to appropriate our own discourses by using Western critical theory uncritically is to substitute one mode of neocolonialism for another. (15)

The conclusion Gates reaches after reflecting on the change that has taken place in his attitude toward the Western critical tradition echoes that of Glissant and so many other ex-colonial scholars: "I once thought it our most important gesture to *master* the canon of criticism, to *imitate* and *apply* it, but I now believe that we must turn to the black tradition itself to develop theories of criticism indigenous to our literatures" (Baker and Redmond 1989:25).

Cheryl W. Wall's (1989) defense of the need for women to make their positionality explicit, as "a response to the false universalism that long defined critical practice and rendered black women and their writing mute" (2), echoes Glissant's rejection of Western European universalist philosophy and carries an important message to even male Caribbean critics. A similar message is conveyed by Valerie Smith (1989), who draws attention to the exclusions and restrictions associated with the term "literature": "the term *literature* as it was commonly understood in the academy referred to a body of texts written by and in the interest of a white male elite" (39). Barbara Christian (1989) carries the notion of explicit positionality beyond the point proposed by Wall and Baker and proposes personal involvement with the writer's work as part of her practice of black feminist criticism (68). But she goes even further, suggesting radical changes in critical discourse itself:

> I thought that black feminist criticism needed to break some of the restricted forms, personalize the staid language associated with the critic — forms that seemed opposed to the works of the writers as well as the culture from which they came — and forms that many readers found intimidating and boring. (68)

The complex negotiation in which ex-colonial critics are often forced to engage because of their paradoxical relationship to colonialism is highlighted by D.S. Izevbaye (1990) in an analysis of the practice of "African" literary criticism:

> Colonialism has ... provided the central focus of the criticism. Even when it has not been the subject of direct attention, it has provided a major point of departure for criticism. Thus, both the literature and its criticism have been governed by an African awareness of its relation to the modern European world and by a preoccupation with the displacement of the West from the center of its universe. Because the African experience has been so closely bound up with colonialism, this literary criticism represents an ironic enterprise, for the means of assailing colonialism and affirming an African identity — the verbal tools of aggression and restoration — are drawn from, or supplied by, the colonial experience itself. (127)

Biodun Jeyifo (1990) raises some of the fundamental issues involved in critical approaches to emergent literatures like African (or Caribbean) literatures. He argues that "the question of an African critical discourse which is self-constituted and self-constituting in line with the forces acting on the production of African literature is intimately connected with the fate of that literature" (35). According to Jeyifo, one of the manifestations of this problematical situation is the claiming and counter-claiming of proprietary rights to critical insights on the part of "foreign"/Africanist and "native"/nationalist scholar-critics, who in any case exist in a state of "unequal power relations between the two camps" (39). What I find particularly compelling, however, is the vital role ascribed by Jeyifo to literary criticism in contexts such as the French Caribbean and the inference that can by drawn of a role of responsibility for literary critics towards the literature they read: "[C]ritical discourse not only assures the survival of literature, it also determines the condition in which it survives and the uses to which it will be put" (34).

The ideas explored by these black critics provide a substantial body of opinion in support of the approach that I have elected to pursue as well as justification for the present study. The approach that I adopt I would designate as diversalist: that is, eclectic, taking into full account the notion of difference, refusing to use Europe as sole or primary referent, and accepting that perspective is usually personal and subjective. My approach involves a combination of contextual (sociocultural, political, and historical), and textual analysis (the reading of both what Gayatri Spivak [1988:102] calls the social and the verbal text), while acknowledging and accepting the two Glissantian opacities (that of the text and my own as reader) that are at play in such reading. One of the claims of the Creolists is that "[French] Caribbean literature does not yet exist, that we are in a state of pre-literature: that of a written production without a home audience, ignorant of the authors/readers interaction which is the primary condition of the development of a literature" (Bernabé et al. 1990:886). Behind this conclusion, which translates the perceived predicament in which many French Caribbean writers find themselves, can be glimpsed aspects of the dilemma by which the French Caribbean and its literature is typified: the space occupied by writing, originally reserved by whites as a sign of the value of black property; the association of books with the colonial power; the restriction of the practice of reading in early colonial societies; the conflict between the oral practice of Creole and the writing of French; an economic problem reflected in the prohibitive cost of books; and the fact that the Caribbean does not constitute a national or linguistic unit. The Creolists' claim does not negate a flourishing of the practice of the production, writing, and publication of all kinds of French Caribbean texts and the growth of an international readership. But critical reading within the context of the Caribbean carries its own problems. The Creolists' claim does point to an urgent need: the need for readers and commentators drawn particularly from the Caribbean who could contribute to the completion of the cycle of recommended interaction. This book is intended to contribute towards filling that need.

This book, therefore, will provide readings of French Antillean poetry colored (the pun is intentional) by my own peculiar consciousness and experience as a black West Indian, trained within a tradition of education and literary analysis intended for Europeans. My aim is to contribute toward the development of the French Caribbean and its literature by giving the work of these writers the respect of attentive reading. I am aware that comparatively few English-speaking readers will have been exposed to such a corpus of literature or to some of the poets represented here. My examination will follow the following format: each chapter will comprise a) introductory biobibliographical information on each author, b) the texts in French of the poems to be explicated, c) English translations of each poem, d) critical readings of each text, and e) a brief conclusion based on all the readings giving a synthesis of and afterthoughts on the foregoing readings. My reading method is that of "classical" analysis informed by a deliberate attempt to avoid reading "through" explicitly European eyes. I consistently seek to highlight problematics of "race" and cultural identity in texts that I consider to be rooted in the complexities of the so-called postcolonial condition.

I decided to concentrate on close readings of a limited number of poems, because I have noted that whereas many French Caribbean novels have been given in-depth analytical study, poetry has rarely benefited from such intensive scholarly activity (Césaire's *Cahier* is a notable exception). This desire to focus on a limited number of poems and poets brought its own problems, not least of which was deciding which poets to include and which to omit. My lack of linguistic competence in Creole limits my access to poems written in Creole, so I chose to focus on poems written in French and on poets writing primarily in French. It was difficult to omit outstanding poets like Georges Desportes, Elie Stéphenson, Christian Rollé, Serge Patient, Ernest Pépin, and so many others. I felt that while the Negritude period (1930s and 1940s) had already received extensive attention by scholars in Europe, Africa, and the Americas, little work had been done on poetic productions in the second half of the century. Certain authors imposed themselves because of their international stature: Césaire, Damas, and Glissant. Marie-Magdeleine Carbet, as the most prolific French Caribbean woman poet to date, was also an obvious choice. Tirolien, as Guadeloupe's foremost poet, also suggested himself. The high quality of the poetry of Padoly and Polius, who are not widely known even in the French Caribbean, recommended itself to me. Also aware that most of the poets were male, I felt it would be interesting to examine some of the poetry of some of the women poets whose names are rarely heard even in the Caribbean, and I therefore included samples from Marcelle Archelon-Pépin, Gilette Bazile, and Michèle Bilavarn.

What I try to do in this book is to investigate the poetic manifestations of a sensibility that may be described as French Caribbean, through close readings of a representative sample of poetic texts, and to make this sample accessible to a wider,

English-speaking public. Even thought I am aware that, as Glissant has indicated, authorial intention is impossible to realize, I intended my commentaries to be part of a dialogue between a Caribbean reader and Caribbean writers, shared with other Caribbean and non-Caribbean readers. I intended to present these from an underrepresented perspective, that of a black West Indian, to introduce English-speaking readers to some of the major qualities, points of interest, and concerns of French Caribbean literature through its poetry, to make a case for acceptance of French Caribbean literature as a literature different from continental French literature, to demonstrate one way of reading this literature, and to demonstrate the relevance of this literature to current social, political, and literary debates in the United States, particularly those related to race and diversity.

W.E.B. Du Bois is among a select group of writers (that includes Aimé Césaire and Edouard Glissant) who have articulated concerns that have supported in a fundamental way hitherto unexpressed notions of myself. The title I have chosen, *Through a Black Veil*, is an allusion to one of these concerns expressed by Du Bois in *The Souls of Black Folk*. While I do not support or agree with all of Du Bois's positions and ideas, and while I know that there are many black people who do not share my emotional and intellectual responses to life, yet many of my own experiences have often left me with the perception that, like Du Bois (1989), "I was different from the others; or like, mayhap, in heart and life and longing, but shut out from their world by a vast veil" (2). I have for a long time been aware that I most often apprehend the world through the veil of my "blackness" and that my consciousness of my "blackness" and all that that signifies informs my literary responses and judgements. This predisposition has become even more firmly entrenched with age and experience, as my sense of self has (I like to think) matured. Du Bois further contends that this veil is also a gift, that of double consciousness (3). I have grown to treasure this gift, which I know others like myself possess, but which is so specifically and uniquely mine. It is this gift that I hope to share with you through the medium of this book.

Notes

[1] On a visit to Martinique in May of 1995, I noticed that the tall statue of d'Esnambuc that stands in the savannah in Fort-de-France facing the harbor has had its name plate removed. The official plaque that carries the inscription "Le Roy a perdu un des plus fidèles serviteurs de son Estat" [The King has lost one of the most faithful servants of his State] still remains. However the following graffiti inscriptions have been added: "Monument français à la gloire du Racisme, de l'Esclavagisme et du Colonialisme" [French monument to the glory of Racism, Pro-Slavery, and Colonialism] and "Mort au colonialisme fwansé" [Death to French colonialism].

[2] Danaho (1985: 46-60) proposes this model to illustrate the difficulty of classifying an individual as Guyanese.

[3] For Glissant's definition of "opacité," see Glissant 1969:13; and 1981:11 ("Nous réclamons le droit à l'opacité" [We claim the right to be opaque]); and 1994: 127-29.

[4] The term "marronnage" refers to the practice of imported Africans who refused to submit to enslavement by running away. They were known as "marrons" [maroons].

2

Marie-Magdeleine CARBET

Marie-Magdeleine Carbet occupies a unique position in the literary history of Martinique of the twentieth century. Born in Martinique August 25, 1902, the woman known as Carbet has been writing and publishing consistently since the middle 1930s in a variety of genres: novels, short stories, children's stories, essays, songs, and recipes, as well as poetry. She has been a vocal activist against racism and anti-semitism and has spoken out about the publication difficulties faced by francophone writers (see Carbet 1973, 1975). Carbet studied at the University of Paris in the 1920s, received her "licence," and became a schoolteacher first in Martinique and later in Paris and the French provinces. In 1937 she launched the first black Caribbean theater in Paris, in collaboration with her woman friend, Claude, with a 1938 production of "Dans sa case."[1] In 1939 she was appointed to collect folklore as a cultural representative of France's Overseas ministry. She was for a long time an active contributor to *Droit et Liberté*, the clandestine organ of MRAP, le Mouvement contre le Racisme et pour l'Amitié des Peuples (a movement against racism and anti-semitism), as well as to several literary journals. She attracted the suspicion of the collaborationist Vichy government, which removed her from her teaching position, to which she was not reinstated until 1955. According to her niece, Dr. Yolande Marie-Magdeleine, Carbet returned to Martinique on a vacation in 1939 and was prevented from returning to teach in France because of her anti-Pétain activities. She did not return to France until 1951. Carbet has traveled extensively, and has lectured in France, Africa, and Canada on issues related to the situation of the Caribbean. Carbet returned finally to Martinique in 1990.

Carbet has been Martinique's most prolific woman writer to date, originally collaborating with a school-teacher friend, known as Claude Carbet,[2] to publish books on Martinique. Since the late 1950s, when the literary collaboration ended, Marie-Magdeleine has published several novels, including *Au péril de ta joie* (1972), *D'une rive à l'autre* (1975), and *Au sommet de la sérénité* (1980), and several collections of poetry, including *Point d'orgue* (1958), *Ecoute, soleil-dieu* (1961), *Viens voir ma ville* (1963), and *Rose de ta grâce* (1970), for which she was awarded the Prix des Caraïbes by the Association des Ecrivains de Langue Française, Paris, in 1971. Since then she published another volume of poetry, *Mini-poèmes sur trois méridiens* (1977). Carbet was awarded France's Grand Prix Humanitaire for services to arts and letters and the sheer volume of her creative output can rival that of Césaire or Glissant. Yet she has received little attention from anthologists, literary historians or critics,[3] perhaps because her work seems curiously anachronistic and because she appears to have ignored the major social, cultural, and political issues that are reflected in the voices of other French Caribbean writers of her generation, particularly Surrealism, Negritude, and the on-going political struggles of the French Caribbean.

Carbet's real name is Anna Marie-Magdeleine and "Carbet" is a pseudonym she adopted because she considered it a uniquely

Martinican designation, since it is the name of an administrative district in the north of Martinique and also denotes the huts (still found in the north of the island) of the aboriginal inhabitants of Martinique. Thus the writer's chosen identity as a writer is one that insists on a Martinican specificity.

The two collections studied in this chapter, *Point d'orgue* and *Rose de ta grâce*, comprising poems written during the 50s and 60s (as well as undoubtedly some earlier poems), represent a Carbet already approaching the middle years of her life, at a time when she may be considered to have found her "real" voice. Certainly, as a female Martinican poet, Carbet stands alone. The poems that appear in these two collections reveal the way in which her gender informs both the cultural model she adopts as a poet and the poetic choices she makes, as she attempts to forge a new and authentic French Caribbean voice that is different from that of the male poets.

Carbet's *Point d'orgue* (1958) is a collection of 34 poems, eight of which are designated as "chansons." The titles of many of the poems in this collection give some indication of the intellectual and poetic orientation of the poet: seven poems bear brief, abstract titles ("Tourment" [Torment], "La jolie folie" [Fine Folly], "Le doute" [Doubt], "Rancune" [Resentment] "Caprice" [Caprice], "Sagesse" [Wisdom], "Absence" [Absence]); four pose questions ("Je renierais?" [Would I deny?], "Et puis, après?" [And What Then?], "Vous souvient-il?" [Do You Remember?], "Pourquoi pas une autre?" [Why Not Someone Else?]); two others are ironic imperatives ("Mentez encore" [Lie again], "N'ayez point doute" [Don't Doubt]); all appear within the textual framework of "Ta voix" [Your Voice] and "Votre rire" [Your Laughter], respectively the first and last poems of the collection. The shift from the familiar possessive pronoun "Ta" [Your] at the beginning to the more formal "Votre" [Your] at the end point to a shift in intimacy, which is an important part of the code of social interaction maintained by the French language. These titles suggest the adoption of a stance of increasing emotional and intellectual distance on the part of the poet and a tendency to focus on the attitudes and attributes of an "other" to whom the poetic communication is generally addressed.

These poems, consisting mainly of rhymed octosyllabic verses, are in their form very "traditional," from the perspective of metropolitan literary practices, and present few direct indications, if any, of a specific Caribbean poetic presence. The landscape is generally non-tropical and the thematic orientation revive echoes of some nineteenth century Romantic poetry, particularly that of Marceline Desbordes-Valmore, in relation to the primacy of suffering, the representation of nature, and the presentation of a loving, passive, poetic subject, and of Baudelaire, in relation to a *fin de siècle* sensibility, to feelings of exile, and to the longing for a tropical paradise. Even the identity of the poetic persona, often not clearly female, seems somehow masked or muted, lacking definition and precision.

The title of the collection, *Point d'orgue*, bears the double association of, on the one hand, the literal sign of a period of silence within a musical composition, and, on the other, a suspension of sound and of time which creates tension. This tension, which may be characterized as a tension of voice, is reflected also in the geographical and sociocultural situation of Carbet, as she finds herself oscillating between the rival attractions of her native Caribbean island and mainland France. There is, moreover, an implication, in the choice of this title, that the poet is aware at some level that these poems do not constitute the sound of her real "voice." This collection, therefore, may be considered a concrete indicator of the poet's conscious silence, a moment, for her, of suspended sound.

TA VOIX

Dans le ramage des oiseaux
Au faîte des sapins tranquilles,
Dans la course allègre des eaux
Sur les racines immobiles,

Quoi que j'écoute, où que je sois,
Je retrouve toujours ta voix.

Dans le bruit du vent, qu'il traînaille
Au long de la sente mouillée,
Ou qu'obstinément, il travaille
A trouer la robe rouillée
Des chênes noircis, c'est ta voix,
Ta voix, toujours, que je perçois.

Le souffle court du feu de bois,
Le soupir chaud du saxophone,
Le rire de l'enfant narquois,
L'appel rythmé du téléphone,
Tout me l'annonce ou me la rend.
Et je l'attends, et je l'entends,

Ta voix qui peut, tout à coup sèche,
D'une inflexion, glacer mon sang;
Qui vient toucher mon âme fraîche
Comme une main aux doigts brûlants;

Qui fait de moi un pur ruisseau
Jasant de joie en la lumière,
Une urne, un précieux vaisseau
Où fume l'encens en prière;

Ta voix ronde, profonde, grave,
Qui coule en moi comme du lait,
Qui m'envahit comme une lave,
Qui me tuerait... si tu voulais.

❦

YOUR VOICE

In the warbling of birds
Atop the tranquil firs
In the cheer of waters running
Over motionless roots,
Whatever I listen to, wherever I am,
I always find your voice.

In the noise of the wind, drawling
Along the sodden path,
Or laboring stubbornly
To pierce the rusted dresses
Of blackened oaks, it's your voice,
Your voice, always, that I perceive.

The short breathing of the wood fire,
The warm sighing of the saxophone,
The laughter of the teasing child,
The rhythmic ringing of the telephone,
Everything proclaims it or brings it back to me.
And I wait for, and I hear it,

Your voice, that can, suddenly dry,
With an inflexion, turn my blood to ice;
That comes and touches my cool soul
Like a hand with burning fingers;
That turns me into a pure brook
Prattling joyfully in the light,
An urn, a precious vessel
With incense prayerfully smoking;

Your voice, round, deep, and low,
That within me flows like milk,
That overruns me like a lava flood,

That would kill me ... if you wanted.

This opening poem of the collection immediately raises issues of eroticism and gender.[4] The dominant voice here is not that of the poet but of an Other ("ta" [your]), whose gender is unspecified within the poem, with whom the poetic persona enjoys an erotic relationship. This fact acquires even greater significance when a similarly dominant "Other" is seen to be implicit in the title of the last poem in the collection, "Votre rire" [Your Laughter](71). An Other, a sexual partner whose role is dominant, therefore, serves both as the implied starting point for the first poem and as the closing point for the collection as a whole.

"Ta voix" is thus a "love" poem, expressing the poet's obsession with and nostalgia for the absent lover's voice. Love, however, is never mentioned in the poem. As the collection opens, the temporary interruption of sound, the moment of silence implicit in the title of the collection, is immediately filled by "ta voix," so that the dominating other voice forms part of the period of suspended sound. The poetic voice, that of the "je"[I]-subject of the poetic discourse, is literally subordinated (through the repetition of "dans" [in] in opposition to "au faîte" [atop] and "sur" [on] in the first stanza) to the voice of the Other. The images of the first stanza establish a contrast between sound and silence, between movement and immobility, and a metonymic link between the tensile strength of firs and the fixity of roots. The Other's voice is thus an indicator of the power and security the poet seeks.

The impression of serenity and joy associated with the Other's voice and suggested in the dominant adjectives "tranquilles" [tranquil], "allègre" [cheerful], and "immobiles" [immobile] of the first stanza is altered in the second stanza: "ramage" [warbling] changes to "bruit" [noise] and the stanza becomes overlaid with a sense of effort and exertion, conveyed through "traînaille" [drawling], "obstinément" [stubbornly], and "travaille" [laboring]. In the central third stanza, the poem and its voices move from the schematic natural exterior of the first two stanzas, characterized in the first two stanzas by "oiseaux" [birds], "sapins" [firs], "eaux" [waters],"racines" [roots], "vent" [wind], "la sente" [the path], and "chênes" [oaks], to an equally schematic interior, characterized by "feu de bois" [wood fire], "saxophone" [saxophone], "enfant" [child], and "téléphone" [telephone], and by their accompanying sounds: "souffle" [breathing], "soupir" [sighing], "rire" [laughter], and "appel rythmé" [rhythmic ringing].   Objects are thus transformed by the poet and assume significance only as metonyms of voice.

    In the last three shorter stanzas of the poem, the relationship between the poet and the Other becomes more defined, more complex, and more problematical. The poet moves from an attitude of passive waiting in the third stanza, to excited sensual anticipation, based on the memory of the contradictory physical and spiritual effects of the Other's voice. While the poet's voice is associated with stereotypically feminine characteristics of innocence and purity ("mon âme fraîche" [my cool soul], "pur ruisseau" [pure brook]), the Other's voice is invested metaphorically with the (masculine?) potential for producing extremes of emotion ("glacer" [turn to ice], "brûlants" [burning]), for purification and creativity ("qui fait de moi un pur ruisseau..., un précieux vaisseau" [That turns me into a pure brook ..., a precious vessel]), for life-giving ("lait" [milk]), as well as for destruction ("m'envahit" [overruns], "lave" [lava], "me tuerait" [would kill me]). The poet emerges above all as a relatively passive receptacle and a channel for the activity of the Other ("vaisseau" [vessel], "urne" [urn], "coule en moi" [flows within me], "m'envahit comme une lave" [overruns me like a lava flood]), ultimately dependent for survival on her partner's will ("si tu voulais" [if you wanted]).

    The reference to the volcanic power of the voice that serves as the poet's muse in this poem sets up extratextual resonances recalling the history of Martinique, and the destruction of Saint-Pierre following the eruption of Mount Pelée in 1902, which functions for many Martinican writers as a defining and characteristic symbol of their Caribbean reality. The reference also, however, suggests the powerful impact that erotic (orgasmic) experiences hold for the poet and her desire to find a poetic outlet for the expression of her pleasure. This opening poem is thus born implicitly out of the poetic acceptance of the dominance of the voice of these experiences. It sets the scene for the exploration of a series of situations in which the deceptively fragile identity of the woman poet appears fearful of asserting itself and in which the voice of this hidden Other/lover (Martinique/ Another woman) is revealed through the poet's voice, itself hidden, within the text.

à Clément

Crépuscule antillais

LA PRIERE DES MERLES

L'horizon saigne. L'astre nu,
Comme au sein d'un immense nid,
Glisse dans l'eau. Bientôt, la nuit
Tendra le ciel blessé de noir.

Dans l'air encor chaud, l'angélus
S'étire, le rythme alourdi
Du flux quotidien de souci.
Le clocher semble un encensoir.

Ecoute au palmier chevelu,
Comme au cœur d'un immense nid,
Des légions de merles unis
Chanter l'hymne fervent du soir.

Laisse nos vieux rêves perclus,
Masqués des voiles de la nuit,
Du fond de leur douloureux nid,
Dire au vent nos défunts espoirs.

ॐ

To Clement

Antillean Twilight

THE BLACKBIRDS' PRAYER

The horizon is bleeding. The naked star,
As if in the bosom of a huge nest,
Slips into the water. Soon, night
Will drape the wounded sky in black.

In the yet warm air, the angelus
Stretches, its rhythm heavy
From the daily flow of worries.
The church tower seems like a censer.

Listen, in the longhaired palm-tree,
As if in the heart of a huge nest,
To legions of blackbirds united
Singing the evening's fervent hymn.

Let our old crippled dreams,
Masked in the veils of night,
From the depth of their painful nest,
Tell our defunct hopes to the wind.

In "La prière des merles" [The Blackbirds' Prayer](9), the concealment of the poetic identity parallels the muffling of the poetic voice. The notation above the title of the poem indicates that the scene described depicts a Caribbean twilight ("crépuscule antillais"). This notation echoes the title of the collection, *Point d'orgue*, in that, since in the Caribbean darkness descends very quickly after the sun sets, twilight is a comparatively brief period, comparable to a musical pause between day and night. This notation, which insists on a Caribbean connection, is necessary. The description of the scene contains only one element which may be regarded as typical of the Caribbean: the "palmier chevelu" [longhaired palm-tree] of the third stanza. The specification is therefore useful within the context of an expected metropolitan French readership. There is a tension in the text between the attractions of the Caribbean and of metropolitan France, and the poet finds it necessary to mark the text with a definite Caribbean inscription in "Crépuscule antillais."

There is further but similar tension, implicit in the title, between exposure and concealment. The identity of the poet is concealed behind that of the "merles" [blackbirds], the birds whose voiced prayer provide the focus for this poem. "Merles" are characterized by typically dark-colored plumage, black for males and brown for females, to the extent that the French expression "merle blanc" [literally a white blackbird] has come to represent someone or something that is impossible to find. This hidden color/racial association literally illuminates the whole poem, and has implications for the poet's situation as a Martinican woman of color, living and writing in a "white," French, cultural context.

In the first three stanzas, "nid" [nest] carries its familiar connotation of security, as the poet establishes parallel associations between the situations of the sun and the birds, all of which find a secure resting-place ("immense nid" [huge nest]) in the sea and in the palm-trees ("l'astre nu"/"l'eau": "merles"/"palmier chevelu" [the naked star/the water: blackbirds/long-haired palm-tree]). The impression of security is negated, however, in the final stanza, by the introduction of "douloureux" [painful], which becomes descriptive of the existence of the birds, when they sing, not of "l'hymne fervent du soir" [the evening's fervent hymn], but more authentically of "nos défunts espoirs" [our defunct hopes]. The poet, whose textual presence is felt in the familiar imperatives "écoute" [listen] and "laisse" [let], emerges in this final stanza not as an individual but as part of a plurality in the possessive pronoun "nos" [our], reminiscent of the group of "merles unis" [blackbirds united] of the third stanza. The disappointment and disillusionment evident in "vieux rêves perclus" [old crippled dreams] and "défunts espoirs" [defunct hopes] are presented as part of the experience of the poet and of the "merles," whose voice is evoked in the poem. The force of "Masqués" [Masked], which may be linked syntactically both to "rêves perclus" [crippled dreams] and to "merles" [blackbirds], dominates the final stanza, suggesting that the poet's identity and voice are, in this poem, concealed, and that the poet is conscious of the possible futility of poetic activity ("dire au vent"), within the context of the "douloureux nid" [painful nest] of a Caribbean island.

This poem illustrates two components of Carbet's poetic practice. On the one hand, the poem, built around the idea of a prayer, translates a personal search for security that is consistently resolved for Carbet through religious faith. On the other hand, the poem functions as the means whereby the poet's situation is externalized and masked. It reflects the dilemma of a woman and a poet, who is troubled by conflicting desires for exposure and concealment, between imitation and authenticity, inscribing her frustration and her disillusionment directly and indirectly within the poem.

JE RENIERAIS ?

Je renierais, serait-il vrai,
Le vermillon de ton argile,
Tes plages, tes ombrages frais,
Ton odeur, ton sel, ô mon île ?

Ingrate, j'oublierais ainsi
Tes longs filaos en musique,
La saveur du punch de midi,
Le fouet du vent sur l'Atlantique ?

Je ne saurais plus la chanson

Du petit marchand d'écrevisses
Dont la pêche grouille dans son
Panier tressé de bambous lisses ?

Et si j'abaissais la paupière,
Le colibri, ne verrais plus,
Poudré d'arc-en-ciel en poussière,
Puisant au cœur de l'hibiscus ?

A mon coucher, de mon logis,
Je fixerais les fermetures,
Je m'endormirais dans un lit
Sous de pesantes couvertures,

Sans un retour vers les soirs calmes
Où, dans le velours bleu des airs,
Parmi le froissement des palmes,
Danse la luciole aux feux verts ?

Peu me chaut d'étaler au jour
Les menus drames de ma vie
Sous ce ciel aux pâles amours,
Mais, avouer ta nostalgie,
Mon pays, pétri de ma chair,
Tout volupté dans ta misère,
Mon pays, fruit doré de mer
Noyé d'azur et de lumière.

Comment dirais-je ta douceur,
Tes brusques accès de violence ?
Où trouver les sons, la couleur,
Pour exprimer ton opulence ?

Tel une femme dont le charme
Voile vaillance et passion,

Tu veux, par pudeur, que tes larmes
Parent de perles tes haillons.

Tu veux que nos rires, nos chants,
Poignants ou non, rythment ta vie,
Que, jusqu'au dernier, tes enfants,
Marqués du feu de ton génie,

A l'univers fassent la preuve
Que nous, tes bâtards va-nu-pieds,
Nous nous forgeons en tes épreuves
Orgueil farouche et cœurs altiers.

❧

WOULD I DENY ?

Would I deny, could it be true,
The vermilion of your clay,
Your beaches, your cool shades,
Your smell, your salt, O my island?

Would I be so ungrateful as to forget
Your long casuarinas in music,
The flavor of the midday punch,
The whip of the wind on the Atlantic ?

Would I no longer know the song
Of the little crayfish seller,
His catch swarming in his
Shiny woven bamboo basket ?

And were I to lower my eyelid,
Would I no longer see the humming bird,

Powdered in a dusty rainbow,
Sucking at the hibiscus' heart ?

At my bedtime, my house
Latches would I fasten,
Would I fall asleep in a bed
Under heavy blankets,

Without returning to the calm evenings
Where, in the blue velvet of the air,
Among the rustling of the palms,
The green lighted firefly dances.

It matters little to me to expose
The petty dramas of my life
Under this sky of pale loves,
But, to confess nostalgia for you,

My country, kneaded from my flesh,
All sensual in your poverty,
My country, golden sea food
Bathed in azure and in light.

How would I tell of your gentleness,
Your sudden fits of violence ?
Where to find the sounds, the color,
To express your opulence ?

Like a woman whose charm
Masks valor and passion,
In your modesty, you want your tears
To adorn your rags with pearls.

You want our laughter, our songs,
Poignant or not, to give rhythm to your life,

And every last one of your children,
Branded with the fire of your genius,

To give proof to the universe
That we, your barefoot bastards,
Are in your trials forging for ourselves
Fierce pride and haughty hearts.

"Je renierais?" (10-11) represents one of the strongest affirmations of the poet's identification with her native land in this collection. This affirmation is expressed in the title through a semi-rhetorical question which anticipates the answer "No." This is a forceful but indirect way of claiming undeniable links with her beloved island. The first half of the poem (the first six stanzas) is composed entirely of a series of questions indicating aspects of life in her native island which the poet considers as unforgettable and personally meaningful. The poet's affirmative stance, however, bears traces of the guilt any exile would experience, as she lists reasons why denial would be out of the question. This underlying guilt is reflected in the very first line of the poem: "serait-il vrai" [could it be true].

The poet's psychological separation from the native island is ironically implicit even in the affectionate and familiar use of the personal pronouns "ton" and "tes" [your] of the first stanza, and is reinforced by the possessive assertion of "ô mon île" [O my island]. The island is evoked by the poet, over the first six stanzas, in terms of physical characteristics, sensory impressions of sights, sounds, smells, and tastes which the poet may be in danger of forgetting ("argile" [clay], "plages" [beaches], "ombrages" [shade], "odeur" [smell], "sel" [salt], "filaos" [casuarinas], "punch" [(rum-)punch], "vent" [wind], "marchand d'écrevisses" [crayfish seller], "bambou" [bamboo], "colibri" [hummingbird], "hibiscus" [hibiscus], "palmes" [palms], and "luciole" [firefly]). The articulation of this possibility ("j'oublierais ainsi" [would I thus forget]) is an indication of the poet's physical separation from the island, and it is the force of this possibility that engenders the feelings of guilt evident in the self-castigatory stance ("ingrate" [ungrateful]) in the second stanza, where the poet reveals herself textually as a woman.

In the seventh stanza, a contrast is proposed between the island already evoked and "ce ciel aux pâles amours" [this sky of pale loves], suggesting metropolitan France, with which the poet can evidently not identify. Implicitly, the poet's geographical situation determines, she claims, the orientation of her poetry. She is evidently only too conscious of the frustrations of life in the metropolis and convinced of the personal futility of sharing current emotional experiences in her poetry: "Peu me chaut d'étaler au jour / Les menus drames de ma vie" [It matters little to me to expose / The minor dramas of my life]. The poem is therefore the means of combating alienation and of establishing identity linkages by entering into direct communication with her native island ("avouer ta nostalgie / Mon pays, pétri de ma chair" [confess nostalgia for you / My country, kneaded from my flesh]). The chiasmatic equation "mon pays"/"misère" [my country/poverty] = "ma chair"/"volupté" [my flesh/ sensuality] contrasts with the impression of the island created in the first half of the poem, as well as with the visual picture drawn in the second half of the eighth stanza: "fruit doré de mer / Noyé d'azur et de lumière" [golden sea food / Bathed in azure and in light], and implies a complexity about her native land that provokes doubt in relation to her capacity as a writer: "Comment dirais-je ta douceur, / Tes brusques accès de violence? / Où trouver les sons, la couleur, / Pour exprimer ton opulence?" [How could I tell of your gentleness, / Your sudden fits of violence? / Where to find the sounds, the color, / To express your opulence?]

The earlier intimate association between her native land and her own flesh is reinforced in the tenth stanza by the association drawn between the island and a woman with a deceptively charming exterior, and a new impression of the island emerges, as a place characterized not only by "vaillance et passion" [valor and passion] but also by "larmes" [tears] and "haillons" [rags]. The verb "voile" [masks] indicates that the effect of concealment applies equally to the woman/poet, to the island, as well as to the poem itself. The final two stanzas point to the underlying concern of the poet, in relation to the question of how far may her poetry be considered as a true reflection of her native island: "Tu veux que nos rires, nos chants, / Poignants ou non, rythment ta vie" [You want our laughter, our songs, / Poignant or not, to give rhythm to your life]. Her reference to herself as one of the island's "bâtards" [bastards] indicates that the poet's doubts arise not so much because she is tempted to reject her native land, but rather because of her fear of herself being rejected. The insularity of her land is thus related to her own feeling of isolation.

In this important poem, the poet is able to accept and assert her identity as a woman and as a Caribbean woman, physically separated from her native land, struggling with the constant threat of alienation, feeling vulnerable, defensive, and even somewhat guilty. Through the simile of the tenth stanza ("Tel une femme" [Like a woman]), which is a good self-description of Carbet, she appropriates the identity of her native island and effectively becomes its incarnation. Within this context, the poem is "masked" means of exploring her fears of rejection and at the same time of investing herself with pride and self-esteem ("orgueil farouche et cœurs altiers") by literally formalizing in verse her intimate relationship with her native land.

à Madeleine

LETTRE A UNE AMIE INCONNUE

Il faut des yeux, des mains, des lèvres,
Pour atteindre au secret des êtres.

Une prière, une souffrance,
Dans un regard plus appuyé,
Et déjà tremble l'amitié
Dans l'ombre de l'indifférence.

Une légère altération
Au timbre habituel d'une voix,
Un mot plus tendre, insinuance
Dans un: «Bonjour» «Merci». Parfois
Un soupir surpris, un silence,
Et puis voilà: c'est la passion!

Ce désir de percer à jour
L'étranger plongé dans son drame,
De limiter à notre amour
L'immense horizon de son âme;
Ce besoin de s'évanouir
Comme un bouquet léger de bulles
Parmi le souffle qu'il respire;
De s'approprier, d'envahir,
L'eau de ses vivantes cellules;
De l'absorber, de le détruire,
Et d'en mourir...

Il faut des lèvres, une voix,
Pour atteindre au secret des âmes
Et permettre à l'amour son choix...

Il faut des paupières, des larmes
Pour mettre un sceau à l'amitié
Et pardonner à la pitié.
Mais, savez-vous pire folie
Que chérir au long d'une vie
Un mythe, un nom, une pensée?

Dois-je risquer de confronter
Votre rêve avec mon visage?
Et ne serait-il pas plus sage
A mon amitié d'éviter

La peur terrible, inavouée,
Ma peur de n'être pas aimée?

❧

to Madeleine

LETTER TO AN UNKNOWN GIRL FRIEND

Eyes, hands, lips, are needed
To reach the secret part of people.

A prayer, a hint of suffering,
In a look that's more intent,
And already friendship flickers
In the shadow of indifference.

A slight alteration
In the usual tone of a voice,
A tenderer word, suggestiveness
In a "Hello" or "Thanks." Sometimes
An unexpected sigh, a silence,
And, what do you know, it's passion!

This desire to see through
The stranger engrossed in his own drama,
To reduce to the limits of our own love
The vast horizon of his soul;
This need to dissolve
Like a light bouquet of bubbles
Amidst the breath he breathes;
To appropriate, to invade,
The water of his living cells;
To absorb him, to destroy him,
And then to die from doing so...

Lips, a voice, are needed
To reach the secret part of souls
And to let love have its choice...

Eyelids, tears, are needed
To put a seal on friendship
and grant forgiveness to pity.
But, do you know a worse folly
Than cherishing all life long
A myth, a name, a thought?

Must I risk confronting
Your dream with my face?
And would it not be wiser
For my friendship to avoid
The terrible, unadmitted fear,
My fear of not being loved?

"Lettre à une amie inconnue" [Letter to an Unknown Girl Friend](50-51) is, as the repetition of "amitié" [friendship] in the second, sixth, and final stanzas indicates, a philosophical meditation on the issue of friendship between women, as well as the exploration of a personal dilemma confronted by the poet. The central question posed by the poet is: Should I let our friendship remain at the level of friendship, or should I confess my love and risk the pain of its not being reciprocated? The tension between the philosophical and the personal is reflected in the movement within the text from concealment to self-disclosure, and is enhanced by the nature of the poetic communication, which, as both poem and letter, is inherently self-disclosing. While the gender of the addressee is clearly indicated in the dedication ("à Madeleine" [to Madeleine]) and in the title ("à une amie inconnue" [to an unknown girl friend]), that of the poetic persona is concealed for most of the poem, and is revealed, graphically, only in the feminine past participle ("aimée") of the final line of the poem.

The tension between the philosophical and the personal is played out at the level of the formal arrangement of the poem. The poem begins with a philosophical assertion introduced by the impersonal "Il faut" [(literally) there is need for]. This assertion subverts its own assertiveness by the questions it raises: What is the significance of, and relationship between, "des yeux, des mains, des lèvres" [eyes, hands, lips]? Are these terms metonymies of sensual contact or of communication? What "secret" is referred to here? Friendship is represented in the second and third stanzas as the middle stage between indifference and "passion." The poet, moreover, evinces sensitivity to nuances of "voice," as indicators of changes in the nature of relationships between individuals ("Une légère altération / Au timbre habituel d'une voix" [A slight alteration / in the usual tone of a voice]).

In the middle (fourth) stanza of the poem, sexual and gender tension reaches a peak. It is interesting to note that the addressee is clearly female, but up to this point of the poem there is no textual indication of the gender of the poetic persona. The fourth stanza, however, introduces a discussion of the dynamics of a passionate relationship with an "étranger" [stranger], the textually masculine counterpart of the "amie inconnue" of the title. Similarly, "Ce désir de percer à jour / L'étranger" [This desire to see through / The stranger] echoes the poet's opening aspiration, "Pour atteindre au secret des êtres" [To reach the secret part of people]. Passion, comprising both "désir" [desire] and uncontrollable "besoin" [need], is partly hermeneutical activity, which the poet recognizes as restrictive ("limiter" [limit]), predatory ("s'approprier" [appropriate], "envahir" [invade]), destructive ("l'absorber" [absorb him], "le détruire" [destroy him]), and potentially self-destructive ("de s'évanouir" [to dissolve]), "d'en mourir" [to die from doing so]). The expiration at the end of the paroxysm of passionate absorption is marked by the suspension points at the end of the stanza. Once again, as in the opening poem of the collection, "Ta voix" [Your Voice], erotic pleasure becomes the stimulus for poetic expression.

The poem returns to the impersonal restatement of the opening assertions, emphasizing this time the metonymic link between "lèvres" [lips] and "voix" [voice]. For the first time love ("l'amour") is mentioned explicitly in the poem, as the umbrella under which its variants "amitié" and "passion" appear. From this point the poem becomes more intensely personal, as assertive statements give way to questions. By the final stanza, as personal pronouns, first "vous" [you], then "je," appear, the dilemma of the poetic persona, cast in a feminine gender role against a more masculine lover, is disclosed. The dilemma is literary rather than real, since the poem itself discloses the poet's love. By writing the poem the poet has already confronted and confessed (in contradiction to "inavouée" [unadmitted] in the text) her fear of rejection. The movement from concealment to self-disclosure is now at one level completed. While, however, the association between the "amie" of the title and the "amitié" of the final stanza suggests the possibility that the poem could be an admission of passion for this unknown friend ("Madeleine" ?), the evocation of intense passion for a male "étranger" in the middle stanza creates an atmosphere of sexual (and interpretative) ambiguity. Within the poem, the dilemma of the sexual and gender role of the poet remains unresolved.

TOURMENT

Tes lèvres font ouvrir des fleurs
De joie au vaisseau de mes reins;
Sous mon front tremblent des lueurs,
Quand tu les poses sur mes seins.

Quand tu les poses sur mes seins,
Tes lèvres me vident les veines,
Et me font danser des essaims
D'abeilles tout au long des aînes.

Des essaims d'abeilles sur l'aîne,
Dans les entrailles du piment,
Dedans mon cœur et miel et peine;
Un cuisant, délicieux tourment.

Un cuisant, délicieux tourment
Que j'endure les dents serrées,
Tandis que s'enfle, sourdement,
Ton souffle ample et lent de marée.

❦

TORMENT

Your lips open flowers of joy
In the vessel of my loins;
Glimmers tremble under my brow,
When you lay them on my breasts.

When you lay them on my breasts,
Your lips cause my veins to drain,
And set swarms of bees
Dancing all along my groin.

Swarms of bees on my groin,
Pepper in my belly,
Inside my heart both honey and pain;
A burning, delightful torment.

A burning, delightful torment
That I endure with clenched teeth,
As all the while dully rises
Your breath, slow and ample like a tide.

Many poems in this collection give no explicit indication of a connection with the Caribbean,[5] and are constructed in response to experiences that are essentially personal. "Tourment" [Torment] (16), for example, celebrates the painful pleasure of a sexual encounter. The poetic voice here is one of unapologetic sensuality, unconcerned with issues of geography, race, or politics. While the gender of the poetic persona is feminine, the sex of the sexual partners is ambiguous. The poem derives its intensity from the formal economy with which it is constructed. The use of octosyllabic lines and alternating rhymes produces a harmonious effect that is enhanced by the reprise of the last line of each stanza as the opening line of the following stanza.

This economy extends to the representation of people and objects. The poetic persona's partner is represented, for example, through only two elements: "tes lèvres" [your lips] and "ton souffle" [your breath]. It is the lips that create intense sensual effects on the poetic persona, whose presence is perceived through the specific body parts listed: "reins" [loins], "front" [brow], "seins" [breasts], "veines" [veins], "aînes" [groin], "entrailles" [belly], "cœur" [heart], and "dents" [teeth]. Objects such as "fleurs" [flowers], "abeilles" [bees], "piment" [pepper], and "miel" [honey] are used as metaphors of sensation, the suggestive quality of which is enhanced by alliterations in "f," "v," and "r." Only two adjectives are needed to describe the sensation experienced, "cuisant" [burning] and "délicieux" [delightful]. These economical elements convey the poet's unrepressed pleasure in sexuality.

Such a poem points to the enormity of the risk taken, particularly by a female poet, to exercise her right to treat a subject, related to intimate sexual experience, not often treated so directly by male Martinican poets. This poem represents a movement away from a literary tradition (Romanticism) that tended to avoid any mention of sex and often depicted woman as suffering and sentimentally passive. The poet here, by appropriating her sexual experience and asserting herself as a sexual being, breaks with the dominant Christian, Western tradition, and produces an incredibly new, unrepressed voice with which many late twentieth century feminists would identify.[6]

RANCUNE

Le sable chaud où tu te reposes
　　Moule ton corps
D'un lin fluide à reflets roses
　　Pailleté d'or.

Ce voile mouvant rend plus nue
　　Ta nudité.
Tu prends conscience plus aiguë
　　De ta beauté.

Au fond de tes yeux impassibles
　　Tremblent, secrets,
Des rêves d'amours impossibles
　　Et des regrets.

Ta main tendre comme une joue,
　　Lorsque tu veux,
Etrangement hostile, joue
　　Dans mes cheveux.

Tu me gardes un peu rancune
　　Du don de moi,
D'avoir limité ta fortune,
　　Fixé ton choix.

D'avoir chargé tes bras d'offrandes,
　　Calmé ta faim
Du fruit sans nom que tu demandes
　　Au jour qui vient.

Tu m'en veux. Je tiens prisonnière,
Encor battant,
L'aile vive de ta chimère
Rouge de sang.

Jusqu'où ton épuisante course?
Vers quels sommets?
Je te retiens près d'une source,
Malgré toi; mais

Telle est ta fièvre de poursuivre
Un rêve vain,
Que tu remets le soin de vivre
Au lendemain.

Sache bien toute âme alourdie
D'espoirs anciens.
Ecoute la vague attiédie
Pleurer les siens.

Regarde, en ce couchant tragique,
Mourir le jour.
Qui sait s'il croyait, magnifique,
Durer toujours?

Si la mer rêvait, soulevée,
D'atteindre au ciel,
Et moi, d'une ardente envolée,
A l'irréel?

❧

RESENTMENT

The warm sand on which you lie
Moulds your body
In a fluid sheet with pink flecks
Spangled with gold.

This moving veil makes your nakedness
More naked.

You become more acutely aware
Of your beauty.

In the depths of your impassive eyes
Secretly tremble
Dreams of impossible loves
And regrets.

Your hand tender as a cheek,
When you choose,
Plays, with strange hostility,
In my hair.

You hold some resentment towards me
For the gift of myself,
For limiting your prospects,
Fixing your choice.

For loading your arms with offerings,
Appeasing your hunger
With the nameless fruit you ask for
From the coming day.

You are angry with me. I hold prisoner,
Flapping still,

The living wing of your chimera
Red with blood.

How far will your exhausting rush take you ?
Toward what peaks ?
I hold you back near a spring,
Despite yourself; but

Such is your fever to pursue
An empty dream,
That you put off the care of living
Until the morrow.

Know well every soul weighed down
With ancient hopes.
Listen to the warmed up wave
Weeping for its own.

Look, in this tragic sunset,
At the dying day.
What if it thought, in its magnificence,
It would last forever ?

What if the sea dreamed, as it rose,
Of reaching the sky,
And I, with an ardent flight,
Of unreality ?

"Rancune" [Resentment](25-27) is another very individual
post-coital reflection, without any explicit linkage to the Caribbean
or even to a communal or racial experience. The location is
indeterminate, identified only in the first stanza by "le sable chaud"
[the warm sand], although the outdoors, the beach, the sun, and the
heat indicate the Caribbean rather than Paris. Similarly, the physical
indicators of the two human presences in the poem are

indeterminate: the only physical attribute by which the poet is identified is "mes cheveux" [my hair], while the partner is represented with reference to unparticularized physical traits: "ton corps" [your body], "ta beauté" [your beauty, "tes yeux impassibles" [your impassive eyes], "Ta main tendre comme une joue" [Your hand tender as a cheek], and "tes bras" [your arms]. There is, furthermore, no textual inscription of gender in the poem. The gender identity of the poetic persona is veiled and vague, although the reference to the "don de moi" [gift of myself], within the context of a patriarchal convention in which the woman is considered as commodity that can be "given" to the man particularly in marriage, would tend to suggest that the poetic persona is feminine. The gender of the naked partner is similarly indeterminate, although the references to "ta beauté" [your beauty] and "Ta main tendre comme une joue" [Your hand tender as a cheek] would stereotypically be characteristic of women rather than of men. Thus, although the sexual partners are not explicitly gendered as female, there are sufficient indicators in the text, however masked, to suggest that they are. Indeed, the text itself functions, as the second stanza suggests, as a "voile mouvant" [moving veil], masking and unmasking the poet, and thereby enhancing the effect of the poet's self-disclosing "nudity."

This poem represents a moment of fearful lucidity, arrested and intensified by the use of the present tense, as the poet evokes her awareness of some of the complexities surfacing after sex in this intimate relationship. Her poetic vision is able to penetrate the impassive veil of her partner's eyes and grasp the partner's secret realization that this encounter has effectively compromised the future: "Des rêves d'amours impossibles / Et des regrets" [Dreams of impossible loves / And regrets]. She is also aware of the change in her partner's caresses, from accustomed tenderness to a strange hostility ("étrangement hostile"), which she is able to name as "rancune" [resentment].

The poet's sensitivity to the negative emotion experienced by her sexual partner provides the springboard for the poem. It is the poet's voice, and hers only, we hear throughout the poem speaking to her partner. She is in control of the communication, as she was of the sexual encounter. The fifth stanza indicates a clear articulation of the of what the partner considers as the underlying causes of her resentful attitude: "Tu me gardes un peu rancune / Du don de moi, / D'avoir limité ta fortune, / Fixé ton choix." [You hold some resentment towards me / For the gift of myself, / For limiting your prospects / Fixing your choice.] Sex, in this context, is perceived as a threat to the realization of aspirations, and thus generates resentment. The poet's clarity about her partner's perceptions, however, carries no hint of defensiveness, no acknowledgement of the validity of her partner's attitude. Instead, the claims of limitation and fixity are replaced by contrasting images of positive spiritual and emotional contributions made by the poetic subject to her partner's development: "Chargé tes bras d'offrandes, / Calmé ta faim" [loading your arms with offerings, / Appeasing your hunger]. The poet gives a new twist to the *carpe diem* philosophy that has inspired European lyric poets for centuries. The horrific image of the seventh stanza translates the poet persona's own "rancune" [resentment], as she exacts sadistic vengeance on her partner's dream: "Je tiens prisonnière, / Encor battant, / L'aile vive de ta chimère / Rouge de sang" [I hold prisoner / Flapping still, / The living wing of your chimera / Red with blood]. What the poet berates in her partner is the latter's failure to live fully in the present moment: "tu remets le soin de vivre / Au lendemain" [you put off the care of living / Until the morrow]. Every "rêve vain" [empty dream] is castigated, and the poet turns to nature for metaphorical illustration of the futility of unrealistic yearnings. Resentment is finally self-directed (last stanza), as the poet contemplates the possible failure of her presumably poetic aspirations: "Si la mer rêvait, soulevée / D'atteindre au ciel, / Et moi, d'une ardente envolée, / A l'irréel." [What if the sea dreamed, as it rose, / Of reaching the sky, / And I, with an ardent flight, / Of unreality ?].

This is a highly personal poem in which the sexual act alluded to in the text provides the context for the poet to take the risk of exploring some of the complexities of her individual situation as a woman and as a poet. The negative emotion of resentment unconventionally associated with this act furnishes the energy for the poet to affirm and justify her right to exploit the present within her intimate relationship. This poem is a wonderful example of the poet's lucidity and courage in adopting and textualizing what is after all an unusual stance for a woman.

à mon frère, tué en Indochine

JE TE TIENS VIF...

Dans la clairière, en la forêt,
J'ai découvert un cimetière
Enfoui dans la neige, discret.
Croix de bois et stèles de pierre

Disent que là, des militaires,
Loin du pays où ils sont nés,
Dorment, doublement solitaires,
Et doublement abandonnés.

J'ai cru te retrouver, mon frère,
Toi dont on m'apprit le décès,
Toi qui gis en terre étrangère,
Sous herbe ou granit, je ne sais.

Brusquement, je voulus savoir
Quelle main ferma ta paupière,
Qui, par amitié ou devoir,
Tendit le linceul dans ta bière,

Si seulement on te la fit,
Cette humble charité dernière,
Et si tu mourus dans un lit

Ou, comme un chien, dans la poussière.

Mon cœur crevait. Mes pas, pourtant,
Ecrasant la couche légère
D'humus, rebondissaient, heurtant
Le ventre ferme de la terre.

Et je sentais la vie en elle,
Fatale, invisible, agitant,
Dans l'air blême et le rameau frêle,
Les premiers signes du printemps.

Je l'entendais en moi, la vie,
Exalter l'ardeur des matins
Où nous cherchions dans la prairie
La «liane douce» des lapins.

Nous avions, moi, sept, toi, neuf ans.
Nous poursuivions tout ce qui bouge
Parmi les «cabouillas» mouvants
Où se dressaient de grands lys rouges.

Pour franchir les fossés d'un bond,
Grimper après les mangotines,
Je t'empruntais des pantalons,
Et nous délacions nos bottines.

Tu veillais à ce que j'évite
De m'égratigner les mollets,
A ce que mon pied nu ne quitte
Le sentier bordé de galets.

Contre le soleil trop ardent,
Le vent, le froid, la guêpe vive,
Tu me protégeais en grondant,

Bourru, la tendresse attentive.

Pas une heure de notre enfance
Ne peut s'arracher de mon corps.
Ni le silence, ni l'absence
Ne me sont preuves de ta mort.

Je dors avec toi dans la boue,
Sinon, tu vis de ma misère;
Tes larmes coulent sur ma joue,
Dans mon cri perce ta colère.

Je te tiens vif au plus profond
De la source où mon souffle puise.
Approche, incline ici le front,
Revêtons nos longues chemises,

Rangés autour de notre mère,
À ses genoux, comme autrefois,
Nous reprendrons notre prière,
Mot à mot, en suivant sa voix:

«Seigneur, dans ta bonté, accorde
Grâce à ceux qui se sont aimés
Et que ta main a séparés.
Fais à nous tous miséricorde.»

❦

to my brother, killed in Indochina

I KEEP YOU ALIVE...

In the clearing, in the forest,
I discovered a graveyard

Buried in snow, secluded.
Crosses of wood and steles of stone

Declare that soldiers, there,
Far from the countries of their birth,
Sleep, doubly alone,
And doubly abandoned.

I thought I'd find you again, my brother,
You whose death they told me of,
You who are lying in a foreign land,
Under grass or granite, I know not which.

Suddenly, I wanted to know
Whose hand closed your eyelid,
Who, out of friendship or duty,
Straightened the shroud in your casket,

Whether at least you had it done,
This last humble act of charity,
And whether you died in a bed
Or, like a dog, in the dust.

My heart was breaking. My steps, however,
Crushing the thin layer
Of humus, bounced back, as they struck
The firm belly of the earth.

And in it I felt life,
Fateful and invisible, shaking,
In the pallid air and the frail branch,
The first signs of spring.

I heard life within me
Exalting the ardor of those mornings

When we went looking in the meadows for
Rabbits' "sweet bush."

We were, I, seven, you, nine years old.
We chased everything that stirred
Among the moving *cabouillas*
Where tall red lilies stood.

To jump over ditches,
Or climb for baby mangoes
I would borrow your trousers,
And we would unlace our boots.

You made sure that I avoided
Scraping my calves,
That my feet stayed inside
The pebble-lined path.

From the too hot sun,
From wind, cold, and lively wasps,
You protected me, grumbling,
Surly, with watchful tenderness.

Not an hour of our childhood
Can be taken from my body.
Neither silence, nor absence
Are proof to me that you are dead.

I sleep with you in the mud,
Or else you live on my woe;
Your tears flow on my cheek,
Your anger shows in my cry.

I keep you alive in the deepest part
Of the spring from which my breath is drawn.

Come closer, here bow your head,
Let's put our long shirts on again,

Grouped around our mother,
At her knees, like long ago,
We will say our prayer again,
Word by word, following her voice:

"Lord, in thy kindness, give
Grace to those who have loved one other
And who have been separated by thine hand.
Have mercy on us all."

"Je te tiens vif ..." [I keep you alive..](17-19), dedicated to the poet's dead brother ("à mon frère, tué en Indochine" [To my brother, killed in Indochina]), is an elaboration of another personal experience. Here, the poet explores the links, both in life and in death, that bind her to her brother, who, I am told, died in 1944 of dysentery in a concentration camp. In the first two stanzas, it is against a backdrop of significantly white snow ("dans la neige"), here associated with death, that the poet finds concrete signs ("Croix de bois et stèles de pierre" [Crosses of wood and steles of stone]) of generalized exile and alienation from the native land ("Loin du pays où ils sont nés" [Far from the countries of their birth], "solitaires" [alone], "abandonnés" [abandoned]). The poet's hope, therefore, is to re-establish contact with her brother separated by death and by geography ("Toi qui gis en terre étrangère" [You who are lying in a foreign land]).

The poet's immediate first concern is with the observance of traditional rituals associated with dying, which would have mitigated her brother's alienation and protected his dignity as a human being: "Brusquement, je voulus savoir / Quelle main ferma ta paupière.... [Suddenly, I wanted to know / Whose hand closed your eyelid]. It is through the poet's sense of a physical contact with the earth that awareness of life is re-awakened: "... heurtant / Le ventre ferme de la terre. / Et je sentais la vie en elle... [striking / The firm belly of the earth. / And in it I felt life]. Whereas snow was associated with death in the opening stanza of the poem, life comes to be related, in stanzas 8 - 12, to childhood experiences, which include "liane douce" (a bush used to feed rabbits), "cabouillas" (a variety of wild grass), "mangotines," "soleil trop ardent" [too hot sun], all of which evoke memories of the Caribbean. The insertion of creole vocabulary, in inverted commas, into the French text insists on a non-French reality in which she and her brother participate.

Memories of experiences shared with her brother during childhood are therefore affirmed as an integral part of the poet's physical identity and as indications of the survival, beyond the tomb, of her brother within her own being: "Pas une heure de notre enfance / Ne peut s'arracher de mon corps" [Not an hour of our childhood / Can be taken from my body]. This joining of identity is presented, in the fourteenth stanza, as an interpenetration of identity between her brother and herself, to the extent that her poetic voice is projected as the expression of her brother's emotions: "Dans mon cri perce ta colère" [Your anger shows in my cry]. This adoption of her (male) brother's emotion points to her assumption, as a woman poet, of responsibility for transmitting her sibling's voice as well as her own.

The fifteenth stanza, which contains the phrase used as the title of this poem, provides a climax to the poetic elaboration of the significance which her dead brother holds for the poet: "Je te tiens vif au plus profond / De la source où mon souffle puise" [I keep you alive in the deepest part / Of the spring from which my breath is drawn]. The inference here is that the source of the poet's creativity is connected to the island life of childhood, shared with her brother, and beyond him to the voice of their mother ("en suivant sa voix" [following her voice]), heard in a childhood ritual of repeated prayer.

This poem is a statement of the poet's awareness, even in the face of the threat of exile and alienation in foreign soil, of the strength and importance of her connection to her brother and behind him to their mother and to her memories of her Caribbean native island. Through the poem, this connection is re-established and contributes toward the emergence of the poet's Caribbean poetic voice.

à Jasmine

CHANSON

LA JOLIE FOLIE

I

« Cré nom de dieu! la belle femme! »
Te détournant de ton chemin
Tu m'as suivie au long des rues.

Folle et fou, la jolie folie!

II

Devant toi mes hanches tanguaient,
Et tu sentais brûler ton sang.
Longtemps au soleil de midi,

Folle et fou, la jolie folie,

III

Tu m'as suivie. Quand à la fin
J'ai pris ta main, ton pouls chantait,
Criait, hurlait que désormais,

Folle et fou, la jolie folie,

IV

Dans mes veines coulait ta vie.
Noire j'étais; noire de peau,
Dents nacrées et cheveux crépus.

Folle et fou, la jolie folie,

V
Par malheur, par malheur, en plus
J'avais une âme, une âme en trop.
Au fait, qu'es-tu donc devenu?

Folle et fou, la jolie folie!

❦

to *Jasmine*

SONG

FINE FOLLY
I
"Gosh! What a lovely woman!"
Turning from your path
You followed me along the streets.

Crazy woman and crazy man, fine folly!

II
In front of you my hips were swinging
And you felt your blood catch fire.
For a long time in the midday sun,

Crazy woman and crazy man, fine folly,

III
You followed me. When at last
I took your hand, your pulse sang,
Shouted, screamed that from now on,

Crazy woman and crazy man, fine folly,

IV

Your life flowed in my veins.
Black I was; black of skin,
Pearly teeth and kinky hair.

Crazy woman and crazy man, fine folly,

V

Unfortunately, unfortunately, as well
I had a soul, one soul too much.
By the way, what became of you?

Crazy woman and crazy man, fine folly!

Among the eight poems in this collection designated as songs ("chansons"), "La jolie folie" [Fine Folly] (20-21) deserves particular attention. The inclusion of so many "chansons" in the collection points to the poet's interest in adopting an "oral" model for some of her poetry, and this poem is a excellent example of Caribbean orality. It is, moreover, the only poem in the collection in which the poetic persona identifies herself explicitly as beautiful and as black.

The song opens, lightheartedly, with the voice of a man attracted by the sight of a beautiful woman: « Cré nom de Dieu! la belle femme! » [Gosh! What a lovely woman!]. It is the woman/ poet who leads in this suggestive encounter, as she recounts the physical effect she has on the man: "Devant toi mes hanches tanguaient, / Et tu sentais brûler ton sang" [In front of you my hips were swinging, / And you felt your blood catch fire]. Her control continues in the third verse, where it is she who initiates the first physical contact ("j'ai pris ta main" [I took your hand]), which immediately shows promise of future durable intimacy between the couple: " ... désormais, / Dans mes veines coulait ta vie" [...from now on / ... / Your life flowed in my veins].

It is at this point of hope that the woman/poet describes herself, first generally, then with specific reference to features which would stereotypically identify her as a black woman: "Noire j'étais; noire de peau, / Dents nacrées et cheveux crépus" [Black I was; black of skin, / Pearly teeth and kinky hair]. The syntactical fluidity of "noire," which could be adjective or noun, emphasizes both race and gender. The final verse, which follows this disclosure, transmits, through the repetition of "par malheur" [unfortunately] and "âme" [soul], all the pain that a (stereotyped black) woman feels to discover that acceptance by a male is too often conditional on her own acceptance of her role as merely a physical object. This light-hearted song ends on a deeply ironic note of resigned rejection: "Au fait, qu'es-tu donc devenu?" [By the way, what became of you?]

"La jolie folie" is in many ways a breakthrough poem. Its dialogue and its formal arrangement, as a song of three-line verse and single-line chorus, emphasize its orality, and make it wonderfully playful and light. It is a funny poem, presenting a black woman indulging, without illusion or self-deception, in frank sexual play. Its humor, climaxed by the turn-around at the end, is typically Caribbean, reminiscent of "picong"[7] associated with Caribbean calypso. This poem therefore reveals a voice, recognizably that of a Caribbean woman, which continues the voice of "Tourment," and contrasts sharply with the stereotypical French Romantic female voice of many of Carbet's other poems.

Twelve years separate the publication of *Point d'orgue* from *Rose de ta grâce*. During that period, Carbet made several trips to West Africa on her own, out of personal interest. Significantly, in Rose de ta grâce, the 1970 collection of 35 poems, Carbet, for the first time in her poetry, acknowledges the existence of Africa as a source for some of her verse. Indeed, five poems ("Hautes eaux" [High Waters], "Greffe" [Transplant], "Civilisation" [Civilization], "Au roseau" [To the Reed], and "Beau piroguier" [Fine Pirogue-man]), two of them ("Greffe" and "Civilisation") among the longest in the collection, directly address aspects of life in Africa. Four other poems are just as clearly set in the Caribbean:

"Verger" [Orchard] (13), "La Vendeuse des rues" [Woman Street-Vendor](24), "Folklore" (63), and "La Saison des mangues" [Mango Season](69). The inclusion of these clearly Africa- and Caribbean-oriented poems indicates a movement on the part of the poet towards a reconciliation of these two aspects of her identity and a greater and clearer acknowledgement of the native land and Africa as axes for the generation of poetic activity. At the same time, Carbet's verse has become more liberated from the constraints of formal versification. Although she retains a fondness for the octosyllabic line, she employs more variations of rhyme than she had used in *Point d'orgue*, and often dispenses with rhymes altogether. The following poems point to ways in which Carbet, while transforming elements that link her to metropolitan poetic traditions, and discovering in Africa a new source of inspiration, ultimately finds personal and poetic resolution for all her problems in expressions of religious faith.

À Claire Delattre.

TOI QUI NOUS AS PROMIS MERCI...

Mon cœur est un sépulcre gris
Où sous les ronces, les débris
D'âges divers gisent en vrac.

Rameaux moisis, les amours mortes
Sans relief, sans poids, sans couleur...
Cinq, sept ou dix dans le fagot?
Comment savoir, il est enfoui
Sous cendre en monceaux refroidis
Où la rouille et le vert-de-gris
Endeuillent la flèche épointée
Des jeunes amours avortées.

En bas de leurs stèles tronquées

Des éclats d'amitiés trahies...
Des restes d'offrandes jetées
En mille pièces dans la suie.
Mon cœur est un sépulcre gris
Qui refuse asile à l'oubli.

Toi qui nous a promis merci,
Seigneur, d'un rayon fais éclore
Rose de ta grâce en sa nuit,
Mon cœur sera jardin nouveau.

❦

To Claire Delattre

THOU WHO PROMISED US MERCY...

My heart is a grey sepulcher
Where the ruins of different ages
Lie pell-mell beneath the thorns.

Moldy branches, loves dead
Without contour, weight, or color...
Five, seven or ten in the bundle ?
How is one to know? It is buried
Under ashes in cold piles
Where rust and verdigris
Add a mournful cast to the blunted dart
Of young abortive loves.

Beneath their truncated pillars
Shards of friendships betrayed...
Remains of offerings thrown
By the thousands of pieces into the soot.
My heart is a gray sepulcher

Refusing to give sanctuary to forgetting.

Thou who promised us mercy,
O Lord, with a beam make
The rose of your grace flower in its night.
My heart will be a garden new.

To any student of literature educated, as Carbet was, within the French tradition, the opening lines of this poem would appear to be very familiar in its Baudelairian echoes of vocabulary and image. Because of this immediate impression of familiarity, I felt it might be interesting to undertake a reading of this poem from the perspective of intertextual linkages between Carbet and Baudelaire.

A little more than a century before this Martinican woman of color had published her volume of thirty-five poems entitled *Rose de ta grâce* [Rose of Thy Grace], Charles Baudelaire, a Frenchman, who conducted a long-time affair with a woman of color from one of the French dependencies, had published (in 1857) a volume of poetry entitled *Les Fleurs du Mal [Flowers of Evil].*[8] The title of Carbet's collection is a phrase which appears in the penultimate line of "Toi qui nous a promis merci... [Thou Who Promised Us Mercy]," a poem whose tone and emotional climate are far from Baudelairian, but which is nevertheless replete with textual Baudelairian resonances. There are striking similarities between this poem and some of the "spleen" poems of Baudelaire which cannot be ignored,[9] to the point where it appears that the male, metropolitan French, *fin de siècle*, Baudelairian sensibility serves as a point of departure for a Caribbean woman to address her own personal and cultural dilemma and find a poetic resolution through a transforming religious and creative experience.

The title of Carbet's collection, *Rose de ta grâce* suggests paradoxically contrasting metonymic linkages with the Baudelairian title, *Les Fleurs du Mal*: the singular Carbetian rose asserts its specificity among the generality of Baudelairian "flowers," while the acknowledgement of an intimate relationship with God, as the source of the poetic gift, implicit in "ta grâce" [thy grace], contrasts with a similar acknowledgement of an impersonal Evil as the source of the Baudelairian poetic product. This initial point of convergence between Carbet and Baudelaire could be considered as accidental and even irrelevant, were it not for other textual intersections which permit an appreciation of the deep connections between the male French and female Martinican poets. These Baudelairian flowers, an early manifestation of a decadent, *fin de siècle* sensibility, are in a sense replanted by Carbet and transformed into *Rose de ta grâce*.

The opening lines of Carbet's poem metaphorically identify a condition of death and decay as the state of the poet's heart. This introduction evokes a mood of depression, disillusionment, and world-weariness that is highly reminiscent of Baudelairian "spleen." The terms used to create this mood provide interesting intersections with several of Baudelaire's poems: "Du fond du gouffre obscur où mon cœur est tombé" [From the bottom of the dark gulf into which my heart has fallen] (*"De profundis clamavi"*, 51); "Moisir parmi les ossements" [Grow moldy among the bones], "Mes amours décomposés" [My decomposed loves] (Une charogne," 51); "Leur peau fleurira l'aridité des ronces" [Their skin will make the aridity of thorns bloom]("Duellum," 55); "quelque vieux débris gisant" [some old debris lying]("A une mendiante rousse," 96).

The starting point for Carbet is "mon cœur" [my heart], the traditional seat of the emotions, here metaphorically represented as "un sépulcre" [a sepulcher], the literary equivalent of a tomb, the concrete symbol that ensures a form of immortality. The literary resonance of this image, which establishes a significant linkage between the poet and the tomb, recalls the Baudelairian statement in "Remords posthume" [Posthumous Remorse]: "Car le tombeau toujours comprendra le poète" [For the tomb will always understand the poet](54). Baudelaire's expressed attitude in this poem reflects an awareness of problems in relating, as a man and as a poet, to women, as well as to the conditions of "modern" life. The Baudelairian suggestion that absolution and justification will come after death establishes the expectation of a successful communication with a future beyond his lifetime. The Carbet text provides confirmation of the validity of Baudelaire's suggestion. The description of the state of Carbet's heart, characterized by confusion, by lack of care, and by abandonment, reflects a sadness similar to that expressed by Baudelaire in describing the state of his heart: "Mon cœur est un palais flétri par la cohue" [My heart is a palace condemned by the mob] ("Causerie", 73). However, the proud stance of a noble victim implicit in the Baudelairian image is missing in Carbet, whose attitude of acceptance leaves no room for the bitterness and violence conveyed in the Baudelairian text. While problems of the heart lead Baudelaire to experience the sensation of a descent into the depths of a depression reminiscent of Hell ("*De Profundis clamavi*," 52), in Carbet there is no sensation of descent; her heart does not "fall." What is for Baudelaire a "gouffre obscur" [dark gulf] is for Carbet merely a "sépulcre gris" [gray sepulcher]. The title of Baudelaire's poem, borrowed from the Psalms, transmits the poet's religious fervor. The "Toi" [Thee] whom he addresses, however, fuses religiosity with sexuality. For Carbet, the "Toi" addressed in the final stanza is the Christian "Seigneur" [Lord]. Her attitude is far from the self-castigatory prostration of Baudelaire, as he appeals to an implicitly pitiless power. Carbet is secure in her faith, in her belief in the divine promise, anticipating, not Baudelaire's suggested emotion of "pity," but the more productive gift of "merci" [mercy].

The impression created by Carbet, of an emotional condition of depression, conveyed through references to a tomb, to thorny bushes, to the débris of past ages, to mildew, ashes, rust, and past loves, is similar to the condition of "spleen" evoked by Baudelaire in one of his "Spleen" poems, "J'ai plus de souvenirs que si j'avais mille ans" [I have more memories than if I were a thousand years old] (87). The contents of Baudelaire's "gros meuble à tiroirs" [large chest of drawers] match what Carbet calls "les débris / D'âges divers" [ruins / Of different ages]. Significantly, in his poem Baudelaire describes himself not only as "un cimetière" [a cemetery], which forms a metonymic link with Carbet's "sépulcre" [sepulcher], but also as "un vieux boudoir plein de roses fanées" [an old boudoir full of faded roses]. It is precisely the "rose" that Carbet uses as an emblem of her own emotional, spiritual, and creative transformation.

Within the Carbet poem, the relationship established in the last stanza between "cœur" [heart] and "Seigneur" [Lord] invests "cœur" with a spiritual as well as an emotional significance. The Carbet equation "cœur" [heart] = "sépulcre" [sepulcher] parallels Baudelaire's statement, "Mon âme est un tombeau" [My soul is a tomb] ("Le mauvais moine,"(37). In this poem, Baudelaire does not entertain any prospect of change but remains concerned about his literary sterility. Although he uses his awareness of the creative difficulties he experiences as the subject matter of his poem, Baudelaire remains emotionally and spiritually stuck, the victim of his own impotence. In Carbet, on the other hand, awareness of the metaphorical equation leads rather to action and to a solution, through reliance on a sure source of creative power. The image of the "ronces" [thorns] used by Carbet to describe the situation of her heart suggests difficulty of access through the protective thorns. Interestingly, Baudelaire used "ronces" to suggest dryness of soil, difficult for cultivating flowers ("Duellum," 55). The Baudelairian poem will grow out of the sexual battle-to-the-death of the lover-warriors. For Carbet, the "ronces" will disappear, as her heart becomes a new garden, in which the poetic rose will flower.

Disillusionment in relation to love is transmitted by Carbet in two references in this poem: "les amours mortes" [dead loves] and "jeunes amours avortées" [young abortive loves]. Her preference for the literary feminine plural contrasts with Baudelaire's practice in transmitting similar sentiments: the Baudelairian poem "Une charogne" [A Decaying Carcass] is the immortalized essence of the male poet's "amours décomposés" [decomposed loves] (51). The discussion of "leurs amours défunts" [their defunct loves] is a manifestation of "Spleen" (87). Thus the problems of the feminine experience in love are textually implicit in Carbet's choice.

Baudelaire's "Un voyage à Cythère" [A Journey to Cythera] (133) opens, as does the Carbet poem, with an image of the poet's heart: "Mon cœur, comme un oiseau" [My heart, like a bird]. The setting for this poem is an island, represented as "pleine de fleurs écloses" [full of flowers that have opened], "Où les soupirs des cœurs en adoration / Roulent comme l'encens sur un jardin de roses" [Where the sighs of hearts in adoration / Roll like incense over a garden of roses]. At the end of the poem, the poet appeals to a "Seigneur" [Lord] to provide him with strength and courage. The nouns "cœur" [heart], "jardin" [garden], "rose" [rose], and "Seigneur" [Lord], which have strong symbolic associations in the Baudelairian poem, all have similarly important functions in Carbet's poem. It is the "Seigneur" who is called upon to provide the creative force by which the poetic "rose" is produced. Within the course of the poem the poet's heart is transformed from "un sépulcre gris" [gray sepulcher] into a "jardin nouveau" [new garden] within which the poem can find life.

What, however, is the significance of all these textual intersections between Carbet and Baudelaire? It would be a profound disservice to Carbet as a woman, as a poet, and as an Antillean, to suggest that her poetry is merely a re-writing of Baudelaire. It clearly is not. It is evident that Baudelaire was confronted with problems for which he chose to seek solutions in his poetic creations: problems related to life, love, spirituality, and art. Carbet's problems were similar, yet different. Carbet, as a woman of color writing in French within a culture which even in the twentieth century tended to deny her a voice both as a woman and as a woman of color must have experienced a version of the Baudelairian spleen. Isolated within a literary climate that favored male Surrealist attitudes and practices, which treated Woman as an object and an Other, she must have found difficulty in seeing herself as a poetic subject. Baudelaire's longing for a tropical paradise far away from the problems of metropolitan France parallels that of

Carbet, who was led in her poetry to recreate the folkloric voices of her island homeland. Baudelaire's sexual frustration and ambivalence finds an echo in Carbet's own poetic ambivalence and reticence in relation to sex, evidenced in the fact that in her love poems her lovers are rarely clearly identifiable as male or female. Baudelaire's nineteenth century existential malaise, expressed as "spleen," prefigures the malaise of a Martinican woman of color in twentieth century France. This malaise is reflected in Carbet's tendency towards textually masking her identity as a woman of color, even while exploring her identity dilemma and her relationship to the white world.

Within the poem a transformation takes place: the opening "Mon cœur est un sépulcre gris" [My heart is a gray sepulcher] becomes at the end "Mon cœur sera jardin nouveau" [My heart will be a garden new], indicating a movement from despair to hope. This suggests that the collection as a whole is the voice of hope. This poem moves away from morbidity and depression to embrace signs of hope and rebirth, as the poet becomes effectively the channel for the word of God. The poem thereby indicates that the resolution of all the problems confronting the poet, as a daughter, a brother, a woman, a poet, and as an "Antillaise," lies ultimately in religious faith.

The intersections between Carbet and Baudelaire indicate her turning away from the dominant contemporary literary practice of the early twentieth century towards a traditional expression with which she was more comfortable. Even the Baudelairian tradition, however, was not entirely suitable to express her own sensibility. She could use it, however, as a point of departure to address her own personal and cultural dilemma, and find a poetic resolution through a transforming religious and creative experience. Carbet's collection thus takes as its name the "rose" of divine grace, produced in the new garden of the poet's heart. Carbet can share with Baudelaire a sensibility that is bruised by the sociocultural context within which it exists. Carbet, however, survives and transcends the difficulties of her position, moves beyond the *fin-de-siècle* tendency to spleen and despair to affirm a positive vision of hope, as both woman and poet.

A Paulette Nardal.
En Afrique du Sud, un cœur de nègre a été greffé sur un blanc
par le professeur Barnard.
(Les journaux, janvier 1968).

GREFFE

Et si mon cœur se souvenait?
Marqué à jamais en ses fibres
Du sceau des brûlures anciennes
S'il se révélait étranger
A tes angoisses, à ta haine?

Désormais stricte mécanique
Ni plus ni moins qu'ordinateur,
Rebelle au jeu de ton cerveau,
S'il rejetait le poids nouveau
De tes amours et de ta joie ?

Si mon cœur de nègre emmuré
Sanglé en poitrine de blanc
Refusait d'endosser ta peau ?
Si de mon rire bafoué
Il suffoquait... à t'étrangler ?

S'il te renvoyait à la gorge
Crachats et mépris encaissés ?
Si brusquement en toi, montait
Le fiel des humiliations
Qui furent mon pain quotidien?

Si, retrouvant, impérieux
Le devoir de se surpasser

Pour émerger de l'infamie,
Mon cœur persistait dans l'effort
D'honorer la justice qui
Gît flagellée, front dans la boue ?

Quelques consciences alertées
Ont confessé crainte timide
Que le proche destin du nègre
En lieux supercivilisés
Se réduise à pourvoir aux greffes.

Seigneur qui, depuis deux mille ans
Bras ouverts sur la croix attends,
Aurais-tu choisi de sauver
A ce prix tes brebis perdues ?

Si l'étoile jaune, les camps,
La famine, les crématoires,
La bombe-joujou, le napalm,
Si la terre gorgée du sang
Des infirmes et des enfants
Laissent le Blanc encor au chaud
A l'aise, en confort dans sa peau,
Et si tu décides qu'il faut
Greffer un cœur nègre à tous ceux
Dont la disgrâce est d'en manquer,

S'il te faut nous sacrifier
Pour qu'enfin règne ton amour
Christ, nous briguons la faveur d'être
Volontaires à ton service.

❦

To Paulette Nardal.
In South Africa, a negro heart has been transplanted into a white man
by Professor Barnard.
(Newspaper reports, January 1968).

TRANSPLANT

And what if my heart remembered ?
Marked forever in its fibers
With the stamp of ancient burns
What if it showed itself alien
To your anguish, and to your hate ?

Henceforth strictly mechanical
A computer neither more nor less
Resistant to the workings of your brain,
What if it rejected the new burden
Of your loves and of your joy ?

What if my negro's heart immured
Strapped into a white man's chest
Refused to endorse your skin ?
What if on the jibes of my laughter
It choked ... to the point of strangling you ?

What if it threw back in your throat
The spit and scorn it had received ?
What if in you suddenly rose up
The gall of the humiliations
That were my daily bread ?

What if, seeing again as urgent
The duty to outdo itself
So as to emerge from infamy,
My heart persisted in the effort
Of honoring justice which

Lies flogged, face down in the mud ?

Some informed consciences
Have confessed a timid fear
That soon the negro's fate
In supercivilized places
May simply be to provide transplants.

Lord, who for two thousand years now
Have been waiting with open arms upon the cross,
Could this be your chosen price
For saving your lost sheep ?

If the yellow star, the camps,
Famine, the crematoria,
Toy bombs, napalm,
If the earth gorged with the blood
Of cripples and of children
Leave the White man still cozy
At ease, comfortable in his skin,
And if you decide that it is necessary
To transplant a negro heart into all those
Whose disgrace it is not to have one,

If you need to sacrifice us
For your love at last to reign,
Christ, we crave the favor of being
Volunteers in your service.

"Greffe" (19-21) is a unique poem for Carbet, since it is the only poem in this collection where she assumes the identity and voice of a (South African) "nègre" [negro]. The adoption of the identity of a "nègre" contrasts with her characterization of herself as "noire" [black] in "La jolie folie," and represents an increased sensitivity to issues of social and economic deprivation and exploitation that are part of the condition of the "nègre."

The poem is dedicated, significantly, to Paulette Nardal, one of the four Martinican Nardal sisters who held a literary and artistic salon in Paris in the late 1920s-early 1930s. It was Paulette who organized the ephemeral *Revue du monde noir* (1931-32), in collaboration with the Haitian, Dr. Sajous. In the notation at the head of the poem, the poet indicates the context for the poem: newspaper reports of the transplant operation, performed in South Africa by Dr. Christian Barnard, of a black man's heart into a white man. The poem poses a series of hypothetical questions, first to the white man (stanzas 1-5) and then to Christ (stanza 7), in relation to the implications of such an operation, before proposing an attitude of conditional self-sacrifice.

The preliminary question ("Et si mon cœur se souvenait" [And what if my heart remembered]) forms the link between the newspaper reports and the activity of the poet: the poem is a result of the survival of the poet's own memories of experiences as a "nègre," the emotional effects of which (implicit in "mon cœur" [my heart]) have been triggered and brought to life by the newspaper reports. The combination of the physical and emotional connotations of "cœur" [heart] is continued in this stanza. The poet contends that such painful memories, of physical and emotional "brûlures anciennes" [ancient burns] are literally ineradicable, both for the poet and for the black man's heart ("Marqué à jamais en ses fibres" [Marked forever in its fibers]). "Etranger" [alien] (of the fourth line), is invested with highly ironic resonances: it expresses the physical rejection of the transplant by the black man's heart, in contradiction to the more common rejection of the heart by the body; it also implies a moral rejection by the black man of "white" attitudes, characterized by "angoisses" [anguish] and "haine" [hate]. This first stanza, addressed to the white man, thus introduces the notion, through the symbol of the heart, of the possible moral superiority of the black poet.

In the second stanza, the transplanted heart becomes a symbol of the further emotional exploitation of blacks by whites, as "tes amours" [your loves] echoes "tes angoisses' [your anguish] of the first stanza, and "ta joie" [your joy] reflects "ta haine" [your hate]. The attitude of rejection hypothesized by the poetic persona ("S'il rejetait" [What if it rejected]) implies a threat to the emotional security of the white man, and suggests a new choice for blacks. The threat implicit in the first two stanzas becomes clearer in the third, where the oppositions only hinted at earlier are now stated more explicitly. Moreover, "mon cœur" [my heart] of the first stanza becomes "mon cœur de nègre" [my negro heart], as the poet fully adopts the identity of a "nègre." The second stanza introduces a new hypothesis -- a new role for the black heart, that of "rebelle" [resistant], with connotations of political as well as emotional and biological resistance. What is implied is the acquisition of a measure of freedom from the control, literally and figuratively, of the white man's rationalism, "ton cerveau" [your brain]. "Poids nouveau" [new burden] echoes "brûlures anciennes" [ancient burns] of the first stanza, intimating that historically the role of whites has been to heap burdens upon blacks. This transplanted heart therefore becomes a symbol of the further emotional exploitation of blacks by whites. The attitude of rejection hypothesized by the poet implies a threat to the emotional security of the white man, and indicates a new choice for blacks.

The developing threat implicit in the first two stanzas becomes clearer in the third. Whereas the first stanza presented the revelation of the true nature of the black heart ("se révélait étranger" [showed itself alien]), and the second stanza expressed an attitude of emotional rejection ("S'il rejetait" [What if it rejected]), the third stanza, while contemplating total refusal ("refusait d'endosser ta peau" [refused to endorse your skin]) proposes the poet's ironic laughter as a powerful instrument of destruction ("Il suffoquait... à t'étrangler" [It choked ... to the point of strangling you]). Suggestions for retaliatory and subversive activities continue in the fourth stanza, as the poetic persona speculates with bitter irony on biological manifestations of revenge for the past humiliations. The fifth stanza, however, presents the black heart as operating under the influence of moral imperatives diametrically opposed to those of whites ("Le devoir de se surpasser / Pour émerger de l'infamie" [The duty to outdo itself / So as to emerge from infamy]; "l'effort / D'honorer la justice" [the effort / Of honoring justice]).

In the sixth stanza, the poetic persona suspends his questions to the white man in order to make a bitter declaration of the implication of the transplant operation for the future role of black people in the white industrialized world: "... le proche destin du nègre / En lieux supercivilisés / Se réduise à pourvoir aux greffes" [soon the nigger's fate / In supercivilized places / May simply be to provide transplants]. The articulation of this prospect prepares for the last section of the poem, where the poet, in the role of a doubting Christian, enters into communication with Christ: "Seigneur qui, depuis deux mille ans / Bras ouverts sur la croix attends" [Lord, who for two thousand years now / Have been waiting with open arms upon the cross], presenting blacks as "brebis perdues" [lost sheep], and posing the frightening question of whether the price of the salvation of blacks is their exploitation as transplant sources.

In the last two stanzas, the poet introduces a new series of hypotheses to validate the position espoused at the end of the poem. The first set of hypotheses relates to the enviably comfortable situation of whites ("le Blanc encor au chaud / À l'aise, en confort dans sa peau" [the White man still cozy / At ease, comfortable in his skin]), despite the havoc they have caused. The second hypothesis relates to the proposition already advanced in the sixth stanza of the function of blacks: "Et si tu décides qu'il faut / Greffer un cœur nègre à tous ceux / Dont la disgrâce est d'en manquer" [And if you decide that it is necessary / To transplant a negro heart into all those / Whose disgrace it is not to have one]. "Un cœur nègre" [a negro heart] is presented as a desirable quality and the antithesis of the cruelties and abuses associated with whites. The final hypothesis makes even more radical assumptions about the desirability of "black" qualities, establishing an association between the black heart and divine love, and presenting blacks in the saintly role of sacrificial victim: "S'il te faut nous sacrifier / Pour qu'enfin règne ton amour" [If you need to sacrifice us / For your love at last to reign]. The use of "nous" [us] highlights the poet's total identification at this point with all blacks, in the suggested role of eager servants of Christ: "Christ, nous briguons la faveur d'être / Volontaires à ton service" [Christ, we crave the favor of being / Volunteers in your service].

The evocation, in the third stanza, of the excruciatingly painful situation of a "black" heart firmly fixed within a white skin raises the extratextual question of the relevance of this situation to Carbet herself as a woman of color. The whole poem is doubtlessly to some extent an exploration of a personal dilemma. "Greffe" is used as a metaphor of the poet's awareness both of physical and emotional exploitation by whites, and of assimilation into an alien cultural "body." Through the poem, the poet affirms the moral superiority of blacks over whites, and appropriates for blacks a courageous and divine role as well as the freedom to choose, and she becomes a willing and eager religious volunteer. In this way, the poet transcends the emotions of resentment prescribed by the role of powerless victim to produce the authentic voice of "un cœur nègre." The poem at the same time raises the question of Carbet's own presumably painful choice of poetic assimilation as a device adopted in order to be heard, and offers concrete justification for the insertion of a "black" poetic heart within a "white" cultural body. The poet's voice in "Greffe" is ironic and even bitter, as she names the reality of the cultural suffering imposed by whites on blacks. While the Christian motif runs throughout the poem and fits into the theme of suffering, explicit references to money, class, and exploitation make this poem radically different from other poems in the collection.

CIVILISATION

En demi-sommeil, noyé dans la brume,
Le bois rêve, amer, des aubes d'été.
Et le chêne-vert, corset éclaté,
Et le châtaignier aux limbes étroits
    Pleurent d'avoir froid.

    Tout dernier venu,
    Né de cette nuit,
    Simplet et lourdaud,
    Sous son grand chapeau,
    Champignon moussu
    Elève la voix:
    «Dans l'herbe bleuie
    Traînent des joyaux
    Voici des lambeaux
    De tulle perlé
    Quelqu'un a passé...

—   Ouvre bien les yeux,
    Champignon tout rond,
    Foi de Puceron,
    Tu verras comment
    Sans se soucier
    De fil ni métier
    L'araignée habile
    Joue au tisserand.

—   Puceron gentil,
    Que tisse la dame,
    Voile d'épousée
    Ou robe de fée ?

—   L'araignée travaille

A tendre les mailles
D'un piège candide.
S'y prendront les ailes
Du premier passant
Féru de beauté
Où chaud d'amitié.
Elle en fera son déjeuner.»

Ecolier crépu
Tout naïf éclos
Au champ des nations
Sais-tu pas le sort
Du peuple neuf qui
Bardé d'illusion
S'apprêtait, ravi,
A danser en rond
Autour de la terre
La main dans la main
Des hommes ses frères.
Toile d'araignée
Perlée de rosée
Le guettait aussi.
Le piège avait nom civilisation.

❧

CIVILIZATION

Half asleep, shrouded in fog,
The wood dreams, bitterly, about summer yawns.
Both the holm oak, its corset burst,
And the narrow-limbed chestnut tree
        Are shedding tears because they are cold.

The latest arrival,

Born last night,
Simple and oafish,
Under his big hat,
Mossy Mushroom
Raises his voice:
"In the grass turned blue
There are jewels lying around
Here are scraps
Of beaded tulle.
Someone has passed by...

— Open your eyes wide,
Round Mushroom,
On my word as a Greenfly,
You'll see how
Not worrying
About thread or craft
Skillful spider
Is playing weaver.

— Nice Greenfly,
What's the lady weaving,
A bridal veil
Or a fairy dress ?

— The spider is working
On tightening the meshes
Of a candid trap.
It will catch the wings
Of the first passerby
Smitten by beauty
Or warm with friendship.
She'll have him for lunch."

Natty-haired schoolboy

Just naively hatched
On to the field of nations
Don't you know what happened
To the new country which
Cloaked in illusion
Was getting ready, in rapture,
To dance in a circle
Around the earth
Holding hands
With its brother men.
Spider's web
Beaded with dew
Was watching it too.
The name of the trap was civilization.

"Civilisation" (41-43), related by the notation at the top of the page ("Chissay-Abidjan") to Côte d'Ivoire, which became an independent republic in 1960, represents the poet's response to the new political situation of this state, within the context of possible danger from Western European "civilization." This response, in effect a warning, is transmitted by the device of a fable, narrated by the poetic persona-storyteller, who adopts in turn the voices of the two characters, Mushroom and Greenfly, involved in a dialogue in the tale.

The poet-narrator first uses the regular, heavier rhythm of the decasyllable to introduce in the opening scene the unhappy wood, represented through the allusions to flora and climate as typically European: it is "noyé dans la brume" [shrouded in fog], it "rêve, amer, des aubes d'été" [dreams, bitterly, about summer dawns], and in it trees "[p]leurent d'avoir froid" [are shedding tears because they are cold]. In the second stanza, the story-teller switches to the lighter five-syllable lines and to a question-response nursery rhyme format to present the significant dialogue that is to follow, introducing and then reproducing the voice of the most recent character to become part of this wood of civilization, the

"Champignon moussu" [Mossy Mushroom]. This character, represented as "[s]implet et lourdaud" [simple and oafish], is particularly attracted to what he thinks are the "joyaux" [jewels] and "lambeaux / De tulle perlé" [scraps / Of beaded tulle] he sees in the grass. His vision, however, is distorted, and it is left to the more astute "Puceron [Greenfly] to recognize the signs left by "l'araignée habile" [skillful spider]. The nursery-rhyme tone of the poem continues with the naïve request for clarification made by Champignon ("Que tisse la dame, / Voile d'épousée / Ou robe de fée? [What's the lady weaving, / A bridal veil / Or a fairy dress?]). This interplay ends with the response of Puceron, who interprets for Champignon the significance and real danger of the spider's actions.

In the final stanza, the voice of the poet-narrator reappears, drawing the moral to this fairy-tale, addressing her comments to "[Ecolier crépu / Tout naïf éclos / Au champ des nations" [Natty-haired schoolboy / Just naïvely hatched / On to the field of nations]. Direct correspondences are established between the "bois" [wood] of the first stanza and this "champ des nations" [field of nations], as "tout naïf éclos" [just naïvely hatched] echoes "Tout dernier venu, / Né de cette nuit" [The latest arrival, / Born last night] of the second stanza, and "naïf" [naïve] echoes the earlier description of the "champignon" as "simplet" [simple]. The African is presented as "bardé d'illusion" [cloaked in illusion], lacking the qualities of judgement and maturity necessary to survive in the new community of "civilized" nations. The poet leaves little to the imagination, ending with an explanation of the central analogy, civilization as a trap, around which the whole poem is built: "Le piège avait nom civilisation" [The name of the trap was civilization]. As the poem ends, the "araignée" [spider] lies in wait, but Africa is not (yet?) caught in her web.

This poem is a carefully constructed fable, drawing a moral about the danger of Western European civilization particularly for newly independent African states. It poses interesting questions in relation to identity as well as gender. The poet's empathy with Africa and her rejection of Europe and "civilisation" are quite evident. Indeed, this poem awakens memories of several of the "négritude" poems of Damas, in which this Caribbean poet expressed his rejection of European "civilisation."[11] There is, however, no textual identification between the poet and Africa. It is also worthy of note that in this poetic fable the poet and Africa are gendered as male ("puceron" and "champignon"), while Europe is gendered as female ("araignée"). This suggests the ambiguity that accompanies the role of the female French Caribbean poet, confronted not only with the issue of rejecting Europe in order to assume an authentic identity, but also with the historical need to subordinate her own voice to that of the male.

> *De Gao, à Emma*
> *et Noumou Kounda Konaté.*

HAUTES EAUX

Du Niger en crue
La plaine est noyée.
Troupeaux en pâture,
Pattes effacées,
Ne sont plus que dos
Arrondis sur l'eau.

Cases sur la rive,
Coupes renversées,
Ne sont que toitures
Emergeant de l'eau.

Viendra la saison
Où le fleuve, las,
Tout doux descendra
Au creux de son lit.

Alors le soleil

Ne moirera plus
Qu'un étroit ruban,
Fil d'argent, perdu
Dans le sable chaud.

ॐ

From Gao, to Emma
and Noumou Kounda Konaté

HIGH WATER

The plain of the Niger
in spate is flooded.
Grazing herds,
Legs blotted out,
Are now just rounded
Backs on the water.

Shacks on the river bank,
Inverted bowls,
Are just rooftops
Emerging from the water.

The season will come
When the river, grown tired,
Will very gently sink
Into the hollow of its bed.

Then the sun
Will cast a shimmer no wider
Than a narrow ribbon,
A silver thread, lost
In the warm sand.

"Hautes eaux" (10), if we accept the dedication as accurate, was written in Gao, a town on the Niger in Mali. Here, the poet is subjectively absent (as a "je" [I]), and hence of unstated gender. In the first two stanzas, the poet is all eyes, using her voice to describe in brief, quick strokes the fleeting impression of the river overflowing its banks, allowing commonplace objects to acquire freshness in the, for her, new context of the African landscape. In the second half of the poem, the poet moves beyond the description of the present to envisage the change that will come in the future, in terms that reflect a more familiar, Caribbean-like, landscape.

The Niger's rise in height is illustrated with reference to two characteristics of the African scenery: "troupeaux" (herds) and "cases" (shacks). The effect of the river is transmitted through the verbal negatives occurring in the first and second stanzas ("ne sont plus que" [are now just], "ne sont que" [are just]), while in the fourth stanza ("Ne moirera plus / Qu'..." [will cast a shimmer no wider / Than...]), the same device is used to illustrate the contrasting effect of the river's fall. This use of negatives results in an almost photographic reduction of the scene described. Thus herds of animals are reduced to "dos" [backs], homes are reduced to "toitures" [roof tops]; even the mass of the water of the river Niger is reduced, in the future within the poem, to nothing more than "un étroit ruban" [a narrow ribbon]. This reduction of the scene described is paralleled by the poet's use of four-syllable lines, which may be considered a reduction, a halving, of octosyllables. The first two stanzas may in fact be read as five octosyllabic lines, with rhymes of "noyée"/"effacées"/"renversées" [flooded/ blotted out / overturned], and of "sur l'eau"/ "de l'eau" [on the water/ from the water].

When the poet moves away from the present scene, in the first two stanzas, to the future, in the final two, and from the actuality of the dominance of the "Niger en crue" [Niger in spate] to the probability of the future dominance of "le sable chaud" [the warm sand], the familiarity of the scene which has as its principal features sun and sand forms a link with the Martinican landscape.

What, however, is most conspicuously absent from this picture of present water and future sand is a human presence, whether of Africans or of the poet herself. There is no textual (pronominal) self-identification on the part of the poet: the poet effaces and distances herself, virtually disappears, when confronted with Africa. This poetic response to the new experience of a natural phenomenon in Africa, characterized by self-effacement and a concern for "objectivity," indicates a step taken by the poet towards representing Africa without the mediating screen of the romantic exile.

Des bords du Niger, à Emile Dervain

BEAU PIROGUIER

Piroguier droit et fier
Dressé comme un rhonier
Sur ton étroite nef,
Pèse de tout ton poids
Sur ta perche tendue.
Pèse et sous le soleil
Luiront tes bras musclés,
Brilleront tes dents claires.

Pousse, beau piroguier,
Ta barque glissera
Sur son chemin d'eau douce
Jusqu'au seuil où t'attend
Le dîner en famille,
En reposant la nuit,
De forces pour demain.

❦

From the shores of the Niger, to Emile Dervain

HANDSOME PIROGUE-MAN

Pirogue-man straight and proud
Standing like a Rhone-man
On your narrow bark,
Press with all your weight
On your braced pole.
Press and under the sun
Your muscular arms will gleam,
Your bright teeth will shine.

Push, handsome pirogue-man,
Your craft will glide
On its fresh water path
Right to the doorway where
Family dinner awaits you,
Where, by resting at night,
You will harvest
Strength for tomorrow.

"Beau piroguier" (65), written, according to the dedicatory notation, on the shores of the Niger, bears similarities with "Hautes eaux." It is one of the very few Carbet poems where an African human being appears, and the only one in which the poet uses her voice to address directly an African man. The poetic voice here is one of admiration, encouragement, appreciation, and respect. The picture drawn by the poet is to some extent idealized, as she celebrates the exotic beauty of the "beau piroguier" [handsome pirogue-man], standing "droit et fier" [straight and proud], and possessed of "bras musclés" [muscular arms] and "dents claires" [bright teeth]. This picture, particularly within the context of the 1960s, is a revisualization of the black man, presented here as noble, proud, and handsome, a figure of both beauty and dignity, as he rows back to his family. Thus the poem represents a revolutionary vision of the black man as a positive figure, and a revalorization of the black man in relation to his family. It is worthy of note that it is the figure of the male, not the female, whom the poet encourages in his journey. The use, however, of an African as an ideal of beauty and pride affirms an extension of Carbet's frame of reference beyond European and even Caribbean criteria. It is difficult, however, not to read in this picture of the African a transposition of the frequently absent father figure who was and is such a common feature of the Caribbean reality.

A la mémoire de mes morts

LITANIES

Des appels laissés sans écho,
Des ferveurs, des espoirs déçus,
Je viens faire contrition.

De l'aveuglement, des absences
Et de la surdité du cœur,
Accepte, Seigneur, de m'absoudre.

Des amours que je n'ai pas eues
Au long des saisons d'opulence,
Daigne aujourd'hui me pardonner.

Pour le détournement, l'abus
Des jeunes années de ma mère,
Pour la servitude imposée
Aux forces vives de mon père,
O Dieu ! ne me tiens pas rigueur.

De leurs regrets et leurs silences,
Leur quotidienne abdication

Payés d'ingrate impatience,
Seigneur, accorde-moi quittance.

Veuille rendre en lumière et joie
Tous les biens dont je fus comblée,
Tous les dons que j'ai piétinés.

Du martyre discret de l'un,
Du mutisme éloquent de l'autre,
De l'abnégation par-ci,
La générosité par là,
Seigneur, dispense à tous le prix.

A ceux qui déjà t'ont rejoint,
A ceux qui, ton appel, attendent,
Consens de payer mon tribut,
Et rends à leur éternité
L'amour qu'ils m'ont en vain donné.

❧

In memory of those of mine who died

LITANIES

For the calls left with no response,
For the fervors, for the disappointed hopes,
I have come to make contrition.

For the blindness, for the absences
And for the deafness of the heart,
Please, O Lord, absolve me.

For the loves I did not have
All through the times of plenty

Deign to forgive me today.

For the misdirection, the abuse
Of my mother's early years,
For the servitude imposed
On my father's vital strength,
O God ! hold that not against me.

For their regrets and their silences,
Their daily abdication
Repaid with impatient ingratitude,
O Lord, grant me quittance.

Please return in light and joy
All the goods with which I was showered,
All the gifts on which I trampled.

For one's discreet martyrdom,
For the other's eloquent silence,
For this one's abnegation,
That one's generosity,
O Lord, exempt them all from paying.

To those who have rejoined thee,
To those who thy call await,
Vouchsafe to pay my tribute,
And render to them in eternity
The love they gave me in vain.

"Litanies" (70-71), the poem that closes the collection, announces itself through its title as an oral communication using the form of a Catholic ritual, transmitting the voice of the praying subject in a series of invocations addressed to God. The form, however, is not uniform, with stanzas varying between three, four, and five lines each. The dedication "A la mémoire de mes morts" [In memory of those of mine who died] indicates that the poetic voice is also the voice of love, immortalizing memories and establishing contact beyond the grave.

In the first three stanzas the poet seeks absolution for her shortcomings in the past, her failure to open herself up to emotional opportunities offered. In the fourth stanza, the poet curiously is seeking forgiveness for occurrences clearly outside her sphere of responsibility: her mother's early experience of "détournement" [misdirection] and "abus" [abuse], and the servitude imposed on her father. What is implied is comparatively late awareness on the part of the poet of the conditions that determined her parents' existence, as people of color in a nineteenth century French colony. It is thus for her former lack of understanding, conveyed in "ingrate impatience" [impatient ingratitude], that she now seeks absolution.
The poem moves beyond being simply a cry for forgiveness to become an acknowledgement of and a celebration of her parents' heroism, expressed as "martyre discret" [discreet martyrdom], "mutisme éloquent" [eloquent silence], "abnégation" [abnegation], and "générosité" [generosity]. It becomes the medium by which the poet is able to make reparation ("payer mon tribut" [pay my tribute]) for her past sins of omission. As the closing lines of the poem indicate, this poem and the whole collection represent a communication link with childhood and a permanent gift of love at last returned: "Et rends à leur éternité / L'amour qu'ils m'ont en vain donné" [And render to them in eternity / The love they gave me in vain].

These studies of Carbet's poems indicate the nature of her response as a poet to the conditions of her life as a Martinican, as black, and as a woman. The implicit perception of *Point d'orgue* that this earlier collection may not constitute her real voice suggests, at one level, a measure of poetic and personal insecurity. In *Rose de ta grâce*, Carbet's dilemma finds a clearer, though still largely indirect, articulation. Her poems reflect the tension of a Martinican who is still attracted to the metropolis, where she experiences feelings of exile and alienation, but for whom the native island is the axis around which poetic production develops, and whose pride in her native land takes the form of poems celebrating its beauty and folklore. The cultural dilemma within which she operates exacerbates her feelings of self-doubt and uncertainty, and her fragile self-esteem is reflected in her tendency toward the concealment, toward the muffling, of her voice, and toward the subordination of her voice to that of the male Other. At the same time, Carbet finds the courage to move toward an acceptance and a celebration of Africa, to identify physically and emotionally with Africa, and even to assume the voice of a "nègre." Moreover, as a woman she is able to express her consciousness of oppression and rejection, and to translate personal experiences into themes of love, friendship, childhood, and family. It is in the variety and complexity of these responses that the peculiar voice of this authentic female Martinican poet is to be heard. These responses by Carbet are connected, not only to the problematical situation of the Caribbean writer in general, but also to the additional personal frustrations of being black and female.

At another level, Carbet's perceived reluctance to adopt a clearly expressed female identity may be linked to the stance of other women writers before her who subordinate themselves in their poetry. Carbet's self-effacement may be compared, too, to the practice of some black writers who appropriate equality with whites by not identifying themselves as "black" in their literary discourse. The seemingly fragile and fearful identity projected at one level by the poet is, in a way, misleading. The fact is that Carbet dared to write and to publish for many many years. This suggests that Carbet's response to the cultural dilemma facing writers like herself was to mask her poetic language, in a similar way that Césaire deliberately masked his in the early 1940s when producing *Tropiques*, in order to ensure publication within a potentially hostile environment. Carbet may have needed to hide in order to be heard. This may also explain why the poetic identity of *Rose de ta grâce* is more clearly articulated than in *Point d'orgue*.

Carbet's concern for issues related to the emotions, to the family, and to friendship, her feelings of exile and distance from Martinique, her adoption of Martinican orality, her revisualization of the black man and of Africa, her hesitations in projecting a firm poetic identity, may all be considered as her poetic response as a Martinican woman to the social and cultural complexities of her life. Underlying Carbet's poetic practice is the question: "Will I be heard?" It is ironic that to a large extent she has not been. Not only has she been largely ignored by critics and scholars in France and the Caribbean, but the hearing of her voice requires sensitivity both to the general cultural problematic confronting French Caribbean writers, and to the even more intense and complex dilemma of a woman writer. Carbet remains a fiercely independent character, courageously challenging the limitations consciously or unconsciously imposed on women writers, daring to treat in her poetry taboo subjects, situations, and emotions, moving without apology from light-hearted banter to heavy irony, from extreme sensuality to fervent religiosity. She is above all a passionate woman, deeply committed to life, to her family, to the people, culture, and geography of her native land. I will always remember her sitting up in her bed in a nursing home in Martinique at the age of nearly 93 in 1995, still a strikingly beautiful woman, warning me flirtatiously that she was still capable of being "inflamed."

Notes

[1] Carbet states that she and her friend Claude reacted strongly against the exotic and undignified representations of the tropics in the popular French media of the 1930s and pledged to present a more realistic picture: "unmask the difficult life of men and women capable of singing of their poverty but very touchy about their dignity" (Carbet 1985: 66).

[2] According to M.-M. Carbet's niece, Yolande Marie-Magdeleine, Claude's real name was Claude Tricot. M.-M. For a brief account of Claude's literary life, see Carbet 1985:66.

[3] The main exceptions are: Condé 1977:19, 29-30; Corzani 1978 (Vol.5): 336-41; and Zimra 1984:53-77.

[4] For earlier versions of readings of this poem as well as of "La prière des merles," "Lettre à une amie inconnue," and "Rancune," see Hurley 1992 b.

[5] See particularly "Et puis après" (12), "Réveil au Wiedeneck" (14), "Le chien" (30), "Heure féminine" (33), "Prière du matin" (41), "En retard" (42), "Pourquoi pas une autre?" (44), "Deux heures après minuit" (46), "Un jour, la mésange dit..." (48), "Lettre à une amie inconnue" (50), "Caprice" (52), "Sagesse" (54), "Flirt" (55), Absence" (56), "Amours, délices" (58), "Mentez encor" (60), "Il a venté" (62), "Adieu" (63), "Lits jumeaux" (64), "N'ayez point doute" (67), and "Mes trois fourmis" (70).

[6] It must be cautioned, however, that Carbet, in an unpublished interview with me in May 1995, strongly objected to being labeled a feminist.

[7] "Picong" is a term employed in Trinidadian dialect to refer to a form of verbal banter often used for humorous and dramatic effect in calypsos.

[8] Page citations refer to Baudelaire, 1927.

[9] See particularly "J'ai plus de souvenirs..." (Baudelaire 1975:73), and "Quand le ciel bas et lourd..." (74).

[10] For an account of the Nardal salon and Paulette Nardal's contribution to *La Revue du monde noir* see Vaillant 1990:91-98 and Arnold 1981:11.

[11] See particularly "Solde," in Damas 1962:39-40.

3

Léon-Gontran DAMAS

Damas was born in Cayenne, French Guyana, in 1912. At the age of twelve he was sent to Martinique for his secondary education at the Lycée Schœlcher where for the first time he met Césaire, who was later to become his best friend. Damas left Martinique in 1926 and was sent to the Collège Meaux, near Paris, to complete his secondary education (Racine 1988). Césaire and Damas met again in Paris, where Damas went to study law and anthropology. Damas followed courses at the School of Oriental Languages and developed an interest in African culture, reading the works of ethnologists such as Léo Frobénius and Maurice Delafosse. When his parents learned that he was pursuing these interests rather than law they cut off his allowance. It was around this period that he met Léopold Sédar Senghor. Damas, Césaire, and Senghor founded *L'Etudiant Noir*, to provide an outlet for all black students in Paris. In 1934 Damas left on an ethnographic field trip to Guyane to study the Bush Negroes and

African cultural survivals. The result was *Retour de Guyane [Return From Guyana]* of 1938. Damas reports that out of the 1500 copies published, over 1000 were bought by the local government of French Guyana and burnt. In 1937 *Pigments* was published, the text that was the first literary manifestation of the sensibility that was soon to be known as Négritude. The poems were quickly translated into several African languages, but the text was seized and banned by the French authorities in 1939 as a threat to the security of the state. Later Damas was asked by the journal *Vu et Lu* to do a story on French Guyana and in 1943, published *Veillées noires [Black Vigil]*, a collection of authentic folk tales gathered during his field trip to French Guyana. In 1947, he edited the first anthology of overseas francophone poets, *Poètes d'expression française.* During the period 1948-51, Damas represented French Guyana in the Chambres des Députés. He visited Africa for the first time in 1950, as a delegate of the French National Assembly. He worked later as technical advisor to French Overseas Radio, until he found himself dismissed after a trip to the Congo. He later got a job with UNESCO as a representative of the African Society of Culture. He became the main editor of the *Nouvelle Somme de poésie du monde noir*, published by Présence Africaine in 1966, the same year in which he organized the First Negro Arts Festival in Dakar. In 1970 he accepted a temporary position at Georgetown University in the United States. He later took up a position at Howard University, where he later became Acting Director of the African Studies and Research Program and Professor of African Literature. He died in January 1978. His principal works are: *Pigments* (1937); *Retour de Guyane* (1938); *Veillées noires* (1943); *Graffiti* (1952); *Black-Label* (1956); and *Névralgies* (1966).

Damas's poetry, particularly the poems of *Pigments*, have been the subject of considerable critical analysis. Competent translations of many of the *Pigments* poems appear in Ellen Conroy Kennedy's *The Negritude Poets* (1975) and in Keith Q. Warner's *Critical Perspectives on Léon-Gontran Damas* (1988).

Consequently, while I have included a poem from *Pigments* that has not been overexposed, I have focused on a collection that has received comparatively little attention from scholars, *Névralgies*.

S.O.S.[1]

A ce moment-là seul
comprendrez-vous donc tous
quand leur viendra l'idée
bientôt cette idée leur viendra
de vouloir vous en bouffer du nègre
à la manière d'Hitler
bouffant du juif
sept jours fascistes
sur
sept

A ce moment-là seul
comprendrez-vous donc tous
quand leur supériorité
s'étalera
d'un bout à l'autre de leurs boulevards
et qu'alors
vous les verrez
vraiment tout se permettre
ne plus se contenter de rire avec l'index inquiet
de voir passer un nègre
mais
froidement matraquer
mais
froidement descendre
mais
froidement étendre
mais froidement
matraquer

descendre
étendre
et
couper leur sexe aux nègres
pour en faire des bougies pour leurs églises

❧

S.O.S.

Then and only then
will all of you understand
when the idea occurs to them
soon this idea will occur to them

to want to have you gobble up negroes
just like Hitler
gobbling up jews
seven fascist days
a
week

Then and only then
will all of you understand
when their superiority
is flaunted
from one end of their boulevards to the other
and then
you will see them
really doing whatever they want
not being satisfied any more just to laugh with
restless forefinger
when they see a negro pass by
but
coldly beating up

but
coldly knocking down
but
coldly laying out
but coldly
beating up
knocking down
laying out
and
cutting off negroes' penises
to make into candles for their churches

The elliptical title of this poem[2] (*Pigments*, 49) exemplifies some of the complexity of the techniques often employed by Damas. This Morse code abbreviation, though a common one, requires, if it is to be understood, a correct interpretation of the basic elements provided. Similarly the whole poem is an appeal for an understanding, based on a correct interpretation of elements provided by the poet. The poem, as the title indicates, develops out of the awareness of imminent danger. The danger alluded to is racism. This urgent poetic appeal implies a plural addressee, represented by the "vous ... tous" [you ... all] of the second line, whose cultural identity is ambiguous. The poet presupposes addressees who are opposed to the "leur" [them] of line three and who participate in the identity of the Jew, the Negro, and the Aryan. The world conjured by the poet consists of three components: the fully conscious poet, the unaware composite group, and the group of racists. The force of the comparison, "à la manière d'" [just like], establishes the link between anti-Jewish Hitlerian fascism in the Europe of the 1930s and anti-black racism. But the thrust of the poet's message emerges only slowly, becoming clear only in the fifth line ("de vouloir vous en bouffer du nègre" [to want to have you gobble up negroes], which serves as a climax in this first stanza. This is the longest line of the stanza, and it is preceded by four shorter lines that convey only incomplete thoughts and thus serve to build up suspense by the fact that none of them allows for total comprehension. The tension is further heightened by the parenthetical reconstructed repetition that occurs in the fourth line, which again serves to defer the moment of revelation that will be given in the fifth: "quand leur viendra l'idée / bientôt cette idée leur viendra" [when the idea occurs to them / soon this idea will occur to them]. The repetition and the placing of "bientôt" [soon] in a strong position at the beginning of the line enhance the urgency of the poet's appeal. The comparison on which the stanza ends is constructed in decrescendo, ending in deliberately isolated single-word lines that are thereby invested with greater autonomy and weight.

Repetition of the two opening lines in the second stanza provides coherence and harmony, and establishes the basis for the introduction of a new idea: "leur supériorité" [their superiority]. It is this characteristic element, noticed by the poet, which serves as the red flag, warning of urgent danger. Once again, the group indicated by "leur" [their] is not specified, but they enjoy a proprietorial relationship to the typically French "boulevards" that the poet does not share. The adverb, "froidement" [coldly], refers to a manner of action that is particularly sinister, and its repetition emphasizes the frightening effect. Similarly, the repetition of the conjunction ("mais" [but]) is used effectively in separate lines to add force to the anti-black violence conjured up by the poet. The little conjunction "et" [and] also used as a separate line creates a pause that adds to the force of the final image of emasculation. It is here that the real fear, implicit in the appeal for help of the title, is expressed. But the poem is not yet over. The possessive used in the final line, "pour en faire des bougies pour leurs églises" [to make into candles for their churches], echoes the "leurs boulevards" and indicates a similar rejection of a shared identity. The whole line reflects further the poet's condemnation of the religiosity (Catholic) he associates with these racists. However farfetched the prospect evoked by the poet may appear, it should be noted that the post-war discoveries of the use of the skins of Jews as lampshades take the poet's warning out of the realm of hyperbole.

This poem is representative of Damas' first collection, in that its inspiration is in the awareness of the situation of blacks in an often hostile white world. It also illustrates characteristics such as the poetic exploitation of orality, a tendency towards the vernacular, the effective use of repetition, an ironic even bitter sense of humor, and an intense emotional expressivity, which will typify Damas's poetic practice.

IL NE FAIT PAS L'OMBRE D'UN DOUTE[3]

Il ne fait pas l'ombre d'un doute
qu'une fois de plus la question
aura été bien mal posée
de savoir
q u a n d

Et parce qu'il ne fait pas l'ombre d'un doute
qu'une fois de plus la question
aura été bien mal posée
de savoir
q u a n d

il était à prévoir autant qu'à redouter
qu'elle répondrait
q u o i

à la question bien mal posée
de savoir
q u a n d

Alors chien battu
penaud et cois
je me suis bien gardé

de demander

o ù

❧

THERE'S NOT A SHADOW OF A DOUBT

There's not a shadow of a doubt
that once again the wrong question
will have been asked
to know
w h e n

And because there's not a shadow of a doubt
that once again the wrong question
will have been asked
to know
w h e n

it was to be expected as much as to be feared
that She would answer
w h a t

to the wrong question asked
to know
w h e n

Therefore a beaten dog
abashed and shy
I was very careful not
to ask

w h e r e

While the title of Damas's first collection of poetry, *Pigments*, drew attention to external (physical) characteristics, the title of this later collection, *Névralgies*, points to internal (emotional) conditions, and this poem, "Il ne fait pas l'ombre..." (*Névralgies*, 18) exemplifies the kind of "névralgie" [neuralgia] from which the poet is suffering. The reader is drawn into an experience far removed from the direct cultural and sociopolitical involvement that characterized *Pigments*. Here the focus is on the poet's difficulty in establishing communication with, of getting satisfactory answers from, and of being understood by, a member of the opposite sex. Language itself, the very basis of poetry, is at issue here, and in this apparently very simple poem the poet explores his reaction to the problem of language as well as to a human situation that dramatizes the problem.

The opening line introduces the contradiction upon which the whole poem is based: "Il ne fait pas l'ombre d'un doute" [There's not a shadow of a doubt]. The affirmation of certainty, which the sentence appears to make, is mitigated by the negative form in which it is presented. The whole poem is in fact enveloped in doubt. Little is clear or certain. None of the questions, introduced by "quand" [when], "quoi" [what], and "où" [where], is completed in the poem. The introduction of spaces between the letters of these interrogatives, however, contributes to an increase in the physical space they occupy and coincidentally to their significance, and the indentation and separation of the final "où" [where] place an ironic emphasis on the little word. Even the identity of the woman is hazy, suggested only by the capitalized "Elle" [She] of the third stanza. Thus the notion of the difficulty of communicating and of the limitations and contradictions of language is already mooted.

The phrase "une fois de plus" [once again] of the first stanza indicates that the poet's failure to find the right question to ask is not a single incident but represents a recurring situation, an ongoing problem that the poet has not been able to solve. The propositional statement of the first stanza is repeated in the second, with a slight, but significant, change in the opening phrase: "Et parce qu'..." [And because]. This prepares us for what seems to be a logically developed argument, the conclusion of which will be introduced by "Alors" [Therefore] in the final stanza. The repetition of "la question ... bien mal posée" [the wrong question] and of "de savoir / q u a n d" [to know / w h e n] in the second and fourth stanzas make these elements the most substantial in the poem. Asking the question of when that produced what the poet interprets as rejection returns like an obsession to haunt him, a constant reminder of his inadequacy.

What is presented therefore, through the progression "Et parce qu'..." [And because] to "Alors" [Therefore], is a logical explanation for the poet's action or lack of it. He reveals himself to be supersensitive and insecure, a "chien battu / penaud et coi" [a beaten dog / abashed and shy], suffering from emotional abuse at the hands of a woman. The metaphor of the beaten dog emphasizes the element of humiliation and self-deprecation but paradoxically also invites humor, because it is a contrived exaggeration of the rejection perceived by the poet. The woman is not shown to be at fault in the poem. It is the poet who blames and even laughs at himself ("il était à prévoir autant qu'à redouter" [it was to be expected as much as to be feared]) for his failure to ask the right question.

The awareness of the failure of language in a human relationship is the catalyst that serves to stimulate poet. The insecurity he displays is matched by his lucidity as he takes full responsibility for the frustration of his love and frustration is ironically creative. It is this frustration at both the linguistic and the emotional level that the poet consciously transmutes into poetry. Damas demonstrates his ability to use language with humor and with deceptively casual expertise to capture a moment of emotional insecurity with which virtually anyone can identify.

CONTRE NOTRE AMOUR
QUI NE VOULAIT RIEN D'AUTRE

Contre notre amour qui ne voulait rien d'autre
que d'être beau comme un croissant de lune au
beau mitan du Ciel à minuit
et pur comme le premier ris du nouveau-né
et vrai comme le verbe être
et fort comme la Mort d'où nous vient toute vie

contre notre amour
qui rêvait de vivre à l'air libre
qui rêvait de vivre sa vie
de vivre une vie
qui ne fut
ni
honteuse
ni lépreuse
ni truquée
ni tronquée
ni traquée
ils ont invoqué NOE
et NOE en appela à SEM
et SEM en appela à JAPHET
et JAPHET s'en remit à NOE
et NOE en appela à MATHUSALEM
alors MATHUSALEM ressortit de l'arsenal
tous les oripeaux
tous les tabous
tous les interdits en fanal rouge

Attention
Ici Danger
Déviation
Chasse gardée

Terrain privé
Domaine réservé
Défense d'entrer
Ni chiens ni nègre sur le gazon

❦

AGAINST OUR LOVE
THAT WANTED NOTHING ELSE

Against our love that wanted nothing else
but to be beautiful like a crescent moon right in the
center of the Heaven at midnight
and pure like the first laugh of a new-born babe
and true like the verb to be
and strong like Death whence comes to us all life

Against our love
that dreamed of living in the open air
that dreamed of living its own life
of living a life
that was
neither shameful
nor leprous
nor rigged
nor cut short
nor tracked down
they invoked NOAH
and NOAH called upon SHEM
and JAPHETH referred back to NOAH
and NOAH called upon METHUSELAH
then METHUSELAH brought back up out of the
arsenal
all the old gear
all the taboos

all the red lantern prohibitions

Beware
Danger
Detour
Game preserve
Private property
Restricted area
No entry
No dogs or negroes on the grass

The visual and spatial arrangement of this poem[4] (*Névralgies*, 32) draws attention to a ternary structure that is repeated with variations in its syntactical and semantic arrangement. Visually, the poem consists of a short but wide section of long lines, followed by a long, narrower section of shorter lines, punctuated by uppercase names, and a third narrow section in italics of mainly short lines (the final line is an exception). Syntactically, the poem consists of one long sentence divided into three parts. The first part comprises the two sections introduced by a prepositional phrase, "Contre notre amour" [Against our love], with relative clauses attached. The second part contains the main clause, with a succession of subjects, beginning with "ils" [they], and main verbs ("ont invoqué" [invoked], "en appela à" [called upon], "s'en remit à" [referred back], etc.). The third part comprises the italicized examples of the prohibitions ["interdits"] mentioned at the end of the second part. In the spatial arrangement of the poem, the middle section makes no separation between the second of the "Contre notre amour" [Against our love] propositions and the main clause. This section thus constitutes a semantic (and spatial) expansion of the proposition introduced in the first section. This expansion has the effect of tightening the syntactical link. Because the poem is just one sentence, comprehension is necessarily deferred and the total sense of the poem is incomplete and unavailable until the last line. This rhetorical structure provides the framework for the generation of the poet's emotion and for the development of a persuasive stance.

The theme of forbidden love is introduced by the first three words of the poem. All we know at the beginning is that the poet's love has met with some opposition. The presence of both lover and loved one is revealed only in the possessive pronoun, "notre" [our]. No physical or other details are given about either partner. Consequently emphasis is placed on the experience of love rather than on the personality of the lovers. The abstraction of love is invested with a capacity for desire that renders it sympathetically human, especially since the attributes desired ("beau" [beautiful], "pur" [pure], "vrai" [true], and "fort" [strong]) represent basic qualities associated with courtly and romantic love in the French literary tradition. The first comparison, "comme un croissant de lune au beau mitan du Ciel à minuit" [like a crescent moon right in the center of the Heaven at midnight], contains a Creole term, "mitan" [center], which has the effect, together with the repetition of "beau" [beautiful], of indicating the Caribbean as the location for this love. The capitalization of "Ciel," a word that signifies both sky and heaven, points to an association with divinity and with the notion of life after death, and thus prepares us for the three other comparisons that follow, which are concerned respectively with birth, life, and death.

The repetition of the opening phrase of the poem at the beginning of the second stanza before there is closure to the sentence that had been started imparts an oratorical quality to the poem. The new relative clause, "qui rêvait" [that dreamed], introduces the element of illusion that is itself part of the lore of romantic love: the dream that is doomed to die unrealized. The thematic note on which the first stanza ends, "vie" [life], is taken up again in the second and forms the basis for rapid musical variations or riffs in the form of word-play on the noun "vie" [life] and the verb "vivre" [to live]: "qui rêvait de vivre à l'air libre / qui rêvait de vivre sa vie / de vivre une vie" [that dreamed of living in the open air / that dreamed of living its own life / of living a life].

Conjunctions have their own musical role to play. The repeated "et" [and] in strong positions at the beginning of the line is contrasted and enhanced by the repeated "ni" [nor]. The short adjectives ("beau" [beautiful], "pur" [pure], "vrai" [true], and "fort" [strong]) give way to longer rhyming adjectives of progressive intensity ("honteuse" [shameful] and "lépreuse" [leprous]) and alliterative past participles ("truquée" [rigged], "tronquée" [cut short], and "traquée" [cut down]), the last one of which evokes the experience of escaping slaves. It is only with this term that the idea of a love that is prohibited by a slave society begins to take shape.

The capitalized references that follow refer to an account of the origins of humanity given in the book of Genesis in the Bible.[5] What is striking in the references in the poem is the absence of Ham, who according to biblical legend, was the ancestor of all the black races. The exclusion of Ham is therefore a further indication that the prohibition suffered by the poet is related to race. The ironic capitalization of names and the repetition of "et" [and] and "en appela à" [called upon] that echoes the biblical format (e.g., "... and Noah begat...") underline the poet's rejection of intolerance based on religiosity. The final section in italics enumerates a series of commonly seen notices of prohibition, the last of which, dramatically different from all the others in its length and in its sound (note the rhymes that predominate in the first seven: "attention"/"déviation" and "danger"/"gardée"/ "privé"/"réservé"), drives home the deep sense of rejection felt by the poet in relation to his race. The transgression with which the poem is concerned is now clearly revealed to be that of interracial love.

Thus even in a poem that treats a theme (thwarted love) that is a commonplace in the tradition of lyric poetry, the problem of race intrudes. It is virtually impossible for this black Caribbean poet to live in a space that is unaffected by racial prejudice. It is this fact that accounts for the bitterness that characterizes so much of Damas's poetry.

SI DEPUIS PEU

Si

     depuis

         peu
je trouve à ta larme en détresse
le goût âcre de l'eau de sang-mêlé des TROIS
FLEUVES
c'est qu'il est midi pour deux
midi qui ne connaît ni angélus ni crépuscule
midi qui se rit d'avant
midi qui se rit d'après
midi vieux de tant de midis
midi qui échappe à sa propre ombre
midi qui ramène à soi la pirogue aux deux pagayes
créoles
midi qui la ramène sur la digue dominant de haut
et de loin
l'eau de sang-mêlé des TROIS FLEUVES
dont ta larme en détresse a depuis peu
ce goût âcre
que je lui trouve
lui trouverai
aussi longtemps que ne serai point seul
à danser au soleil
debout dans ma triple fierté de sang-mêlé

❦

IF JUST LATELY

If

     just

         lately
I've been finding in your anguished tears

the acrid taste of the mixed-race water of the
THREE RIVERS
it's because it's noon for two
noon that knows not angelus nor gloaming
noon that laughs at before
noon that laughs at after
noon old from so many noons
noon that escapes from its own shadow
noon that pulls back in the pirogue with its two
creole paddles
noon that pulls it back in to the dyke towering far
and high
over the mixed-race water of the THREE RIVERS
of which just lately your anguished tears have
this acrid taste
that I've been finding they have
will find they have
as long as I'm not alone
dancing in the sun
upright in my threefold pride as a mixed-race man

The opening three short single-word lines of this poem (*Névralgies*, 46), staggered in a descending pattern, point to a mood of progressive depression as the poet proffers an explanation for a recent change in his relationship with his lover. The capitalized words "TROIS FLEUVES" [THREE RIVERS] stand out graphically in the text as the focal point around which the poem is constructed. They represent the combination of geography and culture through which the poet's identity is revealed. The three rivers have as their referent not merely the geographical features of the poet's native Guyana, including the Mana, Marouni, and Oyapock rivers, but also the cultural and racial components of the poet's identity, the African, Amerindian, and European. "TROIS FLEUVES" thus acts as a symbol for the composite and complex reality of both the native land and the poet. It is this condition that generates the emotional reactions of the two personas in the poem, the poet and his lover, identified only in the possessive pronoun, "ta" [your]. The lover is represented as sad, shedding anguished tears ("ta larme en détresse"). These tears, for which the combined water of the three rivers serves as a metaphor, are related to the condition of being of mixed race, while the adjective "âcre" [acrid] hints at the bothersome potential of such a condition.

The dominant term of the middle section of the poem is "midi" [noon], its importance highlighted by repetition and by its position at the beginning of the line. Noon acts as a powerful symbol for this poet, as it did for Césaire (see particularly "Couteaux midi" [Noon Knives]), because of its significance within the tropics, a moment of absolute clarity with the sun directly overhead. The explanation given by the poet, "c'est qu'il est midi pour deux" [it's because it's noon for two], is based on the association of noon with a moment of truth. This is the point of the confrontation of reality in the relationship between the two lovers. The succeeding descriptive clauses emphasize aspects of the significance of noon: its perfect distance from morning and evening ("qui ne connaît ne angélus ni crépuscule" [that knows not angelus nor gloaming], its complete focus on the present ("qui se rit d'avant / ... qui se rit d'après" [that laughs at before / ... that laughs at after]), its self-confidence and wisdom derived from the fact that that moment occurs every day ("vieux de tant de midis" [old from so many noons]), and the fact that the sun when it is directly overhead casts no shadow ("qui échappe à sa propre ombre" [that escapes from its own shadow]). It is this phenomenon, the capacity to eliminate shadows, that creates the optical illusions referred to in "midi qui ramène à soi la pirogue aux deux pagayes créoles" [noon that pulls back in the pirogue with its two creole paddles] and "midi qui la ramène sur la digue" [noon that draws it back in to the dyke]. The adjective "créoles" [creole] assumes particular significance in light of the central drama, the drama of a "creole" society, that lies at the heart of the poem and the two creole paddles function as metaphors of the two personas in the poem. The physically dominant position of the sun at noon is shown to be an indicator of its symbolic power ("dominant de haut et de loin / l'eau de sang-mêlé des TROIS FELUVES" [towering far and high over / the mixed-race water of the THREE RIVERS]).

The poem ends on an ambiguous note as the poet looks toward the future. The tears will remain, the acrid taste associated with racial mixing will persist. The early tone of depression is however gone. The earlier menace of "midi pour deux" [noon for two] is transmuted into the hope that "ne serai point seul / à danser au soleil" [I won't be alone / dancing in the sun]. The poet can finally experience pride in his mixed racial heritage: "debout dans ma triple fierté de sang-mêlé" [upright in my threefold pride as a mixed-race man].

While Damas is renowned for his contribution to the revalorization of the African heritage in the name of Negritude, the pride expressed here is not limited to the African element. Once again Damas shows himself to be in the forefront of cultural and racial consciousness. His implied acknowledgement of his Amerindian heritage and his acceptance of his European links foreshadow the importance attached to "métissage" [racial mixing] as a characteristic of Caribbean societies, emphasized by Edouard Glissant and by the Creolists, Patrick Chamoiseau and Raphaël Confiant. But Damas also indicates through this poem that "métissage" brings its own problems: racial pride also involves pain. The inference is that no relationship in the context of a so-called creole society is exempt from the discomfort associated with the hierarchization of racial affiliation. The poem is thus the site where Damas confronts and expresses the emotional turmoil stirred up by "race" in Caribbean societies.

TU M'AS BEL ET BIEN DIT

Tu m'as dit bel et bien dit
ne plus
ne plus vouloir

ne plus vouloir être *ma chose*
pour l'avoir été
pour l'avoir été l'avoir été si peu
si peu
au point que le Ciel qui s'aime en son miroir
en est venu lui-même à s'interroger de doute

A mon tour
A mon tour de dire
toujours
toujours tu seras *ma chose*
quand bien même
tu croirais
tu croirais pouvoir dire
bel et bien dire
l'avoir été
l'avoir été si peu si peu
Car las de s'interroger de doute
le Ciel qui s'aime tant en son miroir en est venu à
prophétiser
à tout vent
Quoique tu fasses
      où que tu sois
      quoique tu veuilles
et surtout
      quoique l'on dise
      quoique l'on fasse
      quoique l'on veuille
      et dise
      et fasse
      et veuille
tu seras *ma chose*

Car fut-il nazaréen et nègre de surcroît
mon Dieu mien dont nul être au monde

n'eût à porter la Croix

Mon Dieu mien qui de mémoire mienne
jamais ne fut traqué
jamais persiflé
jamais hué
ni
cru
      ci
          fié
pour avoir à la passion
aimé à la fois
Marthe
Marie-Magdeleine
et Véronique

Mon Dieu mien
magnifié en tout ce qui vibre
magnifié en tout ce qui vit

Mon Dieu mien
que l'on invoque
non pas à genoux
les yeux faussement baissés
les mains menteusement jointes

Mon Dieu mien
que l'on invoque
dans la joie de l'amour
dans l'amour de la joie
dans l'amour de la vie
dans la vie de l'amour

Mon Dieu mien
qui se rit

de l'encens et des ors
et qui se rit
de cette grande lithurgie de mots

Mon Dieu mien
dont le corps ni le sang
ne sont à prendre à jeun
en hostie blanche
en vin de messe

Mon Dieu mien
n'en prie pas moins
pour que vive l'amour
pour que vive notre amour

❧

YOU WELL AND TRULY TOLD ME

You told me well and truly told me
you no longer
no longer wanted
no longer wanted to be *my thing*
because you'd been that
because you'd been that been that so little
so little
that Heaven which loves itself in its mirror
even reached the point of having doubts about itself

My turn
My turn to say
forever
forever you'll be *my thing*
even if
you thought

you thought you could say
well and truly say
you'd been that
you'd been that so little so little
For tired of having doubts about itself
Heaven which loves itself so much in its mirror
reached the point of prophesying

to the four winds
Whatever you do
       wherever you are
       whatever you want
and above all
       whatever they say
       whatever they do
       whatever they want
       and say
       and do
       and want
you'll be *my thing*

For even if he were a Nazarene and a negro to boot
my God of mine for whom nobody in the world
had to carry his Cross

My God of mine who if my memory serves me
right
never was hunted down
never mocked
never booed
nor
cru
      ci
           fied
for having passionately

loved all at the same time
Martha
Mary Magdalene
and Veronica

My God of mine
magnified in all that vibrates
magnified in all that lives

My God of mine
who is called upon
not on your knees
eyes deceitfully lowered
hands mendaciously clasped

My God of mine
who is called upon
in joy of love
in love of joy
in love of life
in life of love

My God of mine
who laughs
at incense and gold
and who laughs
at this great liturgy of words

My God of mine
of whom neither body nor blood
is to be taken on an empty stomach
as white host
as communion wine

My God of mine

nevertheless prays
that love lives on
that our love lives on

This love poem (*Névralgies*, 47) shows the poet in a more light-hearted mood than that normally manifested in *Pigments*. The poem is a response to a rejection that is evidently not taken seriously by the poet. It is addressed directly to a lover, identified in the very first word of the poem as "Tu" [You]. The opening line sets the tone of the whole poem. The repetition of "dit" [told] and the use of the vernacular expression "bel et bien" [well and truly] indicates a privileging of the oral in this communication. The word play that follows ("ne plus / ne plus vouloir / ne plus vouloir être..." [you no longer / no longer wanted / no longer wanted to be...]) mimics a form of shyness that manifests itself in difficulty in getting words out and introduces an element of jocularity that will continue throughout the poem. The italicized expression "*ma chose*" [*my thing*], a term of affection used within the black vernacular, reinforces the orality and humor, but also, because it represents directly the actual words supposedly used by the poet, gives increased weight of sincerity to the communication. The repetition of the sound of "oir" in "vouloir," "avoir," and "miroir" adds to the musical harmony created by the other rhythmic repetitions of "ne plus" [no longer] and "pour l'avoir été" [when you'd been that]. The reference to "le Ciel" [Heaven] in the penultimate line of the stanza introduces a religious element in a humorous vein that will be developed further in the second half of the poem. The double connotation in French of "Ciel" (both sky and heaven) plays on the paradox of absolute certainty attached to the sky (a permanent indisputable global reality) and uncertainty accompanying the notion of heaven. It is this awareness of the contradictory nature of language, implicit in the title, that contributes to the verbal wit generated in the poem.

Thus the lover's words reported in the first stanza are contradicted in the second, while the verbal humor is transmitted through the repetition of new word groups "A mon tour" [My turn], "toujours" [forever], "tu croirais" [you thought], as well as through the reprise of "l'avoir été" [you'd been that], and "si peu" [so little] from the first stanza. The main contradiction is conveyed through "toujours" [forever], which directly opposes "ne plus" [no longer]. The assertive "toujours tu seras *ma chose*" [forever you'll be *my thing*] becomes the poet's declaration of eternal love, in which humor and the vernacular contribute paradoxically to the poet's sincerity. His insistence on the validity of an expression that is consistent with his cultural identity is an affirmation not only of love but also of cultural pride. The poet's conviction of undying love is given justification, as the conjunction "Car" [For] indicates, by the divine authority of a public prophesy from Heaven. This prepares us for the climax that occurs in the third stanza, where the form of the proclamation "tu seras *ma chose*" [you'll be *my thing*] prevails and is made triumphantly at the end of this stanza, in the face of opposition from two quarters, the lover, "tu" [you] and an unspecified "l'on" [they].

After this insistent expression of love the tone of the poem changes. The vaguely religious concern that was implicit in the references to "le Ciel" [Heaven] now becomes more clearly articulated. The phrase "Car fut-il nazaréen et nègre de surcroît" [For even if he were a Nazarene and a negro to boot] introduces the elements of Christian religiosity and racism which by implication are seen as sources of the opposition encountered by the poet in the pursuit of his love relationship. The possessiveness of "mon Dieu mien" [my God of mine] echoes that of "*ma chose*" [*my thing*], and this phrase is going to be repeated insistently at the beginning of every stanza for the remainder of the poem. The declaration of love gives way to a declaration of faith as the poet asserts his belief in a divinity different from that associated with traditional Christianity. He rejects and pokes fun at some of the major tenets and rituals of the Christian faith. First he rejects the notion of people having to carry Jesus's cross: "dont nul être au monde / n'eût à porter la Croix" [for whom nobody in the world / had to carry his Cross]. He pokes fun at the biblical account of Jesus's sufferings, using the fragmentation and progressive indentation of "cru / ci / fié " [cru / ci / fied] to underline the irony arising from the fact that these experiences ("traqué" [hunted down], "persiflé" [mocked], "hué" [booed]) have been endured by African slaves in the Americas. The expression "à la passion" is a *double entendre*, signifying both "passionately" and the "passion" [sufferings] of Christ. This ironic humor reaches a peak at the end of the stanza where the name of "Véronique" is joined to the list of two biblical women, Martha and Mary-Magdalene, reputedly loved by Jesus.

The poet's rejection of organized Christianity continues in his appropriation of the term "magnifié" [magnified], often used with reference to God in Christian ritual. The practices of praying "à genoux" [on your knees], "les yeux ... baissés" [eyes lowered], and "les mains ... jointes" [hands clasped] are similarly ridiculed, with the adverbs "faussement" [deceitfully] and "menteusement" [mendaciously] used to indicate the hypocrisy of such practices. It becomes evident that this form of religion presents an obstacle to the poet's love relationship and this is why he moves to predicate a personal religion founded on "l'amour" [love]. The playful repetition of this word conveys the poet's conviction and his ecstasy: "dans la joie de l'amour / dans l'amour de la joie / dans l'amour de la vie / dans la vie de l'amour" [in joy of love / in love of joy / in love of life / in life of love].

The poet's humor is directed not only against religious elements that he rejects (the use of incense and gold) but even against himself. The phrase "cette grande lithurgie de mots" [this great liturgy of words] may be read as referring both to religious ritual and to Damas's own predilection for word play. This self-directed irony mitigates the potential bitterness of the disapproval of the practice referred to in the penultimate stanza that forms such a fundamental part of Catholic doctrine: the belief in the transformation of the body and blood of Christ into the wafers and wine offered during Mass and the injunction that these should be taken on an empty stomach. The tone on which the poem ends is not at all bitter. It is quiet but insistent reaffirmation of the poet's love, a statement of faith that this love can survive the obstacles of racism and religious intolerance.

The intrusion of race into what is supposed to be (in *Névralgies*) a discourse of love and of personal emotion is significant, especially when we consider the fact that nearly thirty years separate the publication of these poems from those produced in the youthful fervor of Negritude. It is an indication of the extent to which "race," the prime motivator at a conscious level of the earlier collection, *Pigments*, affects so many aspects, often unconsciously, of an individual's life in the Caribbean. Damas's importance within the literary history of the French Caribbean is considerable, though often undervalued. Not only was he the first to publish a literary text that manifested the principles and expressed the emotional and cultural dimensions of Negritude, but his active involvement in the propagation of black culture in Paris, Africa, his native Guyana, and in the United States, has contributed, more than any of his contemporaries in the French Caribbean, to the global perception of a "black" literary expression. He has succeeded in producing unforgettable poetry, whose deceptive simplicity deliberately and skillfully exploits black traditions of orality and music in the Caribbean, Africa, and the United States. Damas has established models of poetic style and cultural sensitivity that will endure for generations to come.

Notes

¹ Damas 1962: 49.

² For commentaries on this poem see Cartey 1988:70 and Warner 1988b:95. For other brief commentaries, see Walker 1989:146 and Chemain 1989:175.

³ Damas 1966:16. Page citations for subsequent poems from *Névralgies* refer to this edition.

⁴ Hodge 1988:123-124 offers a brief comment on this poem as well as a translation.

⁵ According to this account, Noah had three sons, Shem, Ham, and Japheth, who were the ancestors of the whole earth. Noah got drunk one day and lay naked in his tent. Ham discovered him and told his brothers who then covered their father's nakedness. When Noah awoke and discovered what Ham had done he cursed him, condemning his race to be a perpetual servant of servants, while blessing Shem and Japheth who had taken care not to look at their father's nakedness. Methuselah was Noah's grandfather, the oldest living man at 969 years.

4

Aimé CÉSAIRE

Born June 26, 1913, in Basse-Pointe in the north of Martinique, Césaire has been the most renowned figure in French Caribbean letters and politics since the early 1940s. In 1924 he moved to the capital town of Fort-de-France on a scholarship to undertake his secondary education at the Lycée Schœlcher, where he was to meet his fellow student Léon Damas for the first time. He left Martinique for Paris in 1932 on another scholarship to further his education. He enrolled at the Lycée Louis-Le-Grand to prepare to enter the Ecole Normale Supérieure. There he met and started a lifelong friendship with the Senegalese Léopold-Sédar Senghor, who was preparing for the same examination, and renewed his acquaintance with Léon Damas from Guyane. The collaboration between these three resulted in the launching of an ephemeral student newspaper, *L'Etudiant noir [The Black Student]* in 1935, which featured a number of articles that placed emphasis on a common African dimension in the cultural expression of black people. That same year Césaire gained admission to the Ecole Normale Supérieure from which he later obtained his Diplôme d'Etudes Supérieures with a thesis on the theme of the South in Black American literature. After a trip to Yugoslavia with his friend Petar Guberina that included a visit to an island with the evocative name of Martinska, Césaire started working on a poem that was to become his first published poetic work, *Cahier d'un retour au pays natal [Return to My native Land]*. This publication was virtually unnoticed when it first appeared in August 1939 in the journal, *Volontés*. Césaire returned to Martinique in 1939 a little before the outbreak of the Second World War. He taught at his old high school, the Lycée Schœlcher, and founded a journal, *Tropiques*, with the help of his wife, Suzanne, René Ménil, and Aristide Maugée. In 1941 the French Surrealist leader, André Breton, on a brief visit to Martinique, was impressed by a poem of Césaire's which he came across in *Tropiques*. Césaire's literary reputation in metropolitan France was confirmed by laudatory articles by Breton and Jean-Paul Sartre, and he became highly respected as both a poet and a dramatist within the metropolitan French mainstream literary tradition. Césaire rose to political prominence in Martinique in 1945, when he was elected Mayor of Fort-de-France and Deputy to the Constituent Assembly as a member of the Communist Party. In 1946 he piloted a bill through the Assembly transforming the Caribbean colonies of Martinique, Guadeloupe, Guyane, as well as the Indian Ocean colony of Reunion into departments. In 1956 he resigned in disillusionment from the Communist Party to found his own Parti Progressiste Martiniquais (PPM), of which he has remained undisputed leader. Césaire has exercised the functions of both Mayor and Deputy ever since, until in 1993 he decided to retire from contesting the legislative elections for deputies. He has however retained his mayoral position, and in June 1995 was preparing to be returned once again as Mayor.

Césaire's voluminous writings include historical and political texts, including *Discours sur le colonialisme* (1950) and

Toussaint Louverture: La Révolution française et le problème colonial (1962); several plays, including *La Tragédie du roi Christophe* (1963), *Une saison au Congo* (1966), and *Une tempête* (1969); critical and theoretical articles on poetry and literature, as well as several volumes of poetry, including *Cahier d'un retour au pays natal* (1939), *Les Armes miraculeuses* (1946), *Cadastre* (1961) — a re-edition and emendation of two previously published collections, *Soleil cou-coupé* of 1948 and *Corps perdu* of 1950 —, *Ferrements* (1960), *Noria* (1976), and *Moi, laminaire* (1982).

All French Caribbean writers acknowledge the monumental importance of Césaire to the cultural development of the Caribbean no matter what they think of his politics or of Negritude. In fact it is not unusual to criticize Césaire for his failure to lead the French Caribbean ex-colonies towards a meaningful autonomy or full independence. Undoubtedly he could have done it if he had chosen to do it. He seems to have deliberately avoided the role as political leader of an independent nation that appeared destined to be his — the role embraced by his friend and colleague Senghor in Senegal and by other similarly situated and endowed colleagues din the English-speaking Caribbean, such as Eric Williams in Trinidad, Normal Manley in Jamaica, Eric Gairy in Grenada, and Grantley Adams in Barbados. Césaire has settled for what may be called comparatively meager pickings: the mayorship of Fort-de-France. Only time will be able to estimate the true measure of Césaire's political choices. The assertiveness and boldness of his writing stands in sharp contrast to his cautious, conciliatory, even assimilationist political behavior. However, despite all the opposition and criticism from respected intellectuals within Martinique and outside, Césaire still (in 1995) exercises a charismatic influence on masses of Martinicans who for fifty years have consistently demonstrated their support of him at the polls. Even his most vocal detractors concede his power as a literary figure and join the Martinican masses in paying homage to him for putting Martinique on the global map as a center of literary excellence. Criticism of what seems to be his political timidity and poor judgement has in no way challenged his literary standing. He is the pre-eminent poet of the French Caribbean.

Cadastre, published in 1961, is the re-edition of poems from two previously published collections, *Soleil cou-coupé* of 1948 and *Corps perdu* of 1950, with some of the original poems removed completely and others revised.[1] As the title indicates, the poet is concerned with making a cadastral survey — taking an inventory of his situation as a black man and as a poet. This collection explores and articulates the issues faced by the poet in relation to alienation and identity, as he searches within himself and attempts to solidify his commitment to his people. The poems evoke the tension implicit in the ambivalence of the relationship between the poet and the social order within which he functions, and serve to concretize the message of liberation.

MAGIQUE[2]

avec une lèche de ciel sur un quignon de terre
vous bêtes qui sifflez sur le visage de cette morte
vous libres fougères parmi les roches assassines
à l'extrême de l'île parmi les conques trop vastes
pour leur destin
lorsque midi colle ses mauvais timbres sur les plis
tempétueux de la louve
hors cadre de science nulle
et la bouche aux parois du nid suffète des îles
englouties comme un sou

avec une lèche de ciel sur un quignon de terre
prophète des îles oubliées comme un sou
sans sommeil sans veille sans doigt sans palancre
quand la tornade passe rongeur du pain des cases

vous bêtes qui sifflez sur le visage de cette morte
la belle once de la luxure et la coquille operculée

mol glissement des grains de l'été que nous fûmes
belles chairs à transpercer du trident des aras
lorsque les étoiles chancelières de cinq branches
trèfles au ciel comme des gouttes de lait chu
réajustent un dieu noir mal né de son tonnerre

❦

MAGICAL

With a slice of sky on a lump of earth
you beasts hissing on this dead woman's face
you ferns free among the murderous rocks
at the island's edge amid the conchs whose fate
cannot contain them
when noon pastes its used stamps on the lioness's
stormy folds
no science that
and the mouth at the walls of the nest suffete of
islands squandered
like a cent

with a slice of sky on a lump of earth
prophet of islands forgotten like a cent
no sleep no wake no catch-pin no trawl-line
when comes the tornado eating the hovels' bread

you beasts hissing on this dead woman's face
beautiful ounce of lust and operculated shell
soft shifting of the summer grain we once were
fine flesh to be pierced by the aras' trident
when the stars five-branched chancellors
clover in the sky like drops of fallen milk
readjust a black god ill born from its thunder

The title of this opening poem of the collection (*Cadastre*, 9) anticipates the magical metamorphosis that occurs at the end of the poem: the repositioning of a black god. This metamorphosis takes place against a background of metaphors of natural phenomena, associated with the hurricane season in the Caribbean: an overcast sky in which only a thin slice of blue ("une lèche de ciel") is visible, and high winds ("vous bêtes qui sifflez") [you beasts hissing], which are characteristic of the destructive tornado ("rongeur du pain des cases") [eating the hovels' bread). The island, a mere "lump of earth" ("ce quignon de terre"), is represented as virtually dead ("cette morte") [this dead woman], threatened by and at the mercy of the wind-beasts ("vous bêtes"), and of "vous libres fougères," the ferns that are shown to be already free. The feminizing of the island points to a desire on Césaire's part to invest the island with those attributes that he associates with the feminine — particularly the vulnerability in the roles of mother, daughter, and wife/lover. In this context, the viewing of the dead island reflects the poet's frustrated affection (paternal, filial, and sexual) and his grief at the loss of the woman/island's (pro)creative potential. The metaphors also signify a geopolitical context of conflict, between "vous bêtes" [you beasts] and "cette morte" [this dead woman]; between "vous libres fougères" [you ferns free] and "les roches assassines" [the murderous rocks]; between "les conques" [the conchs], a seafood delicacy common in the Caribbean islands, and "leur destin" [their fate]; even between the implied light of "midi" [noon] and the darkness associated with "les étoiles" [the stars]. The negative attributes of noon ("mauvais timbres" [used stamps]) in this poem contrast with the positive association of absolute clarity signaled by Damas in "Si depuis peu" (see p. 176 above). The images here are opaque, not immediately or directly accessible. The referent for "la louve" [the lioness] is unclear. Out of this opacity, however, emerges the impression of a conflict between forces of oppression and destruction and other forces with an impulse toward liberation. The struggle takes place on an island, one that shares a situational bond of worthlessness with other islands, in that they have all been, like a worthless coin ("comme un sou"), "englouties" [squandered] and "oubliées" [forgotten].

Against this background, the poetic persona identifies itself through the plural "nous" [we] of line 14. This poetic subject is significantly plural and collective, possessing an already realized potential for regeneration and metamorphosis: the grains have already shifted, and we are no longer what we were. The poet has several roles to play: he is the "bouche" [mouth], "suffète" [suffete], and "prophète" [prophet], with creative, political, and visionary responsibilities, as he attempts to communicate with an audience, whom he addresses directly, using the vocatives, as "vous bêtes" [you beasts] and "vous libres fougères" [you free ferns].

The dilemma of the poet in this situation is that of a potential voice confronted by the practical limitations associated with the island: "la bouche aux parois du nid" [the mouth at the walls of the nest]. In order to resolve this dilemma, the poet assumes the role of responsibility and leadership, that of "suffète," but also that of "prophète," announcing the future of his people. It is through the vision, the prophetic voice, of the poet that the dead island, "cette morte" [this dead woman], is restored to life; it is through the poetic activity implicit in the poem that a metamorphosis takes place, "mol glissement des grains d'été que nous fumes" [soft shifting of the summer grain we once were]. For even in the midst of the atmosphere of menace and danger there were signs of hope: even the "lèche de ciel" [thin slice of sky] bore within itself signs of good weather to come; the "étoiles" [stars] imply not only darkness, but also light, with associations of good fortune ("trèfles au ciel") [clover in the sky] and vitality ("gouttes de lait chu") [drops of fallen milk]. These are all signs of hope, the hope which is at the heart of the message of this poem: the restoration of the divinity of the black man ("réadjustent un dieu noir mal né de son tonnerre") [readjust a black god ill born from its thunder].

In this opening poem, therefore, the poet communicates his acceptance of responsibility based on awareness and his decision to focus on the situation of the island and on "black" needs and potential. In executing this decision, the poet virtually rewrites and reconstructs the geographical and climatic situation of the island in relation to an opposing Other ("vous"). In this way the poem becomes the magical voice of hope through which the dilemma of identity will be articulated. The poet as a linking voice magically emerges out of the silence historically imposed on blacks in a neo-colonial situation. It must however be cautioned that the almost messianic leadership and prophetic role that Césaire envisions for the poet is one that most other Caribbean poets, including Glissant, Padoly, Polius, and all the women, will reject.

LE GRIFFON

Je suis un souvenir qui n'atteint pas le seuil
et erre dans les limbes où le reflet d'absinthe
quand le cœur de la nuit souffle par ses évents
bouge l'étoile tombée où nous nous contemplons

Le ciel lingual a pris sa neuve consistance de crême
de noix
fraîche
ouverte du coco

Andes crachant et Mayumbé sacré
seul naufrage que l'œil bon voilier nous soudoie
quand âme folle déchiquetée folle
      par les nuages qui m'arrivent dans les
poissons bien clos
je remonte hanter la sinistre épaisseur des choses

❦

THE GRIFFIN

I am a memory that fails to reach the threshold
and wanders in limbo where the glint of absinthe
when night's heart blows through its vents
stirs the fallen star in which we view ourselves

The lingual sky has taken on its new consistency
of freshly opened
coconut milk

the only wreck the eye fine sailboat hires for us
when I crazed soul torn to pieces crazed
       by the clouds that come to me in tightly
closed fish
climb up again to haunt the sinister thickness of
things

The poet adopts the persona of "Le griffon" (19)[3] the fabulous
winged beast, usually depicted as having primarily a lion's body,
and an eagle's head and wings. The griffin's hybrid composition
immediately suggests that complexity of identity be at least partly
at issue here. This complexity is increased by the associated
connotations of the term "griffe" which is inscribed in "griffon." As
Gregson Davis indicates in his commentary on this poem, "griffe"
indicates racial hybridization, associated with colonization:

> [T]he French *griffe* (the basis of *griffon*) designates
> the offspring of a negro and a mulatto in colonial
> society. (The feminine form of the diminutive,
> *griffonne*, denotes a woman who is three-quarters
> negro and one quarter white.) Thus the
> mythological monster joins with the racial
> construct to produce an emblem of cultural
> indeterminacy. (*Non-Vicious Circle*, 127).

At the same time, "griffe" is used in French to connote the special label or "signature" of a creator, which suggests that the poet's specific identity is located in the image of the griffin.

This complexity is elaborated poetically within the text by the contrast between the first section of the poem, where the rhythm of the traditional French alexandrine (12-syllable lines) predominates, and the middle section, which alludes to a change in relation to language: "Le ciel lingual a pris sa neuve consistance de crême de noix / fraîche / ouverte du coco" [The lingual sky now has its new consistency / of freshly opened / coconut milk]. This complexity is reflected syntactically too in the fluidity of agreement between "fraîche" [fresh], "crême" [milk], and "noix" [nut], and in the ambivalence of relationships created by the "de" in "de crême" [milky], "de noix" [of nut], and "du coco" [of the coco(nut)] and by the separation between "noix" [nut] and "coco" [coco(nut)]. Significantly this reference to a coconut is the only allusion in the text to an object which evokes the Caribbean, but it signifies the poet's effort to endow the text with a specifically Caribbean flavor.

The poet's frustration is reflected in the situation of the poet-griffin, whose existence in the present is problematical: "Je suis un souvenir qui n'atteint pas le seuil" [I am a memory that fails to reach the threshold]. He is, like the griffin, forced to wander in the nether regions between death and life ("erre dans les limbes" [wanders in limbo]), and it is in the awareness of a common fall from grace that the poet's own duality meets that of the griffin ("l'étoile tombée où nous nous contemplons" [the fallen star in which we view ourselves]).

In the third section the poet presents himself as "âme folle déchiquetée folle" [crazed soul torn to pieces crazed]. This description announces physical, spiritual, and cultural fragmentation as well as mental disorder in a "je" [I] whose very existence as a living creature is being called into question. The context within which the poet appears is that of "Andes crachant et Mayumbé sacré" [belching Andes and sacred Mayombe], evocations of destructive volcanic power in the Americas and of religious veneration associated with Africa. Hence, the poet-griffin becomes invested with conflicting powers for good and evil, for life and death. At the end, however, there is no solution for the poet, who remains caught between two worlds, a disturbed and disturbing presence, still searching for answers, hovering above the plane of human reality: "je remonte hanter la sinistre épaisseur des choses" [I climb up again to haunt the sinister thickness of things].

Within this poem, the poet acts as both a demystifier and a demythifier, by identifying himself with, and reconstructing the dilemma of, the mythical griffin. This poem transcribes the sense of failure and frustration experienced by the poet out of his inability to meet the expectations that he has imposed on himself. While the role he has chosen is reminiscent of that adopted by Baudelaire, Rimbaud, and Mallarmé, and associated with Symbolism, of a decipherer of the "épaisseur des choses" [thickness of things], the insecurity manifested by the poet is linked firmly to an aspect of the Caribbean tradition later identified by Glissant, who points to the effort to supplement the rupture of impossible memory as a manifestation of creative marronnage and as an expression of the third moment in French Caribbean literature (see page 40 above).

The density of the griffin image creates the impression that racial hybridization has contributed to the rupture of memory and thus to the limbo state in which the poet finds himself. Such an intense expression of psychic dislocation is rare in French Caribbean literature.

A L'AFRIQUE

Paysan frappe le sol de ta daba
dans le sol il y a une hâte que la syllabe de l'événement
ne dénoue pas
je me souviens de la fameuse peste
il n'y avait pas eu d'étoile annoncière
mais seulement la terre en un flot sans galet pétrissant
d'espace

un pain d'herbe et de réclusion
frappe paysan frappe
le premier jour les oiseaux moururent
le second jour les poissons échouèrent
le troisième jour les animaux sortirent des bois
et faisaient aux villes une grande ceinture chaude très
forte
frappe le sol de ta daba
il y a dans le sol la carte des transmutations et des ruses
de la mort
le quatrième jour la végétation se fana
et tout tourna à l'aigre de l'agave à l'acacia
en aigrettes en orgues végétales
où le vent épineux jouait des flûtes et des odeurs
tranchantes
Frappe paysan frappe
il naît au ciel des fenêtres qui sont mes yeux giclés
et dont la herse dans ma poitrine fait le rempart d'une
ville qui refuse de donner la passe aux muletiers de la
désespérance
Famine et de toi-même houle
ramas où se risque d'un salut la colère du futur
frappe Colère
il y a au pied de nos châteaux-de-fées pour la rencontre
du sang et du paysage la salle de bal où des nains
braquant leurs miroirs écoutent dans les plis de la
pierre ou du sel croître le sexe du regard
Paysan pour que débouche de la tête de la montagne
celle que blesse le vent
pour que tiédisse dans sa gorge une gorgée de cloches
pour que ma vague se dévore en sa vague et nous
ramène sur le sable en noyés en chair de goyaves
déchirés en une main d'épure en belles algues en graine
volante en bulle en souvenance en arbre précatoire

soit ton geste une vague qui hurle et se reprend vers le
creux de rocs aimés comme pour parfaire une île
rebelle à naître
il y a dans le sol demain en scrupule et la parole à
charger aussi bien que le silence

Paysan le vent où glissent des carènes arrête autour de
mon visage la main lointaine d'un songe
ton champ dans son saccage éclate debout de monstres
marins
que je n'ai garde d'écarter
et mon geste est pur autant qu'un front d'oubli
frappe paysan je suis ton fils
à l'heure du soleil qui se couche le crépuscule sous ma
paupière clapote vert jaune et tiède d'iguanes
inassoupis
mais la belle autruche courrière qui subitement naît des
formes émues de la femme me fait de l'avenir les signes
de l'amitié

❦

TO AFRICA

Farmer pound the ground with your daba
in the ground there is an urgent knot that is not untied
by the syllable of the event
I recall the famous plague
there had been no foretelling star
only earth in a pebble-free gush kneading with space
a loaf of grass and reclusion
pound farmer pound
on the first day the birds died
on the second day the fish were washed up
on the third day the animals came out of the woods

and formed a great warm girdle very strong around the
cities
pound the ground with your daba
there is in the ground the map of death's transmutations
and tricks
on the fourth day the vegetation withered
and everything turned bitter from the agave to the
acacia
into egret plumes into vegetable organs
on which the prickly wind played flutes and sharp
odors
pound farmer pound
in the sky windows are born which are my squirted
eyes
and their harrow in my chest forms the rampart of a
city that refuses to let the mule-drivers of despair pass
through
Famine and your own billow
heap in which the future's anger risks a salvation
pound Anger
at the foot of our fairy castles there is the ballroom for
blood and landscape to come together where dwarfs
aiming their mirrors listen in the folds of stone or salt
to the sex of the gaze growing hard

Farmer so that she whom the wind wounds may come
forth from the mountain's head
so that a mouthful of bells may grow warm in her
throat
so that my wave may be consumed in her wave and
take us back to the sand like drowned people torn like
guava flesh like the rough sketch of a hand like
beautiful algae like flying seed like a bubble like a
recollection like a precatory tree

may whatever you do be a wave that roars and pulls
itself together near the hollow of beloved rocks as if to
perfect a rebellious island at its birth
in the ground there is tomorrow in the balance and the
spoken word as well as silence to load

Farmer the wind in which the hulls glide stays the
distant hand of a dream
around my face
your field in its havoc explodes erect with sea
monsters
which I take care not to send away
and my action is as pure as a brow of oblivion
pound farmer I am your son
at the time of the setting sun twilight under my eyelid
splashes yellow green and warm with iguanas roused
from their doze
but the beautiful courier ostrich suddenly born from the
moved forms of the woman makes signs of friendship
to me from the future

This poem (39) illustrates Césaire's concern with articulating his
awareness of his connection to Africa. The dedication of the poem
to Wilfredo Lam is a reminder of the complex cultural identity of
the Afro-Chinese Cuban painter, who shares with Césaire the
ancestral linkage to Africa. The reference to Lam also serves as a
reminder that one characteristic of this painter's work, heavily
influenced by European Surrealism, was its hybrid creatures,[4] and,
as we have seen in "Le griffon," Césaire was well aware of the
negative effects of racial hybridization on Caribbean people.

    The primary and dominant link established by the poet in
the poem is with the African farmer ("paysan"), identified as
African only through the agricultural tool ("ta daba") he wields, and
with whom the poet communicates throughout the whole poem.
The soil is presented as a creative source that the poet encourages

the farmer to stimulate by pounding with the "daba." The association between the activity of the farmer and that of the poet is heightened through the alliterations in "le sol de ta daba" and "la syllabe." The characteristic of the soil emphasized by the poet is "une hâte" [an urgency]. In other words, Africa represents for the poet a source of hope, the rapid realization of which cannot be prevented by any negative analysis of the African situation. Continued activity by the African farmer ("frappe"[pound]) is proposed as a means of averting the catastrophe evoked ("je me souviens de la fameuse peste" [I recall the famous plague]), since the medium on which the peasant works contains the potential for the magical transformation necessary to survival and rebirth ("il y a dans le sol la carte des transmutations et des ruses de la mort" [there is in the ground the map of death's transmutations and tricks]).

As the farmer's activity persists and as the poetic activity continues, a transformation takes place within the poet himself: "il naît au ciel des fenêtres qui sont mes yeux giclés" [in the sky windows are born which are my squirted eyes]. This new openness may be contrasted with the confinement and restriction connoted earlier in "réclusion" [reclusion] and "ceinture" [girdle]. Thus the action of the farmer becomes a metaphor for hope and endows the poet with the protective capacity to defend both himself and his country: " ... la herse dans ma poitrine fait le rempart d'une ville qui refuse de donner la passe aux muletiers de la désespérance" [their harrow in my chest forms the rampart of a city that refuses to let the mule-drivers of despair pass through].

The evocation of "Famine" immediately after the mention of "désespérance" [despair] points to a causal relationship and this link reinforces the earlier association of a threat to survival. Thus the line "ramas où se risque d'un salut la colère du futur" [heap in which the future's anger risks a salvation] indicates that what is at issue here, for both the poet and the African, is their survival and salvation. It is at this point in the poem that a new association is established between the African farmer and anger personified, as the earlier "frappe paysan" [pound farmer] is replaced by "frappe Colère" [pound Anger]. The objective of the poet is articulated in "pour la rencontre du sang et du paysage" [for blood and landscape to come together] which signifies a state of convergence between racial identity and country. This objective is further elaborated in a series of anaphoric clauses, introduced by "pour que" [so that], which refer to a relationship between an as yet unspecified woman and the poet. It is only when the objective is clearly articulated in "pour parfaire une île rebelle à naître" [to perfect a rebellious island at its birth] that it becomes clear that the poet is concerned about his own Caribbean island, evoked as being volcanic and subject to hurricanes ("pour que débouche de la tête de la montagne celle que blesse le vent" [so that she whom the wind wounds may come forth from the mountain's head]). Even the poet's name is inscribed in the poem, in "aimés," and this subjectivity is enhanced by "rebelle" which is linked intertextually to the main character in Césaire's dramatic poem, *Et les chiens se taisaient*, who has no name but is identified simply as "Le Rebelle." The island, Africa, and the poet are thus inextricably entwined. The action of the African farmer becomes symbolically creative, in that it contributes toward the emergence of the poet's native island. The African farmer's choice of action over inaction mirrors the poet's own need to be given a voice ("la parole" [the spoken word]) rather than to be silent, and it is on this voice that the future depends: "il y a dans le sol demain en scrupule et la parole à charger aussi bien que le silence" [in the ground there is tomorrow in the balance and the spoken word as well as silence to load].

In the final section of the poem the poet evokes nightmarish memories of slave-ships and of the rape of Africa (" ... la main lointaine d'un songe / ton champ dans son saccage éclate debout de monstres marins" [the distant hand of a dream / your field in its havoc explodes erect with sea monsters]). The alliterative consonants, "t," "d," "c," and "m," translate an intensity of emotion. It is through the transcending of these negative memories that the poet is able to create an ancestral affiliation with the African farmer ("mon geste est pur autant qu'un front d'oubli / frappe paysan je suis ton fils" [my action is as pure as a brow of oblivion / pound farmer I am your son]). As the poem ends, the African ostrich becomes a phoenix-like symbol of hope for the future: "la belle autruche courrière qui subitement naît des formes émues de la femme me fait de l'avenir les signes de l'amitié" [the beautiful courier ostrich suddenly born from the moved forms of the woman makes signs of friendship to me from the future].

In "A l'Afrique," the poet claims a definite African identity, beyond the breach created by slavery. He implies that it is on this cultural linkage that his own survival and that of his native island depend. He further intimates that his poetic lineage is essentially African, and that traditional cultural activity in Africa, represented in the dominant symbol of the "daba," associated metonymically with the Césairian lance, is needed to stimulate and foster creative activity by Africans in the Caribbean. The poem as a communication addressed directly to Africa acts both as a declaration of chosen identity and as a communication bridge between the Caribbean poet and his African heritage. It therefore supplements the loss of oral contact effected as a result of slavery and colonization. Such a direct expression of African connectedness will become increasingly rare in French Caribbean poetry.

COUTEAUX MIDI

Quand les Nègres font la Révolution ils commencent par arracher du Champ de Mars des arbres géants qu'ils lancent à la face du ciel comme des aboiements et qui couchent dans le plus chaud de l'air de purs courants d'oiseaux frais où ils tirent à blanc. Ils tirent à blanc ? Oui ma foi parce que le blanc est la juste force controversée du noir qu'ils portent dans le cœur et qui ne cesse de conspirer dans les petits hexagones trop bien faits de leurs pores. Les coups de feu blancs plantent alors dans le ciel des belles de nuit qui ne sont pas sans rapport avec les cornettes des sœurs de Saint Joseph de Cluny qu'elles lessivent sous les espèces de midi dans la jubilation solaire du savon tropical.

Midi ? Oui, Midi qui disperse dans le ciel la ouate trop complaisante qui capitonne mes paroles et où mes cris se prennent. Midi ? Oui Midi amande de la nuit et langue entre mes crocs de poivre. Midi ? Oui Midi qui porte sur son dos de galeux et de vitrier toute la sensibilité qui compte de la haine et des ruines. Midi ? pardieu Midi qui après s'être recueilli sur mes lèvres le temps d'un blasphème et aux limites cathédrales de l'oisiveté met sur toutes les lignes de toutes les mains les trains que la repentance gardait en réserve dans les coffres-forts du temps sévère. Midi ? Oui Midi somptueux qui de ce monde m'absente.

Doux Seigneur !

durement je crache. Au visage des affameurs, au visage des insulteurs, au visage des paraschites et des éventreurs.

Seigneur dur !

doux je siffle; je siffle doux

Doux comme l'hièble

doux comme le verre de catastrophe

doux comme la houppelande faite de plumes d'oiseau que la vengeance vêt après le crime

doux comme le salut des petites vagues surprises en jupes dans les chambres du mancenillier

doux comme un fleuve de mandibules et la paupière du perroquet

doux comme une pluie de cendre emperlée de petits feux.

Oh! je tiens mon pacte

debout dans mes blessures où mon sang bat contre les fûts du naufrage des cadavres de chiens crevés d'où fusent des colibris, c'est le jour,

un jour pour nos pieds fraternels

un jour pour nos mains sans rancunes

un jour pour nos souffles sans méfiance

un jour pour nos faces sans vergogne

et les Nègres vont cherchant dans la poussière — à leur oreille à pleins poumons les pierres précieuses chantant — les échardes dont on fait le mica dont on fait les lunes et l'ardoise lamelleuse dont les sorciers font l'intime férocité des étoiles.

ꙮ

NOON KNIVES

When Negroes make a Revolution they start by pulling up giant trees from the Champ de Mars and throwing them like the barking of dogs into the face of the sky, as these trees lie in the warmest air of pure currents of cool birds where they fire (white) blanks. They fire (white) blanks? Yes indeed yes because white (blank)is the righteous and controversial force of the black which they bear in their hearts and which is always conspiring in the too perfectly formed little hexagons of their pores. The white blank shots then plant ladies- of-the-night in the sky which are not unlike the coifs worn by the Sisters of Saint Joseph of Cluny washed by the nuns under inferior noons in the solar jubilation of tropical soap.

Noon? Yes, Noon that scatters in the sky the too complacent cotton wool that muffles my words and in which my cries get trapped. Noon? Yes Noon night almond and tongue between my fangs of pepper. Noon? Yes Noon like a leper or window-cleaner bears on his back all the sensitivity to hatred and ruins that matters. Noon? by god Noon which after resting on my lips just long enough for a curse and at the cathedral limits of idleness places on all the lines of every hand the trains held in reserve by repentance in the strongboxes of hard times. Yes sumptuous Noon that absents me from this world.

Gentle Lord!
I spit hard. In the faces of the hunger-givers, in the faces of the insulters, in the faces of the paraschites and the debowellers. Hard Lord!
gentle I whistle; I whistle gentle
gentle like the elder-bush
gentle like the glass of catastrophe
gentle like the greatcoat of bird feathers donned by vengeance after the crime
gentle like the greeting of small waves caught by surprise in their skirts in the bedrooms of the manchineel tree
gentle like a river of mandibles and the eyelid of a parrot
gentle like a shower of ash pearly with little fires.
Oh! I am sticking to the pact I made
erect in my wounds in which my blood throbs against the casks of the shipwreck of corpses of dead dogs from which humming birds spurt out, today's the day,
a day for our fraternal feet
a day for our hands free of rancor
a day for our breath free of distrust
a day for our faces free of shame

and the Negroes go searching in the dust — in their ears as loud as they can the precious stones singing — looking for the splinters from which mica is made from which moons are made and the flaky slate from which sorcerers make the intimate ferocity of the stars.

In the first part of this poem (44), the subjective presence of the poet appears in the possessive and object pronouns of "mes paroles" [my words], "mes cris" [my cries], "mes crocs de poivre" [my fangs of pepper], "mes lèvres" [my lips], and "m'absente" [absents me]. The poet is evoked as a disembodied voice and mouth, involved in a dialogue, as the questions "Ils tirent à blanc?" [They fire (white) blanks?] and "Midi?" [Noon?] (posed five times) indicate. The poetic replies to the questions are always an affirmative "oui" [yes], which suggests the validity of the propositions advanced.

These propositions are related to the activities of blacks, and specifically to what the poet suggests occurs "quand les Nègres font la Révolution" [when Negroes make a Revolution]. He intimates, with evident irony, playing on common connotations of "white" and "black," that the ineffectual blank bullets they fire are white, supporting the validity of this paradox by explaining that "le blanc est la juste force controversée du noir qu'ils portent dans le cœur" [the white (blank) is the righteous and controversial force of the black which they bear in their hearts]. Metropolitan Frenchmen are clearly indicated in the reference to "les petits hexagones trop bien faits de leurs pores" [the too perfectly formed little hexagons of their pores], since "l'Hexagone" is common designation used to refer to continental France because of its shape. The text implies that the poet considers this an abortive pseudo-revolution, doomed from the start by its own endemic contradictions, equivalent to a white-washing process taking place under a pseudo-midday sun, so pale in comparison to the tropical sun that it is to be greeted only with derisive laughter: "les cornettes des sœurs de Saint Joseph de Cluny qu'elles lessivent sous les espèces de midi dans la jubilation solaire d'un savon tropical" [the coifs worn by the Sisters of Saint Joseph of Cluny washed by the nuns under inferior noons in the solar jubilation of tropical soap].

The poet, struck by the contrast between these two different noons, explores the significance that the tropical noon holds for him. A contrast may be made with Damas in "Si depuis peu" (see page 135 above), where Damas focuses on associations based largely on observable visual characteristics (position, light, shadow). Both poets allude to and develop the essential quality of lucidity they associate with noon. The associations drawn by Césaire are more unusual. Césaire suggests that noon provides a natural avenue of escape from the muzzling of his voice and limitations of a complacent and comfortable life: "Midi qui disperse dans le ciel la ouate trop complaisante qui capitonne mes paroles et où mes cris se prennent" [Noon that scatters in the sky the too complacent cotton-wool that muffles my words and in which my cries get trapped]. The poetic voice shifts to a more assertive and affirmative mode, corresponding to the graphic shift from the common noun, "midi" [noon], disdain for which is suggested by the contemptuous expression "espèces de ...," to the proper (capitalized) "Midi" [Noon]. This contrasting "Midi" is invested with capacities which stand in opposition to the other "midi": the capacity for a presence affirmed even in darkness, like the almond whose scent is recognizable even at night, and the capacity for speech ("langue" [tongue]). This "Midi," too, is associated with the sensitivity that comes from emotional and social humiliations: " ... qui porte sur son dos de galeux ...." [bearing on its outcast's back]. This "Midi" is a metaphor for courageous patience, endurance, and the potential for problem-solving which may be read " sur toutes les lignes de toutes les mains " [on all the lines of every hand]. It is this "Midi" that, significantly, makes possible a break with the (white) world ("Midi somptueux qui de ce monde m'absente") [sumptuous Noon which absents me from this world].

The attitude and activities of the poet change with the movement within the poem away from "ce monde" [this world]. As the poem assumes a poetic "form" in the middle section of the poem the poet becomes active and assumes the voice of revolt. The opposites of "doux" [gentle], and "dur" [hard] are indications of the extreme nature and completeness of the revolt: "Doux Seigneur! / durement je crache. Au visage des affameurs, au visage des insulteurs, au visage des paraschites et des éventreurs. Seigneur dur! doux je siffle; je siffle doux ..." [Gentle Lord! / I spit hard. In the faces of the hunger-givers, in the faces of the insulters, in the faces of the paraschites and the debowellers. Hard Lord! Gentle I whistle; I whistle gentle...]. This new attitude is presented by the poet as indicative of a sense of self, characterized by painful experiences, but founded on dignity and commitment: "Oh! je tiens mon pacte / debout dans mes blessures où mon sang bat contre les fûts" [Oh! I am sticking to the pact I made / erect in my wounds in which my blood throbs against the casks...]. This sense of self includes solidarity with others of his race and is expressed through a message of hope and humanitarianism. This brings into existence, at the end of this section, the dawn of a new revolution that transcends hatred: "... c'est le jour, / un jour pour nos pieds fraternels / un jour pour nos mains sans rancunes / un jour pour nos souffles sans méfiance / un jour pour nos faces sans vergogne" [today's the day, / a day for our fraternal feet / a day for our hands free of rancor / a day for our breath free of distrust / a day for our faces free of shame]. The final short prose section, which continues the discussion of the opening section, links the role of the poet to that of "les sorciers" [sorcerers]. This metonymic link signifies the involvement of both poet and sorcerer in harnessing powers of potential ferocity and in creatively exploiting intimacy with the dark forces of nature: "l'intime férocité des étoiles" [the intimate ferocity of the stars].

The poet, in this poem, establishes a contrast, implicit in the title, between violent physical pseudo-revolution represented metaphorically as "couteaux" [knives] and the lucidity ("Midi" [Noon]) of true revolt, in order to resolve what the poet sees as a sociocultural and political problem confronting "Negroes." The poetic solution is to move beyond embracing violence, and to transform the knife into a kind of magic wand. Thus the poet finally assumes the voice of a prophet to predict a future of hope, dignity and love, and that of a sorcerer, relying on the supportive chorus of his brother "Nègres" to participate in the creative activity of the cosmos. This poem is an example of the way in which Césaire's rhetoric of violence tends to negate action. Even within the poem the word, however violent, is a producer ultimately of beauty rather than destruction. For Césaire, revolution finds its proper place within the creative imagination.

AUX ÉCLUSES DU VIDE

Au premier plan et fuite longitudinale un ruisseau desséché sommeilleux rouleur de galets d'obsidiennes. Au fond une point quiète architecture de burgs démantelés de montagnes érodées sur le fantôme deviné desquels naissent serpents chariots œil de chat des constellations alarmantes. C'est un étrange gâteau de lucioles lancé contre la face grise du temps, un grand éboulis de tessons d'icones et de blasons de poux dans la barbe de Saturne. A droite très curieusement debout à la paroi squameuse de papillons crucifiés ailes ouvertes dans la gloire une gigantesque bouteille dont le goulot d'or très long boit dans les nuages une goutte de sang. Pour ma part je n'ai pas soif. Il m'est doux de penser le monde défait comme un vieux matelas à coprah comme un vieux collier vaudou comme le parfum du pécari abattu. Je n'ai plus soif.

> par le ciel ébranlé
> par les étoiles éclatées
> par le silence tutélaire
> de très loin d'outre moi je viens vers toi
> femme surgie d'un bel aubier
> et tes yeux blessures mal fermées
> sur ta pudeur d'être née.

C'est moi qui chante d'une voix prise encore dans le balbutiement des éléments. Il est doux d'être un morceau de bois un bouchon une goutte d'eau dans les eaux torrentielles de la fin et du recommencement. Il est doux de s'assoupir au cœur brisé des choses. Je n'ai plus aucune espèce de soif. Mon épée faite d'un sourire de dents de requin devient terriblement inutile. Ma masse d'armes est très visiblement hors saison et hors de jeu. La pluie tombe. C'est un croisement de gravats, c'est un incroyable arrimage de

l'invisible par des liens de toute qualité, c'est une ramure de syphilis, c'est le diagramme d'une saoulerie à l'eau-de-vie, c'est un complot de cuscutes, c'est la tête du cauchemar fichée sur la pointe de lance d'une foule en délire.
J'avance jusqu'à la région des lacs bleus. J'avance jusqu'à la région des solfatares
j'avance jusqu'à ma bouche cratériforme vers laquelle ai-je assez peiné? Qu'ai-je à jeter? Tout ma foi tout. Je suis tout nu. J'ai tout jeté. Ma généalogie. Ma veuve. Mes compagnons. J'attends le bouillonnement. J'attends le coup d'aile du grand albatros séminal qui doit faire de moi un homme nouveau. J'attends l'immense tape, le soufflet vertigineux qui me sacrera chevalier d'un ordre plutonien.

Et subitement c'est le débouché des grands fleuves
c'est l'amitié des yeux de toucans
c'est l'érection au fulminate de montagnes vierges
je suis investi. L'Europe patrouille dans mes veines comme une meute de filaires sur le coup de minuit.

Europe éclat de fonte
Europe tunnel bas d'où suinte une rosée de sang
Europe vieux chien Europe calèche à vers
Europe tatouage pelé Europe ton nom est un gloussement rauque et un choc assourdi

je déplie mon mouchoir c'est un drapeau
j'ai mis ma belle peau
j'ai ajusté mes belles pattes onglées

Nom ancien
je donne mon adhésion à tout ce qui poudroie le ciel de son insolence à tout ce qui est loyal et fraternel à tout ce qui a le courage d'être éternellement neuf à tout ce qui sait

donner son cœur au feu à tout ce qui a la force de sortir
d'une sève inépuisable à tout ce qui est calme et sûr
à tout ce qui n'est pas toi
hoquet considérable

❧

AT THE LOCKS OF THE VOID

In the foreground the longitudinal passage of a dried up
stream sleepily rolling obsidian pebbles. In the background
a far from tranquil architecture of demolished burgs of
eroded mountains on whose dimly glimpsed ghostly form
are born chariots serpents a cat's eye of alarming
constellations. It is a strange pie of fireflies thrown into the
gray face of time, a great landslide of shards of icons and of
blazons of lice in Saturn's beard. On the right very
curiously standing at the squamous wall of crucified
butterflies their wings open in glory a gigantic bottle its
very long golden neck drinking a drop of blood in the
clouds. As for me I am not thirsty anymore. I take pleasure
in imagining the world undone like an old copra mattress
like an old voodoo necklace like the scent of a slain
peccary. I am not thirsty any more.

by the shattered sky
by the exploded stars
by the tutelary silence
from far far outside myself I am coming towards
you
woman sprung from a fine sapwood
and your eyes wounds not well closed
on your modesty at being born

It is I singing in a voice still stuck in elemental stuttering. It is nice to be a piece of wood a cork a drop of water in the torrential waters of the end and of the new beginning. It is nice to doze off at the broken heart of things. I am not the slightest bit thirsty anymore. My sword made from a smile of shark's teeth is becoming terribly useless. My mace is very clearly out of season and out of bounds. Rain is falling. It is a crossing of rubble, it is an incredible stowing of the invisible using all sorts of bonds, it is a branchwork of syphilis, it is the diagram of a brandy bender, it is a conspiracy of cuscutae, it is the nightmare's head stuck on the lance tip of a crowd gone wild.
I go forward as far as the area of the blue lakes. I go forward as far as the area of the sulfur springs
I go forward as far as my crater-shaped mouth to reach which have I worked hard enough? What do I have to get rid of? Everything yes indeed everything. I am completely naked. I have got rid of everything. My genealogy. My widow. My companions. I am waiting for the bubbling to start. I am waiting for the wing beat of the great seminal albatross that is to make me into a new man. I am waiting for the immense tap, for the vertiginous slap that will consecrate me knight of a Plutonian order.

And suddenly it is the opening of the great rivers
it is the friendship in toucans' eyes
it is the erection at the fulminate of virgin mountains
I am invested. Europe patrols in my veins like a host of filaria on the stroke of midnight.
Europe a cast-iron explosion
Europe a low tunnel with a dew of blood seeping from it
Europe an old dog Europe a worm carriage
Europe a skinned tattoo Europe your name is a raspy gurgle and a muffled shock

I am opening my handkerchief it is a flag
I have donned my beautiful skin
I have adjusted my beautiful clawed paws

Ancient name
I give my support to everything that raises flurries in the
sky with its insolence to everything loyal and fraternal to
everything that has the courage to be eternally new to
everything that can give its heart to fire to everything strong
enough to emerge from an inexhaustible sap to everything
calm and sure to everything that is not you
considerable hiccup

This poem (46) is a figurative exploration, conducted with often
ironic humor, of the poet's problematical relationship with Europe.
The first section of the poem is a methodical and analytical
description ("Au premier plan," "Au fond," "A droite" [In the
foreground, In the background, On the right]) in prose of the poet's
imaginative conception of Europe as an empty sluice. The
accumulated images suggest dilapidation and death ("ruisseau
desséché" [dried up stream], "burgs démantelés" [demolished
burgs], "montagnes érodées" [eroded mountains], "éboulis de
tessons" [landslide of shards], "paroi squameuse" [squamous wall],
"papillons crucifiés" [crucified butterflies], "goutte de sang" [drop
of blood]). The references to crucifixion, wings open in glory, and
the drinking of blood, create savagely humorous evocations of
Catholic rituals. The poet's insistently repeated assertion, "je n'ai
plus soif" [I am not thirsty any more], emphasizes both his
awareness that Europe has nothing to offer, already implicit in the
"vide" [void] of the title, and the finality of his rejection of cultural
practices associated with Europe. The reflexive commentary with
which this section ends highlights the poet's pleasure in activity of
the creative imagination which permits him to draw on imagery and
alternative African religious manifestations related to his native
land: "Il m'est doux de penser le monde défait comme un vieux

matelas à coprah comme un vieux collier vaudou comme le parfum du pécari abattu"[5] [I take pleasure in imagining the world undone like an old copra mattress like an old voodoo necklace like the scent of a slain peccary]. These familiarly Caribbean images are nevertheless ambiguous; they are not entirely sources of security ("défait" [undone], "vieux" [old], and "abattu" [slain]), even though they sate his thirst.

The second section, in free verse, begins with a rhythmic incantation in suggestively cataclysmic phrases ("ciel ébranlé" [shattered sky], "étoiles éclatées" [exploded stars]). The regular and similar rhythm of the first three lines and their similar form add to the solemnity of the incantation, as a result of which the spirit of the poet appears before the conjured woman to whom the communication is addressed: "de très loin d'outre moi je viens vers toi / femme" [from far outside myself I am coming towards you / woman]. This woman, characterized by "blessures mal fermées" [wounds not well closed] is an incarnation of the poet's native island, while the distant external source of the poet's magical power evokes the geographically and historically distant cultural source of ancestral Africa.

In the third section, the poet appears as a self-conscious poet ("C'est moi qui chante ..."[It is I singing...]), who recognizes the limited maturity and effectiveness of his poetic voice ("d'une voix prise encore dans le balbutiement des éléments" [in a voice still stuck in elemental stuttering]). His faith in the power of this eschatological source is reflected in the pleasure he expresses in the experience of passive creative activity: "Il est doux d'être un morceau de bois un bouchon une goutte d'eau dans les eaux torrentielles de la fin et du recommencement. Il est doux de s'assoupir au cœur brisé des choses." [It is nice to be a piece of wood a cork a drop of water in the torrential waters of the end and of the new beginning. It is nice to doze off at the broken heart of things]. This activity is strongly reminiscent of Rimbaud's experimental practices and the distinction he established between "bois" and "violon" in the "Lettre du Voyant." The poet's link with this "natural" source of power evidently relieves him of the need for direct aggression: "Mon épée faite d'un sourire de dents de requin devient terriblement inutile. Ma masse d'armes est très visiblement hors de saison et hors de jeu" [My sword made from a smile of shark's teeth is becoming terribly useless. My mace is very clearly out of season and out of bounds]. This reference to "armes" recalls Césaire's previous collection of poems, *Les Armes miraculeuses [Miraculous Weapons]* of 1946, and permits the speculation that Césaire may, at this stage of his poetic development, now be rejecting the notion of a directly aggressive poetic practice.

As the poem continues, it becomes evident that the poet is engaged in tracing the progress he is making in defining his voice. The self-referential nature of this painful journey is rendered syntactically by the juxtaposition of indicative and interrogative forms within the same sentence ("j'avance jusqu'à ma bouche cratériforme vers laquelle ai-je assez peiné?" [I go forward as far as my crater-shaped mouth to reach which have I worked hard enough?]). Thus an affirmation is interrupted rhetorically and involuntarily by a question. The account of the poet's progress both complements and opposes the movement toward the "femme" [woman] of the second section, as details of the sacrifices involved are given: "Qu'ai-je à jeter? Tout ma foi tout. Je suis tout nu. J'ai tout jeté. Ma généalogie. Ma veuve. Mes compagnons" [What do I have to get rid of? Everything yes indeed everything. I am completely naked. I have got rid of everything. My genealogy. My widow. My companions.] This section ends in the expression of ironic humor, as the poet prepares himself for the expected rewards of his heroic efforts: "J'attends le coup d'aile du grand albatros séminal qui doit faire de moi un homme nouveau. J'attends l'immense tape, le soufflet vertigineux qui me sacrera chevalier d'un ordre plutonien." [I am waiting for the wing beat of the great seminal albatross that is to make me into a new man. I am waiting for the immense tap, for the vertiginous slap that will consecrate me knight of a Plutonian order]. The white albatross and the "chevalier" allude to the poet's expectation of approbation and validation from Europe. This expectation is nullified, however, in the following section, which gives the result for the poet of a successful entry into the European world : "je suis investi. L'Europe patrouille dans mes veines comme une meute de filaires sur le coup de minuit" [I am invested. Europe patrols in my veins like a host of filaria on the stroke of midnight]. However since "investi" bears the double connotation of siege and investiture, its use emphasizes Césaire's sensitivity to the problematical potential and mortal danger of such success.

Awareness of the danger represented by Europe leads to an aggressive stance that contrasts with the earlier passivity and rejection of arms. Europe now becomes a dominant term of profanity in the second incantatory passage of the poem: "Europe éclat de fonte..." [Europe a cast-iron explosion...]. The poet exploits the phonemic composition of the word "Europe" (in French) as a basis for his rejection even at the level of poetic language: "Europe ton nom est un gloussement rauque et un choc assourdi" [Your name is a raspy gurgle and a muffled shock]. The final section of the poem is a personal manifesto, a strong declaration of the philosophical and cultural position adopted by the poet, particularly in relation to Europe: "je donne mon adhésion ... à tout ce qui n'est pas toi" [I give my support ... to everything that is not you].

The poet's response in this poem is clearly to define himself negatively in relation to Europe and positively in relation to qualities of rebelliousness, loyalty, creativity, self-sacrifice, and courage. The poem is not only the means by which the poet is able to trace and clarify his journey of separation from Europe, but also the concrete documentation of the stand he has adopted. It is significant that his most direct rejection of Europe is at the oral level: Europe represents a collection of sounds that are physically repugnant to his voice. In the final analysis, the involuntary rejection of Europe, implicit in "hoquet" ["hiccup"] and earlier suggested in the interruption of an affirmation, is both physical and cultural. This attitude clearly echoes that expressed even more directly by Césaire's old friend, Damas, in his famous poem,

"Hoquet" (*Pigments*, 33-36). Césaire meets Damas in affirming the rejection of assimilation on the part of poets from another (i.e. non-European) oral tradition.

ODE À LA GUINÉE

Et par le soleil installant sous ma peau une usine de force
et d'aigles
et par le vent sur ma force de dent de sel compliquant ses
passes les mieux sues
et par le noir le long de mes muscles en douces insolences
de sèves montant
et par la femme couchée comme une montagne descellée et
sucée par les lianes
et par la femme au cadastre mal connu où le jour et la nuit
jouent à la mourre des eaux de source et des métaux rares
et par le feu de la femme où je cherche le chemin des
fougères du Fouta-Djallon
et par la femme fermée sur la nostalgie s'ouvrant
         JE TE SALUE
Guinée dont les pluies fracassent du haut grumeleux
des volcans un sacrifice de vaches pour mille faims
et soifs d'enfants dénaturés
Guinée de ton cri de ta main de ta patience
il nous reste toujours des terres arbitraires
et quand tué vers Ophir ils m'auront jamais muet
de mes dents de ma peau que l'on fasse
un fétiche féroce gardien du mauvais œil
comme m'ébranle me frappe et me dévore ton solstice
en chacun de tes pas Guinée
muette en moi-même d'une profondeur astrale de méduses

ODE TO GUINEA

And by the sun setting up a factory of strength and of
eagles under my skin
and by the wind on my tooth and salt strength complicating
its best known passes
and by the blackness along my muscles rising in gentle
insolences of sap
and by the woman reclining like a mountain unsealed with
vines sucking at her breast
and by the woman with a little known cadaster in which
night and day spring waters and rare metals play a game of
mora
and by the woman's fire in which I seek the path to ferns
and to Fouta-Djallon
and by the closed woman opening herself up on nostalgia
     I GREET YOU
Guinea whose rains shatter a sacrifice of cows from the
curdled top of volcanoes for a thousand hungers and thirsts
of denatured children

Guinea from your cry from your hand from your
patience
we still have arbitrary lands left
and even when killed me near Ophir they may have never
silent
from my teeth from my skin may there be made
a fierce fetish guardian of the evil eye
as your solstice shakes me strikes me and devours me
in each step of yours Guinea
you silent within me as deep as the astral depth of
medusas

This poem[6] (50) represents another attempt (as in "A l'Afrique") to re-establish the poet's cultural link to Africa, through what is essentially an oral communication with Guinea as the symbol of the motherland. Orality is implicit in the flowing incantatory phrases introduced by "et par..." [and by...], as well as in the graphic centerpiece of the poem, "JE TE SALUE" [I GREET YOU]. Indeed the elliptical opening "et" [and] suggests that the whole poem is the continuation of a communication that has already been engaged.

The poet invokes two principal links as justifications for his right to salute Guinea: aspects of his self (in the first three rhetorical phrases) and aspects of the unspecified woman (in the following four phrases). The personal qualifications relate to characteristics of strength ("sous ma peau une usine de force" [a factory of strength under my skin], "ma force de dent" [my tooth and salt strength], "mes muscles" [my muscles]), derived from such "natural" forces as sun and wind ("le soleil" and "le vent") as well as from skin color, "le noir" [blackness]. "Insolences" ironically alludes to the attitude of whites who stereotypically consider as insolent or "uppity" the manifestations of black dignity, vigor, and creative potential implicit in the image of rising sap. Woman is evoked in terms that point to a direct connection between this poem and the central theme of the whole collection: "la femme au cadastre mal connu" [woman with a little known cadaster]. Since the title of the collection, which connotes the poet's concern with evaluating his native island and his own journey in relation to the native land, is inscribed in this poem, it is reasonable to infer that "la femme" [the woman] is a metaphor and an allegory of Martinique. Thus "couchée comme une montagne descellée" [reclining like a mountain unsealed] alludes to a Martinique after the eruption of Mount Pelée.

Similarly, the "feu" [fire] of the Martinican volcano is for the poet a reminder of, and a link to, the mountain range of the Fouta-Djallon in Guinea. It is through Martinique that the poet finds his way back ("je cherche le chemin" [I seek the path]) to

Africa. The final line of this first part of the poem ("et par la femme fermée sur la nostalgie s'ouvrant" [and by the woman closed opening herself up on nostalgia]) indicates the poet's evaluation of the situation of Martinique, where "sur la nostalgie" [on nostalgia] is linked syntactically to both "fermée" [closed] and "s'ouvrant" [opening herself up]. This syntactical ambiguity indicates both that Martinicans have been sadly limited by their separation from their cultural motherland and that Martinique is now opening itself up to the realization of the cultural connection it has been missing.

In the final section of the poem, Guinea is addressed directly by the poet as the haven for "mille faims et soifs d'enfants dénaturés" [a thousand hungers and thirsts of denatured children]. This allusion indicates the poet's acknowledgement of an original identity that has been bastardized by assimilation into an alien culture. The poet, however, firmly aligns himself with Guinea to form a unified "nous" [we] in opposition to an unspecific "ils" [they] in the contrived density of the line "et quand tué vers Ophir ils m'auront jamais muet" [even when killed me near Ophir they may have never silent], where the poet assumes the role of rebellious sacrificial victim, impenitent, and above all stubbornly vocal ("jamais muet" [never silent]). The syntactical density of this phrase, highly reminiscent of Mallarmé, geometrically increases its evocative potential, and draws attention to the magical power of the language. It is indeed the poet's capacity as a poet that qualifies him to be used as a "fétiche féroce gardien" [fierce fetish guardian] and Guinea becomes the unspoken inner voice that guarantees his integrity "(Guinée / muette en moi-même" [Guinea / you silent within me]).

Guinea functions as an effective symbol for both the mountainous motherland of Africa and the similarly mountainous native island of Martinique. The reference to the "ode" in the title indicates that Césaire is seeking here to coopt an established (European) literary tradition while effectively subverting that tradition by displacing the cultural center of the poem from Europe to Africa. By establishing Guinea symbolically as a fit object of lyrical desire and by appropriating but not subordinating himself to the literary practices of Europe, Césaire validates not only the African cultural heritage but his own practice as a French Caribbean writer.

BARBARE

C'est le mot qui me soutient
et frappe sur ma carcasse de cuivre jaune
où la lune dévore dans la soupente de la rouille
les os barbares
des lâches bêtes rôdeuses du mensonge

Barbare
du langage sommaire
et nos faces belles comme le vrai pouvoir opératoire
de la négation
Barbare
des morts qui circulent dans les veines de la terre
et viennent se briser parfois la tête contre les murs
de nos oreilles
et les cris de révolte jamais entendus
qui tournent à mesure et à timbres de musique

Barbare
l'article unique
barbare le tapaya
barbare l'amphisbène blanche
barbare moi le serpent cracheur
qui de mes putrifiantes chairs me réveille
soudain gekko volant
soudain gekko frangé
et me colle si bien aux lieux mêmes de la force
qu'il vous faudra pour m'oublier
jeter aux chiens la chair velue de vos poitrines

❦

BARBARIAN

This is the word that sustains me
and knocks on my carcass of brass
in which the moon devours in the closet of rust
the barbarian bones
of the cowardly prowling beasts of the lie

Barbarian
summary in language
and our faces beautiful like the true operating
power
of negation

Barbarian
dead men moving about in the veins of the earth
and sometimes coming and breaking their heads
against the walls of our ears
and the cries of revolt never heard
dancing to sounds and beat of music

Barbarian
the single article
barbarian the tapaya
barbarian the white amphisbena
barbarian I the spitting snake
waking up from my putrefying flesh
suddenly a flying gecko
suddenly a fringed gecko
and so well do I stick to the very spots of strength
that to forget me you will have
to throw the hairy flesh of your chests to the dogs

The title of this poem, "Barbare" (956), provides a visual focus and the oral stimulus to which the poet reacts. The visual aspect will be reinforced throughout the poem by the position of the word. But it is in response to the oral stimulus that the poetic voice makes itself heard from the first line of the poem, in "C'est le mot qui me soutient" [This is the word that sustains me]. This statement immediately indicates the nature of the relationship between the poet and "le mot" [the word], which functions as a source of needed support for the poet. The poet is represented metonymically as "ma carcasse" [my carcass], a lifeless drum-like receptacle on whom the word, as voice, strikes to produce sound and, by extension, life. In the second and third stanzas, the voice of the poet becomes identified and fused with the voices of others, sharing with them "nos faces belles" [our faces beautiful] and "nos oreilles" [our ears], within the context of the word that introduces and dominates even visually those two stanzas, "Barbare" [Barbarian]. In the final stanza, the poet subverts the notion of barbarity. He fully assumes the identity of a barbarian and at the same time that of "le serpent cracheur" [the spitting snake], as he addresses a "vous" [you] whose physical presence is indicated in "la chair velue de vos poitrines" [the hairy flesh of your chests].

Contrast and conflict between the barbarian group that includes the poet and the other hairy-chested group are clearly indicated by the text. The poem therefore sends a message of revolt, different from "les cris de révolte jamais entendus" [the cries of revolt never heard]. The revolt in the poem involves using a word with pejorative and insulting resonances and investing it with an aura of new nobility and power. The resonance of the word "barbare" is a reminder of psychological debasement, represented metaphorically in the text as the rusting effect of the noon on the poet's carcass, in which ironically only true barbarism, characterized by cowardice and dishonesty, is being destroyed.

In the second stanza, the poet alludes to the magical power of language as a means of affirming the validity and beauty of "nos faces" [our faces]. The metonymic association between "du langage sommaire" [summary in language] and "de la negation" [of negation] implies that poetic practice involves an attitude of rejection which bears within itself the power of creation. In the following stanza, the poet uses the word "barbare" as a reminder of the past suffering and present condition of people who have been characterized as dead, but who are yet the life-blood of the earth, reminiscent of the situation of black South African miners: "des morts qui circulent dans les veines de la terre" [dead men moving about in the veins of the earth]. "Barbare" is used also as a reminder of a spirit of revolt concealed behind a facade of dance and music, which whites stereotypically associate with blacks: "et les cris de révolte jamais entendus / qui tournent à mesure et à timbres de musique" [and the cries of revolt never heard / dancing to musical sounds and beat].

The poet exploits the regenerative potential intrinsic in the word "barbare," so that it is represented as the magical and beautiful principle of life concealed in savage and reptilian forms normally regarded as loathsome ("amphisbène" [amphisbena], "serpent" [snake], "gekko" [gecko]) and with which he completely identifies: "Barbare moi ..." [Barbarian I...]. It is this vital principle that enables the poet to metamorphose ("qui de mes putrifiantes chairs me réveille" [waking up from my putrefying flesh]) and adopt an attitude of direct and violent revolt ("me coller ... aux lieux mêmes de la force" [stick to the very spots of strength]).

Through the use of the explicit and implicit "barbare"-"moi"-"poète" [barbarian-I-poet] linkage, the poem itself functions as the theatre where a subversive linguistic revolution takes place, and as the means by which the word "barbare" achieves a truly healing significance.

MOT

Parmi moi
de moi-même
à moi-même

hors toute constellation
en mes mains serré seulement
le rare hoquet d'un ultime spasme délirant
vibre mot
      j'aurai chance hors du labyrinthe
plus long plus large vibre
en ondes de plus en plus serrées
en lasso où me prendre
en corde où me pendre
et que me clouent toutes les flèches
et leur curare le plus amer
au beau poteau-mitan des très fraîches étoiles

vibre
vibre essence même de l'ombre
en aile en gosier c'est à force de périr
le mot nègre
sorti tout armé du hurlement
d'une fleur vénéneuse
le mot nègre
tout pouacre de parasites
le mot nègre
tout plein de brigands qui rôdent
des mères qui crient
d'enfants qui pleurent
le mot nègre
un grésillement de chairs qui brûlent
âcre et de corne
le mot nègre
comme le soleil qui saigne de la griffe
sur le trottoir des nuages
le mot nègre
comme le dernier rire vêlé de l'innocence
entre les crocs du tigre
et comme le mot soleil est un claquement de balles

et comme le mot nuit un taffetas qu'on déchire
le mot nègre
dru savez-vous
du tonnerre d'un été
que s'arrogent
des libertés incrédules

ૐ

WORD

Among me
from myself
to myself
outside every constellation
nothing clasped in my hands
but the rare hiccup of a final spasm of delirium
vibrate word
I will have a chance out of the labyrinth
longer wider vibrate
in waves tighter and tighter
in a lasso to catch me with
in a rope to hang me with
and for all the arrows to impale me
and their bitterest curare
right on the center stake of the cool cool stars

vibrate
vibrate very essence of the dark
like a wing like a throat it's by dint of dying
the word nigger
sprung fully armed from the howling
of a poisonous flower
the word nigger
all putrid with parasites

the word nigger
all full of bandits prowling
of mothers screaming
of children crying
the word nigger
a sizzling of burning flesh
acrid and horny
the word nigger
like the sun bleeding from its claw
on to the sidewalk of the clouds
the word nigger
like the last calved laugh of innocence
between the tiger's fangs
and just as the word sun is a blast of bullets
and just as the word night a tearing of taffeta
the word nigger
       dense you know
from a summer's thunder
      appropriated by
          incredulous liberties

This poem, "Mot" (71), forms an obvious link with "Barbare" since both are responses to the destructive force of words used by whites to refer to blacks. The poet refers to himself directly only in the first two shorter sections of the poem. At the beginning of the poem, the poet's self ("moi") serves as the point of departure for the poem, as the context, as source or sender, and as receiver of the "word": "Parmi moi / de moi-même / à moi-même / .... / en mes mains" [Among me / from myself / to myself / .... / in my hands]. The prepositions define and limit the space within which poetic activity takes place. At the beginning of the second section, the poet becomes a voice of hope: "j'aurai chance hors du labyrinthe" [I will have a chance out of the labyrinth]. Very soon afterwards, however, the poet becomes the object to be acted upon, at the mercy of, increasingly possessed by, the word ("me prendre," "me pendre," "que me clouent" [to catch me with, to hang me with, to impale me]). After this point the poet virtually disappears from the poem as a self-referential voice and there are no further explicit references to a "moi" [me]. The only direct indication of a subjective presence is in "savez-vous" [you know], while the vibration of the word "nègre" [nigger][7] gathers momentum and dominates the remainder of the poem.

The word, unspecified at the opening of the poem, is lodged deep in the poet's psyche, inseparable from his identity, and is evoked as a vital instinct, an automatic impulse of revolt: "le rare hoquet d'un ultime spasme délirant" [the rare hiccup of a final spasm of delirium]. The word becomes active and vibrates ("vibre") more and more throughout the poem. It is this vibration that gives the poet hope of escaping from the "labyrinth" of his present situation. His willingness to submit to the emotional vibration is translated into a series of circular images that indicate the delirium of magical possession as he assumes the role of poet-priest and scapegoat at the center-stake of the voodoo temple: "au beau poteau-mitan des très fraîches étoiles."

As the poem develops, the poet's being is possessed by the word "nègre" [nigger], which assumes an independent force of its own, evoking and conjuring, to the rhythm of a drum, images of humiliations, lynchings, horrible sufferings of mothers and children, and the burning of black bodies. The evocation of these horrors produces its own metamorphosis; the word "nègre," vibrating in the poet's unconscious, magically emerges as a symbol of resistance and revolt, of virility and dignity, successful beyond all expectation in obtaining liberty: "dru savez-vous / du tonnerre d'un été / que s'arrogent / des libertés incrédules" [dense you know / from a summer's thunder / appropriated by / incredulous liberties].

The whole poem, therefore, concretely represents the transformation of the poetic "moi" into "le mot nègre," from the first to the second half of the poem, under the influence of a literal vibration within the poem itself. Hence, the poem functions as the arena within which this creative and liberating transformation takes place. The orthographic transformation of "M-O-I" into "M-O-T" parallels the semantic and metaphoric fusion of "mot" [word] and "le mot nègre" [the word nigger]. This poem expresses with rare lucidity the dilemma faced by many blacks who live in societies largely defined linguistically and culturally by whites: that of constructing positive values in a language and power system that that imposes negative characteristics and expectations on blacks. But the poem does more that expose a problem. It also provides within itself a solution. It is the "word," inscribed within and throughout the poem, that symbolizes the problem of debasement and enslavement of blacks by whites. It is also the written "word" that is transformed by the poet into a triumphant expression of transcendence and liberation.

ELÉGIE

L'hibiscus qui n'est pas autre chose qu'un œil éclaté
d'où pend le fil d'un long regard, les trompettes des
solandres,
le grand sabre noir des flamboyants, le crépuscule
qui est un trousseau de clefs toujours sonnant,
les aréquiers qui sont de nonchalants soleils jamais
couchés parce qu'outrepercés d'une épingle que les
terres à cervelle brûlée n'hésitent jamais à se
fourrer
jusqu'au cœur, les souklyans effrayants, Orion
l'extatique papillon que les pollens magiques
crucifièrent sur la porte des nuits tremblantes
les belles boucles noires des canéfices qui sont des
mûlâtresses
très fières dont le cou tremble un peu sous la
guillotine,

et ne t'étonne pas si la nuit je geins plus lourdement
ou si mes mains étranglent plus sourdement

c'est le troupeau des vieilles peines qui vers mon
odeur
noir et rouge
en scolopendre
allonge la tête et d'une insistance du museau
encore molle et maladroite
cherche plus profond mon cœur
alors rien ne me sert de serrer mon cœur contre le
tien
et de me perdre dans le feuillage de tes bras
il le trouve
et très gravement
de manière toujours nouvelle
le lèche
amoureusement
jusqu'à l'apparition sauvage du premier sang
aux brusques griffes ouvertes du
DÉSASTRE

❧

ELEGY

The hibiscus which is nothing but an exploded eye
with the thread of a long look hanging from it, the
solandras' trumpets,
the flamboyants' large black sabers, dusk that is a
bunch of keys ever jangling,
the areca palms which are nonchalant suns never
setting because they have been transfixed by a pin
which the lands their brains blown out are never
loath to shove
right up to their own hearts, the frightening
soucouyants, Orion
the ecstatic butterfly that magic pollens

crucified on the door of trembling nights
the beautiful black tresses of the cassias that are
mulatto women
very proud whose necks tremble slightly under the
guillotine

and don't be surprised if at night my moans are
heavier
or if my hands are strangling more silently
it's the drove of old sorrows stretching its head out
toward my scent
black and red
like a centipede
and with insistent muzzle
still soft and clumsy
searches deeper for my heart
then it helps me none to press my heart against
yours
and to lose myself in the foliage of your arms
it finds it
and very earnestly
in a manner ever new
licks it
lovingly
until the first blood savagely appears
on the crude open claws of
DISASTER

In "Elégie" (75), the poet is sad, uncharacteristically almost self-pitying. The poem comprises two main sections: the first, an evocative enumeration of images of Caribbean flora viewed through the sensibility of the poet; the second, in which the poet addresses an apparent lover and reveals as well as explains his night-time insecurity and fears. The three references to "cœur" [heart] in the poem indicate that what is at issue in this sad poem, which ends in a graphically forceful "DÉSASTRE" [DISASTER], is the core of being, represented figuratively as the poet's "heart."

A mood of horror, associated unexpectedly with the innocuously beautiful hibiscus, is established from the first line of the poem: "L'hibiscus qui n'est pas autre chose qu'un œil éclaté" [The hibiscus which is nothing but an exploded eye] and prepares for the incongruities of the menace ("grand sabre noir") [large black sabers] of the flamboyants, the agony of the Areca palm trees, and the terror of the "canéfices" [cassias], personified as "des mûlâtresses / très fières dont le cou tremble un peu sous la guillotine" [mulatto women / very proud whose necks tremble slightly under the guillotine]. These impressionistic descriptions are brilliantly accurate and the suggestion of danger in typical examples of Caribbean flora is heightened by an associated reference to the terrifying vampire-type figures ("souklyans" also known as "soucouyants") of Caribbean folklore. Thus the notion of the Caribbean as an exotic tropical paradise and as a source for romantic, idyllic poetic creation is subverted.

In the second part of the poem, the poetic subject appears as a voice of lamentation ("je geins")[I moan], addressing an unspecified individual ("t'"), presumably a lover whom he embraces at night ("serrer mon cœur contre le tien" [press my heart against yours]). Here the poet is invested with the potential for violence ("mes mains étranglent" [my hands are strangling more silently]), which is attributed to and justified by the resurgent memory of past experiences of suffering ("vieilles peines"). The lover's embrace becomes fused with the dangerous and obscene activity of a centipede ("scolopendre"), which succeeds in its sexual assault on the poet's heart ("le lèche / amoureusement" [licks it / lovingly]).

This poem points not only to the poet's intimations of personal disaster, but also to his association of characteristically Caribbean elements with suffering and terror. The personifications of Caribbean flora suggest that the beauty of the Caribbean and the emotional security of the poet are subject to the effect of "vieilles peines" [old sorrows] which threaten to destroy their "heart." Thus the classical song of mourning (elegeia) implied by the title is given a typically Caribbean flavor and is effectively subverted and transformed into an essentially Caribbean lamentation.

CORPS PERDU

Moi qui Krakatoa
moi qui tout mieux que mousson
moi qui poitrine ouverte
moi qui laïlape
moi qui bêle mieux que cloaque
moi qui hors de gamme
moi qui Zambèze ou frénétique ou rhombe ou
cannibale
je voudrais être de plus en plus humble et plus bas
toujours plus grave sans vertige ni vestige
jusqu'à me perdre tomber
dans la vivante semoule d'une terre bien ouverte.
Dehors une belle brume au lieu d'atmosphère serait
point sale
chaque goutte d'eau y faisant un soleil
dont le nom le même pour toutes choses
serait RENCONTRE BIEN TOTALE
si bien que l'on ne saurait plus qui passe
ou d'une étoile ou d'un espoir
ou d'un pétale de l'arbre flamboyant
ou d'une retraite sous-marine
courue par les flambeaux des méduses-aurélies
Alors la vie j'imagine me baignerait tout entier
mieux je la sentirais qui me palpe ou me mord
couché je verrais venir à moi les odeurs enfin libres
comme des mains secourables
qui se feraient passage en moi
pour y balancer de longs cheveux

plus longs que ce passé que je ne peux pas
atteindre.
Choses écartez-vous faites place entre vous
place à mon repos qui porte en vague
ma terrible crête de racines ancreuses
qui cherchent où se prendre
Choses je sonde je sonde
moi le porte-faix je suis porte racines
et je pèse et je force et j'arcane
     j'omphale
Ah qui vers les harpons me ramène
     je suis très faible
je siffle oui je siffle des choses très anciennes
de serpents de choses caverneuses
Je or vent paix-là
et contre mon museau instable et frais
pose contre ma face érodée
ta froide face de rire défait.
Le vent hélas je l'entendrai encore
nègre nègre nègre depuis le fond
du ciel immémorial
un peu moins fort qu'aujourd'hui
mais trop fort cependant
et ce fou hurlement de chiens et de chevaux
qu'il pousse à notre poursuite toujours marronne
mais à mon tour dans l'air
je me lèverai un cri et si violent
que tout entier j'éclabousserai le ciel
et par mes branches déchiquetées
et par le jet insolent de mon fût blessé et solennel

     je commanderai aux îles d'exister

❦

LOST BODY

I who Krakatoa
I who much better than monsoon
I who chest open
I who Laëlaps
I who bleating better than a cloaca
I who off-scale
I who Zambezi or frenetic or rhombus or cannibal
I would like to be humbler and humbler and lower
always graver with neither vestige nor vertigo
until I lose myself fall
into the living semolina of well opened soil.
Outside a beautiful mist instead of atmosphere
would be not dirty
each drop of water in it making a sun
whose name the same for all things
would   be   TOTAL   AND   COMPLETE
ENCOUNTER
so that one could not be sure what is passing
whether a star or a hope
or a petal from the flamboyant tree
or an underwater retreat
streaked by the torches of the medusa aurelias
Then life I imagine would bathe me all over
better would I feel it touching me or biting me
As I lie I would see approaching me scents finally
free
like helpful hands
and they would find a way to pass within me
to swing their long hair
longer than this past that I cannot reach.
Things move aside make space between you
space for my rest that bears like a wave
my terrible crest of anchoring roots

looking for somewhere to hold on to
Things I probe I probe
I the burden-bearer I am the root-bearer
and I weigh and I force and I arcane
     I omphale
Ah which takes me back towards the harpoons
     I am very weak
I whistle yes I whistle very ancient things
of snakes of cavernous things
I gold now wind be still
and against my cool unstable muzzle
place against my eroded face
your cold face of canceled laughter.
The wind alas I shall hear it still
nigger nigger nigger from the depth
of the immemorial sky
not quite as loud as today
but too loud yet
and this mad howling of hounds and horses
that it sets on our ever-runaway trail
but when my turn comes into the air
I will raise up a cry so violent
that I will spatter the sky utterly
and by my shredded branches
and by the insolent jet of my solemn wounded bole

     I shall command the islands to exist

The position of this poem, "Corps perdu" (80), in the center of the collection to which it lends its title, the significance of the title, and the themes treated in the poem, all indicate that this is an important poem. Consequently, it has attracted the attention of many commentators.[8] This poem is in a way a rewriting of *Cahier d'un retour au pays natal,* presenting the poet's imaginative journey from the starting-point of self-consciousness or self-confrontation.

The issue of self is raised immediately with the first word of the poem, "Moi" [I]. The combination of "moi" with the relative pronoun ("qui" [who]) forms an anaphora that indicates and emphasizes the diverse dimensions of a self-conscious poetic persona. It is perhaps significant that the characteristics of the self-identified by the poet all betoken an identity that is different from the norm (particularly "Krakatoa," "laïlape" [Laëlaps], and "Zambèze ou frénétique ou rhombe ou cannibale" [Zambezi or frenetic or rhombus or cannibal]). Krakatoa and Zambezi signify power, the former referring to the Indonesian island that was partly destroyed in 1883 by the explosion of its volcano and the latter to the powerful river in southern Africa that is famous for its rapids and falls. The poetic persona is invested with the potential for explosive power (implicit in the oral (phonic) and geographical qualities of "Krakatoa"), and manifests, through the rhythm of the opening lines, an almost lyrical sense of pride in the personal possibilities of metamorphosis.

The suggestion of arrogance in the first seven lines is quickly moderated as the poet takes voice as a subjective presence expressing desire and consequently lack: "je voudrais" [I would like]. This first verb of the poem draws attention to the lack of verbs indicating essence or action in the opening phrases and to the contradiction between the expressed desire for humility and the tone of conceit with which the poem opens. The poet therefore expresses both pride and humility, desiring to move downward toward a condition that would ensure closer communion with the life-force of earth: "je voudrais être de plus en plus humble et plus bas / toujours plus grave sans vertige ni vestige / jusqu'à me perdre tomber / dans la vivante semoule d'une terre bien ouverte" [I would like to be humbler and humbler and lower / always graver with neither vestige nor vertigo / until I lose myself fall / into the living semolina of well opened soil]. The creative experience, represented symbolically as fusion with the vitality of the earth, replaces the reaction of self-assertion.

The expression of desire for fusion is immediately transformed into an exercise of the imagination in which the poet acts as poet-magus, using the power of the word to envision a situation of total communion: "chaque goutte d'eau y faisant un soleil / dont le nom le même pour toutes choses / serait RENCONTRE BIEN TOTALE" [Each drop of water in it making a sun / whose name the same for all things / would be TOTAL AND COMPLETE ENCOUNTER]. This image implies the freedom and equality of an open confrontation between phenomena on the microcosmic plane where difference is no longer relevant. The poet's desire, therefore, is implicitly for the dissolution of a painful sense of identity.

At this point of the poem, the poet participates both as the subject of an imaginative journey ("j'imagine" [[I imagine]) and as the object of the activity imagined ("me baignerait" [would bathe me]). The poet's desire is implicitly to be a "corps perdu" [lost body], passive rather than active, as he evokes an ideal situation characterized by true freedom ("les odeurs enfin libres" [scents finally free]), conscious of his own failure to affix himself to a traditional past ("ce passé que je ne peux atteindre" [this past that I cannot reach]). It is the poet's imaginative experience within this poem, his submitting himself to the inanimate forces he senses around him ("Choses écartez-vous faites place entre vous" [Things move aside make space between you]), that enables him to find his voice. He voluntarily undertakes the search for his past but finds himself at its mercy since he is incapable of finding peace except through rootedness: "place à mon repos qui porte en vague / ma terrible crête de racines ancreuses" [space for my rest which bears like a wave / my terrible crest of anchoring roots]. This experience defines his role as a poet: one who has the responsibility not merely of prophesying the future but also of preserving his links with the past. The poet is therefore able, by employing verbs of essence and activity, in sharp contrast to the verbless assertions of the opening lines of the poem, to articulate the dimensions of his poetic self: "Choses je sonde je sonde / moi le porte-faix je suis porte racines /

et je pèse et je force et j'arcane / j'omphale" [Things I probe I probe / I the burden-bearer I am the root-bearer / and I weigh and I force and I arcane / I omphale].

Experiences, however, affect the strength of the poet as well as the tonality of his communication even when he is linked orally to his past: "je suis très faible / je siffle oui je siffle des choses très anciennes" [I am very weak / I whistle yes I whistle very ancient things]. The resultant breach in articulation becomes reflected, within the poem, in the syntactic obscurity of "Je or vent paix-là" [I gold now wind be still]. The obscurity is related particularly to "or" which may be either a noun, "gold," or a conjunction, "now." The rest of the line indicates that the poet is uttering a command, rather in the manner of a biblical prophet commanding the elements, in order to create the desired silence.

As the final movement of the poem begins, "vent" is associated with the voice of an Other, and with the continuing unpleasant sound and destructive force of the word "nègre": "Le vent hélas je l'entendrai encore / nègre nègre nègre depuis le fond / du ciel immémorial / un peu moins fort qu'aujourd'hui / mais trop fort cependant" [The wind alas I shall hear it still / nigger nigger nigger from the depth / of the immemorial sky / not quite as loud as today / but too loud yet]. Here the poet assumes the communal mantle ("notre" [our]) of an escaping slave conscious of the sounds of pursuing dogs and horses which he associates with the voice of the Other ("il" [it]): "et ce fou hurlement de chiens et de chevaux / qu'il pousse à notre poursuite toujours marronne" [and this mad howling of hounds and horses / that it sets on our ever runaway trail]. This image recalls Césaire's earlier prose tragedy, *Et les chiens se taisaient*, which opens with the prophetic line: "Bien sûr qu'il va mourir le Rebelle" ["Of course the Rebel is going to die"]. The poem ends with the promise of a rebellious poet ("je me lèverai un cri et si violent" [I will raise up a cry so violent]), dedicated to use his voice creatively to bring the Caribbean islands into existence: "je commanderai aux îles d'exister" [I shall command the islands to exist].

This poem presents imaginatively the dilemma of the poet, conscious of his situation as a "corps perdu" [lost body], and of the force of the negative voice of the Other. The poet fuses past, present, and future as the various facets of his persona, proud, explosive, different, passive, weak, and prophetic, are allowed to speak in the poem. The liberties he takes with syntax (as in "Je or vent paix-là) and with vocabulary (as in the neologism "j'omphale") are indications of his desire to subvert the linguistic and cultural system which has made him into a "corps perdu" [lost body]. It is against this corrosive system that the poet envisions and constructs the future existence of the Caribbean.

DIT D'ERRANCE

Tout ce qui jamais fut déchiré
en moi s'est déchiré
tout ce qui jamais fut mutilé
en moi s'est mutilé
au milieu de l'assiette de son souffle dénudé
le fruit coupé de la lune toujours en allée
vers le contour à inventer de l'autre moitié

Et pourtant que te reste-t-il du temps ancien

à peine peut-être certain sens
dans la pluie de la nuit de chauvir ou trembler
et quand d'aucuns chantent Noël revenu
de songer aux astres
égarés

voici le jour le plus court de l'année
ordre assigné tout est du tout déchu
les paroles les visages les songes
l'air lui-même s'est envenimé

quand une main vers moi s'avance
j'en ramène à peine l'idée
j'ai bien en tête la saison si lacrimeuse
le jour avait un goût d'enfance
de chose profonde de muqueuse
vers le soleil mal tourné
fer contre fer une gare vide
où pour prendre rien
s'enrouait à vide à toujours geindre le même bras

Ciel éclaté courbe écorchée
de dos d'esclaves fustigés
peine trésorière des alizés
grimoire fermé mots oubliés
j'interroge mon passé muet

Ile de sang de sargasses
île morsure de remora
île arrière-rire des cétacés
île fin mot de bulle montée
île grand cœur déversé
haute la plus lointaine la mieux cachée
ivre lasse pêcheuse exténuée
ivre belle main oiselée
île maljointe île disjointe
toute île appelle
toute île est veuve
Bénin Bénin ô pierre d'aigris
Ifé qui fut Ouphas
une embouchure de Zambèze
vers une Ophir sans Albuquerque
tendrons-nous toujours les bras ?

jadis ô déchiré
Elle pièce par morceau

rassembla son dépecé
et les quatorze morceaux
s'assirent triomphants dans les rayons du soir.

J'ai inventé un culte secret
mon soleil est celui que toujours on attend

le plus beau des soleils est le soleil nocturne

Corps féminin île retournée
corps féminin bien nolisé
corps féminin écume-né
corps féminin île retrouvée
et qui jamais assez ne s'emporte
qu'au ciel il n'emporte
ô nuit renonculée
un secret de polypier
corps féminin marche de palmier
par le soleil d'un nid coiffé
où le phénix meurt et renaît
nous sommes âmes de bon parage
corps nocturnes vifs de lignage
arbres fidèles vin jaillissant
moi sybille flébilant.

Eaux figées de mes enfances
où les avirons à peine s'enfoncèrent
millions d'oiseaux de mes enfances
où fut jamais l'île parfumée
de grands soleils illuminée
la saison l'aire tant délicieuse
l'année pavée de pierres précieuses ?
Aux crises des zones écartelé
en plein cri mélange ténébreux
j'ai vu un oiseau mâle sombrer

la pierre dans son front s'est fichée
je regarde le plus bas de l'année

Corps souillé d'ordure savamment mué
espace vent de foi mentie
espace faux orgueil planétaire
lent rustique prince diamantaire
serai-je jouet de nigromance ?
Or mieux qu'Antilia ni que Brazil
pierre milliaire dans la distance
épée d'une flamme qui me bourrelle
j'abats les arbres du Paradis

❦

WANDERING WORDS

All that has ever been torn
in me has been torn
all that has ever been mutilated
in me has been mutilated
in the middle of the plate stripped of its breath
the cut fruit of the moon always gone away
towards the not yet invented contour of the other
half

And yet what do you have left of the old
days

scarcely perhaps a certain sense
in the rain at night of pricking up my ears
or trembling
and when some sing of Christmas back
here again
thinking of the stars

gone astray

this is the shortest day of the year
assigned order all is totally fallen
words faces dreams
the air itself has become poisoned
when a hand reaches out towards me
I can scarcely grasp the idea of it
I am well aware of the so tearful season
the day had a taste of infancy
of something deep like mucosa
towards the ill-turned sun
steel against steel an empty station
where to take nothing
the same arm grew hoarse to no avail from
constant moaning

Exploded sky flayed curve
of backs of whipped slaves
treasurer punishment of the tradewinds
closed grimorium forgotten words
I question my silent past

Island of blood of sargasso
island shark bite
island last laugh of the cetaceas
island last word of a risen bubble
island great heart poured forth
tall the furthest the best hidden
drunk tired exhausted fisherwoman
drunk beautiful gauntleted hand
maljointed island disjointed island
every island calls
every island is a widow
Benin Benin O stone of bitterness

Ife that was Ouphas
a mouth of the Zambezi
towards an Ophir with no Albuquerque
shall we always be holding out our hands?

once o torn one
She piece by strip
reassembled her dismemberment
and the fourteen bits
sat down triumphant in the evening rays.

I have invented a secret cult
my sun is the one that one is always waiting for

the most beautiful of the suns is the nocturnal sun

Feminine body island found
feminine body well charted
feminine body born from the sea-spray
feminine body island recovered
and who never gets mad enough
for it to matter to the sky
o night of buttercups
a secret of polypary
feminine body palm tree step
by the sun coifed in a nest
in which the phœnix dies and is reborn
we are souls of good background
nocturnal bodies alive with lineage
faithful trees gushing wine
I a plaintive sybil.

Congealed waters of my infancies
into which the oars could barely sink
millions of birds of my infancies

when was ever the perfumed island
illuminated with great suns
the season the area so delicious
the year paved with precious stones?

Torn apart at the crises of the zones
in full cry a gloomy mixture
I have seen a male bird go down
the stone embedded itself in its forehead
I am looking at the lowest point of the year

Body soiled with filth skillfully transformed
space wind of faith falsified
space planetary false pride
slow rustic diamond-merchant prince
would I be the plaything of nigromancy?
So better than Antilia or Brazil
milliary stone in the distance
sword of a flame that racks me
I cut down the trees of Paradise

This poem, "Dit d'errance" (89), whose position makes it the poet's final statement in this collection, may be said to indicate a summary as well as a conclusion of the poet's response at this stage of his literary career to his dilemma as a black French Caribbean poet. As the title indicates, the poem is an oral communication, serving both as a means of clarifying the poet's own situation and as a catalyst for other blacks, universally, to explore and validate their position as black people in a white-dominated society. "Errance" [Wandering] signifies the poet's doubt about his ability to effect a fusion between inner exploration and outward, political commitment to his island and his people.

At the beginning of the poem, the poet assumes the microcosmic mantle of all suffering, fragmented humanity and of all alienation from self: "Tout ce qui jamais fut déchiré / en moi s'est déchiré / tout ce qui jamais fut mutilé / en moi s'est mutilé" [All that has ever been torn / in me has been torn / all that has ever been mutilated / in me has been mutilated]. This personal alienation is associated with an alienation in cosmic terms and necessitates an invention of the other half of the self: "au milieu de l'assiette de son souffle dénudé / le fruit coupé de la lune toujours en allée / vers le contour à inventer de l'autre moitié" [in the middle of the plate stripped of its breath / the cut fruit of the moon always gone away / towards the not yet invented contour of the other half].

The poet's response ("à peine peut-être certain sens ..." [scarcely perhaps a certain sense]) to his own reappraisal of the past ("Et pourtant que te reste-t-il du temps ancien" [And yet what do you have left of the old days]) indicates tentativeness and doubt in relation to the significance of what has been achieved. He even has to consider the possibility of having been led astray: "et quand d'aucuns chantent Noël revenu / de songer aux astres / égarés" [and when some sing of Christmas back here again / to think of the stars / gone astray]. At this point, the poet appears to be oppressed by a sense of failure, of lamentation: " ... tout est du tout déchu ...;" " ... j'ai bien en tête la saison si lacrimeuse ..." [all is totally fallen; I am well aware of the so tearful season]. Indeed, the dominant characteristic of one part of the poet's fragmented self, represented by his past experience of slavery, seems to be silence: "Ciel éclaté courbe écorchée / de dos d'esclaves fustigés / peine trésorière des alizés / grimoire fermé mots oubliés / j'interroge mon passé muet" [Exploded sky flayed curve / of backs of whipped slaves / treasurer punishment of the tradewinds / closed grimorium forgotten words / I question my silent past].

As the poet evokes the island which is part of his being, "île de sang" [island of blood], the island, like every island, is represented as sharing in the same condition of alienation and loss as the poet himself: "île maljointe île disjointe / toute île appelle / toute île est veuve" [maljointed island disjointed island / every island calls / every island is a widow]. The loss for the island, as it is for the poet, is related to separation from the source of identity,

Africa, represented by the civilizations of Bénin and Ifé, and his rhetorical question, in the name of all alienated Africans ("nous" [we]), expresses his own doubt of ever being able to heal this breach: "tendrons-nous toujours les bras?" [shall we always be holding out our hands?].

In the apostrophe which follows ("ô déchiré" [O torn one]), the poet addresses his wounded and divided self, as he conjures up an image of triumphant reunification and healing. This leads him to a new state of consciousness, in which he dons the priestly mask of hope: "J'ai inventé un culte secret / mon soleil est celui que toujours on attend" [I have invented a secret cult / my sun is the one that one is always waiting for]. The poet then adopts another persona, that of lover ("corps féminin île retrouvée" [feminine body island found]), which becomes fused with the plaintive persona of his prophetic role ("moi sybille flébilant" [I a plaintive sybil]). When he turns again to look back on his (shared) childhood past ("mes enfances" [my infancies]), the painful memories of communal failure with which he identifies ("j'ai vu un oiseau mâle sombrer" [I have seen a male bird go down]) produce in him a sense of disillusionment: "je regarde le plus bas de l'année" [I am looking at the lowest point of the year].

The poet's rather depressing impression of his past life, his doubts about his identity and his role, about whether he is indeed agent or victim, and about the validity of his concern with "black" issues, are translated into lucid, self-reflexive, ironic wit: "serais-je jouet de nigromance?" [would I be the plaything of nigromancy?]. The process of rigorous self-examination leads unerringly to an awareness of the importance of his linkages to Africa and his native island. From this process the image of the "pierre" [stone] emerges to suggest both fixity and power, and the poem ends on a triumphant note, with the poet adopting the proud, resonant, and heroic voice of a personified lance: "Or mieux qu'Antilia ni que Brazil / pierre milliaire dans la distance / épée d'une flamme qui me bourrelle / j'abats les arbres du Paradis" [So better than Antilia or Brazil / milliary stone in the distance / sword of a flame that racks me / I cut down the trees of Paradise]. The images of these concluding lines are not immediately accessible. Transparent sense is subordinated to suggestive sound.[9] The apparent conclusion is inconclusive. The word with all its evocative potential holds sway. The pen is the poet's sword. The wandering spoken word is written. The final gesture, however, is presumptuously destructive and intentionally subversive. It signifies Césaire's determination to destroy once and for all the European conception of the Caribbean as an exotic tropical paradise.

Cadastre represents the emergence of Césaire's mature poetic voice, as he gives responses to his situation as a self-conscious and experienced black Martinican poet. In this collection, he adopts and accepts his roles as leader, magician, and prophet, giving voice to revolt, articulating the sufferings of his people, prophesying and creating their integrity and destiny as an authentic people, and proclaiming the survival and eventual triumph of the people on whom his identity depends. The constant message voiced in the poems is one of hope: hope in the restoration of the dignity and divinity of the black man, hope in the triumph of humanitarianism, hope in the validity of true revolt, and hope in the future liberation of the Caribbean.

The poet addresses an individual self, "moi" [me], or a plural (Caribbean) "nous" [us] more often than he does an opposing (European) "vous" [you]. In other words, the communication is directed not so much to the representatives of the oppressive and alienating social order but rather to the poet's self and to the French Caribbean people with whom the poet chooses to identify. The poems function as affirmations: of solidarity and humanitarianism, of dignity, divinity, and power, and above all of an authentic black and Caribbean imaginary. They presuppose a problematical cultural context of alienation from self, of loss of identity, dignity, nobility, beauty, and power, of divisiveness and inhumanity. It is precisely because these conditions are taken for granted, are part and parcel of the social order within which the poem itself functions, that the poetic act becomes an affirmation of contrary values. In itself, therefore, Césaire's poetry is the concretization of dignity, nobility, hope, change, revolt, and liberation. It operates in two directions simultaneously, inwardly and personally, and outwardly and politically: inwardly, the poetry serves as a vehicle for the poet to explore and resolve issues of personal identity and liberation, and as a means of personal salvation; and outwardly, the poetry operates as a means of communicating with his people and with the supporters of the alienating social order, and as a means of affirmation, education, disalienation, and even of subversion. These two functions represent the personal and political thrusts of Césaire's poetry. Underlying and linking these functions is a conception of poetry as ritual, with its magical and prophetic potential.

In his 1943 article in *Tropiques*, "Maintenir la poésie" [Maintaining Poetry], Césaire had indicated that poetry as he conceived and practiced it had a deliberately subversive function, in relation to the existing social order: "To defend oneself from the social by creating a zone of incandescence, beyond which and within which the unheard of flower of the "I" flourishes in a terrible security; ... to win, through revolt, one's fair share in which one can raise up oneself, integrally. These are some of the requirements that tend to be essential to every poet.... Here poetry equals insurrection...." (*Tropiques* 8-9 (Octobre 1943, 7-8). This revolutionary function of poetry, related to a need to affirm and protect the threatened integrity of identity, has remained a constant in Césaire's poetry. At the same time, Césaire has retained his conception of the poet as leader and prophet for a people. In a 1989 interview, discussing a poem entitled "Dyâli" which he had written in honor of his long time friend and colleague, Léopold Sédar Senghor, Césaire explains: "'Dyâli' autrement dit 'le diseur de parole', le 'poète' ... Le Dyâli c'est aussi celui qui montre le chemin ...." [Dyâli, or in other words, "the speaker of words," the "poet" .... The Dyâli is also the one who shows the way...] (Rowell 1989:52). Césaire himself, by his continued literary and political activity, has also been showing the way. What he has shown, what his poetry shows, by its very existence and by its function as a literary creation that expresses and embodies an alternative imaginary to that of metropolitan France, is that French Caribbean poetry exists.

Notes

[1] For a discussion of changes from the original collections to the revised edition, see Arnold 1981:191-251.

[2] Page citations for poems in this chapter refer to Césaire, *Cadastre* (Paris: Seuil, 1961). An earlier version of this essay previously appeared in Hurley 1992a.

[3] For another commentary on this poem see Davis 1984.

[4] Césaire's fascination with and admiration for his Cuban artist friend is reflected in the ten poems of *moi, laminaire* devoted to Lam. For comments, see Arnold 1990:xxxviii-xxxix.

[5] "Coprah," often used to designate dried coconut, refers here to the fiber of the dried coconut shell used as stuffing for mattresses; the "pécari" is a wild pig, found in some Caribbean territories.

[6] For interesting commentaries on this poem see Arnold 1981: 217-219, and Davis 1984:96-100.

[7] The word "nègre" in French, often translated as "negro," is not generally considered by francophone blacks as profoundly insulting as "nigger" is by African Americans. However, Césaire's reaction to the word in this poem is closer to the African American attitude and so I think "nigger" is a more appropriate translation than "negro."

[8] For other illuminating, detailed commentaries on this poem see particularly Cailler 1976:97-95; Scharfmann 1980: 74-85; and Arnold 1981: 235-42.

[9] Césaire once told me, for instance, that he used the English spelling and pronunciation of Brazil instead of the French "Brésil" simply because it sounded better.

5

Edouard GLISSANT

Glissant occupies a conspicuous position in the Caribbean world, because of the volume and variety of his output as a poet, novelist, playwright, and essayist, and because of the influence he has exercised on Martinican intellectual and cultural life as an educator, theorist, and political activist since the mid-1960s. Born in a small village, Bezaudin, in the northeast of Martinique on September 21, 1928, Glissant at an early age went to live with his mother in Lamentin. From 1938 he attended the Lycée Schœlcher in Fort-de-France while Césaire was a teacher there and was for some time an ardent supporter of Césaire. Glissant went to Paris in 1946 to complete his university education at the Sorbonne. He abandoned his formal studies after two years and devoted his time to reading and writing. In 1951 he returned to a formal program in philosophy at the Sorbonne and in ethnology at the Musée de l'Homme. After obtaining his Diplôme d'Etudes Supérieures he went back for a brief period to Martinique before again returning to Paris where he frequented Antillean intellectual and political circles, started publishing poetry, and became integrated into literary and artistic circles, such as the semiotic avant-garde group that included Roland Barthes and Philippe Sollers. His first volume of poetry, *Champ d'îles*, was published in 1953. In 1954 his first critical article appeared in *Les Lettres nouvelles*. His first novel, *La lézarde*, won the prestigious Prix Renaudot in 1958, which brought him international success and established his developing reputation as an outstanding literary figure. In 1959, he helped to found the Front Antillo-Guyanais, a movement dedicated to the cultural and political liberation of the French Caribbean people, becoming its first president in 1961. His political activity brought him into conflict with the French government of Charles de Gaulle who banned the Front by decree three months after it was formed. Between 1961-62, Glissant found himself expelled from Guadeloupe, placed under virtual house arrest in France, and prevented from travelling freely outside metropolitan France. In 1965, he was finally permitted to return to Martinique, where in 1967, after having taught for a year at the Lycée de Jeunes Filles in Fort-de-France, he opened his own private secondary school, the Institut Martiniquais d'Etudes (I.M.E.), the curriculum of which included Martinican and Caribbean history, geography, and literature. Glissant's Institute was and is both an educational and a cultural center, dedicated to the transformation of Martinican society. An integral part of this cultural project was the companion journal, *Acoma*, which first appeared in 1971. This publication took its name from one of the largest trees found on the island that has the characteristic, reported by DuTertre in his *Histoire générale des Antilles*, of remaining moist and full of sap long after it is cut. From 1982-88 Glissant worked in Paris as director of *Le Courrier de L'UNESCO*. In 1989 he relocated to the United States to take up a position as Director of the Centre Francophone at Louisiana State University. In 1995 he moved to New York as Distinguished Professor of French in the Graduate

School of the City University of New York. He is also establishing an Institute of Caribbean Writers in Lamentin, Martinique.

Since Glissant's return to Martinique in the mid-1960s, he emerged to be accepted as the acknowledged intellectual and ideological leader of large numbers of young Martinican writers and scholars. He is an accomplished novelist, the author of *La Lézarde* (1958), *Le Quatrième Siècle* (1964), *Malemort* (1975), *La Case du Commandeur* (1981), *Mahogany* (1987), and *Tout-Monde* (1993). He has written a play, *Monsieur Toussaint* (1961). His mass of critical and theoretical essays on poetry and poetics have been collected in four major collections of essays, *Soleil de la Conscience* (1956), *L'Intention poétique* (1969), *Le Discours antillais* (1981), and *Poétique de la Relation* (1990). His collections of poetry include *Un champ d'îles* (1953), *La terre inquiète* (1954), and *Les Indes* (1956), all of which are reprinted in *Poèmes* (1965), as well as *Le sel noir* (1960), *Le sang rivé* (1961), *Pays rêvé, pays réel* (1985), and *Fastes* (1991). The edition of *Poèmes complets* (1994) includes, in addition to the previously published collections, *Les grands chaos* (1993).

Glissant's life and work have been dedicated to efforts to find practical and theoretical solutions to the problem of being an Antillean living in a society in which his specificity as an Antillean is constantly challenged by the artificial separation, linguistic and political, from other Caribbean and Central American people to whom he is related not merely in geography but in history and culture. His aim is to contribute to the enrichment of humanity through the cultural liberation of Antillean peoples, a project that requires full integration of the French Caribbean overseas departments into the Caribbean zone.

In the analysis of Glissant's poetry that follows, I examine manifestations of his response to his Antillean situation at the level of actual poetic practice, rather than as articulated in theoretical writings, by examining the roles assumed by the poet and the ways in which poet and poem function. I have chosen selections from *Un champ d'îles* (novembre 1952), *La terre inquiète* (1954), and *Les*

Indes (avril-juin 1955),[1] previous republished together in *Poèmes* (1965). Their republication in one volume under the generic title of *Poèmes* would tend to suggest that they constitute a representative sample of the evolution of Glissant's poetic practice. The titles of the individual collections signal that sensitivity to geography informs Glissant's poetic practice and that geographical factors are for him essential components of the cultural specificity of the Caribbean. Also implicit in the titles is an underlying idea of separateness and connectedness, of disjointed parts and a composite whole, and this idea is, as shall be shown, reflected in the formal arrangement of the individual collections.

1

Tourmentes, feu marin, étendues sans pitié: ce sont les hautes marges des houilles, parfois le vent qui tout doux avive tout doux surprend le cœur et l'empanache; ce sont meutes du vent qui dévolent des mains, vers la coulpe et l'accomplissement du gravier. Ces cavaliers s'éprennent d'une liane, l'entendant croître par le ciel jusqu'aux ultimes étoiles! O de ce langage qu'est toute pierre pourvue de chair et la levant par-dessus elle, de ce langage violent et doucement obscur qu'est la racine douée de chair et la poussant par-dessous elle, voici l'épure. Ce n'est point chaleur du mot qui étincelle, mais peuplades de mains sous la peau: l'attentat massif de la corolle à ses bords d'étang rose, et la montée des folluaires, et la chute meuble des paradisiers. Quel peut être ce cri, cet éclat de vitres dans la voix ! —que de cette chambre où vous voici lovée aux voilures de vie, soudain le jour s'en aille, déflorant, vers ce langage qui se perd, et puis se prend ? Il établit en l'île vos mains atteintes de nuit. Sous les

sombres frondaisons de la peau frêle vous avancez
votre sourire comme un oiseau des bords de mer;
c'est l'éclat de votre silence, c'est la prose tranquille
de vos mains qui font lumière de ce monde, le
conquièrent entre ses haies.

❦

1

Storms, sea fire, pitiless expanses: these
are the tall margins of coal, sometimes it is the
wind that very gently revives very gently surprises
the heart and decks it out in motley colors; these
are hunting packs of wind devolving from the
hands, moving toward the repentance and
fulfillment of the gravel. These riders fall in love
with a vine, hearing it grow in the sky right up to
the furthermost stars! O of this language that is
every stone provided with flesh and raising it over
itself, of this violent and gently obscure language
that is the root endowed with flesh and pushing it
under itself, here is the draft. It is not warmth of
the word that sparkles, but small tribes of hands
under the skin: the massive attack of the corolla at
its pink pond shores, and the rise of the folluaries,
and the loose fall of the birds of paradise. What
can this cry be, this shattering of glass panes in the
voice! — that from this room where here you are
rolled up in the spiral sails of life, suddenly
daylight goes away, deflowering, toward this
language that loses itself and then catches itself?
It establishes in the island your hands stricken with
night. Under the dark foliage of frail skin you put
forth your smile like a seaside bird; it is the

explosion of your silence, it is the quiet prose of those hands of yours which turn this world into light, conquering this world between its hedges.

Un champ d'îles, whose title [*A Field of Islands*] both translates the poet's conception of the Antilles as a geographical and sociocultural unit, similar islands within a common field of sea, and evokes the sugar-cane plantations characteristic of the human and economic exploitation of the Caribbean, is divided into three numbered sections: section 1 consists of six prose poems; section 2 is a long, free-verse poem of 46 stanzas, each of four mainly octosyllabic lines, and a final single line; section 3 consists of four prose poems. This collection, therefore, exhibits a striking, but controlled, variation in form: it is the poet who orchestrates the arrangement in which verse poetry is, as it were, enfolded and contained by prose, and in which, as Glissant has indicated, the prose sections correspond to a personal, imaginary evocation, while the verse section follows the rhythm of reality. In this way, the collection draws attention to itself as a "different" (i.e. non-traditional) form of literary expression, and tries to assert its own individuality and identity. This formal fusion is a reflection of the convergence of cultures which, for Glissant, defines the Antillean identity.

The very first word of this opening prose poem, "Tourmentes" ["Storms"] (55), bears connotations of both meteorological and sociopolitical upheavals, and provides a thematic link between this collection and *La Terre inquiète [The Anxious Land]*. This word sets the tone as well as the context of the collection as a whole, which describes a situation ("un champ d'îles" [a field of islands]) in which meteorological and geographical disturbance reflects disturbance at other levels: economic, social, political, cultural, and even personal. The juxtaposition of "tourmentes" [storms], "feu marin" [sea fire], and "étendues" [expanses] conveys the dominance of a vast and powerful oceanic force, the inexorable nature of which is reinforced by "sans pitié" [pitiless]. The potential for fear and awe implicit in this elemental force is counterbalanced by the gentleness ("tout doux") of the wind, which, though a manifestation of this awesome force, is yet shown to have a positive effect on the poet's emotional being: "avive tout doux surprend le cœur et l'empanache" [very gently surprises the heart and decks it out in motley colors].

The phenomena evoked by the poet are complex in nature and effect and he is concerned with representing them accurately. This concern for clarity is translated in the poem into declarative clauses such as "ce sont les hautes marges ..." [these are the high margins of coal], "ce sont meutes du vent ..." [these are hunting packs of wind], "Ce n'est point chaleur ..." [it is not warmth], "Quel peut être ce cri" [What can this cry be], and "c'est l'éclat ..." [it is the explosion] which help to clarify, identify, define, and interpret the phenomena envisioned by the poet.

The poet's interpretations and definitions are developed around the pivotal image of hands ("mains"), which is employed four times in different contexts in the poem, attesting to the difficulty experienced by the poet in touching reality. In the first reference ("ce sont meutes du vent qui dévolent des mains" [these are hunting packs of wind devolving from the hands]), the loose syntactical relationship between "meutes"[hunting packs] and "mains" [hands] translates the agitation of a mob stimulated by manual activity. In the second reference ("Ce n'est point chaleur du mot qui étincelle, mais peuplades de mains sous la peau" [It is not warmth of the word that sparkles, but small tribes of hands under the skin]), the expression "peuplades de mains" [small tribes of hands] forms a contrast to "chaleur du mot" [warmth of the word]. This contrast indicates the poet's privileging of manual activity over the use of words, and of the communal action of a people linked by the common bond of labor over the exploitation of the emotive potential of the word; in other words, this contrast implies the superiority of communal labor over individual rhetoric. This reflects Glissant's often expressed empathy for agricultural workers in Martinique who embody for him the true cultural spirit of the Caribbean. In the third reference ("Il établit en l'île vos mains ..." [it establishes in the island your hands]), the syntactical association between "ce cri" [this cry] of the previous sentence and "il" [it] creates a link between the poet's voice and the establishment of "hands" in the island. Poetic activity is thus shown to have a constructive, creative, and political function. In the final reference ("c'est l'éclat de votre silence, c'est la prose tranquille de vos mains qui font lumière de ce monde" [it is the explosion of your silence, it is the quiet prose of those hands of yours]), the association drawn between "prose" and "hands" breaks down the separation between the manual and the poetic. The poem is the symbol of the convergence of manual and poetic activity.

Furthermore, this poem is essentially self-referential, drawing attention to itself as a self-conscious linguistic activity: "O de ce langage qu'est toute pierre pourvue de chair et la levant par dessus elle, de ce langage violent et doucement obscur qu'est la racine douée de chair et la poussant par dessous elle, voici l'épure" [O of this language that is every stone provided with flesh and raising it over itself, of this violent and gently obscure language that is the root endowed with flesh and pushing it under itself, this is the draft]. It presents itself as a carefully constructed, multi-dimensional, usable product, both a potential and very human weapon held ready for attack ("pierre pourvue de chair" [stone provided with flesh]), and the link to the poet's human roots ("racine douée de chair" [root endowed with flesh]). This image indicates that the violence and obscurity of the poetic language are related to the problem of its source ("racine" [root]).

The poet's self-consciousness about the oral element in his poetry is reflected in the exclamation "Quel peut être ce cri, cet éclat de vitres dans la voix!" [What can this cry be, this shattering of glass panes in the voice!], which signals a sensitivity to the strident and discordant tonality of the voice that emerges. The implied discomfort experienced by the poet is manifested in the shifts of perspective within the poem, between an implicit "je" [I], "vous" [you], and "il" [it]. Significantly, the poet never constitutes himself fully as a subjective "je"-presence in the poem, but manifests himself rather as an "absent," disembodied persona, whose unstable, fluctuating, emotional reactions may be sensed in "sans pitié" [pitiless], "tout doux" [very gently], and in the exclamatory "O de ce langage..." [O of this language] and "Quel peut être ce cri" [What can this cry be]. At the same time, it is evident that the poet is addressing a female "vous" [you], characterized through the tenderness of the alliterated fricatives in "vous voici lovée aux voilures de vie." This "you," a representation of the land considered as a woman and of a woman considered as the land, develops an increasingly greater presence as the poem nears its end. The multi-dimensional "il" of "il établit" [it establishes] may be linked to "ce cri" [this cry], "le jour" [the day], or "ce langage" [this language], all of which contribute toward the establishment within the island of "vos mains" [your hands]. This linkage is an indication that the poem itself plays an important role in affirming and defining the specificity of the poet's island.

Racial undertones are delicately sketched in the connection drawn between the island and dark skins, in "les sombres frondaisons de la peau" [the dark foliage of skin] which echoes the earlier "peuplades de mains sous la peau" [small tribes of hands under the skin]. The poet, his voice, and the island, therefore, all form part of a dark and fragile entity which all three are trying to define ("conquièrent entre ses haies" [conquering between its hedges]). The dense image with which the poem ends establishes an association between "l'éclat de votre silence" [the explosion of your silence] and "la prose tranquille de vos mains" [the quiet prose of your hands]. This evocation of silence and tranquillity contrasts sharply with the opening "tourmentes" [storms] and suggests a final poetic resolution of the upheaval with which the poem opened.

This opening poem is thus a complex, multi-dimensional evocation of the poet's island and an exploration of the role played by poetic activity within this context. This introductory poem presents some of the dimensions of the dilemma faced by the poet. The complexity of this dilemma is reflected in the density and obscurity of the poetic language used and becomes the literal substance of the poem.

> Ce jour ! — où égalant la Montagne plus proche qu'un nœud de lampes à votre front, il vous leva en lui par dessus les neiges, vous aérant d'un gros discours d'opales, de sensitives. Une patience a grandi dans l'absence, de lui blessé par l'absence et la présence d'une autre voix, non la vôtre, et de vous, qui chavirez vos tours de désespoir, purifiant l'autre (et non pas lui) de vos douceurs. Depuis ce jour, la lumière a avancé d'un pas terrible, la terre est un passé de névadas, un Haut Plateau d'errements sur leurs quilles. Cette argile à nouveau remue ! Serait-ce que l'oiseau guide le ciel vers une source ? Serait-ce, très-lointaine, l'embarquement des rives de la neige vers une foule incendiée ? Ou le cœur, est-ce le cœur, agité comme une gare de populations végétales, qui fume sur la ville sa suée de terres, son ressac tumultueux ? Nul n'avoue, nul ne peut, que cette enfance soit la vielle d'un bivouac. Lui, ne craint plus le sentiment (de dire "je" dans cette terre), mais l'emblave et l'ensemence. Et vous à peine devinant tout ce remous d'étoiles et de lierres, profuse en ce langage, indifférente et soudain calme dans le fruit, faites mystère ainsi que lui de ce silence où bruit la ville. Pour atteindre à votre jour (comme on attente à la douleur, lui brûlant jusqu'à ses étoiles), voici l'argile commuée, ce fruit bougé, l'effraie douce du langage. Fureurs à nu, lances de l'air, forêts ô multitude ! que vient ravir la foi de vous, dans ce champ d'îles non inventées.

☙

That day! — when rivaling the Mountain closer to your forehead than a knot of lamps, he raised you up in himself above the snows, fanning fresh air over you with a big speech of opals, of animal flowers. A patience has grown up in absence, the absence of him wounded by the absence and the presence of another voice, not yours, and the absence of you, capsizing your turns of despair, purifying the other (and not him) with your gentleness. Since that day, light has taken a terrible step forward, the land is a past of nevadas, a High Plateau of erring ways on their keels. This clay is shifting again! Could it be that the bird is guiding the sky toward a spring? Could it be the loading of shores of snow for a crowd, very far away, set on fire? Or the heart, is it the heart, shaken like a station of plant populations, sending out over the town its sweat fumes of lands, its tumultuous backwash? No one admits, no one can, that this childhood may be the viola of a bivouac. As for him, he is no longer afraid of feeling (of saying "I" in this land), but sows it and gives it seed. And you, barely sensing this whole swirl of stars and ivy, you, profuse in this language, indifferent and suddenly calm in the fruit, you make a mystery just like him out of this silence with which the city hums. In order to attain your day (as one makes an attempt at grief, he burning even his stars), here is the commuted clay, this shifted fruit, the gentle barn-owl of language. Rages bared, lances of the air, forests O multitude! that faith for you comes to seize, in this field of uninvented islands.

The exclamation mark that follows the opening two words of the poem, "Ce jour!" [That day!] (56), stresses the significance of a particular moment of consciousness and transformation. The poem develops in three movements related to the importance of this "day." In the first movement the poet describes the situation of that day in the past; the second movement, introduced by "Depuis ce jour" [Since that day], presents a report on the present as it has been affected by the past moment of consciousness; the third movement, introduced by "Pour atteindre à votre jour" [In order to attain your day], looks toward the future offering suggestions for a similar moment of consciousness prepared and provoked by the poet.

The poet here continues to address a "you" (his woman-land), in his account of the association between this "you" and his poetic persona. The capitalized "Montagne" [Mountain] immediately evokes Mount Pelée, which occupies a dominant position in the Martinican geographical, psychosocial, and imaginary landscape. Here its position is subtly reminiscent of that of the American Statue of Liberty with its "nœud de lampes" [knot of lamps], but much nearer to the poet's heart ("plus proche"). The North American connection is further emphasized by "Haut Plateau" [High Plateau] and "nevadas" which are strongly evocative of the topography of the midwest of the U.S.A. This "you" is shown to have been elevated to a position of equal dominance within the "he"-persona's sensibility, towering in importance above "les neiges" [the snows] characteristic of the European north. Thus the "day" evoked by the poet is a day of transformation, reminiscent of Césaire's "au bout du petit matin" [at the end of the fore-day morning], when the awareness comes of a conflict of voices and of interests: "blessé par l'absence et la présence d'une autre voix, non la vôtre ... purifiant l'autre (et non pas lui)" [wounded by the absence and the presence of another voice, not yours ... purifying the other (and not him)].

The second section is marked by the awareness of new movement: "Cette argile à nouveau remue! [This clay is shifting again!] The questions that follow point to the difficulty of interpreting events and reaching conclusions. The reference to past difficulty in assuming a subjective voice ("je" [I]) within the poem underlines the extratextual problems of political and cultural autonomy for the French Caribbean: "Lui, ne craint plus le sentiment (de dire 'je' dans cette terre), mais l'emblave et l'ensemence" [He is no longer afraid of feeling (of saying "I" in this land, but sows it and gives it seed.] The new consciousness evidently brings with it freedom from fear. Here, the blurring of syntactical relationships (since "l'" [it] may refer to both "le sentiment" [feeling] and "terre" [land]) contributes to an impression of the blurring of the roles of the poet, who is presented as a sower of seed both for the land and for the sentiment of pride. This indicates that for the poet, the present poetic activity is perceived as having both a political and an emotive function, contributing to the development of a spirit of nationalistic pride, and more concretely to the sociopolitical and economic development of the "terre" [land].

The final section is profoundly self-referential as the poem presents itself as an offering to a new process of transformation: "voici l'argile commuée, ce fruit bougé, l'effraie douce du langage" [here is the commuted clay, this shifted fruit, the gentle barn-owl of language]. Language becomes fused with landscape in producing movement that is indicative of a change in consciousness.

The deliberate blurring of personas (he, you, and I), the investing of the land with the potential for movement, and the lack of separation between persons, land, and poetic activity give some indication of the poet's project. The obscurity of the poem is an expression of the obscurity of the Caribbean situation. The poem both expresses this obscurity that arises from the confusion of cultural voices and attempts to break through it, to define the real and imaginary parameters of the very complex Caribbean, and to find his own voice. The poem, therefore, is a projection into the future, a visionary depiction of "ce champ d'îles non inventées" [this field of uninvented islands].

Vous, présence, émoi de pierre, ouvrage du soleil quand il est lézard sur la roche. O votre présence est de jour, l'envers miraculeux de celle-ci, malhabile. Et que le souffle hésite, c'est bon signe. Landes, levures du matin. Rade assouvie, une fois franchi le goulet des mots. Votre absence, de même pluie, ouvre la lumière; infinie, après l'intimité cernée de chaque forme; gardienne du mot dans l'allée secrète. O revoici ce champ du jour et de la nuit, assomptions, l'un de chair et puis l'autre de rareté. Ce n'est pas absence de saison, qu'effacent le retour et l'oublieux revoir. Ce n'est présence de raison, le sentier des dialogues, la main dans le cœur comme une épissure de gloire. Acacias rouges sur le rêve. Sang volubile sur le chemin ! Absente qui êtes présence ! Que la parole à l'entrée du poème hésite encore, mûrisse au plus profond les fastes de leurs proches épousailles, c'est témoignage pour l'epoux. O ce n'est point absence, ni présence à demi, mais si pleines que l'être leur est un sillon de terre. Toute chair se divise, à l'aurore et au soir, de présence et d'absence, pour un feu et pour un sevrage. O mangue, image de ses succulences! Chambre du soir, berceuse d'engoulevent, et ta tête de statue blanche, si blanche! Cette image a poussé tout le jour ses lèvres nettes comme une berge. Maintenant que voici le soir, chambre du soir, berceuse d'engoulevent, pose-toi sur la crête et élargis ton rêve. Mais l'élargissant jusqu'aux hauteurs de cette absence, sous l'ogive des filaos, ramène-le cependant vers la foi têtue de cette présence, parmi la foule ! — O poème qui naît de vous, qui naissez à ce labeur du monde entier. (59)

ॐ

You, presence, a stirring of stone, the sun's handiwork when it is a lizard on the rock. O yours is a day-time presence, the miraculous converse of this clumsy one. And it is a good sign that the breath falters. Moorlands, morning yeasts. Harbor satiated once the narrows of words have been cleared. Your absence, of the same rain, turns on the light; infinite absence, after the encircled intimacy of every shape; absence guarding the word in the secret pathway. O here again is this field of day and night, assumptions, one of flesh and then the other of rarity. It is not absence of season that is erased by returning and forgetfully seeing again. It is not presence of reason, the path of dialogues, the hand in the heart like a splice of glory. Red acacias on the dream. Voluble blood on the road! You absent woman who are presence! May speech hesitate again at the entrance of the poem, may it bring to ripeness the deepest splendors of their approaching nuptials: it is a witness for the husband. O it is not absence, nor semi-presence, but they are so full that existence for them is a furrow of earth. All flesh divides, at dawn and in the evening, into presence and absence, for a fire and for a weaning. O mango, image of its succulences! Evening chamber, nighthawk lullaby, and your statue's head, white, so white! All day this image has grown its lips straight as a river's edge. Now that evening is here, evening chamber, nighthawk lullaby, get on to the crest and broaden your dream. But as you broaden it to the heights of this absence, under the arch of the casuarinas, bring it back however toward the

headstrong faith of this presence, among the
people! — O poem who is born of you, who are
born to this toil of the whole world.

In this last poem (59) of this first section of *A Field of Islands*, the
poet continues his exploration of the relationship between the island
as both a "presence" and an "absence" and the birth of the poem.
The poet first addresses the island as a "presence," whose existence,
like the virtually imperceptible movement of a lizard lying on a rock
in the sun, is difficult to perceive: "Vous, présence, émoi de pierre,
ouvrage du soleil quand il est lézard sur la roche" [You, presence,
a stirring of stone, the sun's handiwork when it is a lizard on the
rock]. The contrasting association between the island and the poem
is initiated, with the poem's "presence" presented as being
"malhabile" [clumsy]. The difficulties attending the emergence of
the poem are shown to be expected and even encouraging signs: "Et
que le souffle hésite, c'est bon signe" [And it's a good sign that the
breath falters], since satisfaction is bound to follow: "Rade assouvie,
une fois franchi le goulet des mots" [Harbor satiated once the
narrows of words have been cleared]. This "hesitation" is given
direct encouragement by the poetic persona because of it is evidence
of the consummation of the poetic marriage: "Que la parole à
l'entrée du poème hésite encore, mûrisse au plus profond les fastes
de leurs proches épousailles, c'est témoignage pour l'époux" [May
speech hesitate again at the entrance of the poem, may it bring to
ripeness the deepest splendors of their approaching nuptials: it is a
witness for the husband]. Implicitly, therefore, the difficulty
experienced by the poetic voice becomes a token of the authenticity
of the poem as a product of Antillean specificity.

In a parallel movement, the island's "absence" is shown to
have positive qualities: "Votre absence ... ouvre la lumière" [Your
absence turns on the light]; it is the island's "absence" as "gardienne
du mot" [guardian of the word] that guarantees the survival of the
poem. Thus the island is represented in the middle of the poem as
a woman endowed with the qualities of both presence and absence:

"Absente qui êtes présence" [You absent woman who are presence]. This paradox, the coexistence of apparent opposites in one entity, is represented in images of light and darkness, specifically in the difference between the morning light (which dominates the first half of the poem) and the darkness of evening. It is this paradox that convinces the poet of the inevitable fragmentation that characterizes Caribbean society but which is also a constant in human experience: "Toute chair se divise, à l'aurore et au soir, de présence et d'absence" [All flesh divides, at dawn and in the evening]. The images of light and darkness, of dawn and evening, give way to an image of whiteness, stereotypically European, which has intruded on the poet's consciousness ("ta tête de statue blanche, si blanche! Cette image a poussé tout le jour ses lèvres nettes comme une berge" [your statue's head, white, so white! All day this image has grown its lips straight as a river's edge]). The snow-capped mountains of Europe form a painful contrast with Antillean mountain tops. The creative challenge which confronts the poet, under the dominance of the European image, can best be met by a rededication to the imaginary landscape of the island community: "...pose-toi sur la crête et élargis ton rêve. Mais l'élargissant jusqu'aux hauteurs de cette absence, sous l'ogive des filaos, ramène-le cependant vers la foi têtue de cette présence, parmi la foule!" [...Get on to the crest and broaden your dream. But as you broaden it to the heights of this absence, under the arch of the casuarinas, bring it back however toward the headstrong faith of this presence, among the people!] Finally it is only the island community, itself dependent on its relation to the rest of the world, that can guarantee the birth of the poem: "O poème qui naît de vous, qui naissez à ce labeur du monde entier" [O poem who is born of you, who are born to this toil of the whole world].

> Savoir ce qui dans vos yeux berce
> Une baie de ciel un oiseau
> La mer, une caresse dévolue
> Le soleil ici revenu

Beauté de l'espace ou otage
De l'avenir tentaculaire
Toute parole s'y confond
Avec le silence des Eaux

Beauté des temps pour un mirage
Le temps qui demeure est d'attente
Le temps qui vole est un cyclone
Où c'est la route éparpillée

....

Beauté d'attente Beauté des vagues
L'attente est presque un beaupré
Enlacé d'ailes et de vents
Comme un fouillis sur la berge

Chaque mot vient sans qu'on fasse
A peine bouger l'horizon
Le paysage est un tamis soudain
De mots poussés sous la lune

Savoir ce qui sur vos cheveux
Hagard étrenne ses attelages
Et le sel vient-il de la mer
Ou de cette voix qui circule

....

Les hommes sortent de la terre
Avec leurs visages trop forts
Et l'appétit de leurs regards
Sur la voilure des clairières

Les femmes marchent devant eux

L'île toute est bientôt femme
Apitoyée sur elle-même mais crispant
Son désespoir dans son cœur nu

....

Apitoyée cette île et pitoyable
Elle vit de mots dérivés
Comme un halo de naufragés
A la rencontre des rochers

Elle a besoin de mots qui durent
Et font le ciel et l'horizon
Plus brouillés que les yeux de femmes
Plus nets que regards d'homme seul

Ce sont les mots de la Mesure
Et le tambour à peine tu
Au tréfonds désormais remue
Son attente d'autres rivages

....

Toute parole est une terre
Il est de fouiller son sous-sol
Où un espace meuble est gardé
Brûlant, pour ce que l'arbre dit

C'est là que dorment les tam-tams
Dormant ils rêvent de flambeaux
Leur rêve bruit en marée
Dans le sous-sol des mots mesurés

....

Quelle pensée raide parcourt
Les fibres les sèves les muscles
De la douleur a-t-on fait un mot
Un mot nouveau qui multiplie

Celui qui parmi les neiges enfante
Un paysage une ville des soifs
Celui qui range ses tambours ses étoffes
Dans la sablure des paroles

....

Beauté de ce peuple d'aimants
Dans la limaille végétale et vous
Je vous cerne comme la mer
Avec ses fumures d'épaves

Beauté des routes multicolores
Dans la savane que rumine
L'autan plein de mots à éclore
Je vous mène à votre seuil

Ecoutant ruisseler mes tambours
Attendant l'éclat brusque des lames
L'éveil sur l'eau des danseurs
Et des chiens qui entre les jambes regardent

Dans ce bruit de fraternité
La pierre et son lichen ma parole
Juste mais vive demain pour vous
Telle fureur dans la douceur marine,

Je me fais mer où l'enfant va rêver.

ẽ

To know what cradles in your eyes
A bay of sky a bird
The sea, a caress deserved
The sun back here again

Beauty of space or hostage
Of the tentacular future
Every spoken word merges there
With the silence of the Waters

Beauty of times for a mirage
The time that stays is for waiting
The time that flies is a hurricane
Where it is the road that is scattered

....

Beauty of waiting Beauty of the waves
Waiting is almost a bowsprit
Entwined with wings and winds
Like litter on the bank

Every word comes without scarcely
Making the horizon move
The scenery is a sudden sifting
Of words uttered under the moon

To know what on your hair
Distraught first tries out its yoked team
And does the salt come from the sea
Or from this voice that is going around

....

The men come out of the earth
With their faces too strong
And the appetite of their gazes
On the sails of the clearings

The women walk in front of them
The whole island is soon a woman
Feeling sorry for herself but clenching
Her despair in her naked heart
....

Pitied this island and pitiful
She lives on derived words
Like a halo of castaways
About to meet the rocks

She needs words that last
And make the sky and the horizon
More blurred than women's eyes
Clearer than a lone man's gaze

These are the words of Measure
And the drum hardly silent
In its innermost depths henceforth stirs
Its waiting for other shores

....

Every word is a land
One must dig up its subsoil
Where a soft space is kept
Burning, for what the tree says

It is there the tom-toms sleep
Sleeping they dream of torches

Their dream murmurs like a tide
In the subsoil of measured words

....

What steep thought runs through
The fibers saps muscles
Has a word been made of grief
A new word that multiplies

He who amid the snows gives birth
To a scenery to a town to thirsts
He who sets up his drums his fabrics
In the sanding of spoken words

....

Beauty of this people of magnets
In the plant filings and you
I ring you round like the sea
With its manure of wrecks

Beauty of multicolored roads
In the savannah which the southwind
Ruminates full of words to be hatched
I take you to your threshold

Listening to my drums streaming
Waiting for the sharp slap of the oars
The awakening on the water of the dancers
And of the dogs peering out from between legs

In this noise of fraternity
The stone and its lichen my speech
Right but alive tomorrow for you

Such fury in the marine gentleness,

I make myself into a sea in which the child is going to dream.

In this second section (61-68), the poem assumes a rhythm and a graphically poetic form (46 free-verse quatrains and a single final line), to celebrate the real but deceptive beauty of the Caribbean. The starting point for the poet, however, is not emotion but rather, as the opening word suggests, the probing intellect ("Savoir"), as the poet seeks to find a reconciliation between his own poetic practice and the often contradictory beauties of his native land. Thus in the second stanza the paradoxical nature of the Caribbean is shown to match the contradictory nature of the poetic voice. In this evocation of the different aspects of the beauty of the Caribbean ("Beauté d'attente Beauté des vagues" [Beauty of waiting Beauty of the waves]), the poem becomes explicitly self-referential. The poet comments self-consciously on his own poetic activity, and the visual image of the landscape is transposed into the aural representation of the sound of words:

Chaque mot vient sans qu'on fasse
A peine bouger l'horizon
Le paysage est un tamis soudain
De mots poussés sous la lune

[Each word comes without scarcely / Making the horizon move / The scenery is a sudden sifting / Of words uttered under the moon].

What the poet is searching for is a quality of voice to capture and preserve the special nature of the Caribbean island identity: "le sel vient-il de la mer / Ou de cette voix qui circule" [And does salt come from the sea / Or from this voice that is going around]. In order to acquire this desired quality of voice, the poet's choices have to be narrowed and certain thematic avenues have to be rejected.

Hence, the themes to be rejected by the poet are listed (stanzas 9-11). As a result of these rejections there emerges a more authentic picture of the island, whose profoundly pitiful condition is reflected in the condition of the island's women: "L'île toute est bientôt femme / Apitoyée sur elle-même mais crispant / Son désespoir dans son cœur nu" [The whole island is soon a woman / Feeling sorry for herself but clenching / Her despair in her naked heart]. The state of the island is emphasized by the repetition, over the next four stanzas (14-17), of derivatives of "pitié" [pity]: "Apitoyée cette île et pitoyable / Elle vit de mots dérivés" [Pitied this island and pitiful / She lives on derived words]. The connotative richness of "mots dérivés" [derived words], which associates the inscribed condition of the island, as "rive" [shore], with lack of fixity, lack or loss of direction, otherness, foreign derivation, distortion, displacement, and deviation, accurately translates the cultural dilemma of both the poet and the island. The poet's awareness of this problematic determines the role he proposes for the writer of answering the island's need for fixity and rootedness: "Elle a besoin de mots qui durent" [She needs words that last]. As this section continues, therefore, the poet defines his own poetic role, in relation to both Europe and Africa: he becomes

> Celui qui parmi les neiges enfante
> Un paysage une ville des soifs
> Celui qui range ses tambours ses étoffes
> Dans la sablure des paroles

[He who amid the snows gives birth / To a scenery
to a town to thirsts / He who sets up his drums his
fabrics / In the sanding of spoken words].
Evidently, the poet is seeking a reconciliation, within the orality ("paroles" [spoken words]) of his poetry, of the various components of his cultural heritage, including the European ("neiges" [snows]) and the African ("tambours" [drums]) linkages. His native island is therefore invested with a beauty which resolves issues of

distinctions of color: "Beauté des routes multicolores" [Beauty of multicolored roads]. This poetic resolution of the dilemma permits this section to end on a visionary note of hope:

> Dans ce bruit de fraternité
> La pierre et son lichen ma parole
> Juste mais vive demain pour vous
> Telle fureur dans la douceur marine,
>
> Je me fais mer où l'enfant va rêver.

[In this noise of fraternity / The stone and its lichen my speech / Right but alive tomorrow for you / Such fury in the marine gentleness, / I make myself into a sea in which the child is going to dream.]

Prendra-t-il dans l'inconnu racine, s'effacera-t-il dans la douleur, comme un qui chante? Des ferveurs avoisinaient des lacs sur ton visage — le ciel inquiet des étoiles qui déjà lui manquent. Alors il conduisait des noces à leur havre. Cet oiseau s'envolait de lui, comme d'un fruit. Quel est ce cri, ô quel, sinon du seul pays désenlacé? Il portait sur l'espoir ces vocables des mers: des îles prononcées nettes, des archipels balbutiés, les continents (c'est un cri sourd), disant «j'ouvre pour vous ces rivages...» Et souhaitant «me prenne cette argile,» il s'enlevait de l'Incendie, avril avec ses mots. Voyez-le, voyez-le dériver sur telles splendeurs riveraines. Ses mots, ses épines, ou bien des rocs, si malhabiles, mal taillés. O Blancheurs, où le ciel est sans îles ! Voyez-le sur ce brasier se poser comme le flamant rose (égaré sur les mers) reposerait sans reposer, sur des typhons et des tumultes. D'où surgit-elle, suscitée,

mais étrangère à ce point ? Comme un horizon
illicite? Et ne disait-il pas, il y a si longtemps, «je
n'aime point cette femme,» sans connaître vraiment
s'il parlait encore de femme, ou (tellement l'attente
était vide et sournoise) plutôt de cette terre abusée,
là, où le sang pousse comme un cri?... Maintenant
les sables sont d'autre clarté. Il faut choisir, il faut
venir! soit par la mer, connue des martins-pêcheurs
aux songes funèbres, soit dans la terre, tronc noir
et nu... Et puis, la saviez-vous, cette entreprise de
bâtir le paysage? — parfois le cœur est écrasé, l'air
est hostile; parfois la main s'apaise — et la lumière
monte des choses comme une parole d'architecte.

❦

Will he take root in the unknown, will he
obliterate himself in grief, like someone who
sings? Fervors were close to lakes on your face —
the troubled sky of the stars he already misses.
Then he led nuptials to their haven. This bird flew
away from him, like from a fruit. What is this cry,
O what, if it is not that of the lone country
unloosed? He bore on hope these terms from the
seas: islands spoken clearly, archipelagoes
stammered, the continents (that's a dull cry), saying
"I open these shores for you ...." And wishing
"may this clay take me," he took off from the Fire,
April with his words. See him, see him drift on
such riparian splendors. His words, his thorns, or
else rocks, so awkward, badly carved.   O
Whitenesses, where the sky has no islands! See
him settle on this furnace like the pink flamingo
(lost on the seas) would rest without resting, on
typhoons and on storms. Where does she rise up

from, aroused, but a stranger to this point? Like an illicit horizon? And was he not saying, so long ago, "I do not like this woman," without knowing really whether he was still talking about a woman, or (so empty and cunning was the waiting) rather about this abused land, there, where blood grows like a shout? ... Now the sands are of a different clarity. One has to choose, one has to come! either by the sea, known to the kingfishers with funereal dreams, or in the land, a black and naked trunk ... And then, did you know it, this venture of building the scenery? — sometimes one's heart is crushed, the air is hostile; sometimes one's hand grows calm — and the light rises from things like an architect's saying.

The final section of four prose poems continues the poet's self-examination on the issue of his poetic role. His insecurity about himself and his hesitancy to assume full subjectivity are suggested by his presentation of a third person poetic persona designated as "il" [he] who is having a problem identifying himself as "je" [I]. In "Prendra-t-il dans l'inconnu racine ..." [Will he take root in the unknown...] (70), the poet poses the question of how to satisfy his own need for fixity and specificity and accepts that his own voice is a reflection of the situation of his native island, relative to the other Caribbean islands and to continental mainlands. The problem of an identifiable voice is thus shown to be related to the issue of geographical specificity. What is implied is that his own voice is the product of a specific island, and that clarity, identity, and specificity of voice are lost as the geographical area of identification gets larger: "Quel est le cri, ô quel, sinon du seul pays désenlacé? Il portait sur l'espoir ces vocables des mers: des îles prononcées nettes, des archipels balbutiés, les continents (c'est un cri sourd) ...." [What is this shout, O what, if it is not that of the lone country disentangled? He bore on hope these terms from the seas: islands spoken clearly, archipelagoes stammered, the continents (that's a dull shout)...]. Even his emotional relationship to his native land is presented as problematical, as the earlier association between "terre" [land] and "femme" [woman] is repeated:

> Et ne disait-il pas, il y a si longtemps, «je n'aime point cette femme,» sans connaître vraiment s'il parlait encore de femme, ou (tellement l'attente était vide et sournoise) plutôt de cette terre abusée, là, où le sang pousse comme un cri?

> [And was he not saying, so long ago, "I do not like this woman," without knowing really whether he was still talking about a woman, or (so empty and cunning was the waiting) rather about this abused land, there, where blood grows like a shout?]

The emotional ambivalence which marks the poet's attachment to his native land is compounded by feelings of discouragement resulting from his awareness of the magnitude of the creative task he has set himself: "Et puis, la saviez-vous, cette entreprise de bâtir le paysage? — parfois le cœur est écrasé, l'air est hostile; parfois la main s'apaise" [And then, did you know it, this enterprise of building the scene? — sometimes one's heart is crushed, the air is hostile; sometimes one's hand grows calm]. The frequent questions posed in this poem are indicative of the poet's lack of certainty and his continuing search for answers.

> Blancheurs! moiteurs du mot qui n'interpelle! Fièvre neigeuse, parements! Blancheur qui passe et qui érige. Il reparaît dans sa vie, quand cette voix l'assaille. Il capitule dans sa vie à nouveau droite en lui, mais sa parole est en éveil comme un rosier des jours de fête. Ah! Faudra-t-il enfin que je revienne et nomme, connaissant qu'il est de moi comme de l'arbre après

le vent? Et vous, à peine devinant ce cri des sangs qu'on a émus, ce fleuve allé au long de vous, la vie hélée de tremblements — vous devrai-je nommer afin que l'île vive (en vous)? Est-ce lave, sang, rumeur, sève du bruit, ou le vent, ces cortèges? Est-ce le vent, l'immobile affre des choses (mais voyez comme est déjà revenue blanche la parole), des fureurs sous la peau et des foules? Viendra le temps des capitales — où est la foule incendiée, — sinon le soleil est de neige! Alors, forçant l'écume, j'irai par les plages où meurt le mot, soudain juste. Voyez comme la parole a perdu des ses fouailles, des ses noirceurs. Où sont les îles? Qui amoncelle des boutures?... Il y aura des crispations, et les chants ivres des haies. Des sourires, la main qui offre, le temps clair. Et quelle présence encore, je le demande? Cependant je cherche, lourd et brûlant.

❦

Whitenesses! Clamminess of the word that does not call out! Snowy fever, facings! Whiteness passing and building. He reappears in his life, when this voice hails him. He capitulates in his life that is once again upright within him, but his speech is wide awake like a rosebush on holidays. Ah! Will I then have to come back and give names, knowing that I will be treated like trees after the wind? And you, hardly hearing this cry of bloods that have been moved, this river gone all along you, life greeted with tremblings — will I have to name you so that the island may live (in you)? Is it lava, blood, a rumbling, sap of noise, or is it the wind, these processions? Is it the wind, the

motionless pang of things (but see how speech has
already come back white), of rages under the skin
and of crowds? The time of capitals will surely
come — when the crowd is set on fire, — or else
the sun is of snow! Then, defying the foamy sea,
I will go by the beaches where the word dies,
suddenly right. See how speech has lost some of
its scourges, its blacknesses. Where are the
islands? Who is piling up the cuttings? ... There
will be contractions, and the drunken songs of the
hedges. Smiles, the offering hand, clear weather.
And what other presence, I ask? And yet I am
looking, heavy and burning.

The poet's quest for answers continues in this final prose poem
("Blancheurs! moiteurs du mot ..." [Whitenesses! Clamminess of
the word...] (71), in which the poet is still reflecting on and
tentatively articulating his conception of his poetic role. His
perspective is that of someone dominated linguistically and
culturally, as the opening exclamation indicates, by "blancheurs!"
[whitenesses]. This domination, which threatens the emergence of
his poetic voice, is emphasized by the associated image of "fièvre
neigeuse" [snowy fever] and the repetition of "blancheur"
[whiteness]. The poetic persona is hesitant, apprehensive about the
treatment he might receive, and unsure of his responsibility:
"Faudra-t-il enfin que je revienne et nomme, connaissant qu'il est de
moi comme de l'arbre après le vent?" [Will I then have to come
back and give names, knowing that I will be treated like trees after
the wind?]. The central question which he needs to resolve is:
"vous devrai-je nommer afin que l'île vive (en vous)" [will I have
to name you so that the island may live (in you)?]. The identity of
"vous" [you], continually addressed by the poet, remains obscure.
    The struggle for the poet is to find his own language, but
this is a difficult task. This language is threatened by the
persistence of "whiteness": "mais voyez-vous comme est déjà

revenue blanche la parole" [but see how speech has already come back white]. It is also shown to be in danger of losing its "blackness," thus making the identity of the Antillean islands difficult to establish: "Voyez comme la parole a perdu de ses fouailles, de ses noirceurs. Où sont les îles?" [See how speech has lost some of its scourges, its blacknesses. Where are the islands?]. This may be read in part as an indication of a movement away from the often bitter denunciations of Negritude-inspired poetry as practiced by Damas and Césaire. Glissant, however, is similarly driven by an unshaken determination and faith in the future: "Viendra le temps des capitales -- où est la foule incendiée -- sinon le soleil est de neige!" [The time of capitals will surely come - when the crowd is set on fire, -- or else the sun is of snow!]. He remains committed to his search for a language appropriate to his situation in this field of islands.

Already it is clear that Glissant, in his effort to define poetically the area he has designated as a "field of islands," is moving toward a poetic representation that includes a diversity of forms, both "prose" and "poetry." Within this diversity his personal challenge is to develop a voice that reflects the Antillean reality, not with nostalgic exoticism, but with full consciousness of the pitiful socioeconomic and psychological state of the region. His function, as an Antillean poet, is to recognize and reflect this diversity of cultural images which constitutes the Antillean real and imaginary "field," symbolized most comprehensively by the image of the sea. The poet has not yet satisfactorily identified the object of his poetic communication ("Et quelle présence encore, je le demande" [What other presence, I ask?]. Indeed, no questions are answered definitively in *Champ d'îles*. What emerges, however, even at the end of this final poem, as the poet's consistent response to the cultural issues that confront him, is a commitment to the process of discovery: "Cependant je cherche, lourd et brûlant" [And yet I am looking, heavy and burning].

FALAISE SECRÈTE

1

Pensa-t-il aux livres enfouis
Dans ces pays sans spectacles
Où les femmes n'ont plus de mains?
A ces fulgurances de roches
Que l'on voit aux rivages nus,
Guettant quelles vagues encore?

La mer l'avait envahi
D'un bord à l'autre de son amour.

2

Le mal que fait l'oiseau blessé
Au nuage qui l'achève,
Mais aussi la glace blanche
De tant de fièvres défrichées,
La plage qui troue la plage.
Il vous fait Dame de ce lieu
Ombelle nue que le vent porte,
Mue de brasiers beauté la nôtre.

Puis, si belle, la mer l'emporte.

....

5

En moi vous êtes montagne,
Pays ô visage impur
D'un pur visage fracassé.
L'orage bâtit ces murailles
La mer que tu hantes brûle
Je ne vois d'oiseaux qu'apeurés.

Croyez-vous que l'orage mente?
Ces murailles nous ont traqués.

....

8
Labour, ô pays, pur visage
D'un visage impur et blessé.
Le vent dans l'oiseau fait liesse
L'orage vous a délaissée
Ici commence la cassure.

Et cueillez à l'orgue l'orage,
En vous il mue et n'a de cesse
Que ne soit plus nuit ce murmure.

❦

SECRET CLIFF

1
Did he think about the books buried
In these countries with no shows
Where women no longer have hands?
About these dazzling rocks
One sees on the naked shores
That lie in wait for what other waves?

The sea had invaded him
From edge to edge with its love.

2
The harm the wounded bird does
To the cloud that brings it to a close,
But the white ice too

Of so many fevers cleared,
The beach that makes a hole in the beach.
He makes you Lady of this place
Naked umbel borne by the wind,
Driven by coal-fires our own beauty...

Then, so beautiful, the sea takes him away.

....

5

In me you are a mountain,
Country O impure face
Of a pure face shattered.
The storm builds these walls
The sea you haunt is burning
The only birds I see are scared.
Do you think that the storm may be lying?
These walls have tracked us down.

....

8

Toil, O country, pure face
Of an impure and wounded face.
The wind makes jubilation in the bird
The storm has deserted you
Here begins the break.

And gather the storm on the organ,
In you it moves and will not rest
Till this murmuring be no longer night.

Glissant's second collection, *La Terre inquiète* (1954) [*The Disturbed Land*], consists also of three sections. The first section,

"Le Mouvement, loin des rivages" [Movement, Far Away From the Shores], itself comprises three formally dissimilar poems: "Théâtre" [Theater], a free verse poem with a mixture of italicized and non-italicized type-face; "Océan" [Ocean], a prose poem; and "Incantation" [Incantation], a brief dialogue of mixed verse and prose. The title of the second section lends itself to that of the whole collection, "La terre inquiète," and consists of five verse poems of varying lengths. The third section, "Le Retour à la mer" [Return to the Sea], is also divided into three subsections: "La maison des sables" [The House of Sands], "Versets" [Verses], and the single, short prose poem "Sacre" [Consecration].

The "secret cliff" of "Falaise secrète" (85-88), as Glissant once explained in an unpublished interview with me, refers to a spot in the north of Martinique where a group of Carib "Indians" threw themselves into the sea rather than submit to European colonization. This location thus acts as powerful source of inspiration for the poet and as a symbol of the way in which geography and history have converged to create a specific Antillean reality. By bringing such a little known element of the island's landscape and history back to life, Glissant contributes to the rebirth of his country. There is a constant interplay between the different personas represented by the pronouns "il" [he], "je" [I], "vous" [you], and "nous" [we]. As the poem opens, the poet establishes a distance between himself and an unspecified third-person persona designated in the first line as "il" who could be the poet's *alter ego*: "Pensa-t-il aux livres enfouis / Dans ces pays sans spectacles / Où les femmes n'ont plus de mains?" [Did he think about the books buried / In these countries with no shows / Where women no longer have hands?]. The question serves to focus attention on the subject of literary production ("livres" [books]), in a cultural and geographical context ("ces pays sans spectacles" [these countries with no shows], "ces fulgurances de roches" [these dazzling rocks], and "rivages nus" [naked shores]) that is evocative of the Caribbean islands, which all share a common feature in the omnipresence of the sea. Significantly, the Caribbean connection to the third person "l'" [him] is signaled by the fact that it is the powerful action of the sea which closes the first two sections of the poem: "La mer l'avait envahi / D'un bord à l'autre de son amour" [The sea had invaded him / from edge to edge with its love]; and "Puis, si belle, la mer l'emporte" [Then, so beautiful, the sea takes him away.]

The poet reaches a climax of emotional identification with his native land in the fifth section, where, in three economical lines, he conveys the magnitude and dominance of the role played by his native land in the poet's life and the feelings of love, pride, pain, regret, and compassion which accompany his sensitivity to the fragmentation of his cultural homeland: "En moi vous êtes montagne, / Pays ô visage impur / D'un pur visage fracassé" [In me you are a mountain, / Country O impure face / Of a pure face shattered]. By the end of the poem, however, this negative image becomes reversed, as the poet visualizes the emergence of a new country created out of past suffering and defilement: "Labour, ô pays, pur visage / D'un visage impur et blessé" [Toil, O country, pure face / Of an impure and wounded face.] This last section of the poem indicates that the poet considers his own poetic activity as a means of breaking the cycle of pain and of bringing peace to the storm-tossed island: "L'orage vous a délaissée / Ici commence la cassure" [The storm has deserted you / Here begins the break]. It is with the poem itself ("ce murmure" [this murmuring]) that the process of change begins.

PROMENOIR DE LA MORT SEULE

La baie triste n'a pas bougé
Sur un lac de roses, jonchée
De morts pâlis dans les rosiers
Baie funèbre elle est demeurée

La rive hésite la mer passe
Les barques sont laveuses d'eau
Noir est le sable, la couleur

Est évidente dans ce lieu

Les oiseaux y vêtent de gris
L'azur trouble de leurs envols
Telle évidence a rendu folle
La première vague échouée

Vagues de folie en folie
Hâves les autres ont suivi
Les rosiers ont gardé l'aumône
Des suicidés, à leur surplis

La race blanche des frégates
Jamais ne vient à ces repas
Elles vont sonner d'autres glas
Où le vent ne porte point gants

Ici ne bougent que l'émoi
Du souvenir et ce haut cri
Qu'un midi d'août on entendit
Sur la falaise et son troupeau

Un cri de terre qui déploie
Les nervures de son été
Parce qu'amour l'aura fouillée
Ou que la pluie est avenante

Un cri de femme labourée
A la limite des jachères
Ses seins nubiles partagés
Entre la misère et la mousse

Cri de verrous et cri d'orfraie
Et ce peuple était endormi
L'oiseau rapace fait son nid

Sur la cendre de l'arbre, vive

Et ne bouge encore que lait
Des goémons cette senteur,
La mort vivifie la mort
Baie funèbre elle est demeurée

Mais triste elle n'a bougé
Sur son lac de haines, jonchée
De morts pâlis dans les halliers
Qui vous pardonnent, ô rosiers.

❦

WALKWAY OF LONELY DEATH

The sad bay on a lake of roses
Has not moved, strewn
With corpses grown pale in the rosetrees
A bay of death it has remained

The shore wavers the sea passes
The boats are women washing water
Black is the sand, color
Is obvious in this place

Birds clothe in grey
The murky azure of their flights
The first wave to be wrecked
Has been driven mad by this evidence

Waves from madness to madness
Have wanly followed the others
The rosetrees have kept the alms
Of the suicides, in their surplices

The white race of the frigates
Never comes to these meals
They go to toll other knells
Where the wind wears no gloves

No movement here but the stir
Of memory and this loud cry
Heard one August noon
On the cliff and its flock

The cry of a land unfurling
The nervures of its summer
Because love dug it up
Or because rain is pleasant

The cry of a woman ploughed
To the very limit of her fallows
Her nubile breasts shared
Between poverty and moss

Cry of bolts and an eagle's cry
And this people was asleep
The bird of prey makes its nest
On the live ashes of the tree

And still no movement but the milk
Of wracks this smell,
Death gives life to death
A bay of death it has remained

But sad it has not moved
On its lake of hate, strewn
With corpses grown pale in the thickets
That forgive you, O rosetrees.

"Promenoir de la mort seule" ["Walkway of Lonely Death"] (89-90) presents the highly figurative description of a bay that is associated in the poet's mind with the sadness of abandonment and death: "De morts pâlis dans les rosiers" [With corpses grown pale in the rosetrees]. This description evokes the memory of Martinique's best known natural disaster, the eruption of Mount Pelée in 1902, which completely destroyed the northern town of Saint-Pierre. This association is given validity by the reference to black sand, which typically occurs in volcanic regions: "Noir est le sable" [Black is the sand].

As the poem develops, the poet establishes a link and a contrast between these deaths and others caused by the past (slave-trade) and continuing exploitative activities of whites:

> La race blanche des frégates
> Jamais ne vient à ces repas
> Elles vont sonner d'autres glas
> Où le vent ne porte point gants

[The white race of the frigates / Never comes to these meals / They go to toll other knells / Where the wind wears no gloves].

The historical and geographical context suggested by the poet points to his sensitivity to the need for reawakening the memories associated with this bay and for listening to the voice which issues from such a place of desolation: "Ici ne bougent que l'émoi / Du souvenir et ce haut cri" [No movement here but the stir / Of memory and this loud cry]. The poem explores the different manifestations of this voice: it is at once "un cri de terre" [the cry of a land], and "un cri de femme labourée" [the cry of a woman ploughed], as well as a "cri de verrous et cri d'orfraie" [A cry of bolts and an eagle's cry]. What is particularly significant for the poet, however, is the fact that the voice has remained unheard: "Et ce peuple était endormi" [And this people was asleep].

Once again Glissant turns to an element of the land as a witness to and participant in the country's history. This geographical element is given a voice that speaks to the real experience of the country. The poem serves as a means of compensating for the lack of attention paid to the voice issuing from the bay, which functions as a metonymy of the whole island and by extension even of the whole Caribbean.

LE LIVRE DES OFFRANDES

Réanimée en ce secret
Je vous connais être la rive
Qu'allumèrent sur leur amour
Imperceptibles les vigies

Ils parcouraient des lieux obscurs
Où la parole se devine
Et où les mains prennent racine
Entre des signes séculaires

O animée labour muet
Vous étiez tige hiératique
Victime ou gemme des tempêtes
Je vous connais être mystère

Désir enfance du matin
Le cri noué le sang noué
Sang dénoué de nos douleurs
Et son enfance sans désir

Je vous connais être l'enfance
Encore là, je vous connais
Avoir grandi, rouvre muet
Sur l'équivoque de vos pierres

Epouvantée d'être sur l'eau
Telle une foule solennelle
Désendrapée sur vos autels
Ils vous auront toute traquée

Sur l'amour unique des rives
Vous éparpillez votre corps
En vain: l'orage est déjà mort
Tout est grave sans parenté

O ce lieu est lice d'outrages
La ronce y fleurit bassement
Les amours y vivent de ruines
Je vous connais donjon des eaux

Terre immobile et murée
Dans votre silence, fragile
Il n'est qu'un lieu pour vérité
Qui prenne la douleur, ô dolente

Il n'est qu'un lieu qui pour été
Élise l'homme des collines
L'emplisse d'ardentes victimes
Lui enseigne la cruauté

Où est l'unique tant crié?
Ce peuple meurt, êtes-vous son silence
Éternité d'orages devinée
Sur la souffrance

Splendeur ô raison fugace
Éclaboussure seule manne
Vagues qui êtes l'ouverture
Et veille des corps sans souci

Tout est nu, riche, sauf d'appâts
Vers le gros des terres je peine
O j'abandonne les marées
— Vous connaissant être mystere

Et rivage, quand tout s'éteint.

❦

BOOK OF OFFERTORIES

You reanimated in this secret
I know you to be the shore
The imperceptible watches
Lit up on their love

They traveled through dark places
Where the spoken word is dimly heard
And where hands take root
Between secular signs

O animated one, silent toil
You were a hieratic stem
Victim or gemstone of the storms
I know you to be mystery

Desire childhood of morning
Cry knotted blood knotted
Unknotted blood of our sufferings
And its childhood without desire

I know you to be childhood
Still there, I know you
To have grown up, reopen silent
On the ambiguity of your stones

Terrified at being on water
Like a solemn crowd
Undraped on your altars
They will have utterly tracked you down

On the sole love of the shores
You scatter your body
In vain: the storm is already dead
All is serious without relations

O this place is the arena for insults
Thorns meanly flourish there
Loves live there on ruins
I know you donjon of the waters

Land immobile and immured
In your silence, fragile
There is but one place for truth
Which takes grief, O mournful one

There is but one place which for summer
Elects the man from the hills
Fills him with ardent victims
Teaches him cruelty

Where is the only one shouted for so much?
This people is dying, are you its silence
Eternity of storms glimpsed
On suffering

Splendor O fleeting reason
Splash sole manna
You waves who are the opening
And sleeplessness of bodies without care

All is naked, rich, free from lures
To reach the main part of the lands I toil
O I abandon the tides
— Knowing you to be mystery
And shore, when everything is snuffed out.

In "Le livre des offrandes" ["Book of Offertories"] (91-93), the connotations of the title indicate that the poem is a form of sacred literature, a concrete token of faith. In this poem, faith is demonstrated, and the poet's special knowledge of and relationship with his native land are affirmed, through the repetition of the phrase "je vous connais" [I know you] which runs as a *leitmotif* throughout the poem. In the evocative and hermetic first line of the poem ("Réanimée en ce secret" [Reanimated in this secret]), the poem is represented as a form of secret communication between the poet and the unspecified female entity personified and addressed as "vous" [you] in the second line. It is only in the ninth stanza that "terre" [land] appears as the noun governing the past participles "réanimée" [reanimated] (of the first stanza), "animée" [animated] (of the third stanza), and "épouvantée" [terrified] (of the sixth), emphasizing the "femme"/"terre" [woman/land] equation that runs through Glissant's poetry. The poem, therefore, is presented as the literal means by which the poet's land acquires life.

The first aspect of the land identified by the poet, however, is that of "la rive," the shore line where sea and land converge. The connection between the first and second stanzas is provided by "les vigies" [watches] (normally a feminine noun used to refer to males), who become the masculine "ils" [they] of the second stanza. Here the country is presented in metaphorical terms, which suggest the mysteries of a different and unfamiliar language and way of life:

Ils parcouraient des lieux obscurs
Où la parole se devine
Et où les mains prennent racine
Entre des signes séculaires

[They traveled through dark places / Where the
spoken word is dimly heard / And where hands
take root / Between secular signs]

It is within this context that poetic activity ("parole" [spoken
word], "mains" [hands], "signes" [signs]) takes place. The
characterization of the country as "animée" [animated] invites,
particularly within the context of the allusions to mysterious
manifestations, linkages to the animism often associated with many
African cultures. The change in the poet's connection to this African
heritage is transmitted in his use of the past tense ("Vous étiez tige
hiératique" [You were a hieratic stem]), which contrasts with the
present tense assertion: "Je vous connais être mystère" [I know you
to be mystery]. "Tige hiératique" [hieratic stem], moreover, evokes
an ancient tradition of writing which has been broken, but from
which the poet derives inspiration for his poetic voice.

In the fourth stanza, "le cri" [cry]) and "le sang" [blood])
become fused ("noué" [knotted]), as the poet reflects on the
association between desire and childhood and on the bond of shared
pain ("nos" [our]) that link him to his cultural heritage:

Désir enfance du matin
Le cri noué le sang noué
Sang dénoué de nos douleurs
Et son enfance sans désir

[Desire childhood of morning / Cry knotted blood
knotted / Unknotted blood of our sufferings / And
its childhood without desire]

Significantly, the salient feature that is constant in both childhood
and maturity is the quality of silence, designated through "muet"
[silent] in the third and fifth stanzas. This characterization strongly
implies that the poem is a means by which the need for a voice is
answered. The image of the "rive" [shore] from the first stanza is
repeated in the seventh, where the female persona is represented as

a dispersed body emotionally attached to orphaned "rives." This metonymy signifies the African diaspora, particularly in the context of the Caribbean islands:

> Sur l'amour unique des rives
> Vous éparpillez votre corps
> En vain: l'orage est déjà mort
> Tout est grave sans parenté

> [On the sole love of the shores / You scatter your
> body / In vain: the storm is already dead / All is
> grave without relations].

In the ninth stanza, the female persona to which the poetic communication is addressed is finally named and identified with qualities of lifelessness and vulnerability which contrast with the life and vigor implicit in the opening word ("Réanimée" [reanimated]) of the poem: "Terre immobile et murée / Dans votre silence, fragile [Land immobile and immured / In your silence, fragile]. Indeed it is the quality of silence, associated with death, which impacts most upon the poet: "Où est l'unique tant crié? / Ce peuple meurt, êtes-vous son silence" [Where is the only one talked about so much? / This people is dying, are you its silence?]. The poet here questions the validity of European individualistic philosophy, which is the source of all European writing. It is against this silence, the inappropriateness of European philosophy, that the poet struggles, representing his activity as a movement inward from the shoreline to the more substantial parts of the land:

> Vers le gros des terres je peine
> O j'abandonne les marées
> — Vous connaissant être mystère

> Et rivage, quand tout s'éteint

[To reach the main part of the lands I toil / O I
abandon the tides / — Knowing you to be mystery
/ And shore, when everything is snuffed out]

The frequency with which the self-referential preoccupation
with orality occurs even in the sample of poems we have examined
is too striking to ignore. The word "cri" appears in "Tourmentes...,"
"Prendra-t-il...," "Blancheurs...," and "Promenoir...." References to
"parole," "mot," and "voix" occur in "Vous, présence...," "Savoir...,"
"Prendra-t-il...," and "Blancheurs...." Glissant's poetry presents
itself explicitly and implicitly as an affirmation of the voice needed
to counteract the force of deathly European silence (see
"Tourmentes..." and "Ce jour") which has marked the separation of
the poet's native land from the solidity of Africa. Poetry is the
manifestation of the new life of the Caribbean.

L'APPEL

*1492. Les Grands Découvreurs s'élancent
sur l'Atlantique, à la recherche des Indes. Avec
eux le poème commence. Tous ceux aussi, avant et
après ce Jour Nouveau, qui ont connu leur rêve,
en ont vécu ou en sont morts. L'imagination crée
à l'homme des Indes toujours suscitées, que
l'homme dispute au monde. Ceux qui partirent
d'Espagne et du Portugal, convoitant l'or et les
épices; mais soldats et mystiques aussi. Le Chant
nomme le père Labat, jacobin et corsaire; puis ce
nègre prophète qu'il fit fouetter à sang, lequel
avait vu grandir sur la mer, avant qu'ils eussent
paru, les bateaux; et nomme Toussaint-
Louverture, esclave et libérateur d'Haïti... Mais il
ne faut pas anticiper sur l'histoire: voici le port en
fête, l'aventure qui se noue; le rêve s'épuise dans*

son projet. L'homme a peur de son désir, au moment de le satisfaire.

1

Sur Gênes va s'ouvrir le pré des cloches d'aventures.
O lyre d'airain et de vent, dans l'air lyrique de départs,
L'ancre est à jour!... Et la très douce hébétude,
Qu'on la tarisse! au loin d'une autre salaison.
O le sel de la mer est plus propice ici que l'eau bénite de l'évêque,
Cependant que la foule fait silence; et elle entend la suite de l'histoire...
Ville, écoute; et sois pieuse! Religion te sera faite dans nos cœurs,
Qui avons su l'émoi et la boussole, et d'autres œuvres sur la voile...

ॐ

THE CALL

1492. The Great Discoverers launch themselves on the Atlantic, in search of the Indies. With them the poem begins. All those too, before and after this New Day, who have known their dream, have either lived on this dream or have died from it. Imagination creates for man Indies that are continually being conjured up, over which man fights in the world. Those who set off from Spain or Portugal, lusting after gold and spices; but soldiers and mystics too. The Canto names Father Labat, a Jacobin and a pirate; then this

negro prophet whom he had whipped till he bled,
the one who had seen the boats, before they had
appeared, grow large on the sea; and names
Toussaint-Louverture, slave and liberator of
Haiti... But we must not look ahead into the story:
here is the port celebrating, the adventure which is
beginning; the dream fails in its project. Man is
afraid of his desire, at the moment of satisfying it.

1

On Genoa the meadow of the bells of adventures is
going to open.
O lyre of brass and wind, in the lyrical air of
departures,
The anchor is up to date!... And the very sweet
stupor,
Let it be dried up! in the distance of another
salting.
O the salt of the sea is more propitious here than
the bishop's holy water,
Meanwhile the crowd keeps silent; and hears the
rest of the story...
Listen, town; and be pious! Religion will be made
for you in our hearts,
We who have known agitation and the compass,
and other works on sailing...

Les Indes [The Indies] is a long epic poem, divided into a series of
six main free verse parts, comprising a total of sixty-five numbered
units. Each of these major divisions is preceded by an introductory
prose passage in italics, titled consecutively "L'Appel" [The Call],
"Le Voyage" [The Journey], "La Conquête" [Conquest], "La Traite"
[The Slave Trade], "Les Héros" [The Heroes], and "La Relation"
[Relation]. (In the earlier (1963) edition of *Poèmes*, these sections

were labeled "Chants" [Cantos]. The use of the term "chant" to designate the formal divisions of the poem attests to a privileging of the oral in consonance with the Antillean cultural tradition.) Each introductory prose passage provides a narrative commentary on the subject-matter of the canto, highlighting significant occurrences and personalities, and re-interpreting the traditional (European) version of events.

The introduction to the first part, "L'Appel" [The Call] (109), indicates the direction the whole poem is going to take: "1492. Les Grands Découvreurs s'élancent sur l'Atlantique, à la recherche des Indes. Avec eux le poème commence" [1492. The Great Discoverers launch themselves on the Atlantic, in search of the Indies. With them the poem begins]. The poem presents itself as an imaginative recreation of the development of the cultural and geographical anomaly designated by Europeans as "Les Indes" [the Indies]. Ironically the birth of this Antillean poem is linked directly to the imaginative impulse of Europeans. Moreover, the "Indies" represent a constant in human experience. They serve as a powerful and eternal symbol of man's imagination and desire: "L'imagination crée à l'homme des Indes toujours suscitées, que l'homme dispute au monde" [Imagination creates for man Indies that are continually being conjured up, over which man fights in the world]. Consequently, the poet can appreciate the diversity among the Europeans leaving in search of "Indies": "Ceux qui partirent d'Espagne et du Portugal, convoitant l'or et les épices; mais soldats et mystiques aussi" [Those who set off from Spain or Portugal, lusting after gold and spices; but soldiers and mystics too].

This introduction gives an indication of the intended function of the whole poem: the rewriting of Antillean history, naming individuals who played significant roles in this history, reinterpreting the role of the infamous Father Labat (Père Labat [1663-1738] was a brutal French Dominican priest who has left extensive written accounts of his voyages to the Caribbean), giving prominence and dignity to the African victim of Labat's cruelty, and noting the contribution of Toussaint-Louverture: "Le Chant nomme le père Labat, jacobin et corsaire; puis ce nègre prophète qu'il fit fouetter à sang, lequel avait vu grandir sur la mer, avant qu'ils eussent paru, les bateaux; et nomme Toussaint-Louverture, esclave et libérateur d'Haïti..." [The Canto names Father Labat, a Jacobin and a pirate; then this negro prophet whom he had whipped till he bled, the one who had seen the boats, before they had appeared, grow large on the sea; and names Toussaint-Louverture, slave and liberator of Haiti...]. The tortured African slave forms a link with the poet himself, in their mutual desire to exploit the prophetic potential of language. Thus the slave's vision and heroism in the face of his torture at the hands of Père Labat serve as a model for Glissant. It is evident, however, that his interest is not in condemnation but rather in lucidity. At the end of this first introductory section he drives home the point that the situation of the departing Europeans contains a lesson about the human condition in general: "L'homme a peur de son désir, au moment de le satisfaire" [Man is afraid of his desire, at the moment of satisfying it].

The first numbered section of the poem (111) presents the Mediterranean port city of Genoa as the starting point for the great European adventure ("Sur Gênes va s'ouvrir le pré des cloches d'aventures" [On Genoa the meadow of the bells of adventures is going to open]). In this passage the liquidity of the alliterative "l's" ("le pré," "lyre," "l'air lyrique," "l'ancre" etc.) and the sibilant "s's" ("douce," tarisse," salaison") prepare for the dominance of the central image of the salty sea: "le sel de la mer est plus propice ici que l'eau bénite de l'évêque" [the salt of the sea is more propitious here than the bishop's holy water]. The sea operates in *Les Indes*, as it generally does for Glissant, as a multidimensional symbol, establishing geographical and historical linkages between the Caribbean, Europe and Africa, and indicating a common arena of suffering for blacks. At the same time, its concentrated saltiness, which can act as a preservative, is linked both to the experience of torture itself (literal salt in the wounds) and to the potential for survival.

As this first section ends, the poet adopts, through the use of "nous" [us], the situation of the European masses, identifying with common experiences in relation to upheavals connected to the sea: "Qui avons su l'émoi et la boussole, et d'autres œuvres sur la voile..." [We who have known agitation and the compass, and other works on sailing...]. The symbolic resonance of the statement with which this canto ends ("Les Indes sont éternité" [The Indies are eternity]) (88) indicates that the "Indies" have a symbolic importance for the poet that transcends purely racial or ethnic considerations. The poet's role, within the framework of this recreation, is to gain historical perspective and project a vision that is true for the complex phenomenon known as the Caribbean or West Indies.

XLII

Il dit:
«Tu m'as leurré, femme de ce couchant!   O
vertiges! O trombes!
«L'amant venu de loin, que peut-il boire encore,
quelle ardeur, ô lune?
«Je sais l'amour sauvage qui se dépeuple et
déracine, c'est le mien!
«Tant de sueurs et tant de mers, pour à la fin cette
désolation! O je demeure!
«Et j'écartèlerai ta fiente de jaguars et de serpents!
Moi, entré par la Porte du Soleil!
«Je sais là-bas un peuple, dont je ferai commerce;
que j'attelerai à ta mamelle.
«Amour tenace, pour tes amants que j'ai tués, me
mène où sont les lourds poissons rampants.
«Un peuple, ô femme, qui t'aura toute la nuit pour
sa douleur et son plaisir.
«A l'aurore je gratterai l'écorce noire et ferai choir
la rosée secrète.

«Afin que mon désir prenne forme durable! Afin
que le matin m'apartienne, et la lune aussi!»
Or la terre pleurait, sachant quelle est l'éternité.

ॐ

XLII

He spoke:
"You tricked me, woman of this sunset!   O
vertigos! O waterspouts!
The lover come from afar, what more can he drink,
what ardor, O moon?
I know about wild love having to exile and uproot
itself, that's my love!
So much sweat and so many seas, for at the end
this desolation! O I am staying!
And I shall rip apart your droppings from jaguars
and serpents! I, who came in through the Door of
the Sun!
I know a people over there on whom I'll trade;
whom I shall yoke to your breast.
Tenacious love, for your lovers whom I have
killed, leads me where the heavy crawling fish are.
A people, O woman, who will have you all night
long for its pain and its pleasure.
At dawn I will scrape the black bark and make the
secret dew fall.
So that my desire may take lasting form! So that
morning may belong to me, and the moon too!"
So the land wept, knowing what eternity is.

In the third part of the poem, entitled "La Conquête" [Conquest],
designated in the introductory prose passage as a "Tragique Chant
d'amour avec la terre nouvelle" (129) [Tragic Canto of love with the

new land], the poet evokes the destructive passage of the Conquistadors (Cortez, Pizarro, Almagro, Bilbao) through the "new land." Significantly, he emphasizes that these destructive "Conquerors" are driven by an obsessive dream: "l'homme ne renonce pas au rêve" [man does not give up the dream] (109). This part provides a recreation, in a series of passages introduced by "Il dit" [He spoke], of the voice of the typical European "Conqueror," who in the poem is permitted to justify his lust and the rape and murder of the indigenous populations.

In section XLII (138), the final section of this third part of the poem, both the European speaker and the narrator-poet participate in the persona of the "Il" [He]. This abolition of distance permits the poet to enter more fully into the European imaginary world. The European presents himself as a lover deceived by the geographical displacement of the Indies, while the unexpectedly "western" Indian island is once again represented as a woman, "Tu m'as leurré, femme de ce couchant" [You tricked me, woman of this sunset]. The poet thus implies that the designated identity of the West Indian is an aberration of misguided, frustrated, and disillusioned Europeans. The poet, moreover, characterizes these Europeans, through their own voice, as conscious of their own alienation and deracination : "Je sais l'amour sauvage qui se dépeuple et déracine, c'est le mien!" [I know about wild love having to exile and uproot itself, that's my love!]. Thus the distance between poet and European is completely abolished and the poet is able to establish an emotional and situational bond even with these Europeans. He conveys, furthermore, his understanding that the decision to engage in the slave trade was initiated partly out of the Europeans' need to compensate for their own frustrations and out of their quest, in the exploitation of African culture, for a magical solution to their dissatisfaction: "Je sais là-bas un peuple, dont je ferai commerce; que j'attellerai à ta mamelle. /... / A l'aurore je gratterai l'écorce noire et ferai choir la rosée secrète [I know a people over there on whom I'll trade; whom I shall yoke to your breast. /... / At dawn I will scrape the black bark and make the secret dew fall.] The European persistence in a quest that is ultimately futile provokes the narrator-poet to conclude in the final line of this canto, "Or la terre pleurait, sachant quelle est l'éternité" [So the land wept, knowing what eternity is]. The final word, "l'éternité" [eternity] is used throughout this third part of the poem to end several of the numbered sections, XXXIV (132), XXXV (133), XXXVI (134), XXXVII (134), XXXIX (136), and XL (137). This repetition emphasizes both the eternity of suffering to be endured by the "Indies" as a result of the slave trade which is evoked in the fourth part and the way in which the concepts of history and time are going to be transformed for these slaves and their descendants.

LA TRAITE

La Traite. Ce qu'on n'effacera jamais de la face de la mer. Sur la rive occidentale de l'Afrique, les marchands de chair font provison. Pendant deux siècles le fructueux trafic, plus ou moins avoué, fournit les Iles, le Nord de l'Amérique, et à non moindre proportion, le Centre et le Sud. C'est un massacre ici (au réservoir de l'Afrique) afin de compenser le massacre là-bas. La monstrueuse mobilisation, la traversée oblique, le Chant de Mort. Un langage de déraison, mais qui porte raison nouvelle. Car aussi le commencement d'une Unité, l'autre partie d'un accord enfin commué. C'est l'Inde de souffrance, après les Indes du rêve. Maintenant la réalité est fille de l'homme vraiment: née des contradictions qu'il a vécues et suscitées.

❧

THE SLAVE TRADE

> *The Slave Trade. Which will never be erased from the face of the sea. On the western shore of Africa, the flesh merchants stock up. During two centuries the profitable traffic, more or less admitted, supplied the Islands, the North of America, and to no less an extent, the Center and the South. It is a massacre here (in the reservoir of Africa) to compensate for the massacre over there. The monstrous mobilization, the oblique crossing, the Canto of Death. A language of unreason, but one that carries a new reason. For also the beginning of a Unity, the other part of an agreement finally commuted. It is the India of suffering, after the Indies of dream. Now reality is truly the daughter of man: born from the contradictions he has experienced and aroused.*

The slave trade, the shameful, hidden, experience of Antillean history, is recreated in this fourth part ("La Traite" ["The Slave Trade"]) (139), where it is immortalized and restored to its central importance within the historical and imaginary landscape of Antilleans: "Ce qu'on n'effacera jamais de la face de la mer" [Which will never be erased from the face of the sea]. The narrator presents the Europeans as "marchands de chair" [flesh merchants], engaged in what was for them a profitable commercial venture ("le fructueux trafic"). The historical rewriting draws attention to the fact that as many slaves were sent to Central and South America as to the North ("et à non moindre proportion, le Centre et le Sud" [and to no less an extent, the Center and the South]. This monstrous historical occurrence is translated poetically into "le Chant de Mort" [the Canto of Death]. The narrator as poet is conscious of the paradox implicit in this situation, since his activity as an Antillean writer is related to the occurrence of the slave trade, which is also the starting point for the emergence of the complex cultural community of Antilleans: "Un langage de déraison, mais qui porte raison nouvelle. Car aussi le commencement d'une Unité, l'autre partie d'un accord enfin commué." [A language of unreason, but one that carries a new reason. For also the beginning of a Unity, the other part of an agreement finally commuted.] The poet-narrator is painfully aware that the Antillean reality is the result of the contradictions surrounding the slave trade: "Maintenant la réalité est fille de l'homme vraiment: née des contradictions qu'il a vécues et suscitées" [Now reality is truly the daughter of man: born from the contradictions he has experienced and aroused].

IL

On a cloué un peuple aux bateaux de haut bord, on a vendu, loué, troqué la chair. Et la vieillesse pour le menu, les hommes aux moissons de sucres, et la femme pour le prix de son enfant. Il n'est plus de mystère ni d'audace: les Indes sont marché de mort; le vent le clame maintenant, droit sur la proue! Ceux qui ont incendié l'amour et le désir; ce sont Navigateurs. Ils ont tourné la face vers la forêt, ils demandent, muets, quelque parole. Langage, une autre fois, de nudité. Pour le muscle, tant de mots. O Langage désert, et sa grammaire mortuaire! Pour la denture, encore tant... Jusqu'à l'Oméga du monde nouveau! Or, très-anciennement, je vois Xerxès menant ses gens à l'abreuvoir, à l'heure où tu deviens rouge d'un autre espoir, soleil. Xerxès, maître trahi qui te fustige puis t'insulte, mer. Avez-vous oublié l'abreuvoir de douleurs et le fouet de la lumière? Je vois un soleil cru et une mer de lassitudes, qui entretiennent sur le sang les grandes Indes sans mystère.

ꙮ

IL

They nailed a people to tall-sided boats,
they sold, hired out, bartered flesh. And old age
for meals, men to sugar harvests, and woman for
the price of her child. It is no longer a question of
mystery or daring: the Indies are a death market;
the wind proclaims it now, straight on the prow!
Those who have set fire to love and desire; they
are Navigators. They have turned their faces
toward the forest, silently they ask for something to
be said. A language, once again, of nudity. For
muscles, so many words. O deserted Language,
and its mortuary grammar! For teeth, again so
many .... Right up to the Omega of the new world!
Now, very long ago in the past, I see Xerxes
leading his people to the trough, at the hour when
you, sun, become red with another hope. Xerxes,
betrayed master who thrashes you and then insults
you, sea. Have you forgotten the drinking trough
of pains and the whip of the light? I see a fierce
sun and a sea of lassitude that maintain the great
unmysterious Indies on blood.

In this fourth part, in order to represent this new and harsher
experience, the poet changes from free-verse to adopt the form of
the prose poem: "Choses horribles, prose dure" [horrible things,
hard prose](142). Thus the stylized elegance of the earlier cantos
gives way to a more conversational and declamatory style. In this
section (IL) (145), the experience of slavery is presented in stark
terms, the simplicity of which is conveyed by the use of the
impersonal "on" [they] and the similarly impersonal nouns made
generic by their accompanying definite articles ("la chair" [flesh], la

vieillesse" [old age], "les hommes" [men], and "la femme" [woman]): "On a cloué un peuple aux bateaux de haut bord, on a vendu, loué, troqué la chair. Et la vieillesse pour le menu, les hommes aux moissons de sucres, et la femme pour le prix de son enfant" [They nailed a people to tall-sided boats, they sold, hired out, bartered flesh. And old age for meals, men to sugar harvests, and woman for the price of her child].

The central concern of the poet, literally and figuratively, is the nature and role of "langage" [language] in the context of this slave trade. He subverts transparencies of denotation, establishing more accurate equivalencies: thus, "Les Indes sont marché de mort" [the Indies are a death market], and "Ceux qui ont incendié l'amour et le désir; ce sont Navigateurs" [Those who have set fire to love and desire; they are Navigators]. He explores the process by which language, in the interaction between Europeans and the "Indies," loses its viability as a means of communication, so that only deathly silence results: "Ils ont tourné la face vers la forêt, ils demandent, muets, quelque parole. Langage, une autre fois, de nudité. Pour le muscle, tant de mots. O Langage désert, et sa grammaire mortuaire!" [They have turned their faces toward the forest, silently they ask for something to be said. A language, once again, of nudity. For muscles, so many words. O deserted Language, and its mortuary grammar!].

The accuracy with which the poet-narrator represents the Antillean slave trade stimulates him to project his vision ("je vois" [I see]) back into the past and forward into the future, calling as witnesses to both the past and the future the two constant natural elements of the Antillean reality, the sun and the sea. He moves to the distant past to cite the example of Xerxes, a descendant of the Persian Achemenides dynasty founded by Cyrus and which unified the East between the sixth and fourth centuries BC, who is credited with suppressing revolts in Babylon and Egypt during his reign from 486-465 BC and who was assassinated in a palace plot. He is presented here principally as a slave-master ("je vois Xerxès menant ses gens à l'abreuvoir" [I see Xerxès leading his people to the trough]) against the backdrop of the Antillean constants of sun and sea. The failure of Xerxes is related to his lack of respect for the power of these elements which are presented as active participants in the history of the world: the sun is shows is emotion by becoming red with hope, while the sea reacts to the insult perpetrated by Xerxes. The poet's vision moves forward to a less distant past to share in the response of these two elements to the slave trade. Sun and sea form part of the final demystified picture he draws of the Indies built and maintained on the blood of slaves: "Je vois un soleil cru et une mer de lassitudes, qui entretiennent sur le sang les grandes sans mystère" [I see a fierce sun and a sea of lassitudes, which maintains the great unmysterious Indies on blood].

LI

Cet enfant monte au plus haut de la terre, il voit sur l'horizon grossir la cargaison: «C'est un nouveau! qui arrive pour le marché du carême!»; alors il souffle dans la gorge du lambi, et les marchands là-bas s'apprêtent pour l'acquisition de jeunes filles et de mâles... Où est la flamme, où la splendeur, en ce nouveau Divisement du monde? L'acquéreur se lève; à sa ceinture, la liste qu'il marchandera. J'ai fait la liste, la strophe dure, de ceux qui furent sur l'océan de mort, et voici qu'on me dit: «Liste de rustre, sans mesure!... Histoire ancienne, sans levain! Parole et chant, sans profondeur ni ombre»... Allons! les crieurs paradent sur les tréteaux, ils débitent la vie; les marchands s'empressent; le doux enfant glisse au bas du sentier, abandonnant l'espace d'annonciation. Il ne sait, l'adolescent guetteur de futur, qu'il y aura d'autres criées pour le malheur des prophéties; qu'ils seront quelques-uns, aux talons furieux sur le tambour nocturne, et dont l'ivresse parlera: «Nous sommes fils de ceux qui survécurent.»

ĕ

LI

This child climbs to the top of the land, he sees the cargo growing bigger on the horizon: "It's a new one! that's coming for the Lenten market!"; then he blows into the throat of the conch, and the merchants down below get ready to acquire girls and males... Where is the flame, where is the splendor, in this new Dividing of the world? The purchaser stands up; at his belt, the list that he will haggle over. I made a list, in hard verse, of those who were on the ocean of death, and this is what I was told: "A lout's list, without measure!... Ancient history, without leaven! Word and song, without depth or shade" ... Here we go! The criers parade on the stage, retailing life; the merchants bustle around; the gentle child slides down to the bottom of the path, abandoning the annunciation space. He does not know, this adolescent look-out for the future, that there will be other auctions for the misfortune of prophecies; that they will be some, with heels of fury on the nocturnal drum, and whose intoxication will speak: "We are the sons of those that survived."

In this section (LI) (146), the perspective of the poet changes as he adopts a different role. He puts himself in the position of a boy witnessing and announcing the arrival of a new batch of slaves: "Cet enfant monte au plus haut de la terre, il voit sur l'horizon grossir la cargaison: «C'est un nouveau! qui arrive pour le marché du carême!»; alors il souffle dans la gorge du lambi" [This child climbs to the top of the land, he sees the cargo growing bigger on the horizon: "It's a new one! that's coming for the Lenten market!"; then he blows into the throat of the conch]. His evocation of the preparations for the slave market is interrupted (indicated by the suspension points) by an ironic reflection on the value and historical significance of this activity: "Où est la flamme, où la splendeur de ce nouveau Divisement du monde?" [Where is the flame, where is the splendor, in this new Dividing of the world?]. The poet oscillates between past and present, exploring the link between his own writing and the written inventory ("la liste") drawn up by slave-buyers, anticipating and forestalling criticism from the impersonal Eurocentered other ("on" [they]): "J'ai fait la liste, la strophe dure, de ceux qui furent sur l'océan de mort, et voici qu'on me dit: "Liste de rustre, sans mesure! ... Histoire ancienne, sans levain! Parole et chant, sans profondeur ni ombre ...." [I made a list, in hard verse, of those who were on the ocean of death, and this is what they told me: "A lout's list, without measure!... Ancient history, without leaven! Word and song, without depth or shade"].

The "adolescent guetteur de futur" [adolescent look-out for the future] is presented sympathetically as "le doux enfant" [the gentle child], a poetic ancestor who has given voice to "le malheur des prophéties" [the misfortune of the prophecies]. Above all, however, the poet represents himself as one of the descendants of the African slaves who managed to survive: "ils seront quelques-uns, aux talons furieux sur le tambour nocturne, et dont l'ivresse parlera: «nous sommes fils de ceux qui survécurent»" [they will be some, with heels of fury on the nocturnal drum, and whose intoxication will speak: "We are the sons of those that survived"]. This statement of pride and faith establishes the cultural lineage to which, in Glissant's view, Antillean writing is attached.

LXI

O dans les siècles de ces siècles, plus éternels que
la parole des pythies,
Ainsi les ai-je vus, nombreux parmi les pousses et
les ronces.
L'histoire les oublie, car ils sont morts de ce côté
du monde où le soleil décline.
Je les appelle sur la plage, auprès de ceux partis,
mais qui demeurent cependant.
Ils sont les Conquérants de la nuit nue. Ouvrez les
portes et sonnez
            pour les héros sombres. La mer
Les accueille parmi ses fils, le soleil se lève sur le
souffle de leur âme.
Ils s'appellent, fameux, et oubliés, qui résistèrent
au nocher des caravelles.
Leur cortège pénètre, ils ont brandi les torches de
bambous, et voici le premier,
Delgrès qui tint trois ans la Guadeloupe.

☙

LXI

O in the centuries of these centuries, more eternal
than the words of the pythias,
Thus did I see them, numerous among the shoots
and the brambles.
History forgets them, for they died on this side of
the world where the sun goes down.
I call them on to the beach, beside those who have
left, but who still stay.
They are the Conquerors of naked night. Open
your doors and ring bells

for these dark heroes. The sea
Welcomes them as her sons, the sun rises on the
breath of their soul.
They call each other, famous and forgotten, they
who resisted the pilot of the caravels.
Their procession enters, they have held aloft the
bamboo torches, and here is the first one,
Delgrès who held Guadeloupe for three years.

The fifth main division, entitled "Les Héros" ["The Heroes"], is devoted to an evocation of the struggles that took place in the (West) Indies during the centuries following the initiation of the slave trade and brings to the fore the voices of all past and present arrivals to the (West) Indies. The form of the poem in this section changes once again to long lines of free verse, to translate the solemnity of this rewriting of the history of the (West) Indies as the poet focuses on Antillean heroes. The narrator-poet summons the sons and protectors of Mother (West) Indies and recreates the Haitian revolution and celebrating the emergence of the Haitian heroes, Toussaint L'Ouverture (LIX) (154) and Dessalines (LX) (154), before turning to the Guadeloupean, Louis Delgrès.

The eternity of suffering endured by Africans is implicit in the opening exclamation of this section (LXI) (155), "O dans les siècles de ces siècles, plus éternels..." [O in the centuries of these centuries, more eternal ...]. This implication assumes even greater force in the context of the Antillean Creole saying that Glissant is fond of quoting: "un nègre est un siècle" [a nigger is a century]. The poet assumes subjectivity to attest to direct experience ("Ainsi les ai-je vus" [Thus did I see them]). His vision spans the eternity of time and space as he revives the image of the Caribbean as a field, ("champ") full not only of "pousses" [shoots] and "ronces" [brambles], but also of many heroes ("nombreux" [numerous]). The cultural and linguistic problem in which the poet is enmeshed is manifested in his use of "l'histoire" [history], which inevitably in the context of the French language and culture connotes European history. The subtext within this context is that from the perspective of (European) history, the Caribbean cannot have heroes: "L'histoire les oublie, car ils sont morts de ce côté du monde où le soleil décline" [History forgets them, for they died from this side of the world where the sun goes down]. But it is precisely this subtext that provokes and justifies the poet's activity.

Thus the poem becomes the vehicle by which the poet re-establishes contact with other Caribbean kin as part of a community to which he belongs and creates the conditions in which their presence and their voice may be acknowledged: "Je les appelle sur la plage, auprès de ceux partis, mais qui demeurent cependant" [I call them on to the beach, beside those who have left, but who still stay]. The poet addresses himself also to a presumed audience of contemporary West Indians, exhorting them to honor their forgotten heroes: "Ouvrez les portes et sonnez pour les héros sombres" [Open your doors and ring bells for these dark heroes]. The figures of the sea and sun evoked earlier (see IL, 145) return to validate the importance of these heroes: "La mer / Les accueille parmi ses fils, le soleil se lève sur le souffle de leur âme" [The sea / Welcomes them as her sons, the sun rises on the breath of their soul]. This section closes within the presentation of the Guadeloupean hero, Delgrès who for three years resisted the best attempts of the French army under General Richepanse, which had been sent by Napoleon Bonaparte to reimpose slavery in the French colonies in the Caribbean. Delgrès chose suicide by blowing up his troops and himself rather than surrender. The poem here acquires a distinctly epic dimension in its celebration of Antillean heroes.

LA RELATION

Le poème s'achève lorsque la rive est en vue, d'où s'éloignèrent jadis les Découvreurs. Retour à ce rivage, où l'amarre est toujours fixée. Quelle richesse a grandi, durant ce cycle? Qui revient? Et celui-là, que convoite-t-il à son tour?

Mais peut-être enfin l'homme n'a-t-il que même désir et même ardeur, n'importe soit-il? Et d'où qu'il vienne, même souffrance connaissable? Quelles Indes l'appellent? Ou, si son rêve n'est déjà qu'une passionnée raison, quel océan pourtant s'impose entre elle et lui? — Nul ne peut dire en certitude; mais chacun tente la nouvelle traversée! La mer est éternelle.

ॐ

RELATION

The poem ends when the shore is in sight, from which the Discoverers formerly moved away. A return to this bank, where the mooring line is still fixed. What wealth has increased, during this cycle? Who is coming back? And that one, what is he lusting after in his turn? But perhaps in the end man has only the same desire and the same ardor, no matter who he is? And wherever he comes from, the same knowable suffering? What Indies call him? Or, if his dream is already nothing but an impassioned reason, what ocean however imposes itself between that reason and himself? -- No one can say with certainty; but everyone attempts the new crossing! The sea is eternal.

The italicized introduction, entitled "La Relation" ["Relation"] (159), to the sixth and final part of the poem establishes, through the new title Glissant has given it for the 1994 edition, a connection to his theoretical writing and specifically to *Poétique de la Relation* (1990). The conclusion of this poem is thus for Glissant a manifestation of the philosophical conclusion he has drawn about cultural relativity which he has named "Relation," rejecting the notion of an identity based on a single root and supporting that of an identity based on the "conscious and contradictory lived experience of contacts of cultures" (*Poétique de la Relation*, 158). This kind of contradiction is reflected in the announcement with which this passage opens: "Le poème s'achève lorsque la rive est en vue, d'où s'éloignèrent jadis les Découvreurs" [The poem ends when the shore is in sight, from which the Discoverers formerly moved away]. The poem thus marks the completion of a reverse journey of rediscovery for the poet, retracing in the opposite direction the path taken by the Europeans. The point of fixity to which the poet returns ("Retour à ce rivage, où l'amarre est toujours fixée" [A return to this shore, where the mooring line is still fixed] is Europe, the point of departure for the "Discoverers." Thus the poet acknowledges the European linkage as an undeniable component of the cultural heritage of Antilleans. Europe is incontrovertibly part of "La Relation."

At this stage the poet-narrator becomes reflective, posing a series of questions in relation to his journey, in order to determine the historical and philosophical lessons to be learned about the human condition: "Quelle richesse a grandi, durant ce cycle? Qui revient? Et celui-là, que convoite-il à son tour? Mais peut-être enfin l'homme n'a-t-il que même désir et même ardeur, n'importe soit-il? Et d'où qu'il vienne, même souffrance connaissable? Quelles Indes l'appellent? Ou, si son rêve n'est déjà qu'une passionnée raison, quel océan s'impose entre elle et lui?" [What wealth has increased, during this cycle? Who is coming back? And that one, what is he lusting after in his turn? But perhaps in the end man has only the same desire and the same ardor, no matter who he is? And wherever he comes from, the same knowable suffering? What Indies call him? Or, if his dream is already nothing but an impassioned reason, what ocean however imposes itself between that reason and himself?] These questions are finally unanswerable, but the poet suggests that "chacun tente la nouvelle traversée! La mer est éternelle" [everyone attempts the new crossing! The sea is eternal]. The message that emerges is that Europeans are not that much different from any other human beings. They have in coming to the Caribbean been driven by the same impulses that all humanity shares. The "Indies" are a symbolic object of desire, existing in the imaginations of all. The historical and geographical circumstances surrounding the crossing of the seas by Europeans thus invest the Caribbean with universal significance.

Voici la plage, la nouvelle.   Et elle avance pesamment dans la marée,
La mer! ô la voici, épouse, à la proue, délaissant l'ancre.
Elle roule, très-unie: sur la route non-saccagée.

O course! Ces forêts, ces soleils vierges, ces écumes
Font une seule et même floraison! Nos Indes sont
Par delà toute rage et toute acclamation sur le rivage délaissées,
L'aurore, la clarté courant la vague désormais
Son Soleil, de splendeur, mystère accoutumé, ô nef,
L'âpre douceur de l'horizon en la rumeur du flot,
Et l'éternelle fixation des jours et des sanglots.

꙳

Here is the beach, the new one. And moving heavily forward into the tide,
The sea! O here she is, a wife, at the prow, abandoning the anchor.
She rolls, perfectly calm: on her undevastated road.

O journey! These forests, these virgin suns, these foamy waters
Make a single same flowering! Our Indies are,

Beyond all rage and all acclamation abandoned on
the shore,
Dawn, light henceforth chasing the wave
Its Sun, of splendor, accustomed mystery, O ship,
The bitter sweetness of the horizon in the rumbling
of the tide,
And the eternal fixation of days and sobs.

In the final part of the poem (LXV), Glissant once again adopts the
form of long lines of free verse, repeating the metaphorical linkage
between poetic activity (his own) and voyages of discovery (his
own and Europeans'): "Pour une fois encore je salue l'aube naissant
sur un poème non connu et un désir" [Once again I greet the dawn
rising on an unknown poem and a desire] (162). Indeed it is
through this interpretation of his own motivation that he can
empathize and establish imaginative linkages with the European
"discoverers," celebrating Marco Polo as an "illumineur"
[illuminator]; Vasco da Gama as an "épi éblouissant" [dazzling
spire]; and Magellan "dont le nom fouette la tempête" [whose name
lashes hurricanes](163).
   The final lines of the poem (165) show the poet back aboard
a ship as it arrives once again at the shores of the new (West) Indies,
imagined and brought into existence within and by the poem:
"Voici la plage, la nouvelle" [Here is the beach, the new one]. The
sea reappears as the constant and defining feature of the poet's
landscape, unaffected by all the experiences evoked: "La mer! ô la
voici, épouse, à la proue, délaissant l'ancre. / Elle roule, très-unie:
sur sa route non-saccagée [The sea! O here she is, a wife, at the
prow, abandoning the anchor. / She rolls, perfectly calm: on her
undevastated road]. The Sun, too, reappears to serve as both
metaphor and metonym of the (West) Indies, affirming, as does the
sea, the permanence and survival of these Indies which the poet,
adopting a plural voice ("Nos Indes" [our Indies], claims for himself
and his community. In this final picture, the poet envisions dawn as
a metaphor of the (West) Indies. The last line of the poem

establishes the expression of pain as a constant, like the sun, in the existence of the Antillean: "l'éternelle fixations des jours et des sanglots" [the eternal fixation of days and sobs].

This examination of a sample of Glissant's poetry indicates that his poetic practice represents an attempt to arrive at a representation of the Caribbean undistorted by ideological bias. The problem for him is complicated by a combination of geographical and historical factors, not always friendly or voluntary (e.g. slavery) which have all contributed to the creation of what is now known as the West Indies. Glissant finds a particular symbolic significance in the sea, which links the islands to Europe as well as to Africa, both geographically and historically. However, it is evident that the poet is equally sensitive to the fracturing of the cultural heritage resulting from the same combination of factors that have contributed the virtual obliteration, the "absence," of a coherent Caribbean. This cultural fracture is reflected in Glissant's poetry in a profusion and even confusion of different voices and poetic personas and in what seems to be a deliberate obscurity of language. Indeed, because of Glissant's preoccupation with the transmission of a reality he knows to be complex, his poetry tends to become self-referential, sometimes reflecting on its own effectiveness (or ineffectiveness) to recreate the Caribbean.

Glissant's preoccupation with the problem of language and representation reflects the questioning of the structure of language by avant-garde French writers such as Philippe Sollers and Claude Simon who were associates of Glissant's in Paris in the 1950s. The fact that Glissant has produced a substantial mass of critical and theoretical writings has encouraged critics to comment on his theoretical writings rather than on his poetic texts and even to approach his poetry through the mediation of his theoretical writings. The approach of relying on Glissant's theories (or any author's) to explicate his texts is unsatisfactory because it is restrictive. Glissant's poetry is not an illustration of his poetic theories and Glissant is not necessarily the most reliable authority on his poetic practice. What emerges above all from Glissant's poetry is a multi-dimensional, frequently obscure poetic voice, seeking a means of reconciling the variety of linkages and facets that comprise an often contradictory cultural heritage. It is in this way that the poetry of Glissant projects itself as the recreation of the complex entity known as the Caribbean.

Notes

[1] Page citations in this chapter refer to Édouard Glissant, *Poèmes complets*, Paris: Gallimard, 1994.

6

Guy TIROLIEN

uy Tirolien is a French Caribbean writer who spent the greater part of his adult life (1944-76) in Africa. He was born in Pointe-à-Pitre, Guadeloupe, February 13, 1917. He claims to have had an interest in the "black question" from his youth (Condé & Rutil 1990:59), since his father, a headmaster as well as a politician, had been active in the socialist negrist movement. His father was to become Mayor of Grand-Bourg in the small island dependency of Marie-Galante and later *conseiller général* and deputy. Guy attended the Lycée Carnot in Pointe-à-Pitre. While he was in secondary school, he read French translations of the works of Langston Hughes and Claude MacKay. He left Guadeloupe in 1936 to continue his studies in Paris, winning entry to the Ecole Nationale d'Administration de la France D'Outre-mer at the Lycée Louis-le-Grand. When he arrived in Paris in 1936, he came into contact with Léon-Gontran Damas and Jacques Roumain, the militants of *Cri des Nègres*, and took an active part in the student movement. During the war, from 1940 - 1942, he was imprisoned by the Germans. It was in the stalag that he met, among others, Léopold Sédar Senghor, who introduced him to Negritude. He was not to meet Césaire until 1945. After his liberation in 1942, he created with a group of African students and became President of the General Association of Colonial Students, which included Malagasy, African, Caribbean, and Indochinese students. From 1944, he was sent to Africa as an Administrator. He was a career diplomat and over the next several years served in several African countries, particularly in Guinea, Niger, the Sudan (now Mali), and the Ivory Coast. In 1965 he was attached to the U.N. and was named as U.N. representative to Mali and later to Gabon. Poor health caused him to retire in 1976. He returned to his native land and from 1977 settled in Marie-Galante, where he made an unsuccessful attempt to run for political office. Despite his failure, he continued to be active in politics until he was prevented by illness. He died at his home in Marie-Galante in 1988. Tirolien was twice married, first to Ena Boucolon, from whom he was divorced in 1953, and in 1955 to Thérèse Francfort. He has produced two main works: *Balles d'or* (1961) and *Feuilles vivantes au matin* (1977).

MIRAGES ÉTEINTS

aucun festin d'esprit ne m'a depuis restitué
le sel pur ni l'iode capiteux
repas pour ma félicité de jeune dieu marin
ni
sur les bleues frondaisons des vagues du matin
ce vif parfum de vie
que le vent effeuillait en œillets d'oxygène
ni
ces chants aphones d'oiseaux fabuleux
montant des atlantides de verdure
couchées à la surface du désert profond

le nord était alors le pôle de mes désirs
mon esprit devançait cette flèche qui vole
sur les vieux portulans vers le septentrion
faisant lever
plus proches de mon cœur que les îlets en face
à portée de cailloux les brumes de Thulé

et du nord cependant me venait la lumière
accrochée au flambant visage d'un matelot
à la coque dansante des navires
à l'aile des clairs oiseaux des mers

et les palais de marbre dressaient leur splendeur
sur un fond de collines dorées
Nausicaa aux épaules d'amphore
glissait voile furtive sur les vagues rieuses
et la blanche Ophélie flottait à l'horizon
calice de pureté et lys de clarté

quel soleil quel réveil ont fondu à jamais
mes neiges impossibles?

❦

ERASED MIRAGES

no mental feast has since restored to me
the pure salt nor the heady iodine
that fed my bliss as a young sea god
nor
this sharp fragrance of life
on the blue foliage of the morning waves
whose leaves the wind blew off in nosegays of
oxygen
nor

these voiceless songs of legendary birds
rising from the atlantides of verdure
that lay on the surface of the deep desert

the north was then the pole of my desires
my mind outstripped that arrow that flies
towards the septentrion on old sea charts
lifting
nearer to my heart than the islets across the way
a pebbles' throw away the mists of Thulé

and yet from the north there came to me the light
hanging on a sailor's blazing face
on the dancing hulls of ships
on the wings of bright sea birds

and the marble mansions raised their splendor
against a backdrop of golden hills
Nausicaa with amphora shoulders
glided a furtive bark on the merry waves
and white Ophelia floated on the horizon
a chalice of purity and a lily of light

what sun what awakening have forever melted
my impossible snows?

The two principal elements in the title of the collection, *Balles d'or [Golden Bullets]*, express Tirolien's two main preoccupations in producing this work: the direct expression of a position (cultural and political) and an interest in beauty. As he explained in an interview: "Bullets signify projectiles. Gold expresses quality.... I must reach a maximum of accuracy and precision so that the poems appear like a kind of projectile that by the precision of the shot reach their target. That is, the hearts of readers, the minds, the sense of beauty, etc." (Condé & Rutil 1990:83). The poems are therefore intended to function at two levels simultaneously: the aesthetic and the didactic. There is no separation in Tirolien between creative activity and social responsibility.

"Mirages Éteints" (Tirolien 1961:17) ["Erased Mirages"] is built around a series of oppositions (illusion/reality, past/present, north/south, snow/sun) which illustrate a change that has taken place in the poet's attitudes and perceptions. The sea is the central metaphor through which change in the poet is conveyed. The title derives from the metonymic relationship developed in the poem between sea, sand, and desert, which permits the desert-mirage association: the poet's mirages have been erased, just as the sea erases writing on the sand. Through the title, the poem presents itself as a testimony to the poet's loss of illusions.

The past/present opposition is conveyed in the first line of the poem by "depuis" [since], which marks the separation between two contrasting orders of experience. The first order of experience alluded to in the poem is the "festin d'esprit" [mental feast]. The negative ("aucun" [no]) that is attached to this experience immediately serves to diminish its important in relation to the other experience (sensuous, emotional, imaginative) to which it is set in contrast. On the other hand, the repeated negative ("ni" [nor]) that is used in very strong positions to introduce the privileged experiences of the past adds to the cumulative effect of the importance of these experiences. The sea is an essential element of the poet's past, evoked only indirectly in the poem as a childhood reality ("jeune dieu marin" [young sea god]), through a series of associations: with purity ("le sel pur" [pure salt]), with healthy intoxication ("l'iode capiteux" [heady iodine]), with happiness ("ma félicité"), with life itself ("ce vif parfum de vie" [this sharp fragrance of life], and "oxygène" [oxygen]), and with the creative potential of the islands ("ces chants... montant des atlantides" [these songs ... rising from the atlantides]). In the final line of the first stanza the metaphoric link between sea and desert is completed in the image of "la surface du désert profond" [the surface of the deep desert].

The past/present opposition of the first stanza, conveyed through "depuis" [since], is continued in the second with "alors" [then]. It is here that the poet conveys the nature of the illusion around which the poem is built. The poet's rich sensuous and emotional experience of the past was contradictorily supplanted by a mental attraction toward "le nord" [the north] that displaced the importance of the native geography ("plus proches de mon cœur que les îlets en face" [nearer to my heart than the islets across the way]). The north is evoked through a series of associations that include "esprit" [mind], "brumes" [mists], "palais de marbre" [marble palaces], "collines dorées" [golden hills], as well as "la lumière" [light], "pureté" [purity], "lys" [lily], and "neiges" [snows]. The north is also recreated through three proper names: Thulé, which represented for the Romans an island at the extreme northern limit of the known world; Nausicaa, who, according to Greek mythology, was the daughter of Alcinoüs, who welcomed Ulysses when he was shipwrecked; and Ophelia, Polonius's daughter in Shakespeare's *Hamlet*. These names are all associated closely with European literary and artistic traditions and reinforce the link between the European north and whiteness. It is significant, however, that all these images are underpinned by the omnipresent image of the sea whose presence is felt in the references to "un matelot" [a sailor], "des navires" [ships], and "oiseaux des mers" [sea birds].

The appositional juxtaposition of "soleil" [sun], a metaphor for the Caribbean, and "réveil" [awakening] in the question with which the poem ends suggests that the spiritual and imaginative return to the native land represents a *prise de conscience* which alone can dissipate the illusion of Europe and the temptation of whiteness. Blackness exists only by absent inference in this poem, a silent contrast to all the images of whiteness that inhabit the poem, and yet it is this unmentioned force that finally triumphs. The poet has experienced a permanent change ("à jamais" [forever]) that renders ineffectual the previously dominant illusion of Europe.

"Mirages Éteints" captures a fleeting impression of Tirolien's love for his native land. The poem reveals with touching candor the struggle between attractions to whiteness and blackness, between the north and the native land, for the claiming of his loyalty. Cultural and geographical features intermingle with equal force in the poet's imagination. The overriding emotion, implicit in the title, is one of regret, of sadness at the loss of a dream. Like Carbet, who spent so many years away from her native Martinique, Tirolien experiences feelings of nostalgia and uses the poem to recreate and remind himself of features and memories associated with the native land that are in danger of fading. The poem functions as the site for the immortalization of this indissoluble link.

FRUITS DÉPAREILLÉS

Je suis un fruit veuf de toute mémoire et de tout
cousinage
sans même sur ma joue le chaud reflet
d'une chair congénère
fruit seul dans la corbeille pleine
non pas l'orange douce d'Andalousie
dont s'avive l'éclat
de l'or répercuté des somptueuses orangeries
mais la brune cabosse de cacao
roulant tête sans corps
parmi le peuple bigarré des fruits dépareillés
mangue de feu citron cuivré prune café
pomme acajou grenade ensanglantée

la terre qui m'a nourri
n'a pas la profondeur assurée des continents
je suis une dent mal chaussée dans l'éclatant dentier
des Caraïbes
un triple vouloir m'écartèle
moi que voici cloué
en plein cœur de la rose des vents
qui déploient leur vol polychrome

dans des directions trois fois infécondes

le parler qu'épouse ma voix d'outre-souffrance
a mûri ses racines
dans le tendre calcaire du pays latin
il faudrait à mes lèvres épaisses
des vocables plus lourds des verbes denses
durs comme les galets de nos Lézardes
des adjectifs vénéneux et foudroyants
fleurs de sang fleurs de soufre
à bleuir le cratère de ma bouche

je ne connais que l'histoire inscrite dans ma chair
par le feu des fouets
la brûlure des garrots
des fers rouges
et du viol
pourquoi ce radeau négrier sans mât et sans voilure
largué au large
des Amériques
et qui ouvre sa route aveugle
vers des lendemains que j'ignore?
pourquoi cette calebasse de maléfices portée
jusqu'à mes pieds
sur les flots sans honneur du passé?

mes mains n'ont élévé cathédrale ni mosquée
elles n'ont pas modelé les fines poteries
je n'ai pas connu les soifs rares et les nobles
ivresses
mes mains n'ont pas ciselé les plats ouvragés
ni les lourdes argenteries

ma faim de tout temps fut vorace et grossière
sur les murs d'aucun palais

je n'ai eu loisir d'illustrer mes loisirs en fêtes de
couleurs
ou en festons de formes
les caisses de savon casquées de tôles
déchirées
depuis toujours ont abrité
ma nudité

ma musique n'est que le rythme de mon sang
le cri rauque de ma chair
mes yeux déchiffrent mal ces virgules sonores
que des araignées mélomanes
ont suspendues
à la géométrique élégance
des fils tendus

sans peur et sans bagages je grimpe
agile vigie
au haut mât du présent
dos tourné à mon ombre et à toutes les ombres
je vous salue
formes sans vie et cependant vivantes
millions d'œufs inéclos
future humanité
dieux que l'avenir de ses doigts lumineux
tendrement façonne.

☙

MIXED FRUIT

I am a fruit widowed of all memory and all kin
not even having on my cheek the warm reflection
of flesh of the same stock
a lonely fruit in the full basket

not the sweet Andalusia orange
whose shine is brightened
by the echoes of gold in the sumptuous orangeries
but the brown cacao bean
a bodiless head rolling
among the multicolored crowd of mixed fruit
fire mango copper lemon coffee plum
mahogany apple bloody pomegranate

the land that has nurtured me
does not have the confident depth of continents
I am a badly set tooth in the brilliant denture
of the Caribbean
a threefold desire rips me apart
I whom you see here nailed
right in the heart of the compass card of winds
that unfurl their polychromatic flight
in directions three times unfruitful

the speech that my voice of extreme suffering
adopts
has its roots matured
in the tender limestone of the Latin country
my thick lips would need
heavier nouns denser verbs
hard like the pebbles of our Lézardes
poisonous and thunderous adjectives
blood flowers sulphur flowers
that would turn my mouth's crater blue

the only history I know is that inscribed in my flesh
by the fire of whips
the sear of garrottes
of branding irons
and of rape

why this slave raft without mast or sail
set loose at sea
in the Americas
and which is blindly opening a road
to tomorrows I know not of?
why this calabash of evil spells brought right to my
feet
on the dishonorable waves of the past?

my hands have built neither cathedral nor mosque
they have not moulded fine potteries
I have not known rare thirsts and noble
intoxications
my hands have not chiseled finely worked plates
nor heavy silverware

my hunger has always been gluttonous and vulgar
on no palace walls
did I have the spare time to illustrate my leisure
activities in feasts of colors
or in festoons of forms
torn up
soap boxes with helmets of sheet iron
have always covered
my nakedness

my music is but the rhythm of my blood
the hoarse cry of my flesh
it is hard for my eyes to decipher those resonant
commas
that music-loving spiders
have hung
on the geometrical elegance
of stretched strings

without fear or baggage I climb
an agile look-out
up the high mast of the present
my back turned to my shadow and to all shadows
I greet you
forms lifeless and yet alive
millions of unhatched eggs
future humanity
gods that the future with its luminous fingers
is tenderly forming.

In "Fruits dépareillés" ["Mixed Fruit"] (17), the central image of a basket of mixed fruit provides the initial referent for the poem. The fact, however, that the title is in the plural suggests that the poet's primary concern is not just with his situation as an individual but rather with his relation to the diverse community of which he is a part. Thus, the poem seeks to convey a truth that is applicable both personally and communally. There is an intimate correspondence in the poem between idea and form, but even these support the underlying notion of difference and divergence. It is the idea, represented in an image, that determines the structural divisions in the poem. The self-defining metaphors, "je suis un fruit veuf..." [I am a fruit widowed...] and "je suis une dent mal chaussée" [I am a badly set tooth...] are set in the context of larger images, of the basket and dental plate, each developed within a different stanza. But the poem resists regularity in that these phrases occur in different positions in their respective stanzas. The spatial divisions mark an exploration first of these two images and then of different manifestations of the poet's and his community's culture: language, history, art, economics, and music. The developing pattern of opening the stanza with a noun (stanzas 2, 3, 5, and 6) is interrupted in the fourth stanza, with a return to the poet's appropriation of the discourse with a "je" [I]. This structural irregularity helps to underline the sense of uncomfortable difference that the poet is trying to communicate.

The early part of the poem is penetrated by the poet's consciousness of loss and of solitude. The loss referred to in the first line ("veuf de toute mémoire et de tout cousinage" [widowed of all memory and all kin] spans both the past and the present. It evokes the experience of African slaves forcibly separated from their kin and from their past history, but it also conveys the poet's present sense of isolation. The image developed by the poet only serves to underline the complexity of the situation. While the problem is somehow related to color, the contrast is not explored in terms of a simple white/black opposition. Rather distinctions are drawn between the European ("d'Andalousie" [Andalusia]) golden orange and a mixed collection óf fruit common to the Caribbean of different shades of brown. The use of "orangeries," which refers to the greenhouses used for cultivation in cool climates, hints with subtle irony at an artificiality from which the poet distances himself. The difference that the poet feels even among the Caribbean examples is transmitted in his assumption of the image of the "cacao," since, unlike all the other fruit listed, the cacao is not normally eaten. Furthermore the complexity that characterizes the Caribbean, implicit in the title, is conveyed as well through the illustration of the linguistic practice typical of the Caribbean of creating unusual combinations of names for fruit, so that the names themselves indicate that they are indeed "mixed fruit": "mangues de feu" [fire mangoes], "grenade ensanglantée" [bloody pomegranate], and particularly "citron cuivré" [copper lime], "prune café" [coffee apple], and "pomme acajou" [mahogany apple]. In the following stanzas, the poet reviews aspects of his identity, "la terre qui m'a nourri" [the land that has nurtured me], "le parler qu'épouse ma voix" [the speech my voice adopts], "l'histoire" [history], the works of "mes mains" [my hands], and "ma musique" [my music], which seem to be problematic and sources of his perception of his own difference.

In the second stanza, the Caribbean geology becomes a metaphor for the poet's insecurity as an Antillean relative to the European metropole: "la terre qui m'a nourri / n'a pas la profondeur assurée des continents" [the land that has nurtured me / does not have the confident depth of continents]. The poet's difference even among the group of Caribbean fruit alluded to in the opening stanza is restated in the second stanza, where the poet changes the metaphor of the fruit to that of the tooth to define himself: "je suis une dent mal chaussée dans l'éclatant dentier / des Caraïbes" [I am a badly set tooth in the brilliant denture / of the Caribbean]. The image of the "dentier" [denture]) conveys the artificial beauty of the Caribbean and thus implies that the reality is much less attractive. The poet's pain is presented as a consequence of the frustration he experiences in trying to satisfy three conflicting masters (in "un triple vouloir m'écartèle" [a threefold desire rips me apart] and "dans des directions trois fois infécondes" [in directions three times unfruitful]). This triple pull can be read as that exerted by the Caribbean/America, Africa, and Europe. Significantly, the problem of color referred to in the first stanza is reinscribed in "polychrome" [polychromatic] in the second stanza. For the poet there is no resolution: he remains a Christ-like figure, "cloué" [nailed].

The next area of difference is language. The poet points to the contradiction between the roots of his poetic voice ("outre-souffrance" [extreme suffering]) and the European language training he has had to undergo. Here again geographical difference is used to underscore cultural difference: "le tendre calcaire" [tender limestone] associated with Europe is contrasted with a Caribbean represented by the hard pebbles of the Martinican Lézarde river and by the terms "vénéneux" [poisonous], "foudroyants" [thunderous], "soufre" [sulphur], and "cratère" [crater], which evoke a stereotypical tropical land of poisonous snakes, of hurricanes, and volcanoes. It must be remembered, however, that this distinction is merely poetic, since limestone is equally part of the geological formation of some Caribbean islands, just as snakes and volcanoes are not unknown in Europe. What the poet is trying to convey, however, is that the European language he uses is not suited to his physical or his experiential reality.

The next issue explored by the poet is that of history. What is implied is a rejection of the Euro-centered version taught in (French) schools in favor of an account based on the experience of the slaves and their descendants who constitute the mass of the population of the Caribbean: "je ne connais que l'histoire inscrite dans ma chair / par le feu des fouets" [the only history I know is that inscribed in my flesh / by the fire of whips]. The poet's pain is transmitted through the two unanswered and ultimately unanswerable questions posed in the second half of this stanza which cast doubt on the historical roles played both by the European presence in the Americas, symbolized by the "radeau négrier" [slave raft], and by African cultural practices, symbolized by the "calebasse de maléfices" [calabash of evil spells]. From the poet's perspective both Europe and Africa bear responsibility for his present condition of insecurity.

Tirolien then launches into an echo of Césaire's celebrated (and often severely criticized by African and Caribbean writers and scholars) panegyric to Negritude in *Return To My Native Land* (1971: 114-119), proclaiming a cultural identity based on a lack of technical and artistic accomplishments: "mes mains n'ont élévé cathédrale ni mosquée / elles n'ont pas modelé les fines poteries" [my hands have built neither cathedral nor mosque / they have not moulded fine potteries]. He distances himself from what may be considered as some of the stereotypical representations of the highest forms of European civilization: "soifs rares" [rare thirsts], "nobles ivresses" [noble intoxications], "loisirs" [leisure], "fêtes de couleurs" [feasts of color], and "festons de formes" [festoons of forms]. The adjectives "vorace" [gluttonous] and "grossière" [vulgar] that have such pejorative connotations echo the criticisms of a lack of "civilization" in behavior leveled against blacks by Europeans. The appropriation of these negative qualities is an echo of the process of Negritude as proposed by Césaire and illustrated in the *Cahier*, where Césaire expressed his need to accept the totality of the experience of blacks, even the most humiliating. The cultural experience of extreme poverty that makes Tirolien's poetic persona different is conveyed in the reference to shacks made of soap crates with roofs of galvanized iron. It should be noted that this is not a personal experience, but a symbolic one, similar to the picture drawn by Césaire in the *Cahier* of the house in which he grew up, in which the poet identifies with the experience of poor people who represent the cultural community to which he belongs.

Music is the final vehicle through which difference is articulated in the poem. The musical expression that the poet claims as his own is characterized by its rhythm and its hoarse sound. The possessives "de mon sang" [of my blood] and "de ma chair" [of my flesh] communicate the relation of this type of musical practice to real experience grounded in the physical and the "natural" far removed from the artificiality associated with European system of musical notation: "ces virgules sonores / que des araignées mélomanes / ont suspendues / à la géométrique élégance / des fils tendus" [those resonant commas / that music-loving spiders / have hung / on the geometrical elegance / of stretched strings]. This elegantly humorous representation of European culture recalls Damas's similarly humorous but more bitter denunciation in poems such as "Hoquet" (*Pigments*, 33) and "Solde" (*Pigments*, 39).

The final stanza of the poem presents a view of the poet far different from the sad, conflicted, defensive, and passive persona projected in the earlier stanzas. We are left with an image of the poet liberated from doubt ("sans peur et sans bagages" [without fear or baggage]) and courageously greeting generations to come. The verbs expressing states of the first two stanzas ("je suis un fruit" [I am a fruit]) and "je suis une dent" [I am a tooth]) and those used negatively or restrictively in the succeeding stanzas ("je ne connais que" [I know only], " mes mains n'ont" [my hands have not], "je n'ai pas connu" [I have not known], "je n'ai eu loisir" [I have not had time], and "ma musique n'est que" [my music is only]) finally give way to verbs of positive action ("je grimpe" [I climb] and "je vous salue" [I greet you]). The poem thus ends on a note of confidence and hope, as the poet finds peace with himself and with his role in relation to the past, present, and future.

This poem is a courageous and lucid exploration of the complex psychological and sociocultural problems that Tirolien faces as a black Caribbean poet. Here he is able to articulate and confront through the image of "mixed fruit" the insecurity that he shares with so many other blacks like himself in the aftermath of slavery and colonization with reference to skin color and culture in relation to whites and Europe. The poem serves as a means of self-exploration and provides an avenue for acceptance and transcendence. Through the poem Tirolien is able to move beyond fear, make peace with his cultural past, and dedicate himself with optimism to "future humanity" while fulfilling his aesthetic needs.

BLACK BEAUTY

tes seins de satin noir
frémissant du galop de ton sang
bondissant
tes bras souples et longs dont le lissé ondule
ce blanc sourire
des yeux
dans la nuit du visage
éveillent en moi
ce soir
    les rythmes sourds
        les mains frappés
            les lentes mélopées
dont s'enivrent là-bas au pays de Guinée
nos sœurs
    noires et nues
et font lever en moi
ce soir
des crépuscules nègres lourds d'un sensuel émoi
car l'âme du noir pays où dorment les anciens
vit et parle ce soir
en la force inquiète le long de tes reins creux

en l'indolente allure d'une démarche fière
qui laisse —
       quand tu vas —
           traîner après tes pas
le fauve appel des nuits que dilate
      et qu'emplit
l'immense pulsation des tam —
      tams
         en fièvre
car dans ta voix surtout
      ta voix qui se souvient
vibre et pleure ce soir
l'âme du noir pays où dorment les anciens —

❧

BLACK BEAUTY

your black satin breasts
quivering from the galloping of your blood
leaping
your long lithe arms their sleekness rippling
that white smile
of the eyes
in the night of your face
awaken within me
tonight
      muted rhythms
         clapping hands
            slow tunes
that enchant over there in Guinea land
our sisters
      black and naked
and send up within me
tonight

negro twilights heavy with a sensuous thrill
for the soul of the black land where the old folk
sleep
lives and speaks tonight
in the restless strength along the small of your back
in the indolence of your proud stride
that leaves —
      when you pass —
           lingering behind your steps
the wild call of nights inflated
    and filled by
the tremendous throb of tom —
    toms
        in fever heat
for mainly in your voice
    your voice that remembers
there vibrates and weeps tonight
the soul of the black land where the old folk
sleep —

This poem, "Black Beauty" (41), attempts to make, with its English title, a statement of racial solidarity and pride across boundaries of language. The black woman, the "Black Beauty" to whom this intended tribute is addressed, is used as a means of articulating connections between Africans throughout the diaspora. The title recalls the popular American novel about the adventures of a horse and this animal serves as a point of departure for the representation of the woman in the poem, as the use of the term "galop" [galloping] indicates. This connection is heightened by the descriptive terms "satin noir" [black satin] and "le lissé [sleekness], and by the activity referred to in "bondissant" [leaping].

The beauty the poet celebrates is expressed in the poem by the application of auditory, visual, and oral strategies. The effect of the alliteration of sibilants that dominate the opening lines (sein... satin... frémissant... sang... bondissant... souple... lissé...) is felt throughout the poem and enhances the impression of sensuality that the poet is trying to create. The spatial arrangement of the poem on the page, with a mixture of short and long lines with others staggered, produces its own visual rhythm, which complements the variations in oral rhythms that are generated in the poem.

Curiously, the 12-syllable alexandrine, that most classical of French verse forms, is dominant in direct or concealed forms. The lines "tes bras souples et longs dont le lissé ondule" [your long lithe arms their sleekness rippling] and "l'âme du noir pays où dorment les anciens" [the soul of the black land where the old folk sleep] are alexandrines, while others are concealed: for example, "frémissant du galop de ton sang / bondissant" [quivering from the galloping of your blood / leaping] — 9 + 3 ; "nos sœurs / noires et nues / et font lever en moi" [our sisters / black and naked / and send up within me] — 2 + 4 + 6; "le fauve appel des nuits que dilate / et qu'emplit" [the wild call of nights inflated / and filled] — 9 + 3; "l'immense pulsation des tam — / tams / en fièvre" [by the tremendous throb of tom — / toms / in fever heat] — 8 + 1+ 3; and "car dans ta voix surtout / ta voix qui se souvient" [for particularly in your voice / your voice that remembers] — 6 + 6. Moreover there are a number of six-syllable lines that may be considered as half-alexandrines: "tes seins de satin noir" [your black satin breasts]; "dans la nuit du visage" [in the night of your face]; "et font lever en moi" [and send up within me]; "traîner après tes pas" [lingering behind your steps]; and "vibre et pleure ce soir" [there vibrates and weeps tonight]. It is impossible to determine whether the use of this form is deliberate. What seems clear, however, is that the classical French poetic line is dislocated and made to adapt itself to the new rhythm associated with blacks that is created in the poem.

The placement of "noir" [black] in a strong, stressed, position at the end of the first line provides a bridge across language with the black anglophone American experience suggested in the title. The repetition of "noir" in a similarly strong position in an also repeated key phrase ("l'âme du noir pays où dorment les anciens" [the soul of the black land where the old folk sleep]) with which the poem ends produces a further linkage with Africa. These linkages are reinforced by the echoing of the diphthong or semi-consonant/vowel combination (oi) of "noir" in the repetitions of "en moi" [within me], "ce soir" [tonight], and "ta voix" [your voice].

Thus, through the application of technical resources at the level of language use, the poet succeeds in conveying his awareness of his connections both to Europe and to anglophone America. But it is the memory and influence of Africa, represented as "là-bas au pays de Guinée" [over there in Guinea land] and as the "noir pays où dorment les anciens" [black land where the old folk sleep], and evoked by the rhythms of the tom-toms, that give this poem its coherence and its *raison d'être*. The poem, moreover, provides an intertextual link to Damas's *Pigments*, and particularly to "Ils sont venus ce soir" (11), in its spatial arrangement on the page and in the specific use of "tam-tam" and "rythme." These elements help to connect it to the emerging tradition of Negritude poetry.

AMÉRIQUE

je suis le fer fiché dans les chairs de ta plaie
l'arête coincée dans le goulot
de ton gosier
l'éclat d'anthracite dans la roche de tes os
et nul baptême
nulle ablution ne te lavera de moi
Amérique

les neiges fleurissant tes plaines de coton
c'est ma sueur féconde
      c'est mon sang
           ta richesse

les sèves de douceur
dans tes roseaux aux longs cheveux d'argent

ce sont mes larmes non taries
dans la bruyance de tes machines
de tes mines
de tes usines
dans la violence des voix de cuivre
des voix de nez
des voix enrouées de ta musique

entends l'accent de ma colère
de ma douleur
et de mes hontes

Amérique

les nuées de charbon sur tes banlieues en deuil
non ce n'est pas la suie de ma peau
souillant la lumière des hommes
c'est la cendre de mes os calcinés
dans l'incendie des lynchages

l'acier de tes buildings coule
dans mes muscles de bronze
car je porte sur mes épaules
tout le poids du Nouveau-Monde

je suis l'ombre de ton corps
la nourrice aux mamelles de nuit
dont le lait enrichit la vigueur de ton sang
la pâleur de ton teint
— tu ne peux te défaire de moi
j'ai la fureur des amants éconduits
j'implanterai mes dents
dans ta chair lumineuse
ô terre de viol
terre d'injustice

et d'avenir
je briserai ton échine —
si fragile entre Colon et Panama —
une étroite ceinture d'incandescence
de convoitises

ma voix
      — celle de Césaire et de Mac Kay
        de Robeson et de Guillen
sera plus forte que ton orgueil
plus haute que tes gratte-ciel
car elle jaillit des sombres entrailles de la
souffrance
Amérique

      ॐ

AMERICA

I am the knife driven into the fleshy parts of your
wound
the bone stuck in the neck
of your gullet
the flash of anthracite in the rock of your bones
and no baptism
no ablution will wash me off you
America

the snows that bloom on your cotton fields
that's my fertile sweat
      that's my blood
          your wealth

the saps of sweetness
in your reeds with their long silver hair

are my undried tears
in the noisiness of your machines
of your mines
of your factories
in the violence of the brass voices
of the nasal voices
of the hoarse voices of your music

hear the tone of my anger
of my pain
and of my shame

America

the clouds of coal over your mourning suburbs
no it's not the soot of my skin
soiling the light of men
it's the ash of my bones burned
in the fires of lynchings

the steel in your buildings flows
in my muscles of bronze
for on my shoulders I bear
the whole weight of the New World

I am your body's shadow
the nanny with night breasts
whose milk improves the vigor of your blood
the paleness of your complexion
— you can't get rid of me
I am as full of rage as rejected lovers are
I will sink my teeth
into your luminous skin
o land of rape
land of injustice

and of future
I will break your spine —
so fragile between Colon and Panama —
I will tie around your arched waist
a narrow belt of incandescence
of covetousness

my voice
— that of Césaire and of MacKay
of Robeson and Guillén
will be stronger than your arrogance
higher than your skyscrapers
for it springs from the dark guts of suffering
America

In "Amérique" [America] (67), the poetic persona, the "je" [I] of the discourse, adopts the role of the black man addressing a personified white America. The two opening images ("le fer fiché dans les chairs de ta plaie / l'arête coincée dans le goulot / de ton gosier" [the knife driven into the fleshy parts of your wound / the bone stuck in the neck / of your gullet]) transmit the notion of America as a human being in agony, doomed to intense suffering because of its inability to accommodate the people with whom the poet identifies. This group of people becomes more clearly identifiable in the black color associated with the third image, "l'éclat d'anthracite" [the flash of anthracite], a natural coal noted for its high luster. The stereotypical depiction by whites of the black man as heathen and perhaps aligned with the forces of "darkness" is suggested in the references to "baptême" [baptism] and "ablution" and recalls Césaire's representation of his race toward the end of the *Cahier* as "ma race qu'aucune ablution d'hysope et de lys mêlés ne pourrait purifier" (129) [ma race that no ablution of hyssop and lilies mixed could purify]. This depiction is absorbed and reversed by Tirolien so that here it is white America represented as futilely seeking purification. The subtext of the first stanza is thus the desire of white America to reject blacks as an integral part of that society.

The succeeding stanzas, through a series of bold equations, outline the vital contribution of blacks to America's agricultural, industrial, and cultural accomplishments. Thus the white flowers that signal prosperity in the cotton industry are metaphorically represented as "neiges" [snows], in ironic contrast to the black source of such wealth, as the poet establishes equations between white cotton and black sweat and between white wealth and black blood: "c'est ma sueur féconde / c'est mon sang / ta richesse" [that's my fertile sweat / that's my blood / your wealth]. The second stanza explores the success of sugar cane plantations in the Americas. These plantations are depicted metonymically through the long spires that sprout from mature sugar cane plants ("tes roseaux aux longs cheveux d'argent" [your reeds with their long silver hair], and a further equation is created between white sugar cane juices and black tears.

Unusual associations, rhythm, and metonymy are all used to evoke the presence of blacks and to convey the poetic persona's emotion. The equations that are set up point to the ineradicability of the black presence and the poet draws an unusual parallel between the sounds of industry and the violent quality of the voices often associated with black American music: "des voix de cuivre / des voix de nez / des voix enrouées" [brass voices / nasal voices / hoarse voices]. The emotions that were driving the poem are finally named: "colère" [anger], "douleur" [pain], and "hontes" [shame]. The order in which these emotions are presented may be interpreted as signifying the relationship between them: anger is the outward expression of an inner pain that itself overlays a deep-rooted sense of shame and it is anger in the form of sarcasm that dominates in the following stanza.

The perfect balance of the alexandrine "les nuées de charbon sur tes banlieues en deuil" [the clouds of coal over your mourning suburbs] is immediately contradicted by the irregular rhythms of the lines that follow. The gentle impression of melancholy evoked is erased in the sibilant bitterness of "suie" [soot] and "souillant" [soiling]. The "non" [no] helps to accentuate the poet's pain at the rejection of the humanity of people with black skin. The metonymic linkage between "charbon" [coal], "suie" [soot], "cendre" [ash], "os calcinés" [bones burned], and "incendie" [fire] creates further corroboration that the significance of the black experience in America is indisputable and impossible to erase.

The contribution of black labor to the external signs (tall buildings) that typify American culture is rendered through a literal fusion of images ("l'acier de tes buildings coule / dans mes muscles de bronze" [the steel in your buildings flows / in my muscles of bronze]. The term "bronze" generates a metonymic link with the image of a statue and thus signals that the black contribution has been elevated to heroic proportions. Moreover, the European cultural tradition is coopted as the black poetic persona appropriates the role attributed to Atlas in Greek mythology, condemned by Zeus to bear the weight of the heavens on his shoulders: "car je porte sur mes épaules / tout le poids du Nouveau-Monde" [for on my shoulders I bear / the whole weight of the New World].

The poet moves from the figurative ("l'ombre de ton corps" [your body's shadow]) to the actual ("la nourrice aux mamelles de nuit" [the nanny with night breasts]) to convey the nature of the relationship between whites and blacks in American society, insisting that blacks serve a vital purpose in supplementing the deficiencies of whites ("dont le lait enrichit la vigueur de ton sang / la pâleur de ton teint" [whose milk improves the vigor of your blood / the paleness of your complexion]. This is a patent reference to the role played by black "nannies" in plantation societies throughout the Americas who had primary responsibility for the physical survival, rearing, and care of the white children of their "masters." The simple statement "tu ne peux te défaire de moi" [you can't get rid of me] summarizes in unequivocal and non-poetic language the thrust of the argument the poet has been making throughout the poem. This vernacular element complements the orality that is the driving force in the poem.

At this stage the poet gives direct expression to the emotion of rage he had alluded to earlier: "j'ai la fureur des amants éconduits" [I am as full of rage as rejected lovers are]. The use of "amants" [lovers], however, gives a clue to the fact that the violence contemplated springs not from hatred but from the pain of rejection. Thus the apostrophe that begins with terms of vehement condemnation ends in an expression of admiration: [ô terre de viol / terre d'injustice / et d'avenir" [o land of rape / land of injustice / and of future]. The future tenses ("j'implanterai" [I will sink], "je briserai" [I will break], and "je nouerai" [I will tie]) underline the fact that this violence is only in the mind and reflects only a desire to retaliate for hurts received. The reference to the physical vulnerability of the stretch of land "entre Colon et Panama" [between Colon and Panama], representing the narrowest land mass between North and South America, indicates that the America to which this poem is addressed includes both continents. Thus the poetic voice that he claims as his shares a common bond with other black voices throughout the Americas, from Martinique, the U.S.A., as well as Cuba: "celle de Césaire et de Mac Kay / de Robeson et de Guillen" [that of Césaire and of Mac Kay / of Robeson and Guillén]. Tirolien ends with an echo of Césaire's evolutionary realization in *Return To My Native Land* of a negritude, "non plus un indice céphalique, ou un plasma, ou un soma, mais mesurée au compas de la souffrance" [no longer a cephalic index, or a plasma, or a soma, but measured by the compass of suffering] (137), in asserting that the triumph of the black voice is assured because "elle jaillit des sombres entrailles de la souffrance" [it springs from the dark guts of suffering].

In moving outside the French Caribbean social geography to speak from the perspective of a black person in the African diaspora, Tirolien joins a tradition that is, even within his generation, developing in French Caribbean poetry: that of Carbet who in "Greffe" adopted the voice of a black South African, of Damas and Césaire. Padoly and Polius, as we shall see, continue this practice of extending the individual voice to express empathy and solidarity with others in a similar racial and sociocultural situation.

GHETTO

pourquoi m'enfermerais-je
dans cette image de moi
qu'ils voudraient pétrifier?
pitié je dis pitié !
j'étouffe dans le ghetto de l'exotisme

non je ne suis pas cette idole
d'ébène
humant l'encens profane
qu'on brûle
dans les musées de l'exotisme

je ne suis pas ce cannibale
de foire
roulant des prunelles d'ivoire
pour le frisson des gosses

si je pousse le cri
qui me brûle la gorge
c'est que mon ventre bout
de la faim de mes frères
et si parfois je hurle ma souffrance
c'est que j'ai l'orteil pris
sous la botte des autres

le rossignol chante sur plusieurs notes
finies mes complaintes monocordes !

je ne suis pas l'acteur
tout barbouillé de suie

qui sanglote sa peine
bras levés vers le ciel
sous l'œil des caméras

je ne suis pas non plus
statue figée du révolté
ou de la damnation
je suis bête vivante
bête de proie
toujours prête à bondir

à bondir sur la vie
qui se moque des morts
à bondir sur la joie
qui n'a pas de passeport
à bondir sur l'amour
qui passe devant ma porte

je dirai Beethoven
sourd
au milieu des tumultes
car c'est pour moi
pour moi qui peux mieux le comprendre
qu'il déchaîne ses orages

je chanterai Rimbaud
qui voulut se faire nègre
pour mieux parler aux hommes
le langage des genèses

et je louerai Matisse
et Braque et Picasso
d'avoir su retrouver sous la rigidité
des formes élémentales
le vieux secret des rythmes

qui font chanter la vie

oui j'exalterai l'homme
tous les hommes
j'irai à eux
le cœur plein de chansons
les mains lourdes
d'amitié
car ils sont faits à mon image

❦

GHETTO

why would I shut myself up
in that image of myself
that they'd like to petrify?
have mercy I say have mercy!
I am stifling in the ghetto of exoticism

no I'm not that ebony
idol
inhaling the profane incense
that is burned
in the museums of exoticism

I'm not that fairground
cannibal
rolling ivory eyeballs
to make kids tremble with fright

and if I let out the cry
that burns my throat
it's because my belly boils
from my brothers' hunger

and if at times I bawl my suffering
it's because my toe is caught
under the boot of others

the nightingale sings in several notes
no more of my single-chorded laments !

I'm not the actor
all smeared in soot
sobbing out his sorrow
arms raised to the sky
as the cameras watch

neither am I
a frozen statue of a revolutionary
or of damnation
I'm a living animal
a beast of prey
always ready to pounce

to pounce on life
that laughs at the dead
to pounce on joy
that has no passport
to pounce on love
that passes in front of my door

I will speak about Beethoven
deaf
amid the turmoils
for it's for me
for me who can better understand him
that he lets loose his storms

I will sing about Rimbaud

who wanted to become a negro
to better speak to men
in the language of geneses

and I will praise Matisse
and Braque and Picasso
for rediscovering under the rigidity
of elemental shapes
the old secret of the rhythms
that make life sing

yes I will exalt man
all men
I will go to them
my heart full of songs
my hands heavy
with friendship
for they are made in my image

The title of "Ghetto" (73), with its associations of forced confinement, restriction, separation, exclusion, limitation, and marginalization, establishes the situation against which the poem serves as a protest. The poet's resistance to the pressure to comply in his own self-devaluation is transmitted indirectly in the form of the question with which the poem opens. The strong positions of the terms "m'enfermerais-je" [shut myself up] and "pétrifier" [petrify] at the end of their respective lines reinforce the semantic associations of the title, while "image," itself deriving force if only from the effect of the length of its second vowel within that line, introduces the notion of inauthenticity, another source of the poet's indignation. The unspecified "ils" [they] of the third line transmits the casual power of alienating "others" and "l'exotisme" [exoticism], through its syntactical link to "ghetto" (with "de functioning virtually as an appositional copula), is invested with the connotation of a life-threatening trap. The initial question followed by an exclamation and the final affirmative statement combine to underline the poet's resistance to his being relegated to the margin of a universe of which this "ils" is the center.

The poet's rejection of such a role is expressed in a series of negatives repeated over the next few stanzas: "non je ne suis pas" [no I'm not], "je ne suis pas" [I'm not], "je ne suis pas" [I'm not], "je ne suis pas" [I'm not], "je ne suis pas non plus" [neither am I]. The rejected images, "idole d'ébène" [ebony idol], "cannibale de foire" [fairground cannibal], and "acteur" [actor], all exemplify stereotypical representations of blacks with which whites are comfortable and which all deprive blacks of their essential humanity and variability. The black/African presence is implicit in both "ébène" [ebony] and "ivoire" [ivory], products for which the African continent has long been exploited by Europeans. The poetic denials are interrupted in the fourth stanza, in which the poet gives an explanation for the source, function, and content of his poetry. He presents his poetry as the voicing of a hitherto suppressed cry ("le cri / qui me brûle le gorge" [the cry / that burns my throat]), having its source in his awareness of the condition of black people in the modern world. This conception of poetry is shared by many Caribbean writers, including (as we have seen) particularly Césaire and Glissant. Moreover, the reference to "faim" [hunger] as the characteristic condition of blacks echoes the repeated emphasis given to this term by Césaire in the *Cahier* to describe the condition of his fellow Antilleans. The voice of the poem is a communal one, an expression of empathy with the people the poet considers as "mes frères" [my brothers], sharing in the alienating experience of repression at the hands of "des autres" [others].

The freedom to be different from preconceived stereotype, which is the thrust of the poet's claim in the poem, is reflected in the two lines that form the conclusion of the interruption of emphatic denials: "le rossignol chante sur plusieurs notes / finies mes complaintes monocordes !" [the nightingale sings in several notes / no more of my single-chorded laments !]. These lines are striking in many respects. Visually, they are the two longest successive lines and comprise the shortest stanza in the poem. The reference to the "rossignol" [nightingale], a major symbolic figure in European medieval courtly romances, takes us back to an era and a tradition distinctly different from those evoked in the early stanzas. The subtle irony of this allusion amounts to a deliberate subversion of the European lyric tradition. Moreover, the first of these lines constitutes the only sententious statement of the poem, independent syntactically of the otherwise omnipresent persona, identifiable in the "je" [I] with which every other sentence begins. These lines also represent a demonstration of the freedom exercised by the poet to use or cannibalize European tradition when and how he chooses. This desired freedom is going to be articulated more directly later in the poem.

The final image directly rejected is that of the "statue" whose qualifier, "figée" [frozen], underlines the quality of rigidity that the poet finds most objectionable. The choice of the noun "bête" [animal] as a metaphor for himself curiously reproduces another of the designations typically used by whites to deny the humanity of blacks. But this derogatory term is invested with connotations both of threatening power ("bête de proie" [a beast of prey]) and of an admirably passionate response to life: "à bondir sur la vie ... sur la joie ... sur l'amour" [to pounce on life ... on joy ... on love].

The poem rises to a crescendo in the final stanzas, in verbs of ever increasing force ("je dirai" [I will speak about], "je chanterai" [I will sing about], "je louerai" [I will praise], and "j'exalterai" [I will exalt], as the poet expresses his intention, by the use of the future tense, to exercise his freedom to acknowledge his link to and admiration of some of the most distinguished figures in the modern European cultural tradition, all of whom, ironically, have been reputed to owe a cultural debt to Africa. The earlier articulation of an attitude of rejection is countered in the final stanza by an affirmative "oui" [yes]. The poet transcends the limitations of the ghetto, at least in intention, by asserting his humanistic philosophy. The false "image" of the first stanza ("cette image de moi" [that image of myself]) is finally eradicated by the true image ("mon image" [my image]). The poet has moved from the margin to become the center of his universe.

The rejection of exoticism had been most violently expressed in 1932 by the group of young Martinicans in Paris (particularly René Ménil and Etienne Léro) in the journal *Légitime Défense*. A similar rejection was later to be articulated by Césaire in the *Cahier*: "je lis bien à mon pouls que l'exotisme / n'est pa provende pour moi" (89) [I can clearly read from my pulse that exoticism is no provender for me]. Exoticism represents for all these writers profound alienation and objectification.

Tirolien, by his choice of theme and image, aligns himself firmly within the tradition of Negritude writing. For him, however, this choice is in no way confining. It enables him to express his emotional responses to his condition as a black man as well as his optimistic faith in humanity, while satisfying his taste for artistic beauty. Tirolien exhibits a talent for producing memorable lines, images, and poems. The images he uses rarely conceal or blur comprehension but are usually immediately illuminating without being flatly transparent. Each poem is a gem, finely wrought with careful attention to detail, but creating, as Damas's poems often do, the impression of simplicity. Tirolien's poetry presents itself as that of a gentle figure, who has more questions than answers, and who is willing to explore his contradictory impulses with lucidity and sincerity. As he explained in an interview with Maryse Condé, "the commitment is not the result of an explicit intention to present a demonstration or a plea, but of the even timber of a voice that makes itself heard through the various experiences of a personal autobiography" (Condé & Rutil 1990:61).

7

Yves PADOLY

Y ves Padoly was born in Fort-de-France, Martinique, on June 10, 1937, and, since his father was not around, was raised by his mother. He attended primary school in Terres-Saintville in Fort-de-France and secondary school at the Lycée Schœlcher. He went to work immediately after leaving secondary school, having graduated with the *Brevet supérieur*. Later he took and passed the competitive examination for entry into the civil service. He took some more courses and finally became qualified as a schoolteacher. He followed this career until his retirement. Padoly started writing poetry when he was very young. In fact, in secondary school his nickname was "the Poet." His early writings remained in boxes until one of his friends sent some of his poems off to metropolitan France. Padoly has so far published three volumes of poetry, *Le Missel noir [Black Missal]* (1965), *Poèmes pour adultes [Poems for Adults]* (Paris: La Pensée universelle,

1971), and *L'art d'emmerder (et autres pièces optimistes, de jeunesse)* (1994). Some of his poems have also been published in *Cri et Société: littérature antillaise de combat* (Fort-de-France: SIM, 1978). He has written as well a short novel, *La Mer* (1971), essays, including *L'âme caribéenne* (1973) and *Eloge de la dictature* (n.d.), and a collection of short stories, *Désopilantes "Un": Anecdotes bô caye* (Fort-de-France: Désormeaux, 1994), under the pseudonym of Maloulou. Unlike so many other French Caribbean writers, Padoly has deliberately spent very little of his life outside Martinique. As a result he has remained fully integrated (i.e. relatively free of conflicting outside attachments or temptations) into Martinican traditional day-to-day life. Most of Padoly's works, it should be noticed, have been published locally. Consequently, he has remained relatively unknown, attracting hardly any critical attention either inside or outside of Martinique.

> Et le Peuple d'enfants
> A grandi, a grandi
> Comme les éléphants
> D'Oranda-Oroundi
>
> De sa casaque de bure
> Etriquée, étriquée,
> Les trop faibles coutures,
> Distendues, ont craqué;
>
> Et ses formes authentiques
> Ont paru, ont paru
> Belles et anarchiques
> A tous les coins de rue.

ॐ

> And the People of children
> Have grown up, grown up

Like the elephants
Of Oranda-Oroundi

The too weak stitches
Of their homespun frocks,
Too scant, too scant,
Strained, have burst;

And their authentic forms
Have appeared, appeared
Beautiful and anarchical
On every street corner.

The title of Padoly's collection of sixteen poems, *Le missel noir
[Black Missal]*, gives a clue, in its cluster of associations, to the
significance that this text holds for the poet. The collection presents
itself as a "missal," an "official" record of words and rituals
associated with religious practice. In this way, the collection
attempts to validate itself as something more than the expression of
the attitudes of an individual. The close similarity between this title
and "la messe noire" (black mass], invests the collection with an
iconoclastic and subversive aura and aligns it with satanism in its
rejection of the traditional religious practice of Roman Catholicism.
The connotation of subversion acquires even greater weight within
the historical context of the use made of organized Christianity to
enforce and justify the enslavement of blacks, so that the text forms
a link with Caribbean or South American religions informed by
African religions, such as "vodun" or "santeria," as expressions of
cultural affirmation and anticolonialist resistance. Most directly,
therefore, the text presents itself, through its title, as an essentially
"black" (as opposed to "white") voice. The fusion of these
associations in the title indicates that this collection is in effect an
expression of difference -- a self-consciously "black" alternative to
the words and rituals of the official culture associated with whites.
This notion of difference is implicit, too, in the epigraph from Blaise

Pascal ("Nous sommes pleins de choses qui nous jettent au dehors" [We are full of things that throw us outside]), which alludes to the potential for fragmentation, rejection, and alienation resulting from internal factors.

In this first poem in the collection, "Et le Peuple d'enfants..." [And the People of children] (11), the short six-syllable lines, the alternate rhymes, and the internal rhymed repetition of the second line of each verse, all enhance the poem's regular rhythm and musicality and create the impression that the poem is really a naïve, almost childish, song. This simple form provides the structure within which the poet's deeply ironic response to his situation as a French Caribbean poet is articulated.

The conjunction "Et" [And] with which the poem opens signals that the poem is the continuation of a communication already in progress. The printed text is presented as a different form, a concretized extension, of the poet's voice, as either a resumption or an inscription of orality. This opening thus establishes a link as well as a contrast between orality and literacy. The focus of the poet's textual and pre-textual interest is "le Peuple d'enfants" [the People of children]. In this veiled reference to blacks, the poet ironically adopts the paternalistic term of identification imposed on blacks by racist Europeans to justify the brutality of slavery and colonization, often under the guise of christianization. Furthermore, the designation of blacks as a "peuple" [people] stresses their humanity and their sharing of a common cultural heritage, while the capitalization of the word invests them as a group with importance and dignity. This opening line of the poem thus subtly subverts the traditional European view of blacks. This subversion, transmitted in the irony of the poet's tone, is continued throughout the poem. Thus, the repetition of "a grandi" [have grown up] (I have treated "People" in this context as a collective governing a plural verb) adds a counterpoint of mockery, which is reinforced by the ironic association drawn between the implied weakness of "enfants" [children] and the strength and potential for destruction of African "éléphants" [elephants]. This association discredits the European view of blacks as weak, and proposes an alternative view — of blacks as a possible threatening force. Moreover, the impression of menacing power to be associated with blacks is enhanced by the nasal vowels (in "enfants," "grandi," "éléphants," and "Oranda-Oroundi"), the rumble of which throughout this stanza translates the reverberation of stampeding elephants. At the same time, the metonymic association between "enfants" [children] and "éléphants" [elephants] underscores the irony of a (white) belief system that does not acknowledge the humanity of blacks. These proper names, as Padoly confirmed in an unpublished interview with me, are a barely-concealed reference to the East African territories of Ruanda-Urundi that were occupied by Germany at the end of the nineteenth century, and later by the Belgians, until they became independent as separate nations, Burundi and Rwanda, in 1962. This allusion conveys the poet's resistance to the cultural domination of African peoples by Europeans.

In the second stanza, the implicit low quality of the "casaque de bure" [homespun frock] evidently provided by the parent, is a subtle indication on the part of the poet of his awareness of attempts by Europeans to degrade blacks. Since "bure" [homespun] also refers to monk's clothing, this expression becomes a metaphor of the use of religion to imprison and debase blacks. The repetition of "étriquée" [scant] forms a mocking and contrasting echo to "a grandi" [have grown up] of the first stanza, highlighting the short-sightedness of whites, even within their expressed belief system, in not anticipating what is humanly expected of growing children. The untenable notion of a parent-child relationship between Europeans and blacks thus continues to be ridiculed. Moreover, the connotative force of "Etriquée" [scant] emphasizes the brutality of the Europeans' provision of metaphorical clothing for blacks, which is shown furthermore to be tight and analogous to chains. The "homespun frock" acquires significance, therefore, as a symbol of the violently imposed cultural values of European domination. The weakness and inadequacy of these values as a means of "containing" blacks, as well as associations of violence and suffering, are implied in the multi-dimensional "faibles coutures" [weak stitches], since "coutures" signifies not only sewing, but also scars and sutures. The inevitable effect of the irresistible pressure exercised by the "children" is implicit in "distendues" [strained]. Thus the poet declares the inevitability of the failure of European attempts at permanent domination ("ont craqué" [have burst]), as is illustrated by the earlier reference to the independence of the African territories after so many years of European control.

The priority given to a form based on orality, expressed in the opening "et" [and] of the first stanza, is reaffirmed by the repetition of "et" [and] in the final stanza. The reawakening of the integrity and authenticity of identity ("formes authentiques") is therefore related within the poem to continuity of voice. The rhyme "authentiques" / "anarchiques" [authentic/ anarchic] emphasizes the semantic link between the two terms and signifies that authenticity in this sociocultural context is related to a rejection of Western cultural, religious, and political attitudes. Moreover, the association established between "belles" [beautiful] and "anarchiques" [anarchical], which invests anarchy with attractive connotations, subverts conventional and politically appropriate attitudes, and affirms contrary values. The ironic tone of the poem, therefore, forms the backdrop for the triumphant assertion, with which the poem ends, of the ubiquity ("A tous les coins de rue" [On every street corner]) of the new, grown up, authentic blacks.

This introductory poem is an assertion, underlain with irony, of the emergence to full maturity and to a full sense of their authentic identity of the cultural group (blacks) with whom the poet identifies. This poem both poses and attempts to resolve fundamental issues related to the effects of cultural domination. At the level of language, the poet confronts the debasement inherent in the definition imposed on blacks by whites, and employs irony to affirm his self-worth as a black. The poet also confronts the paternalism of European cultural assimilation and succeeds within the poem in celebrating the acquisition of independence. Perhaps most significantly, the poet breaks through the imposed silence of the centuries to resume an interrupted orality, so that the poem proclaims and exemplifies the re-emergence of a "black" cultural expression.

DONNEZ-MOI!

(Ah! me vient-il souvent ce mot de mendigot)

O vous qui pouvez bien
ô vous qui savez faire,
et qui savez combien
je nous sens tellement frères;
donnez-moi
l'illusion, puisque vous pouvez plus
puisque vous pouvez tant;
de n'être pas que le reclus
qui s'étiole avec le temps...

Ce miroir ... qu'à la main j'ai
d'un autre reflète la face;
les mots que j'ai en idée,
un autre les dit à ma place.
Ah! j'en ai bien assez
de cette double existence:
pour sûr, il me faut casser
cette exécrable faïence
qui me donne sa fraîcheur,
qui me donne son vernis,
qui me donne sa couleur,
qui me prête son fini,
qui me prête ses envies,
qui me prête son amour,
qui me vole toute ma vie.

Il faut bien qu'un de ces jours
je le lance par traîtrise
au fond d'un gouffre perfide.
— C'est là toute ma hantise —
Lors je m'en irai le cœur vide
traînant ma charge de regrets
d'avoir tant tardé à faire
cet acte qui tant importait.
J'en rêve comme d'une affaire
inéluctable comme la mort
et les hymnes que j'entonne
réveillent ce qui ici dort.

❦

GIVE ME !

(Ah! this beggar's phrase often comes to me)

O you who really can
O you who really know how
and who know how much
I feel we are so much like brothers;
give me
the illusion, since you can do more
since you can do so much,
of not being just a recluse
growing pale and sickly with time...

This mirror ... that I have in my hand
reflects another's face;
the words I have in my mind
another says them in my place.
Ah! I have really had enough
of this double existence:

I definitely need to break
this dreadful piece of crockery
that gives me its coolness,
that gives me its glaze,
that gives me its color,
that lends me its finish,
that lends me its envies,
that lends me its love,
that robs me of my whole life.
One of these days I have to
throw it treacherously
into the bottom of a perfidious pit.
— That's all I obsess about —
Then I shall go away with empty heart
dragging my load of regrets
for having waited so long to do
this act that mattered so much.
I dream about it like something
as inescapable as death
and the hymns I start to sing
wake up what is sleeping here.

The poem "Donnez-moi!" (17-18) is presented as a "fragment" of a longer poem, but I have not discovered a longer version among Padoly's published work. The parenthesized notation, appearing under the title of the poem ("Ah! me vient-il souvent ce mot de mendigot" [Ah! this beggar's phrase comes to me often]), expresses the poet's awareness of deprivation and inferiority as characteristics of his situation. The irony implicit in this statement, in which the poet offers a self-mocking comment on the title he has chosen, is heightened by the poetically stylized inversion ("me vient-il" [to me there comes]). This notation suggests an attitude of both separation from and empathy with the experience of a beggar, and prepares for a re-interpretation of the expression "donnez-moi" [give me]. The characteristic utterance of the beggar is therefore to be given a different and more personal significance. The assertion, "je nous sens tellement frères" [I feel we are so much like brothers], eliminates the distance between the poet and an opposing "vous" [you] in relation to power and knowledge ("vous qui pouvez" [you who can] and "vous qui savez" [you who know]). Thus these opening lines reflect a double movement of separation and identification. Implicitly, therefore, the apostrophized "vous" [you], characterized by power and knowledge, reject the equality and fraternity felt by the poet.

It is against this background that the poet's request is produced, a demand not for anything material, but ironically for a specific "illusion." The clauses introduced by "puisque" [since] ("puisque vous pouvez plus" [since you can do more], "puisque vous pouvez tant" [since you can do so much]) enhance the irony of the poet's request. These clauses emphasize the incongruity between the power of the "vous" [you] and the reality of the impotence and isolation of the poet, who characterizes himself as merely a "reclus" [recluse]. The poet's request therefore implies a condemnation of the attitudes and activities of the "vous" [you], whose vaunted power and knowledge are not used to improve the poet's situation of isolation and progressive degeneration, which implicitly was not chosen and is not desired by him.

Within the context of the title of the collection (*Le Missel noir*) and its connotation of religious ritual, the poet's appeal ("Donnez-moi" [Give me], "O vous" [O you]), the form of which recalls Western, Christian, prayers to a deity, acquires even greater poignancy and irony. The poet's prayer becomes a further rejection of traditional religious attitudes and practices as solutions to the peculiar problems experienced by the poet. It is surely not without significance that "étioler" (which I have translated as "growing pale and sickly") is used also to refer to the process of bleaching a plant by excluding sunlight so that it stays white. Degeneration and lactification, as well as separation from a natural source of growth, are therefore implicit in the situation from which the poet is "begging" for a way out.

The dilemma which confronts the poet is presented, as the poem develops, in terms of a loss, of identity and of voice: "Ce miroir ... qu'à la main j'ai / d'un autre reflète la face; / les mots que j'ai en idée / un autre les dit à ma place." (17) [This mirror ... that I have in my hand / reflects another's face; / the words I have in my mind / another says them in my place]. The repetition of "un autre" [another] emphasizes the dominant role played by the "other" as the substitute persona against which the poet rebels but which forms part of the poet's "double existence." The mirror thus becomes, as "cette exécrable faïence" [this dreadful piece of crockery], the hated symbol of the poet's loss of identity, and an emblem of what needs to be destroyed if the poet is ever to achieve the impossible dream of personal integration. Perhaps significantly, one of the characteristics of the "faïence" [piece of crockery] associated with the "other" and given to but rejected by the poet is "sa couleur" [its color]. The enumeration of the attributes which the poet associates with this symbol of otherness reflects a contrast among the ideas of giving ("me donne"), already suggested in the title, lending ("me prête"), and stealing ("me vole"). The identity loss, for the poet, is complete, as apparent gifts and loans become subterfuges for the stealing of everything that makes the poet's life his own: "qui me vole toute ma vie" [that robs me of my whole life]. The repetition of "qui me donne" [that gives me], followed by "qui me prête" [that lends me], emphasizes the poet's intensity of emotion and forms a progression leading to the explosive irony of "qui me vole" [that robs me].

The poet speculates on the means of recapturing his authentic identity by disposing of the "mirror" that contains the false image: "Il faut bien qu'un de ces jours / je le lance par traîtrise / au fond d'un gouffre perfide" [One of these days I needs must / throw it treacherously / into the bottom of a perfidious abyss]. The mirror has been presented as the symbol of the poet's dependence and misdirected loyalty. Thus the act of getting rid of this alienating symbol is presented ironically by the poet as one of treachery. In other words, the poet's dilemma in relation to the mirror in the poem is suggestive of the dilemma of the Martinican. The fact that the Martinican has to define his revolt in terms of metropolitan France is already a limitation on authenticity. From the perspective of Europe the Martinican's action, in rejecting the cultural and political values of the country (metropolitan France) of which he is a citizen, would be defined as "treachery."

The depth of the poet's psychic disturbance is reflected in the physical separation of the line, " -- C'est là toute ma hantise --" [that's all I obsess about], which attests to the poet's preoccupation with the idea of committing an act of "treachery" ("cet acte qui tant importait" [this act that mattered so much]) in order to throw off the image imposed by the West. For the poet, delay in acting will only engender unhappiness and regret ("le cœur vide / traînant ma charge de regrets" [with empty heart / dragging my load of regrets]). The implicit association in the title of the collection of the poet's alignment with forces of darkness, in opposition to the traditional Roman Catholic practices which form part of France's cultural identity, finds an echo in his use of "hantise" [obsessive fear]. The poetic voice, referred to explicitly in "les hymnes que j'entonne" [the hymns I start to sing], is used to combat the death of cultural assimilation and to reawaken the ghost of a repressed cultural otherness ("réveillent ce qui ici dort" [wake up what's sleeping here]).

This poem explores the internal emotional disturbance experienced by the poet as he searches for a resolution of a painful situation in which his self-worth, dignity, and very existence as a human being are constantly under siege. This poem presents the struggle of a poet conscious of the problem of developing an appropriate strategy to resist the assimilation of his personality into that of a rejecting, alienating "other." "Ce miroir" [this mirror] is associated in the text with "les mots" [words]. Hence, the "mirror" is also a metaphor for the act of writing. Thus the poem serves as the mirror in which the poet confronts false images of himself. It is in the poem that the poet's real self finds expression.

PORGY AND SOUL

Sombre...
Une cuisse remue
dans la pénombre.
Des torses nus
font une tache
sur les planches brunes.
Le fond de l'arche
semble un caisson de brunes prunes
quand par moments
un argousin
tire en peinant
l'écoutille qui geint...

En silence,
un genou
se balance
par à-coups.

Du beaupré à l'artimon,
la chanson
triste des drisses
glisse
et verse
dans le trou noir.
Les saisines et les traverses
du bossoir
tintent et craquent
au ressac.

Sans relâche,
en silence
se balance
une tache

de soleil sur planches
de la cale.
Haletant, un buste se penche
berçant son mal
et sa rancœur.

Sans heurt, du cœur
meurtri, monte
une mélopée
syncopée
par l'angoisse de la honte...

Endoloris des nus
entonnent l'air connu
sur ce rythme nouveau
dont l'écho:
plus haut que leurs têtes hirsutes,
plus haut que les voiles jaunies,
plus haut que les nuages contrits, se répercute
à l'infini.

Par delà les temps
la mesure admirable
scande la peine, l'amour, scande le grand
et le minable:
dans la suie des coups de canon
elle scande les psaumes
des hommes;
dans la poussière
du coton,
dans la chaumières
et les ghettos,
dans les palaces, sur les bateaux
et puis sous la nef respectable
des cathédrales hypostyles,

la mesure admirable
ascende les cieux tranquilles
tout embaumés de lilas,
sous l'œil interdit des prélats.

Souvent la douleur est vive
alors souvent l'on danse et chante
sur la note imprécative
pour que la peine se décante.

La fumée d'une cigarette,
une pincée de poudre blanche,
un cadavre dans sa boîte nette
et le ciel dans sa robe pervenche
se trémoussent et s'éparpillent
d'un bout de métal informe;
d'une gueule qui babille
d'un cœur qui cherche sa forme.

Sombre...
La nuit épouse les rôdeurs
elle cache des dangers sans nombre
et des abîmes de douleur
dont le fracas se répercute
aux croisées des riches palaces,
aux portes de la morgue brute
et dont les pavés gardent la trace
jusqu'à la prochaine ondée.

Une trompette abouchée
dans un coin de la rue du bogue
égrène des trilles écorchées
qu'accompagne la basse des dogues;
et le soir tout plein d'émoi
s'écarte pour qu'arrive le bruit,

jusques aux palais des rois
et dans les antres de l'esprit.

Ascender : ce serait monter vers le ciel sans aide
d'aucune sorte; par sublimation en quelque sorte.

❦

PORGY AND SOUL

Dark...
A thigh moves
in the shadows.
Naked chests
make a mark
on the brown planks.
The back of the arch
looks like a crate of brown plums
when from time to time
a guard
tugs at
the groaning hatch...

In silence,
a knee
swings
jerkily.

From bowsprit to mizzen
the sad
song of the halyards
slides
and pours
into the black hole.
The lines and crosspieces

of the davit
jingle and squeak
with the undertow.

Incessantly,
in silence
a spot of sun
swings
on the floorboards
in the hold.
Gasping, a body leans over
rocking its pain
and its resentment.

Smoothly, from the bruised
heart, rises
a melody
syncopated
by anguish and shame...
Naked men in pain
sing the well-known tune
to this new rhythm
whose echo:
louder than their shaggy heads,
louder than the yellowed sails,
louder than the contrite clouds, reverberates
to infinity.

Over the years and beyond
the wonderful beat
marks sorrow, love, marks the great
and the needy:
in the soot of cannon fire
it marks the psalms
of men;

in the dust
of cotton,
in cottages
and ghettos,
in grand hotels, on boats
and even under the respectable naves
of hypostyle cathedrals,
the wonderful beat
ascends into the tranquil skies
that are embalmed with lilac,
under the forbidden eyes of prelates.

The pain is often sharp
so you often dance and sing
on a note of imprecation
for the pain to subside.

Cigarette smoke
a pinch of white powder,
a corpse in its clean box
and the sky in its periwinkle blue dress
wobble and spread
from a piece of shapeless metal;
from a chattering mouth
from a heart looking for its shape.

Dark...
Night gathers prowlers
it hides dangers without number
and abysses of grief
whose din re-echoes
in the casements of the rich hotels
in the doors of the crude mortuary
whose pavements keep the imprint
until the next shower.

An unmuted trumpet
in a corner of chestnut-bur street
sends out raspy trills
accompanied by the mastiffs' bass;
and the evening chock full of commotion
turns aside for the sound to reach
right into the palaces of kings
and into the caves of the mind.

Ascend: that would be rising towards the sky
without help of any kind; by sublimation in some
way.

The non-French title of "Porgy and Soul" (19-23) recalls the popular American song "Body and Soul" and immediately evokes the voice and image of American blacks, through the allusion to the "black" opera "Porgy and Bess," and to "soul," a quality associated with the music, sensibility and cultural heritage primarily of African Americans, and often accepted, with varying degrees of seriousness and humor, as an identifying characteristic among blacks world-wide. These allusions draw attention to "separated" parts of a unit, reflecting the Africans' separation from their homeland.

The isolated adjective with which the poem opens, "Sombre..." [Dark], sets the dominant visual and emotional mood which characterizes the whole poem, within which the various connotations of the word (lacking light, dark in color, melancholy, disturbing) are played out. The impression of darkness is confirmed by "pénombre" ([half-light] or, as I have rendered it, [shadows]), and accentuated by the movement of a disembodied thigh ("une cuisse remue"). Similarly, the dehumanized "torses nus" [naked chests] only serve to highlight the darkness of the "planches brunes" [brown planks]. The repetition of the adjective "brunes" [brown] in an abnormally strong position before "prunes" [plums] further emphasizes the significance of this dark brown color within the poem. Moreover, the implicit comparison between dark brown bodies and "un caisson de brunes prunes" [a crate of brown plums] in this context invites the association of blacks packed into the hold of a slave-ship. The closing movement of this first section, "un argousin / tire en peinant / l'écoutille qui geint...." [a guard / tugs at / the groaning hatch], adds to the impression of pain and disquiet already suggested.

The rhythm marked in the first section by short alternating rhymed lines, and reflected in the movement of the thigh, becomes even more distinct in the second section, through the off-beat movement of a knee: "un genou / se balance / par à-coups" [a knee / swings / jerkily]. In this section, the lines become shorter and the alliteration, particularly of the sibilant consonant, becomes more pronounced, as the musical expression suggested in the title is represented in the poem itself as a sad song: "la chanson / triste des drisses / glisse / et verse [the sad / song of the halyards / slides / and pours]. References to different kinds of masts ("beaupré" [bowsprit] and "artimon" [mizzen]) as well as to other nautical equipment ("drisses" [halyards], "saisines" [lines], "bossoir" [davit]), confirm the context of a ship already evoked in the first section. Thus the idea of "soul," as an expression of sadness in song (rhythm and blues), with origins in traumatic experiences of suffering, is associated here with the experience of "le trou noir" [the black hole] on board a slave-ship.

The rhythm is continued in the short alternating rhymed lines of the third section and in the reprise of the verb "se balance" [swings], the movement of which is emphasized by "berçant" [rocking]. Here "soul," as a rhythmical, musical expression of "blues," is inscribed in the phrase "berçant son mal et sa rancœur" [rocking its pain and its resentment]. This cultural expression is shown to emerge from the profound emotional suffering experienced by blacks ("du cœur meurtri" [from the bruised heart]) and assumes the form of rhythmical "blues": "une mélopée / syncopée / par l'angoisse et la honte.... [a melody / syncopated / by anguish and shame]. The association of suffering and song is also reflected in ("Endoloris des nus" [naked men in pain]), which evokes memories of tortured slaves. Thus the poem becomes an extension ("l'écho" [echo]) of a new voice created from this rhythm ("ce rythme nouveau") of suffering and the confirmation of the survival of this new voice beyond ("plus haut que ...") all expectation.

The following section, introduced by "Par delà les temps" [Over the years and beyond], pays tribute to the persistence of this new rhythm ("la mesure admirable" [the wonderful beat]), and gives an account of the different ways in which it has been manifested. The footnote to the poet's use of the neologism "ascende" indicates: "Ascender : ce serait monter vers le ciel sans aide d'aucune sorte; par sublimation en quelque sorte" [Ascend: that would be rising towards the sky without help of any kind; by sublimation in some way]. This rhythm is conceived of as having a force of its own, which enables it to survive and transcend limitations imposed by social conditions. The quality of poetic expression is presented therefore by the poet as a response to emotional need; consequently the tonality of the poem is affected by the frequency with which pain is experienced: "Souvent la douleur est vive / alors souvent l'on danse et chante / sur la note imprécative / pour que la peine se décante" [The pain is often sharp / so you often dance and sing / on a note of imprecation / for the pain to subside]. The connection between the grouped images of a cigarette, white powder, corpse, and sky is difficult to identify. The relationship, however, of these images to "un bout de métal informe" [a piece of shapeless metal] and to "une gueule qui babille" [a chattering mouth] conjures up the smoky, noisy atmosphere and the drug-related activities often associated with the world of jazz, while "un cœur qui cherche sa forme" [a heart looking for its shape] suggests not only the loneliness that often drives people to seek company in bars but also a more general need for artistic and emotional wholeness.

As the poem draws to a close, the descriptive term with which the poem opened is repeated ("Sombre...." [Dark]), re-emphasizing the dominant mood of the poem. Darkness here is a cloak not only for prowlers ("les rôdeurs") and dangers ("des dangers"), but particularly for the reverberating sounds of pain ("des abîmes de douleur / dont le fracas se répercute" [from abysses of grief / whose din re-echoes]). These sounds are represented metaphorically through the connection and the de-muting of the trumpet ("une trompette abouchée"), which re-introduces the "black" sound inscribed in the title -- the sound of jazz and soul. It is this sound that pierces the darkness, cutting across class lines, to affect the mind: "et le soir tout plein d'émoi / s'écarte pour qu'arrive le bruit, / jusques aux palais des rois / et dans les antres de l'esprit [and the evening chock full of commotion / turns aside for the sound to reach / right into the palaces of kings / and into the caves of the mind].

This poem is thus both an evocation and a demonstration of the source and potential of the "black" voice. The poet borrows images and rhythms from the black American musical experience to illustrate the relationship between this quality of voice and the experience of suffering by blacks on the Middle Passage. The idea of a continuity of voice runs through the poem, as the song born on board the slave ship continues and is heard in other places. The poem thus validates through its connection with the past the unbroken voice associated with the black experience.

PARIS

Paris les Moulin-Rouge;
Les « Caf-concs » et les snacks enfumés;
Paris les ombres qui bougent
Paris les fesses emplumées
J'aime la vie
De Paris
Ah! comme l'on s'y amuse
Les rats dansent même à l'opéra
Le Montmartre est plein de muses
Et tra déri déra ritra

Les nuits vivent mal à Paris
Les jours y sont dégingandés
Le noir y est toujours marri
Même quand il pare les endeuillés.
Ce que j'aime Paris,
A Paris!...

J'ai admiré ses monuments
Et parlé de son caractère
A des gens qui sur le moment
Le regardaient d'un air contraire

Vivent la java et puis les rires,
Les froufrous que l'on y côtoie,
La vie facile, le délire:
L'horizon est le faîte d'un toit
Il n'est de Paris
Qu'à Paris.
Alors pourquoi s'évertuer
A vouloir transformer le monde
Et la bonne ville tuer
Ou en faire quoi d'immonde
Pour mettre un Paris
Au pays...

❦

PARIS

Paris with its Moulin-Rouges;
Its "Caf-concs" and smoky snack bars;
Paris its moving shadows
Paris its feathered bums
I like the life
Of Paris

Ah! how much fun you have there
Rats dance even in the opera
Montmartre is full of muses
And tra-la-la-la-la.

Nights don't do well in Paris
Days there are out of joint
Black there is always woeful
Even when it adorns mourners.
How I like Paris,
In Paris!...
I've admired its monuments
And spoken of its character
To people who at the time
Were looking at it askance

Long live the spreeing and the laughter
The swishing skirts you rub against
The easy life, the frenzy:
The horizon is a rooftop.
There is no Paris
But in Paris.
So why go to such lengths
To try to transform the world,
And to kill a fine town
Or to make it into something filthy
Just to put a Paris
In our country...

In "Paris" (29), a poem overlaid with irony and frustration, the poet begins by evoking some of the attractions, which Paris holds for him. What attract the poet are the external, physical, touristic features of life in the French metropolis. The strangeness of these features, conveyed in "'Caf-concs'," ("cafés-concerts," music-hall cafés where the public are entertained by singers and other performers), "snacks enfumés" [smoky snack bars], "ombres qui bougent" [moving shadows], and "fesses emplumées" [feathered bums], is not only attractive, but also implicitly alienating. The assertions by the poet, "J'aime la vie / de Paris" [I like the life / of Paris] and "Ah! comme l'on s'y amuse" [Ah! how much fun you have there] are contradicted by the irony of the following lines: in "Les rats dansent même à l'opéra / Le Montmartre est plein de muses" [Rats dance even in the opera / Montmartre is full of muses] the poet plays on the *double entendre* of "rat de l'Opéra" which refers to a pupil of the Opéra de Paris ballet class working as an extra and of "muses" which alludes to the presence of prostitutes in this famous section of Paris. The flippancy of "Et tra déri déra ritra" [And tra-la-la-la-la] helps to underline the irony and poke subtle fun at Paris.

The ambiguous reaction on the part of the poet is reinforced in the second stanza, which presents a less superficial and less complimentary picture of Parisian life: "Les nuits vivent mal à Paris / Les jours y sont dégingandés" [Nights don't do well in Paris / Days there are out of joint]. The characteristic of life in the city which is most significant for the black (French Caribbean) poet within the French metropolitan sociocultural and linguistic context is the inescapably sad condition of "blackness": "Le noir y est toujours marri / Même quand il pare les endeuillés" [Black there is always woeful / Even when it adorns mourners]. This negative reaction to "blackness" and implicitly to "black" people, which the poet sees as a feature of Parisian life and which is inscribed within the language, is at the root of the poet's ambivalent response to the city.

Within the poem, the contrast between the poet's attempt to praise Paris and the response which he receives emphasizes his discomfort: "J'ai admiré ses monuments / Et parlé de son caractère / A des gens qui sur le moment / Le regardaient d'un air contraire [I've admired its monuments / And spoken of its character / To people who at the time / Were looking at it askance]. The passage from the present tense of the first two stanzas to the past tense in the third points to a change that has taken place in the poet. This change is reflected also in the direct references to Paris, from the "J'aime la vie / de Paris" [I like the life / of Paris], to the modified approval of "Ce que j'aime Paris, / A Paris!" [How I like Paris, / In Paris!], the modification of which is reinforced further by "Il n'est de Paris / Qu'à Paris" [There is no Paris / But in Paris]. The final stanza provides a return to expressions of admiration: "Vive la java et puis les rires" [Long live the spreeing and the laughter]. But the penultimate reference to Paris presents a conclusion of such unassailable validity that it legitimizes the subversion that follows. In the end Paris becomes simply "un Paris" [a Paris], associated with the defining adjective "immonde" [filthy].

Paris serves, in this poem, as the visible sign of the poet's cultural difficulty. It is through Paris, the center of metropolitan French culture, that the poet is able to confront the basic contradictions, which he experiences in his relationship with the metropole. The poem is an expression of a difference the poet wishes to preserve. The introduction of "Paris" into the Caribbean is seen as threat to the very life of the local town. This poem thus has an understated but strong sociopolitical dimension. There is no condemnation of the metropole as such, merely the recognition of a difference that should be maintained. There is, however, a strong rejection of the imposition of alien cultural values and a spirited defense of the native land against such an imposition. The poem serves as a mark of the poet's involvement in the struggle for cultural autonomy, as an expression of solidarity with the native land, and as vehicle for self-affirmation. The poem acts as the site where Paris is figuratively decentered and literally replaced as the source of poetic inspiration by "le pays" [the native land].

> « Terre ! Terre!... »
> Des humains faméliques
> Sur un rafiot pervers,
> Et, puant à l'envi des vapeurs éthyliques
> Débarquent dans ces eaux vierges...
> O'Waga, dans son antre

Des hauteurs carbétiennes, invoque le sang d'une
vierge
Dont palpite encore le ventre...
Autour d'un grand feu de campêche,
Qui crépite allègrement,
La pythonisse, en transes, prêche
Et débite son boniment...
— « Allez! Fils des Dieux rénovés
Allez, adorez vos maîtres;
Ils savent les secrets introuvés.
Vainqueurs; courez vous soumettre;
Des cieux voilà le châtiment.
Ils portent la mort en tube,
Et le tonnerre en même temps.
Ah! Madinina-Hécube
Verra périr tous ses enfants...
Ah! Si vous vouliez dérechef
Exterminer tous ces faux dieux
Du moussaillon jusqu'au chef:
Vos enfants pourraient vivre vieux...
Ils savent mettre en flacon
Plein de gaîté près du goulot
Et de la colère au fond.
Ah! mes pauvres poulots
Même pas ils ne leur feront
L'honneur de les manger
Et Madinina-Hécube verra noyer
Ses beaux enfants... »
Ayant dit la pythonisse hagarde
Un bûcher dans chaque œil
S'écroule ainsi qu'une outarde
Jabot gonflé de cerfeuil.
Depuis que les femmes aux fesses rondes
Avaient subi les maléfices
De « ceux-aux-tubes-qui-grondent »,

Des hommes avaient tué leurs fils,
Et s'étaient cachés dans la brousse.
— Toute la science des ancêtres
Blémit et puis s'émousse
Quand on l'emploi (sic) contre ces êtres...
Il reste la dernière chance,
L'ultime moyen de victoire:
Le Feu. Déesse de la danse;
Celle qui a vaincu le soir...

Les têtes grimaçantes
Derrière bambous et balisiers
Et fougères arborescentes
Sont des cibles très aisées...
Et Madinina-Hécube a vu pourrir tous ces enfants.

Diapré et chamarré
Malikoko content
Et souverain comblé
Perçoit bel argent comptant:
Vétilles et verroteries
Commerce régulier: patentes;
Os de vie contre eau de vie
Vivent les Dieux de la brocante
Historique bienfait
De sombres négriers, ventre bondé de chair
Grinçaient affreusement au poids de leur forfait
(Doux terreau pour un sol trop longtemps en
jachère)
Cependant que la mer profonde
Renvoyait en écho à tous les cœurs meurtris
Les cris glauques et immondes
D'une humaine cargaison pour une lointaine patrie
« Aux rivages de jade. »
O sombres galéjades!

Piétinement heureux,
La glèbe sulfureuse
Donne un arôme fameux
A la solanacée vénéneuse.

Bien fait
Travail d'esthète
Qu'extirper la moelle
Sans briser le squelette
Et décanter une âme sans que le corps
Se repose.
Tour de main; puissance; record.
Vous savez créer la névrose...

— « Patricide! Patricide!
Ils ont trempé leur plume dans le sang de leur mère;
Ils ont invoqué Homère et Ovide
Et puis ils ont vomi des tirades amères
Et grondé comme des lionnes
Et écrit des poèmes de fiel
Et puis foulé aux pieds la cendre panthéonne.
Ayant bu tout notre miel
Ils nous ont envoyé la cire à la tête
Et brisé nos demeures en criant: « Où sont-ils? »...

Qu'on leur donne alors les os de mes ancêtres
S'il leur manque des projectiles...

❧

"Land! Land!..."
Famished humans
On a perverted tub,
And each one more reeking of alcoholic fumes
than the other

Land on these virgin waters...
O'Waga, in her cave
In the carbetian heights, invokes the blood of a
virgin
Whose belly still quivers...
Around a great logwood fire
That crackles cheerfully,
The prophetess, in a trance, preaches
And spouts her pitch...
— "Go on! Sons of new Gods
Go on, adore your masters;
They know undiscovered secrets.
Victors; run and surrender;
That's the punishment from the heavens.
They carry death in tubes
And thunder at the same time.
Ah! Madinina-Hecuba
Will see all her children perish...
Ah! If you wanted once again
To exterminate all these false gods
From the ship's boy to the chief:
Your children could live to old age
They know how to put stuff in bottles
Full of good cheer near the neck
And of anger in the bottom.
Ah! not even will they
Pay my dear poppets
The honor of eating them
And Madinina-Hecuba will see
Her beautiful children drown..."
Having spoken the frenzied prophetess
A stake in each eye
Collapses like a bustard
Its crop swollen with chervil.
Since the time when the round-bottomed women

Had fallen under the evil spells
Of "those-with-tubes-of-thunder"
Men had killed their sons,
And had hidden out in the brush.
— All the knowledge of the ancestors
Grows pale and blunt
When used against these beings...
The last chance is left,
The only means of victory:
Fire. Goddess of the dance;
She who conquered evening...

Heads grimacing
Behind bamboos and balisiers
And tree ferns
Are very easy targets...
And Madinina-Hecuba saw all her children rot
away

Accoutered in motley colors
Malikoko a contented
And amply satisfied sovereign
Senses ready cash:
Baubles and glass beads
Regular trade: obvious;
Bone of life for water of life
Long live the flea market Gods
Historic benefit
Dark slave-ships, their bellies crammed with flesh

Creaked frightfully under the weight of their infamy
(Sweet compost for a soil too long in fallow)
While the deep sea
Sent back in echo to all bruised hearts
The vile cerulean cries

Of a human cargo for a faraway land
"To the shores of jade."
O gloomy yarns!
Happy stamping,
The sulphurous glebe
Gives the poisonous solanacea
A great aroma.

Well done
The work of an aesthete
Drawing out the marrow
Without breaking the skeleton
And decanting a soul without the body
Resting.
Dexterity; power; a record.
You know how to create neurosis...

— " Patricide! Patricide !
They soaked their pens in their mother's blood;
They invoked Homer and Ovid
And then they spewed forth bitter tirades
And growled like lionesses
And wrote poems of gall
And then trampled on the pantheonic ash.
Having drunk all our honey
They sent us wax in the head
And broke our dwellings, shouting: "Where are
they?"

May they then be given the bones of my ancestors
If they have no projectiles...

"Terre! Terre!" (68-71) is one of the most ambitious and significant
poems of the whole collection.   Here, the poet introduces a
complexity rarely confronted by West Indians: the contribution and

voice of the Caribs, native inhabitants of the Caribbean long before the arrival of Europeans or Africans. Assuming the role of narrator, the poetic persona recounts the first arrival of Europeans to the shores of his native island, at a time when the island was inhabited by Caribs, and transmits the voice of a population rarely recognized in historical or folk accounts. In this way the poet re-writes the history of his country, in order to explore some of the ways in which his attitude as a West Indian has been affected by European contact with his native island.

The poem begins by privileging orality. The opening words, "Terre! Terre!" [Land! Land!] transmit the voices of the European arrivals. The poet's bias is evident in the contrast between the picture he draws of these unattractive Europeans, shipwrecked, hungry, and reeking of alcohol, and his evocation of the purity of the Caribbean: "Des humains faméliques / Sur un rafiot pervers / Et, puant à l'envi des vapeurs éthyliques / Débarquent dans ces eaux vierges" [Famished humans / On a perverted tub / And each one more reeking of alcoholic fumes than the other / Land in these virgin waters]. The poet-narrator introduces the local sibyl, O'Waga ("la pythonisse" [the prophetess]), in a location typical of the mountainous north of Martinique, where Carib huts, referred to as "carbets" in Martinique, survive to this day, and where one of Martinique's administrative districts is named "Carbet": "dans son antre / Des hauteurs carbétiennes" [in her cave / In the carbetian heights]. (It is worth noting parenthetically that the Caribs fiercely resisted the brutality of European attempts at colonization in the fifteenth and sixteenth centuries, but were almost completely exterminated by the end of the seventeenth century. Miniscule populations survive in some of the neighboring islands such as St. Kitts and Dominica). O'Waga is shown to be involved in practicing her religious rituals, in a context of joy and gaiety ("allègrement"). The echoing of "ces eaux vierges" [these virgin waters] in "le sang d'une vierge" [the blood of a virgin] creates an association between the purity of the Caribbean waters and the ritual sacrifice by which the Carib culture is identified. What is implied, therefore, is that there is a link between the "purity" of the Caribbean and the maintenance of traditional non-European cultural practices.

O'Waga provides the second and other dominant voice in the poem. Hers is the voice of the original Martinican/Carib culture, as imagined by the poet. Through O'Waga, the poem becomes the authentic voice of Martinique. This is significantly a female voice, associated with the role of mother as conceiver, nurturer, and caretaker. It is O'Waga who "foretells" the tragic consequences for her people of abandoning their traditional gods and replacing them by making Europeans their new gods: "-- «Allez! Fils des Dieux rénovés / Allez, adorez vos maîtres; / Ils savent les secrets introuvés. / Vainqueurs; courez vous soumettre; / Des cieux voilà le châtiment." [Go on! Sons of new Gods / Go on, adore your masters; / They know undiscovered secrets. / Victors; run and surrender; / That's the punishment from the heavens]. This reference to a conflict between traditional (Carib) and modern (European) practices recalls the conflict implicit in the title of the collection and suggests the poet's desire to reject religious rituals (European, Catholic) which may conflict with what he chooses as his primary cultural heritage.

The poet recreates a composite persona, "Madinina-Hécube," who combines the original Carib name for Martinique and the name of the legendary wife of Priam and mother of Hector who lost her husband and most of her children in the Trojan war. Thus this persona suggests a mother figure that incarnates the cultural identities of both Caribs and Europeans. It is this composite cultural mother who is invoked by O'Waga in predicting the destruction of her own Carib people and of the children of this composite mother: "Ah! Madinina-Hécube / Verra périr tous ses enfants...." [Ah! Madinina-Hecuba / Will see all her children perish]. For O'Waga, Europeans represent false gods, whose destruction is necessary if the children of Martinique are to survive: "Ah! Si vous vouliez derechef / Exterminer tous ces faux dieux / Du moussaillon jusqu'au chef: / Vos enfants pourraient vivre vieux.... " [Ah! If you wanted once again / To exterminate all these false gods / From the ship's boy to the chief: / Your children could live to old age]. The association of Europeans with alcohol use, evoked at the beginning of the poem, is reintroduced by O'Waga to illustrate their potential for deception. Alcohol, through which the promise of joy becomes transformed into anger, becomes a metaphor for European duplicity: "Ils savent mettre en flacon / Plein de gaîté près du goulot / Et de la colère au fond" [They know how to put stuff in bottles / Full of good cheer near the neck / And of anger in the bottom].

O'Waga reintroduces the earlier characterization of Europeans as "faméliques" [famished], but gives it an ironic twist: "«Ah! mes pauvres poulots / Même pas ils ne leur feront / L'honneur de les manger / Et Madinina-Hécube verra noyer / Ses beaux enfants ....»" ["Ah! not even will they / Pay my dear poppets / The honor of eating them / And Madinina-Hecuba will see / Her beautiful children drown..."]. The failure of the Europeans ("ils" [they]) to eat the young Caribs is an indication of lack of respect and a sure sign of coming destruction for the Caribs. "Ils," however, is ambiguous, and could relate to the Caribs, and to their custom, reported by early European colonizers, of cannibalism. In this case, departure from tradition is the signal for coming destruction, since O'Waga believes that survival depends on fidelity to traditional ways. Later in the poem, the voracity and cannibalism of Europeans will become symbolized in the description of the slave-ships: "ventre bondé de chair" [their bellies crammed with flesh].

At the end of O'Waga's prophecy and her choice to commit suicide rather than witness the destruction of her people that she has foretold, the poet-narrator re-emerges to recount the results of the attempted domination of one culture, that of the Caribs, represented as a physical type different from the stereotypical European, by another, that of Europeans, represented as possessors of guns. The conflict between Caribs and Europeans is presented by the poet-narrator as a cultural conflict, in which the traditional practices of the Caribs prove inadequate: "--Toute la science des ancêtres / Blémit et puis s'émousse / Quand on l'emploi (*sic*) contre ces êtres ... [All the knowledge of the ancestors / Grows pale and blunt /

When used against these beings]. Even the final recourse to the power of the goddess of fire ("Celle qui a vaincu le soir" [She who conquered evening]) is unavailing and only serves to make the Caribs easier targets at night for the European guns. As a result, "Madinina-Hécube a vu pourrir tous ces enfants" [Madinina-Hecuba saw all her children rot away].

The poet-narrator then retraces another stage in the history of the Caribbean, hinting that the greed of a local chieftain was a motivator for encouraging the commerce with Europeans which was later to develop into the slave trade: "Os de vie contre eau de vie / Vivent les Dieux de la brocante / Historique bienfait / De sombres négriers, ventre bondé de chair." [Bone of life for water of life / Long live the flea market Gods / Dark slave-ships, their bellies crammed with flesh]. These "Dieux de la brocante" [flea-market Gods] form an ironic echo to the earlier "Dieux rénovés" [new Gods] that attracted the young Carib sons to O'Waga's characterization of Europeans as "faux dieux" [false gods], as well as to the ineffectuality of Fire, represented as "Déesse de la danse" [Goddess of the dance]. A further bitter irony is suggested in the pun "os de vie"/"eau de vie" [bone of life/ brandy (which I have translated as water of life to maintain the word play)] and in the representation of slave-ships as an "historique bienfait" [historic benefit].

The poet's understated but polyvalent description of the slave-ships as "sombres" [dark] is complemented by his evocation of the different sounds he associates with this trade: "Cependant que la mer profonde / Renvoyait en écho à tous les cœurs meurtris / Les cris glauques et immondes / D'une humaine cargaison pour une lointaine patrie" [While the deep sea / Sent back in echo to all bruised hearts / The vile cerulean cries / Of a human cargo for a faraway land]. The same adjective acquires a derisive resonance when repeated in the exclamation "O sombres galéjades!" [O gloomy yarns]. "Bienfait" [benefit], used earlier as a composite noun to provide a sarcastic commentary on slave-ships, is broken down into its component parts of adverb and noun to produce a reflexive and similarly self-mocking commentary on the poet's own poetic activity: "Bien fait / Travail d'esthète / Qu'extirper la moelle / Sans briser le squelette / Et décanter une âme sans que le corps / Se repose." [Well done / The work of an aesthete / Drawing out the marrow / Without breaking the skeleton / And decanting a soul without the body / Resting].

As the poem draws to a close, an unidentified voice, which could be that of O'Waga, is introduced, shouting "Patricide! Patricide!". This cry echoes the shout of "Terre! Terre!" with which the poem opened and suggests a similar new discovery or revelation. What is being revealed in the poem is in effect the process by which a cultural identity has been lost. It is within the poem that the accusation of patricide, the murder of parents and implicitly also of country, is voiced and heard. This accusation is directed at an unspecified "ils" [they], the children of the land, whose list of transgressions all suggest gross disrespect for their cultural heritage. The primary offense listed ("Ils ont trempé leur plume dans le sang de leur mère" [They soaked their pens in their mother's blood]) implies complicity in the destruction of the mother (country) and a violation of the respect owed. This image also indicates a transgression at the level of literary practice: the fact of writing in French. A similar transgression is implicit in the invocation of Homer and Ovid ("Ils ont invoqué Homère et Ovide" [They invoked Homer and Ovid]), prime representatives of epic and elegiac poetry which formed the cornerstone of the classical tradition of Western culture.

The poet's identification with victims of exploitation and violation is reflected in the personal pronoun "nous" [us]: "Ayant bu tout notre miel / Ils nous ont envoyé la cire à la tête / Et brisé nos demeures en criant: 'Où sont-ils?'.... [Having drunk all our honey / They sent us wax in the head / And broke our dwellings, shouting: "Where are they?"]. The poet's response becomes more individual, more personal ("mes" [my]), as the poem ends on a note of intense bitterness: "Qu'on leur donne alors les os de mes ancêtres / S'il leur manque des projectiles.... [May they then be given the bones of my ancestors / If they have no projectiles], in which "os" [bones] echoes the earlier bargain made of "os de vie" [bone of life] for "eau de vie" [brandy].

This poem illustrates in its inner contradictions aspects of the dilemma in which this French Caribbean poet is enmeshed. Padoly's use of "rimes croisées" attaches the poem to conventional French poetry while the subject matter rejects this cultural association. This poem rejoins in a way the emerging epic strain in French Caribbean literature as practiced by Glissant in *Les Indes*. Padoly here similarly coopts the voices of the participants in the history of the Caribbean, including those of Europeans, in order to introduce a new perspective to the Caribbean reality. The link between Glissant and Padoly cannot, however, be pushed too far, since Padoly refuses the notion of Antilleanity, which he regards as an illusion, continuing the illusion of naming the Caribbean territories the "Antilles." Padoly's triumph is in his imaginative recreation of the destruction of the original Carib culture and in his situating his own poetry within the context of a tradition that is definitely "Caribbean."

PRÉSAGE

C'était la musique de rien;
A moins que ce ne fut cette sensation de froid
A moins que ce ne fut le sentiment ancien
A moins que ce fut tout cela à la fois:
Je ne sais.
Musique, remusique; brassage d'effluves et d'âcreté
Douceur d'une peine qu'on essaie
D'oublier, lancinante, spasmodique comme des palpitations
Comme des coliques
Des brassages de boyaux; des triturations
D'entrailles de la femme en gésine
Curieuse doucine
Vision étrange

Que ce trou noir, rectangle de vide encadré de lumière.
Pierre
A briquet... Diamant!
Qui m'aveuglent le cœur dans un chintement*
D'appareil à jambon.
Curieux cœur
Lumineux et ombré, gondolé et strié comme un visage
Derrière des persiennes;
Derrière le grillage
D'un stalag, derrière le rectangle et derrière
Le visage de ma mère
Qui me regarde par ce trou noir.
Il s'époustoufle et puis tombe sur le sol ce visage
Il pleut en gouttes qui moirent
Il dégouline ce présage
En gouttes de cheveux
En gouttes d'oreilles et en gouttes de dents
Et en gouttes d'yeux
Qui me tombent dessus qui me tombent dedans

* *Bruit que fait la lame en coupant la viande en minces
tranches.*

Je déborde d'hideur
Je me rejaillis aux pieds, je suis en crue
Et m'éclabousse d'écume et me monte à la taille, aux épaules, la
gorge; l'odeur
De mon sang fait craquer mes narines. Goût du sang suave et
cru...
Je me laisse m'égarer
M'aveugler
M'immerger
Me noyer
Plutôt...

ॐ

OMEN

It was the music of nothingness;
Unless it was this sensation of coldness
Unless it was the old feeling
Unless it all that at once:
I do not know.
Music, more music; mixing of effluvia and acridity
Sweetness of a hurt one tries
To forget, piercing, spasmodic like palpitations
Like belly pains
Twisting in the guts; grinding
Of the wombs of women in labor
Curious molding
Strange vision
This black hole, rectangle of emptiness framed in light.
Cigarette lighter
Flint... A diamond!
That blind my heart in the squish
Of a ham-slicing machine.
Curious heart
Full of light and shade, warped and streaked like a face
Behind shutters;
Behind the wire mesh
Of a stalag, behind the rectangle and behind
My mother's face
Who looks at me through this black hole.
This face is flabbergasted and then falls on to the ground
It rains in drops that shimmer
It drips this omen
In drops of hair
In drops of ears and in drops of teeth
And in drops of eyes

That fall on me and in me
I overflow with hideousness
I splash back on to my feet, I am in spate
And am spattered in foam and rise up to my waist, to my
shoulders, my throat; the smell
Of my blood makes my nostrils split. Smell of sweet, raw
blood...

                                             I let myself get
lost
                              Blinded
                    Submerged
          Drowned
   Rather...

This final poem in the collection, "Présage" [Omen] (73), is, as its title indicates, a nightmarish projection of what the future is likely to bring. The language and imagery are obscure, reflecting the poet's inability to arrive at or to articulate a clear response to the sociocultural situation that confronts him. However, the attention paid to the graphical arrangement of the poem, characterized by lines of varying lengths centered along a vertical axis and featuring a staggered indentation of the final lines, conveys a sense of fixity, unity, and harmony. This harmony is further enhanced by subtle rhymes and assonances throughout the poem ("rien"/"ancien," "froid"/"fois," "palpitations"/"triturations," "gésine"/"doucine," "visage"/"grillage," "visage"/"présage," "noir"/"moirent," "cheveux"/"d'yeux," "hideur"/"odeur").

As the poem opens, sensory uncertainty prevails, underscored by the poet's inability to distinguish between the confusing impressions with which he is assailed. An association is established between "la musique" [music], "sensation de froid" [sensation of coldness], and "le sentiment ancien" [the old feeling], to the point where differences disappear and the poet loses the ability to differentiate: "Je ne sais" [I do not know]. The repetition of "à moins que" [unless] communicates his groping towards representation and understanding, and his hesitation to be definitive in interpreting his experience. Uncertainty is reflected too in the contradictory reaction of pleasure to the chronic intense pain experienced: "Douceur d'une peine qu'on essaie / D'oublier, lancinante, spasmodique ...." [Sweetness of a hurt one tries / To forget, piercing, spasmodic]. This physical and emotional sensation, which the poet compares to intestinal cramps and labor pains, is translated by the poet into a visual image of contrasting light and darkness, the importance of which is conveyed by the length of the line: "Vision étrange / Que ce trou noir, rectangle de vide encadré de lumière" [Strange vision, rectangle of emptiness framed in light]. This reference to a "trou noir" forms an intertextual linkage with Césaire, who used the same image at the end of the Cahier to indicate his changed attitude to his situation as a black Martinican in resolving the dilemma of identity: "et le grand trou noir où je voulais me noyer l'autre lune / c'est là que je veux pêcher maintenant .... [and the great black hole in which I wanted to drown myself a moon ago / it's there I want to fish now] (155). Here, Padoly uses the image to suggest the same locus of painful self-awareness where the identity dilemma must be confronted.

The pain of self-awareness experienced by the poet is translated into images which convey the effect of a sudden blinding flash of light against the darkness of his heart: "Pierre / A briquet ... Diamant! / Qui m'aveuglent le cœur .... [Cigarette lighter / Flint... A diamond! / That blind my heart]. The poet's disturbance is intensified as the image of the heart, suffering from intense pain as well as from the effect of the blinding flash of intense light, becomes supplanted by that of a face. The horizontal strips of light and darkness reflected on a face behind shutters are immediately replaced metonymically by the vertical strips associated with imprisonment behind bars, while the disembodied face emerges to become more clearly that of the poet's mother:

> Lumineux et ombré, gondolé et strié comme un visage
> Derrière le grillage

D'un stalag, derrière le rectangle et derrière
Le visage de ma mère
Qui me regarde par ce trou noir.

[Full of light and shade / warped and streaked like
a face / Behind shutters; / Behind the wire mesh /
Of a stalag, behind the rectangle and behind / My
mother's face / Who looks at me through this black
hole].

"Ce visage," the poet's mother's face, rhymes and fuses with "ce
présage," the omen of the title, as it literally dissolves into drops of
liquid body parts:

Il pleut en gouttes qui moirent
Il dégouline ce présage
En gouttes de cheveux
En gouttes d'oreilles et en gouttes de dents
Et en gouttes d'yeux
Qui me tombent dessus qui me tombent dedans.

[It rains in drops that shimmer / It drips this omen
/ In drops of hair / In drops of ears and in drops of
teeth / And in drops of eyes / That fall on me and
in me].

This nightmarish image represents the poet's awareness of a
fragmentation of his physical identity, the result of which for him is
a conviction of his ugliness: "Je déborde d'hideur" [I overflow with
hideousness]. This conviction (which is shared by many or even
most blacks in societies which have been subjected to domination
by white cultural values) inevitably produces self-hatred and a
desire to reject the source on which his identity depends: "l'odeur /
de mon sang fait craquer mes narines" [the smell / Of my blood
makes my nostrils split]. As the poem and the collection ends, the
poet is in a state of uncertainty, reluctant to assert himself:

> Je me laisse m'égarer
> M'aveugler
> M'immerger
> Me noyer
> Plutôt....

[I let myself get lost / Blinded / Submerged / Drowned / Rather...]

Significantly, however, where the Césairian poetic persona had grappled with and overcome the suicidal temptation, Padoly's persona, at the end of this poem, is in the process of submitting to the temptation. This poem is thus an indication of the perhaps temporary place Padoly has reached in his attempt to resolve the problems posed by the dilemma of his existence as a French West Indian. The poem suggests that this dilemma is an obsessive, nightmarish, concern of the poet and it is this concern that is explored by the poem, even though no solution is offered. The poem nevertheless becomes the arena within which the poet is able to confront his personal and cultural demons.

It is not without significance that *Le missel noir* was published in Monaco, rather than in Paris or Martinique, which suggests that Padoly may have experienced difficulty in having his voice heard through the usual publishing channels that would have been available to Martinicans. Since the late 1940s, the African-founded publishing house in Paris, Présence Africaine, had provided an outlet for voices from the African diaspora, including those of Césaire and Glissant,[2] while the more mainstream Parisian publishers, Les Editions du Seuil, published Césaire's *Cadastre* and Glissant's *Poèmes*. Both Carbet and Polius found other Parisian publishers: P.J. Oswald, in the case of Polius, and Le Cerf-volant in the case of Carbet. Thus the choice of Monaco indicates a double marginalization of Padoly's work, in relation both to France and to the Caribbean. And yet he has produced a body of poetry, which affirms its own right to be heard as a manifestation of one of the authentic voices of Martinique.

Padoly, it is clear, has not in this collection of poetry reached the level of poetic self-confidence and certainty achieved by either Césaire or Glissant. His poetic program, however, does not lack ambition. His poetry serves, more clearly than for either Césaire or Glissant, as a mirror in which he opposes false self-images and confronts his true self. His poetry reflects a more intense consciousness that his self-esteem is constantly under attack by a "white" world, and a more emphatic representation of his "difference" as a black man. Padoly, like Césaire and Glissant, tries to reconcile poetic practice with political interest. Painfully aware of the dilemma confronting him, he writes through the pain, in an attempt to re-write Martinican cultural history, and to establish this collection of poetry as an authentic "black" book, as a viable and preferred alternative to the "rituals" of the European cultural tradition. In spite of the temptation to submit to the impossibility of the task, Padoly still manages to evoke the almost forgotten voice of the Caribs, and to establish linkage with them as essential to his cultural identity. Padoly's mixture of European and African forms and his use of oral rhythms are part of the ambiguous and problematical identity which he forges. His evocation of Caribs and of American blacks enables him to piece together a voice different from that which was lost. He is thus able to construct a new Caribbean voice from fragments of lost and dispersed peoples.

Notes

[1] Page citations for poems in this chapter refer to Padoly 1965.

[2] Note, for example, that Césaire's *Cahier* and Glissant's *Le sang rivé* were published by Présence Africaine. For comments on the early development and role of Présence Africaine, see Kesteloot 1963:252-72.

8

Joseph POLIUS

Joseph Polius was born December 21, 1942, in Lamentin, Martinique, an area that he considers as "the crucible for the labor consciousness of the Martinican proletariat."[1] His childhood, as he described it in an unpublished interview with me, was one of extreme poverty and deprivation. His mother did day jobs, taking in sewing or working in the cane fields, fighting every day to find the means to support her children, Joseph and his two half-sisters. He lost his mother before he was fourteen and found himself living alone, struggling to support himself and to survive. He was forced to drop out of secondary school in his final year because his homework was not presented in an exercise book but on a single sheet of paper. He did not have the money to buy an exercise book. In 1961 he created La Jeunesse Révolutionnaire Lamentinoise, a group that helped give birth to OJAM, l'Organisation de la Jeunesse Anticolonialiste Martiniquaise (Organization of Martinican Anticolonialist Youth). Polius was arrested and imprisoned in March 1963 when the colonial power banned OJAM and went after its members. He ended up in Paris from 1965 to 1968, where he tried to organize in Paris a party of Martinican emigrants. During this period, Polius also met and established relations with revolutionary anticolonialist leaders including the Vietnamese Le Duc Tho, the Congolese Joseph Soumialof, and Jacques Verges. In 1970, he founded with the help of some others, another activist organization called Groupe Septembre 1970 (named after a peasant revolt). This Group initiated the great strike of February 1974 in Chalvet that resulted in two people dead and more than thirty wounded after being fired upon by the forces of repression. Polius has been active politically in promoting changes in trade union legislation. He now lives and works as a Social Security director in Martinique. He has been writing poetry since age 16, and has had some of it published in journals, including *Nouvelle Somme de poésie du monde noir* (Paris: Présence Africaine, 1966), and N.R. Shapiro's *Negritude: Black Poetry from Africa and the Caribbean* (New York: October House, 1970). He has also published in *Afrique-Actuelle*, *Présence Africaine*, and in the surrealist journal, *Grand Ecart*. He has so far published two collections of poetry, *Bonheur de poche* (1968), and *Martinique debout* (1977).

MON PAYS

Comme
Comme une scolopendre tapie au salon d'une mémoire
Comme l'envers d'une misère
Prise à deux mains
Un soir d'anniversaire
Comme une goutte de sang prise œil de soleil
Dans le goulot du désir
Comme un hoquet dans le tourniquet du rire

Comme une bouche enceinte de mille promesses
cadavériques
Comme deux aiguilles bien sûr
Qui depuis trois siècles marquent la même heure
Comme un soldat marque le pas.
Comme un jupon de femme sur le clocher d'une
église
Comme...
Comme une détresse de canne à sucre
Sur l'espérance qui se givre
Comme un suicide de luciole
Dans un rêve de statue de paix
Comme un chuchotement de pierre dans un désert
de glace
Comme une dent cariée dans une bouche saine
Comme moi parlant à moi-même
A travers la paroi de cette île
Cette Martinique
Miette brisée attendant sa naissance

ೆ

MY COUNTRY

Like
Like a centipede curled up in the living room of a
memory
Like the bottom of a birthday cake
Taken in both hands
On a birthday evening
Like a drop of blood caught a sun's eye
In the bottle's neck of desire
Like a hiccup in the turnstile of laughter
Like a mouth pregnant with a thousand cadaverous
promises

Like two clock hands of course
That for three centuries now have been marking the same hour
Like a soldier marks time.
Like a woman's skirt on a church's steeple
Like...
Like the distress of sugar cane
On hope that's frosting up
Like a firefly's suicide
In a peace statue's dream
Like a whisper of stone in a desert of ice
Like a decayed tooth in a healthy mouth
Like me speaking to myself
Through the wall of this island
This Martinique
A broken crumb waiting to be born

Bonheur de poche[2] [*Pocket Happiness*], a slim volume of 28 poems, establishes a parallel, through the metonymic relationship of the title with "livre de poche" [pocket book], between the text as text and happiness, and draws attention, through "de poche" [pocket], to its small size. Thus, the title indicates that the volume is an emblem of the commodification of happiness, packaged for consumption. The relation of poetry to socialism and the political is reflected also in the dedication of the collection "À tous mes camarades ouvriers, à mon pays" [To all my comrade workers, to my country]. Politically, this dedication signifies, in the use of the term "camarades ouvriers" [comrade workers], the socialist thrust of the poet's sympathies. In practical terms, the dedication announces the poet's decision to align himself with the workers in their struggle as Martinicans for freedom and justice. Culturally, it presents itself as a communication directed exclusively to fellow Martinicans and others who share a bond of "class." In other words, economic considerations supersede bonds of "race."

"Mon pays" (13) presents a textual dramatization of the poet's relationship to his native land. His sense of identification with his country is affirmed in the possessive of the title and in the later reference to "cette Martinique" [this Martinique] toward the end of the poem. It is, however, in the isolated first word ("comme" [like]) of the poem, that the textual drama is initiated. This word, used fifteen times in the poem in the strong position at the beginning of the line, indicates that the poet's dominant concern is to find a way of conveying an essence through the presentation of appropriate similes for his native land, "cette Martinique." The initial isolation of "comme," the later isolation of the word followed by suspension points that emphasize the hesitation of the poet ("comme..."), and the frequency with which the term is repeated, all attest to the difficulty experienced by the poet in finding suitable comparisons. There is, therefore, a problem at the level of language in representing the reality he seeks to articulate.

This problem is reflected also in the nature of the comparative images given, all of which point to some form of incongruity. The first comparison, for example ("Comme une scolopendre tapie au salon d'une mémoire" [Like a centipede curled up in the living room of a memory]), represents Martinique as an embarrassing, unwelcome, loathsome, and potentially dangerous presence. From the perspective of Europe, Martinique is shown to be a disturbing, unexpected, and unwanted historical memory that cannot, however, be ignored. The sense of frustration underlying the incongruous images that the poet associates with his native land becomes clearer in "Comme une bouche enceinte de mille promesses cadavériques" [Like a mouth pregnant with a thousand cadaverous promises], where the dilemma of voice, for which "bouche" [mouth] serves as a metaphor, is presented as a characteristic of the situation of Martinique: the poetic voice, so full of potential, is doomed to be stillborn. Many French Caribbean poets, as we have seen, share the preoccupation with this problem. The image that follows, "Comme deux aiguilles bien sûr / Qui depuis trois siècles marquent la même heure / Comme un soldat marque le pas" [Like two clock hands of course / That for three centuries now have been marking the same hour / Like a soldier marks time], echoes the earlier reference to memory and places this frustration in an historical perspective. This is an allusion to the fact that the present stagnation has been the inevitable result of three hundred years of slavery and colonization. The importance of this historical context is further emphasized by the reference to "canne à sucre" [sugar cane], which is an ironic and visible sign in the Caribbean of the dominance of slave-owners and colonizers. The persistence of sugar cane thus reinforces the hopelessness of the Martinican situation: "Comme une détresse de canne à sucre / Sur l'espérance qui se givre..." [Like the distress of sugar cane / On hope that's frosting up]. This hopelessness is translated into a cluster of images, in which suicide is equated and fused with misplaced trust in Europeans: "Comme un suicide de luciole / Dans un rêve de statue de paix " [Like a firefly's suicide / In a dream about a peace statue]. These metaphors suggest the contrast between the promise of peace in a religious statue and the actuality of death for the firefly in the candle's flame.

While the earlier comparison made between Martinique and "une bouche" [a mouth] had indicated Martinique's disappointing potential as a reliable voice, the return of the image of the mouth in a new context ("Comme une dent cariée dans une bouche saine" [Like a decayed tooth in a healthy mouth]) further emphasizes the problematical situation of the native island. The comparison made between Martinique and a decayed tooth points not only to a condition of decay but also to a perception of incongruity, of disappointing and embarrassing difference. Furthermore, the juxtaposition of the image of "une bouche saine" [a healthy mouth] to the final comparison in the poem forms an intertextual resonance with Césaire's "la bouche aux parois du nid" [the mouth at the walls of the nest] ("Magique," *Cadastre*, 9): "Comme moi parlant à moi-même / À travers la paroi de cette île" [Like me speaking to myself / Through the wall of this island]. This comparison invites the establishment of a direct link between the situation of the island

and the dilemma of the poet. Césaire's dilemma was that of a potential voice confronted by the practical limitations of the island. Polius's comparison also poses the problem of voice. It casts doubt on the effectiveness of poetic communication and implies that the island is itself a barrier to communication.

As the poem ends, the association between "mon pays" [my country] of the title and "Cette Martinique" [This Martinique] is finally established, as the poet's island is given a name. Significantly, although Martinique is presented as a fragment of a larger entity, presumably Africa ("Miette brisée" [broken crumb]), it is invested with a separate identity even before it is born ("attendant sa naissance" [waiting to be born]). "Miette" [crumb], which evokes the picture of a patch of land floating aimlessly in a large sea (Caribbean), also recalls Césaire's reference in *Cahier* to "Îles miettes" [island crumbs](133). This image attests to the fact that the identity of Martinique as an entity existing in the present is problematical for the poet, who can conceive of it only in terms of a future reality.

"Mon pays" represents an attempt to render through a series of comparisons the poet's perception of his native land. It is a concrete illustration of the problem which results from the European view of the historical situation of Martinique, and which causes difficulties for both the island and the poet. The poet experiences difficulty even in articulating, through appropriate terms of comparison, the truth as he sees it about the native land to which he is so firmly attached. The poem is also an expression of love and of commitment. The picture drawn is not a sentimental description of the external beauty of the country. It is a shocking reversal of the European portrayal of tropical paradises, as depicted for example by Charles Baudelaire's "L'Invitation au voyage," where "Là n'est qu'ordre et beauté / Luxe, calme, et volupté" [There is nothing but order and beauty / Luxury, calm, and sensuality]. Polius's view of the Caribbean is that of an insider. It is a lucid view, conducted with love and commitment. This poem represents the appropriation of a perception by someone who belongs and who cares.

MISÈRE DES MOTS

A Emile ANAÏS.

Misère de l'amour et
Des merveilleuses promesses
Misère des airs gelés
Et des douteuses caresses

Misère du bidonville
Rêve noirci d'un décor
Où ça-et-là s'éparpillent
Les cendres du colon mort.

Misère de la jeunesse
Prise au piège de l'espoir
Secouant ses chaînes. Hardiesse!
C'est le temps des soleils noirs.

Misère des filles-mères
Clouées aux terribles sillons
Offrant leur poitrine fière
Aux morsures des saisons

Misère des mots, du sang.
J'écoute alors solitaire
La grande plainte du vent
Le cri du sol, et j'espère.

Mais l'espoir poursuit sa route
La Santé, Fresne, autant
De pièges, d'écueils, de doutes
Sur la route du printemps.

J'ai soif et j'attends l'heure

— Depuis trois siècles j'attends —
Où ma Patrie, majeure,
Epousera son amant.

Est-ce la chanson du ciel
Ou le vent du soir qui pleure?
Donne moi un peu de sel
C'est trop beau! La nuit se meurt.

Sur de merveilleux matins
S'ouvriront nos sacrifices
Fleurira notre destin
Veuf de millions de délices

Vois. Une aube se dénoue
Pour que jamais plus demain
Dans la vie autour de nous
Les gens ne manquent de pain.

Je hais la peur et la haine.
Mon cœur mon âme mes mains
Qu'une passion entraîne
Chantent la fin de la faim.

Ecoute peuple mon Frère
Peuple Martyr, Peuple Roi
Vérité germant sous terre
Debout! Arrache ton droit.

🙂

WOE OF WORDS

Woe of love and
Of wonderful promises

Woe of frozen airs
And of dubious caresses

Woe of the shanty-town
Blackened dream of a setting
Where here and there are being scattered
The ashes of the dead colonist.

Woe of the youth
Caught in hope's trap
Shaking off their chains. Audacity!
It is the time of black suns.

Woe of child mothers
Nailed to the terrible fields
Offering their proud breasts
To the seasons' bites.

Woe of words, of blood.
So I listen, all alone,
To the wind's great lament
To the soil's cry, and I hope.

But hope continues on its way
La Santé, Fresne, so many
Traps, reefs, doubts
On spring's road.

I am thirsty and am waiting for the time
— For three centuries now I have been waiting —
When my Country, come of age,
Will wed her lover.

Is it the sky's song
Or the weeping of the evening wind?

Give me a little salt
It's too beautiful! Night is dying.

Our sacrifices will open
To wonderful mornings
Our destiny will flower
Bereft of millions of delights

Look. A dawn is unfolding
So that never ever again
In life around us
Will people want for bread.

I hate fear and hatred.
My heart my soul my hands
Carried along by a passion
Sing of the end of hunger.

Listen my Brother people
Martyr people, King People
Truth sprouting underground
Up! Seize what's yours by right.

"Misère des mots" (15-16) indicates, through its title, the poet's conception of a problem or an inadequacy that he experiences at the level of language. It is structured on alternating rhymes of "impair" [irregular] seven-syllable lines, suggested by Paul Verlaine in the latter half of the nineteenth century in his attempt to break away from traditional French versification. Polius's twentieth century production thus borrows the structure of some late nineteenth century French poetry. This choice of form, particularly in a poem, which calls, in its final line, for a revolutionary uprising, is an indication of the cultural contradictions experienced by the poet.

The word "misère" [woe] is used as the opening term of a litany in the first five stanzas of the poem to signal the dominant characteristic (of wretchedness and inadequacy) which the poet associates with the "reality" that confronts him. The emotive force of the repeated term of lamentation also signals the ambivalent attitude of the poet — empathy and identification as well as regret and rejection — towards this reality. Different connotations of the term "misère" are used to identify the problematical conditions that the poet observes in the world around him. Thus, in the first stanza, the poet establishes a regrettable parallel between expectations of warm love and the experience of coldness and deceit: "Misère de l'amour et / Des merveilleuses promesses / Misère des airs gelés / Et des douteuses caresses" [Woe of love and / Of wonderful promises / Woe of frozen airs / And of dubious caresses]. The dense imagery of the second stanza conveys the poet's identification with the inevitably wretched condition of blacks living in the Fort-de-France shanty-towns that emerged from the ruins of colonization: "Misère du bidonville / Rêve noirci d'un décor / Où ça-et-là s'éparpillent / Les cendres du colon mort [Woe of the shanty-town / Blackened dream of a setting / Where here and there are being scattered / The ashes of the dead colonist].

The poet's empathy continues in the third stanza, as he identifies with the difficult situation of French Caribbean youth who are rebelling against conditions of hopelessness and enslavement: "Misère de la jeunesse / Prise au piège de l'espoir / Secouant ses chaînes" [Woe of the young / Caught in hope's trap / Shaking off their chains]. The exclamation "Hardiesse!" [Audacity] signifies the poet's approval of and admiration for the young people's liberating activity, which he interprets metaphorically as a sign of the ascendancy of blacks: "C'est le temps des soleils noirs" [It is the time of black suns]. This hope seems negated, however, by the condition of young rural child-mothers, whom he evokes working bare-chested in the fields. They also attract the sympathy of the poet, who presents them ("clouées" [nailed]) as symbols of Christ-like crucifixion: "Misère des filles-mères / Clouées aux terribles sillons / Offrant leur poitrine fière / Aux morsures des saisons" [Woe of child mothers / Nailed to the terrible fields /

Offering their proud breasts / To the season's bites]. This image is subtly subversive. An element often used as an indication of sexual attraction and of lubricious exotic appeal is presented here in such a way as to underscore it sociopolitical significance. Sensuality is subordinated to social consciousness.

The fifth stanza provides a synthesis to the preceding litany of wretchedness, which the poet significantly summarizes in relation to two main categories, words and blood: "Misère des mots, du sang" [Woe of words, of blood]. This categorization indicates that the poet experiences the greatest difficulty in the area of expression ("mots" [words]), and in relation to the complex of race/life/energy ("sang" [blood]) which constitutes his being. It is his awareness of this perplexing situation that contradictorily both isolates him and enables him to find hope through his attunement to the "natural" voices of his universe: "J'écoute alors solitaire / La grande plainte du vent / Le cri du sol, et j'espère " [So I listen, all alone, / To the wind's great lament / To the soil's cry, and I hope]. Even hope, however, is problematical. Just as it had been represented as a "piège" [trap] in the third stanza, the contradiction is indicated between the poet's private hope and the actuality of disappointment. This contradiction is transmitted in the opposition implicit in the "Mais" [But] with which the sixth stanza opens. The journey of hope, represented figuratively as "la route du printemps" [spring's road], reflects the poet's concern, not only in the clashing metaphorical combination of physical and emotional obstacles which he observes ("de pièges, d'écueils, de doutes" [traps, reefs, doubts]), but also in the image of spring, which is more typical of the European geography and culture than of the Caribbean.

In the seventh stanza, the poet identifies himself (through "j'" [I]) as the voice of the non-European (Martinican) community, who are characterized by a need and by an expectation: "J'ai soif et j'attends l'heure / — Depuis trois siècles j'attends — [I am thirsty and am waiting for the time / — For three centuries now I have been waiting]. "Depuis trois siècles" [for three centuries now] is an elliptical reference to the long period during which slave colonies have been maintained in the Caribbean and an indication of the poet's belief that nothing has really changed in the status of the Caribbean people. This belief is linked, in this stanza, to another aspect of the predicament in which the poet is involved. The expression used by the poet to convey his desire for change and his anticipation of the time when his country will attain its majority ("ma Patrie, majeure" [my Country, come of age]) represents self-devaluation, in that the expression borrows the colonizer's voice which, by designating Africans as children, attempted to justify colonization and slavery.

The poet's anticipation becomes transformed into a vision (stanzas 8-9), in which he identifies completely with his people ("nos sacrifices" [our sacrifices], "notre destin" [our destiny]). The increasing concreteness of the vision is reflected in the movement from the future tense to the present ("S'ouvriront" — "fleurira" → "se dénoue" [will open — will blossom → is unfolding]), and a parallel is established between the function of the poetic vision and the social and political purpose of the poetic activity: "Pour que jamais plus demain / Dans la vie autour de nous / Les gens ne manquent de pain" [So that never ever again / In life around us / Will people want for bread].

The paradox in the assertion, "Je hais la peur et la haine" [I hate fear and hatred], is a reflection both of the contradictions inherent in the sociocultural context within which the poet writes and of the emotional crisis faced by the poet. It is out of the need to make sense of these contradictions that his poetry emerges, as the expression of an emotional, spiritual, and physical commitment: "Mon cœur mon âme mes mains / Qu'une passion entraîne / Chantent la fin de la faim" [My heart my soul my hands / Carried along by a passion / Sing of the end of hunger]. The active singing of heart and hands contrasts with the poet's passive listening ("j'écoute solitaire" [I listen, all alone]). The need for a voice, signaled by "chantent" [sing], is at the root of the deliberate ambiguity of the pun "la fin de la faim" [the end of hunger], as the poem becomes the expression of the poet's hope as well as of his doubt, of his need as well as of his vision. The final stanza emphasizes, in "Ecoute peuple" [Listen, people] and "Debout! Arrache ton droit" [Up! Seize what's yours by right], the function of the poem as an oral, motivational communication addressed to the Martinican people, who are invested with dignity and nobility through the capitalizations of "mon Frère / Peuple Martyr, Peuple Roi" [my Brother / Martyr People / King People].

The whole poem presents, therefore, as its title had foreshadowed, some of the basic problems that the poet faces in attempting to find a political and poetic solution to the complex cultural situation of which he is a part. The poet's experience of emotional and cultural contradictions is reflected in the form and the language of the poem. The contradictions within this poem forcefully dramatize the poet's dilemma, a paradox that is at the core of all poetry: the use of words to demand action despite the consciousness of the inadequacy of words (conveyed in the title). The only solution found by the poet is nevertheless to use the poem, however inadequate it may be, to call for social and political upheaval.

CHANSON I

Au pays sombre plus sombre que peau noire
Je vous sens tourmenté non de Terre neuve et
d'Aurores fraîches
Mais de faim de savoir et de soif de liberté
De faim et de soif tout court
Affolantes inconnues d'un quotidien problème
Ile noire de sel noir
Au rire de fin du monde
Dont le bras presqu'île dit
Toute la détresse de l'homme né libre
Fait bête
Pays natal
          Ah vingt fois natal

Au cœur fermé à toute haine
Au regard vierge de tout venin
Quel repos le soir
Quand mains noués sous la nuque
Je pose ma tête lourde
Sur le ventre frais de tes sillons

ॐ

SONG I

Ah! Dark country darker than black skin
I feel you tormented not by new found Land
and cool Dawns
But by hunger for knowledge and by thirst for
liberty
By hunger and by thirst in short
These perturbing unknowns of an everyday
problem
Black island of black sand
With an end-of-the-world laugh
Whose peninsular arm tells
All the distress of man born free
Made into beast
Native land
                         Ah! twenty times native
With a heart closed to all hatred
With a look virgin of all venom
How restful in the evening
When hands clasped behind my neck
I lay my heavy head
On the cool belly of your furrows

"Chanson 1" (17), with its unrhymed lines of varying lengths and
lack of punctuation is more clearly modern in form than "Misère de

mots." Its title draws immediate attention to the orality of the poem, and suggests, in the numerical notation, that this is the first in a series of "chansons" [songs]. However, the expectation of a continuity is not realized in this collection and, in fact, Polius has not to date published any other poem entitled "Chanson." The opening line ("Ah pays sombre plus sombre que peau noire" [Ah! Dark country darker than black skin]) immediately illustrates one aspect of the dilemma which confronts the poet. The word "noire" [black], used to designate the people with whom the poet identifies, is associated metonymically with "sombre" [dark], and thus signifies more than a physical characteristic of skin color, but also negative emotional and social conditions. At the same time, "peau noire" [black skin], particularly within the context of French Caribbean letters, inevitably recalls the title of Fanon's famous *Peau noire masques blancs [Black Skin White Masks]*, which specifically examines the contradictions manifested in the black colonized people of the French Caribbean. Furthermore, the repetition of "sombre," which serves as an umbrella descriptor linking both the people and the country, by emphasizing their common negative characteristic, drives home the fact that the language of identification is itself problematical.

The poetic persona enters (as "je" [I]) to identify and express empathy with the excruciatingly painful situation of this country ("vous" [you]), deprived of knowledge and of liberty: "Je vous sens tourmenté non de Terre neuve et d'Aurores fraîches / Mais de faim de savoir et de soif de liberté / De faim et de soif tout court" [I feel you are tormented not by new found Land and fresh Dawns / But by hunger for knowledge and by thirst for liberty / By hunger and by thirst in short]. It is the basic condition of hunger and thirst, of deprivation and need, that the poet isolates as characteristic of the country. Interestingly, however, the simplification of the problem implied in its reduction to hunger and thirst is negated by the poetic amplification of the appositional phrase "Affolantes inconnues d'un quotidien problème" [Perturbing unknowns of an everyday problem], where the unusually-placed adjectives and deliberate rhythm, as well as the implied personification of the abstract nouns "faim" [hunger] and "soif" [thirst], produce an effect of artificiality.

The blackness associated with skin in the first line of the poem ("peau noire" [black skin]) now returns as a description of the island: "Ile noire de sel noir" [Black island of black sand]. The expression "sel noir" [black sand], both a representation of the geographical reality of Martinique with its volcanic black sand beaches in the northern part of the island and an ironic metaphor of the value of black slaves to Europeans, forms an intertextual linkage with Glissant's 1960 collection of poetry, entitled *Le Sel noir*, which explores on a larger scale the significance of this image to the Caribbean. The attribution of a peninsular arm ("le bras presqu'île") to the island, linking it to a continental land mass, deprives the island of its independent and authentic existence as an island. At the same time, the poet is himself this "arm," which becomes, by a metonymic shift, the sign in the poem of the island's and the people's pain: "... dit / Toute la détresse de l'homme né libre / Fait bête" [tells / All the distress of man born free / Made into beast].

"Pays natal" [Native land] forms a third intertextual linkage in the poem to Martinican letters, and specifically to Césaire's *Cahier d'un retour au pays natal [Return to my Native Land]*. The poetic persona of "Chanson 1" comes, as Césaire did, to accept this "pays sombre" [dark country] as his own, to the point where the country and poet share in the same attitude of tolerance: "Au cœur fermé à toute haine / Au regard vierge de tout venin" [With a heart closed to all hatred / With a look virgin of all venom]. At the end of the poem, the poet's underlying dissatisfaction is resolved and he derives serenity from the physical and figurative contact with his native land: "Quel repos le soir / Quand mains nouées sous la nuque / Je pose ma tête lourde / Sur le ventre frais de tes sillons" [How restful in the evening / When hands clasped behind my neck / I lay may heavy head / On the cool belly of your furrows].

This poem thus poses some of the social and cultural issues which confront French Caribbean people of color, in relation both to the negative connotations associated with blackness and to the condition of material and intellectual deprivation that is part of the heritage of slavery and colonization. It is not without significance, however, that this poem establishes, consciously or unconsciously, identity linkages between this text and other well known French Caribbean texts, and between this poet and three of the most prominent leaders of the French Caribbean literary scene. In this way, it validates the literary tradition that provides the context within which it is produced.

POEME POUR LE GUERRILLERO

Comment dire comment dire
La faim d'un pays de faim
Comment dire Quel dieu maudire
Quand la nuit n'a pas de fin?

Ici un peuple se forge
Et dans la sueur et le sang
Ici l'occident égorge
Des filles qui n'ont pas vingt ans

Ici un peuple se bat
Contre la France du crime
Contre l'oppression qui broie.
Ah! mon peuple! Ah! mon hymne!

Hier décembre, mars puis juin
Toujours au nom de la France
Ils ont du sang sur les mains
Ils vivent de nos souffrances

Mais mon île sait l'histoire
Le vent appelle le vent
Et c'est demain la victoire.
Douboutt' toutt' moune douboutt' zenfants!

č

POEM FOR THE GUERRILLA

How to tell how to tell
The hunger of a land of hunger
How to tell What God to curse
When there is no end to night?

Here a people is being forged
In both sweat and blood
Here the west is slaughtering
Girls who are under twenty

Here a people is fighting
Against criminal France
Against rampant oppression.
Ah! my people! Ah! my anthem!

Yesterday December, March, then June
Always in the name of France
They have blood on their hands
They live off our sufferings

But my island knows history
The wind calls to the wind
And victory is tomorrow.
Get up! Everybody up, children!

The title of "Poème pour le guérillero" [Poem for the Guerrilla](26)
gives an indication of the poet's political leanings: it is a poem not
merely addressed to but also in support of freedom fighters. As the
poem opens, the poet is concerned with the problem of finding an
appropriate mode of expression. The opening line, "Comment dire
comment dire" [How to tell how to tell], introduces and emphasizes

through the repetition the core dilemma facing the poet: the issue of voice. This central problem is developed throughout the first stanza by a series of rhetorical devices. The text immediately exploits the difference between the oral and the written by pointing to the difficulty in recognizing at the aural level the difference between the homophones "faim" [hunger] and "fin" [end] and by extension in recognizing the difference at the philosophical level between a temporary condition (of hunger) and the permanence of destruction. Furthermore, the inscription of "dire" [tell] in "maudire" [curse] determines the consideration of religious rebellion as a possible solution to the poet's problem; the poet, seeking merely to voice the need of his country, is tempted to turn to malediction: "Comment dire Quel dieu maudire" [How to tell What God to curse]. The metaphor of an unending night ("Quand la nuit n'a pas de fin") with which this stanza ends forms a metonymic link with the notion of malediction and thus serves to magnify the nightmarish nature of the poet's situation. This image is a reminder that recognizing and solving the problem of hunger can be even more difficult at night, when one is asleep.

In the second stanza, the poet begins to insist on the difference between his country and an implied Other: "Ici un peuple se forge" [Here a people is being forged]. Since "peuple" [people] implies the sharing of a common culture, it is evident that the poet is concerned about the vulnerability of an embryonic cultural entity. The belief that the threat to the survival of this new people is coming from the "west" is implicit in the contrast established between "Ici" [Here] (repeated at the beginning of the second and third stanzas) and "l'occident" [the west]: "Ici l'occident égorge / Des filles qui n'ont pas vingt ans" [Here the west is slaughtering / Girls who are under twenty]. These "filles" recall the girls working in "sillons" in "Misère des mots" (15). The poet becomes more specific in the third stanza: "Ici un peuple se bat" [Here a people is fighting] echoes the opening line of the preceding stanza, thus establishing the connection between active resistance and the creation of an identity. Similarly, the vague "l'occident" [the west] of the preceding stanza becomes particularized as "la France" [France]. The complement "du crime" [criminal] presents France as an exponent of the criminal oppression and violence of the West. The perfect balance of the exclamatory final line of this stanza ("Ah! mon peuple! Ah! mon hymne!" [Ah! my people! Ah! my anthem!) establishes a parallelism between "peuple" [people] and "hymne" [anthem]. The song of praise ("hymne") celebrates both the heroism of the community and the production of the poetic song. In the final analysis, the poem is a reflection as well as a product of the community's struggle for autonomy.

The continuity of suffering alluded to in the first stanza is articulated less indirectly in the fourth stanza, as the temporal enumeration of "Hier décembre, mars puis juin / Toujours..." [Yesterday December, March, then June / Always...] reflects the "endless night" of the first stanza. Similarly, the difference suggested between the poet's country and France in the second and third stanzas is expressed directly in the fourth stanza: "Toujours au nom de la France / Ils ont du sang sur les mains / Ils vivent de nos souffrances" [Always in the name of France / They have blood on their hands / They live off our sufferings]. This direct expression is mitigated by the vagueness of the pronoun "ils," although in the Caribbean context the enemy is presumed to be known and does not need to be identified with greater precision.

In the final stanza, the poet envisions the eventual victory of his people, indicating for the first time in the poem that the country represented throughout the poem is the island to which he belongs and with which he identifies: "Mais mon île sait l'histoire / Le vent appelle le vent / Et c'est demain la victoire" [But my island knows history / The wind calls to the wind / And victory is tomorrow]. His identification with his island is most strongly stressed by the Creole exhortation with which the poem ends: "Douboutt' toutt' moune douboutt' zenfants!" [Get up! Everybody up, children]. This Creole finale to a poem written in French represents a rebellion against the French cultural tradition within which the poem is produced and an affirmation of the validity of a local cultural identity.

This militant climax in Creole, which asserts its cultural separation from the metropole, contrasts with the form of the poem, which aligns itself with traditional French verse. Despite the apparent contradiction in this formal ambiguity, which is a characteristic feature of much of the production of French Caribbean writers, the poet emerges as the kind of freedom fighter to whom the poem is addressed. He is himself the "guérillero," using the poem as a means of conducting the struggle to liberate and validate French Caribbean people.

POÈME POUR MA PATRIE

Ce jour dit ce jour à n'importe qui jeté
Un jour comme une rose sous le ciel né
On ne garde mémoire que des choses belles:
La vie pour la patrie le cœur sous la tonnelle.

Ce jour dit ce jour pour une Patrie donné
Madiana en mon cœur, ce pays qui saigne
Martinique de ma vie, ce pays sans haine
Au nom de la France, au nom du Blanc, étouffé.

Un homme n'a de sang que le sang de son peuple
Un homme n'a de cœur que pour aimer ses rives
Et cette liberté dont l'oppresseur nous prive
Arrache-la mon peuple, mon peuple, mon peuple.

❦

POEM FOR MY MOTHERLAND

This day proclaims this a day cast to anyone
A day born like a rose under the sky

The only memory one keeps is of beautiful things:
>   One's life for the Motherland one's heart
>   under the bower.

This day proclaims this a day given for a Motherland
Madiana in my heart, this country that is bleeding
Martinique love of my life, this country with no hatred
In the name of France, in the name of the White man, suffocated.

A man has no blood but the blood of his people
A man has no heart but for loving his shores
And this liberty the oppressor keeps from us
Seize it, my people, my people, my people.

"Poème pour ma patrie" [Poem for My Motherland] (27) forms a natural link with the preceding poem, "Poème pour le guérillero" [Poem For the Guerrilla], because of the similarity of their titles and because of the attitude expressed by the poet toward France, toward his native land, and toward his people. The significance of "patrie" as the motherland and as a community of people sharing the same cultural values is exploited in this poem, to explain and justify the poet's attitude. In the first stanza, for example, the expression of nationalistic commitment, "La vie pour la Patrie" [One's life for the Motherland] is given approval: it is presented as an illustration of "des choses belles" [beautiful things] preserved in the memory.

The possessive identification implicit in the title ("ma patrie" [my motherland]) is amplified in the second stanza. "Madiana," one of the variants of the pre-European Carib name for the island (another is Madinina, as in Padoly's "Terre! Terre!"), restores to the island a separate, non-French identity that is lodged within the poet's heart ("en mon cœur"). Inner yearning for the pristine Madiana is contrasted with the lived reality of Martinique, while both Madiana ("ce pays qui saigne" [this country that bleeds]) and Martinique ("ce pays sans haine / Au nom de la France, au nom du Blanc, étouffé" [this country without hatred / In the name of France, in the name of the White man, suffocated]) share in the experience of lethal violence ("saigne," "étouffé" [bleeds, suffocated]) at the hands of the French. The capitalized "Blanc" [White] implies a subtextual "Noir" [Black]. Thus, "Martinique" is presented as a "black" country whose voice has been stifled by the "white" French.

The final stanza summarizes the arguments that form the foundation and justification of the action recommended by the poet. It begins with two assertions: "Un homme n'a de sang que le sang de son peuple / Un homme n'a de cœur que pour aimer ses rives" [A man has no blood but the blood of his people / A man has no heart but for loving his shores]. The first of these statements focuses on the issue of biological connectedness underscores the necessity for a link to the community. The second statement highlights the need for personal responsibility: acceptance of one's Caribbean identity requires the exercise of a protective love of one's country. The poem closes on a note similar to that of "Poème pour le guérillero," as the poet issues a direct call to the people of Martinique, this time in French, for violent revolt. The repetition of "mon peuple" [my people] emphasizes the sense of responsibility the poet feels toward the people of Martinique as well as the intimacy of the link that binds him to them.

This poem, addressed exclusively to "mon peuple," is both a direct expression of the poet's identification with his native land and a call to fellow Martinicans for political action against the white French. It represents a cultural and political choice on the part of the poet, who defines himself emotionally and culturally in relation to Madiana-Martinique, for whose liberty he is prepared to fight. Incongruously, the poet does not apply the same liberty he demands to the poetic form he uses. The poem's formal conservatism (fixed verse form of rhymed alexandrines) is at odds with the revolutionary violence of the final line. The traditional French metropolitan poetic form is applied to the destruction of the political system of which such a form is a part.   In this way, the poem becomes profoundly subversive.

Il pleut doucement sur Harlem
Il fait seul
Il fait froid
Il fait si froid que l'on n'a guère envie
d'être nègre ce soir
dans ces rues noires de misère noire
Il fait si seul
que l'on a peur d'être nigger
dans ce quartier de puces de rats morts
de morpions
ce quartier de claques
de cloaques
ce quartier de dingues
de drogue
ce quartier assis
ce quartier ramassé sur lui-même
comme pour mieux digérer ses tiques
ses crasses
ses peurs
ses lâchetés
Il pleut doucement sur Harlem
et l'on a envie de dire merde à la vie
de se laisser mourir en silence
mais un homme passe
qui parle d'un autre homme
Il parle de Malcolm X
Malcolm
X
X
X

ॐ

It's raining gently on Harlem
It's lonely
It's cold
It's so cold that you hardly feel
like being a negro tonight
in these black streets of black poverty
It's so lonely
that you're afraid to be a nigger
in this neighborhood of fleas of dead rats
                    of crab lice
this neighborhood of slaps
            of sewers
this neighborhood of loonies
        of druggies
this neighborhood set
this neighborhood huddled up on itself
            as if better to digest its ticks
            its filth
its fear
        its funk
        It's raining gently on Harlem
and you feel like saying fuck to life
        like giving up and dying in silence
        but a man goes by
        talking about another man
        He's talking about Malcolm X
        Malcolm
        X
        X
        X

The collection *Martinique debout*[3] contains twenty poems of
varying lengths, from three lines to three pages, in addition to an

obscure short play in prose which features the voices of a variety of real-life characters: Cuban painter, Wilfredo Lam; French Surrealist writer, André Breton; Cuban poet, Nicolás Guillén; American Black Muslim revolutionary, Malcolm X; Martinican psychiatrist and revolutionary, Frantz Fanon; Martinican poet, Georges Desportes; Harlem Renaissance poet, Claude MacKay; and Haitian novelist, Jacques Roumain.

The cover and title page of this edition provide clues to the focus of the collection. The background of the whole cover is white. Against this background, the cover design depicts a dark brown forearm and hand grasping charcoal black manacles that have been broken. The dark brown of the hand matches the brown of "Martinique debout" [Martinique Up] in the title. The author's name and the sub-title, "poésie martiniquaise" [Martinican poetry] are in black. This design thus portrays the liberation struggle of "black" people with dark brown skin, with whom the poet identifies, breaking chains within a context that is "white." On the title page, the sub-title is given as "poésie antillaise" [Antillean poetry] and not as "poésie martiniquaise" [Martinican poetry] as on the cover. This variation, deliberate or not, points to the implication that there is no distinction between the Caribbean and the Martinican identity and that the two terms may be used interchangeably.

In "Il pleut doucement sur Harlem..." (6) [It's raining gently on Harlem], the poet evokes the New York neighborhood identified with a predominantly black community and culture. Significantly, however, the Harlem evoked here is not the center of black cultural activity, not the Harlem of the 1920s Harlem Renaissance that contributed to the awakening of Negritude writers like Césaire. This is a later Harlem, after it suffered from a drug invasion in the 1950s and middle-class flight before it became the mythical American black ghetto. The opening lines, for instance, through a series of impersonal expressions, emphasize the damp, the solitude, and the cold: "Il pleut doucement sur Harlem / Il fait seul / Il fait froid" [It's raining gently on Harlem / It's lonely / It's cold]. These three statements are repeated in reverse order in the poem and become the dominant conditions that affect the emotional reactions of blacks ("l'on n'a guère envie..." [you hardly feel], "l'on a peur..." [you're afraid], "l'on a envie..." [you feel]). The repeated pseudo-diphthong of "froid" [cold] finds an echo in the repetition of "noire" [black], so that this all-pervading cold becomes associated with the condition of "blackness" from which it is impossible to escape; the cold forms a barrier to the black's acceptance of himself and of the condition of socioeconomic depression associated with blackness: "Il fait si froid que l'on n'a guère envie / d'être nègre ce soir / dans ces rues noires de misère noire" [It's so cold that you hardly feel / like being a negro tonight / in these black streets of black poverty].

The poetic persona never assumes full subjectivity in this poem but participates in the general and impersonal identity of "l'on" [you] and of the "nègre" [negro]. The personal and cultural problems that accompany the whole notion of blackness are illustrated in the expressions "rues noires" [black streets] and "misère noire" [black poverty] where the associations of lack of light, danger, depression, and poverty combine to become properties linked to "black" people. The poet demonstrates that this problem of connotation exists not only in French but also in American English, in which the problematical condition of the "nigger" is interchangeable with that of the "nègre": "Il fait si seul / que l'on a peur d'être nigger" [It's so lonely / that you're afraid to be a nigger].

Harlem becomes "ce quartier" [this neighborhood], a repeated, insistent metaphor of the worst possible psychosocial situation for blacks, of which "puces" [fleas], "rats morts" [dead rats], "morpions" [crab lice], "claques" [slaps], "cloaques" [sewers], "dingues" [loonies], and "drogue" [drugs], as well as "crasses" [filth], "peurs" [fears], and "lâchetés" [funk = cowardliness] are characteristic features. The present condition of "ce quartier assis" contrasts with the poet's vision of a future "Martinique debout," emphasizing the poet's identification with the "nigger." The deliberate assonances and careful graphical arrangement create an ambiguity. On the one hand, the deliberate "artistry" points to a concern for beauty and harmony on the part of the poet that runs counter to the ugliness of the scene described; on the other, the formal arrangement resembles "concrete" poetry — a graphic representation of discontinuity and dissonance.

The final temptation of the black "l'on" is a response to the situation that exemplifies how difficult life choices can be for blacks. The impotent voice of frustration is as futile as silent death: "l'on a envie de dire merde à la vie / de se laisser mourir en silence" [you feel like saying fuck to life / like giving up and dying in silence]. This temptation to surrender to hopelessness is erased by the emergence of a new voice in the poem: "mais un homme passe / qui parle d'un autre homme" [but a man goes by / talking about another man]. This act of speaking is the guarantee of the change implied by "mais" [but]: the voice is invested with potential. The poem ends, therefore, with the echo and menacing sibilance of "Malcolm X," one of the primary voices of militant blacks in America and throughout the black diaspora in the middle sixties: "Il parle de Malcolm X / Malcolm / X / X / X ..." [He's talking about Malcolm X / Malcolm / X / X / X]. The graphical separation of the descending and repeated "X" and the suspension points enhance the impression of an unending echo that continues in the present.

The poet, like the man mentioned in the poem, is talking about Malcolm X, who was killed in 1965, twelve years before this collection was published. The poem is thus a *mise en abîme* of the poet's own situation, as he identifies with the degradation and hopelessness of blacks in Harlem, but looks at the legacy of Malcolm X with nostalgia and hope. Implicit, moreover, in the poet's celebration of the importance of Malcolm X is an identification with the early role played by Malcolm of an uncompromising militant, as opposed to the accommodating stance of the other dominant leader of American blacks of that period, Martin Luther King. The poet consequently becomes in this poem the advocate and the voice of black militancy.

Dessus ma peur
à bout d'âge de parole décimée
je suis nègre debout
pour la seule histoire qui vaille d'être écrite
je suis cet homme né à naître
du feu des coutelas
né de la bave d'une nuit d'étranges dormitions
quand l'aube coupe le sang à hauteur d'absence
et mitraille le cri du silex franc de la faim
je suis né assassiné aux premières heures de la vie
par trois siècles d'absence de moi-même
assassiné par assimilation
Matin grillé au couteau de l'ennui quand
je tutoie ton rêve d'être
d'être autre
qu'un sac d'hommes ligotés de famine
qu'un membre d'une cynique équation
car chacun sait que
dix Nègres en sang
plus dix Nègres en sueur
égalent
une usine qui tourne rond
tout en rhum
tout en sucre
Matin grillé au sexe froid de l'humiliation
je vais à routes nouvelles qui me perdent et
m'éparpillent
en promesses d'homme
mon île jet d'étoiles au front des baobabs
mon île
aux yeux d'oiseaux familiers
aux mains d'anciennes caresses
j'ai plus de sept vies
l'une pourtant est morte au Congo avec l'espoir
de Patrice

une autre est vivante comme sang neuf
sous la chair tendre du Mékong
une autre rayonne au soleil de la Sierra Izabal
une autre agonise
battue traquée parquée droguée avec Bob
Kaufmann
à Harlem
et j'attends ah j'attends
cette autre qui fera pousser des étoiles
dans le ciel antillais

Plus jamais chevaucher ton silence de mauvaise
foire
Plus jamais l'aiguille du jour dans le foin de la nuit
mais ton cœur de vingt décembre cinquante neuf
à épingler le rêve à tous les coins de rue
plus jamais l'ivresse blanche des nuits
je te retrouve visage des visages jamais connus
aux quatre coins des mots sans mémoire
où je passais mon temps à séparer
mon rêve de moi-même
Négresse d'amour vacant ma joie liquide
sur tes hanches sans retour
le jour viendra disais-tu
où le Nègre sans surprise reconnaîtra le Nègre
ici comme ailleurs
l'amour d'une seule main recommencé
dans la bouche des frissons d'azur
mille journées pourtant
m'ont surpris hors du rire natal
Besançon Caracas Palaiseau
des mots de climat désaccordé
à mon cœur tropical
matin bouffi d'incertitude une timide tendresse
d'étoile

Reprendre pied dans ton rêve
quand demain ne fait plus les cent pas
aux devantures des promesses
une moitié de nuage
suffirait à te rendre à toi-même
lumière rebelle Antilles sans fatigue
sang debout sur une cicatrice de sang
le poing au défi
Dessus la case
où mon enfance est morte
de t'avoir trop attendue

Boire n'est jamais trahison
quand la soif est utile
pour additionner
mon pas à ton pas
mon poing à ton poing
ma révolte à ta révolte
tu diras
l'incertitude des mots d'exil au front des vagues
tu diras
l'enchantement des rétines
au matin de JUSTICE
toi
ma steatopygie menaçante
ma flamme
mon feu
mon sacre
ma statue Béna Louloua
mon rire sauvage de guerrier congolais
mon bonjour au curare
mon sourire de mort subite
ma poignée de main au plastic
mon regard de serpent déchaîné
mon jazz déposé en révolte

dans chaque homme opprimé
dans chaque cœur noirci du goudron de la faim
ma Patrie ma Patrie c'est Morne-Capot
Calcutta Fu Baï Récife Yaoundé ou Panama
toutes ces terres
où noire misère devient richesse blanche
un jour
en lettres-soleils sur fond nocturne
des mains de terre
écriront ce merveilleux poème
qui ne saura plus rire ni pleurer
et fera l'exact partage
de tendresse et vengeance
j'arrive où tu m'appelles
comme la rime au bout du vers
ce point-critique où la parole
épelle l'action
où le présent s'abolit en futur
mon origine niée reniée
demain mon étendard
SILENCE
ici on construit l'avenir

❦

Above my fear
at life's end with decimated speech
I am a negro standing up
for the only story worth being written
I am this man born to be born
from the fire of cutlasses
born from the drool of a night of strange dormitions
when dawn cuts off the blood at absence level
and guns down the cry of hunger's clear flint
I was born assassinated in the earliest hours of life

by three centuries of absence from myself
out of myself
dispossessed of myself
assassinated by assimilation
Morning roasted on the knife of boredom when
I familiarly greet your dream of being
of being other
than a sack of men tied hand and foot in starvation
than a member of a cynical equation
for everyone knows that
ten Negroes bleeding
plus ten Negroes sweating
equal
a factory running smoothly
full of rum
full of sugar
Morning roasted on the cold genitals of humiliation
I take new roads that lose and scatter me
in manly promises
my island a spray of stars on the forehead of the
baobabs
my island   ·
with eyes of familiar birds
with hands of old caresses
I have more than seven lives
one however died in the Congo with Patrice's
hope
another is alive like new blood
under the tender flesh of the Mekong
another shines in the sun of Sierra Izabal
another is dying
beaten hunted down penned in drugged up with
Bob Kaufmann
in Harlem
and I'm waiting ah I'm waiting

for this other life that will make stars grow
in the Antillean sky

Nevermore to sit astride your silence like on a bad
binge
Nevermore the day's needle in night's hay
but your heart of December twentieth of fifty-nine
to pin up the dream on every street corner
nevermore the sleepless intoxication of nights
I find you again face of faces never known
at the four corners of words without memory
where I spent my time separating
my dream from myself
Negress of vacant love my liquid joy
on your hips irrevocably
the day will come you used to say
when the Negro without surprise will recognize the
Negro
here like elsewhere
love resumed with a single hand
shivers of azure in the mouth
yet a thousand days
have caught me by surprise away from my native
laughter
Besançon Caracas Palaiseau
words of a climate out of harmony
with my tropical heart
a morning puffed up with uncertainty the shy
tenderness of a star

Setting foot again in your dream
when tomorrow no longer paces up and down
outside the shop-windows of promises
half a cloud
would be enough to bring you back to yourself

rebel light tireless Antilles
blood standing up on a scar of blood
fist defiant
Above the shack
where my childhood died
from waiting for you too long

Drinking is never treason
when thirst is useful
for adding
my step to your step
my fist to your fist
my revolt to your revolt
you will speak of
the uncertainty of words of exile on the brows of
the waves
you will speak of
the enchantment of retinas
on the morning of JUSTICE
you
my threatening steatopygia
my flame
my fire
my consecration
my Béna Louloua statue
my Congolese warrior's wild laugh
my curare hello
my sudden death smile
my plastic explosive handshake
my unchained serpent's gaze
my jazz deposited in revolt
in every oppressed man
in every heart blackened with the tar of hunger
my Country my Country is Morne-Capot
Calcutta Fu Baï Récife Yaoundé or Panama

all these lands
where black poverty becomes white wealth
one day
in sun-letters on a nocturnal background
earth hands
will write this wonderful poem
which will no longer be able either to laugh or to
cry
and will share out exact portions of
tenderness and vengeance
I come where you call me
like the rhyme at the end of the line
this critical point where speech
spells action
where present fades into future
my origin denied renounced
tomorrow my banner
SILENCE
here the future is being built

"Dessus ma peur ..." [Above my fear...](10-13) explores several of the issues relating to the poet's identity as a black Antillean and provides an explanation of the poetic and political stance he has chosen to adopt. The first problem presented, which forms the base on which the whole poem is constructed, is the situation of the poet relative to the possible destruction of the voice he is hoping to perpetuate: "Dessus ma peur / à bout d'âge de parole décimée [Above my fear / at life's end with decimated speech]. The problem of the poet's situation is transmitted textually through the ambiguity of the syntactical relationships between "Dessus" [Above] and "ma peur" [my fear] and between "Dessus" and the "je" [I] of the following line. This ambiguity creates doubt as to whether it is the poet or his fear that occupies the dominant position. Furthermore, the identity and dignity of the poetic subject ("je" [I]) are shown to be related directly to his function as a writer: "je suis nègre debout

/ pour la seule histoire qui vaille d'être écrite" [I am a negro standing up / for the only story worth being written]. Thus, the identity he assumes is that of both "nègre" and writer.

The poet attempts to define himself in relation to the significance and strange conditions of his birth as a Martinican: "né de la bave d'une nuit d'étranges dormitions" [born from the drool of a night of strange dormitions]. The term "dormition," used in old Catholic liturgies to refer to the death of the Virgin Mary, hints subtly at the innocence of the women, who in this case are black. This is an indirect reference to the officially taboo but in practice frequent forced sexual contact between colonizing Europeans and enslaved and colonized Africans. The contradiction inherent in "né à naître" [born to be born] and "né assassiné" [born assassinated] is a reflection of the poet's awareness of a troubled sense of existence and of purpose. This profound alienation is presented as the effect of being forced to endure slavery and colonization: "par trois siècles d'absence de moi-même / hors de moi-même / dépossédé de moi-même / assassiné par assimilation [by three centuries of absence from myself / out of myself / dispossessed of myself / assassinated by assimilation]. The poem thus represents an attempt to compensate for this absence from self by recreating an authentic voice.

In the second section of the poem, introduced by "Matin grillé au couteau..." [Morning roasted on the knife..], the poet explores another avenue of freedom by aligning himself with, and becoming the voice of, the socialist worker who resists economic oppression: "je tutoie ton rêve d'être / d'être autre / qu'un sac d'hommes ligotés de famine / qu'un membre d'une cynique équation [I familiarly greet your dream of being / of being other / than a sack of men tied hand and foot in starvation / than a member of a cynical equation]. The line breaks at "être" [being] and "autre" [other] call into question the validity of the present existence of blacks and convey dissatisfaction with the existing conditions of economic exploitation that accompany the identity of blacks.   What is particularly rejected by the poet is an identity imposed for the purpose of the commodification and exploitation of blacks on the sugar plantations of the Caribbean: "car chacun sait que / dix Nègres en sang / plus dix Nègres en sueur / égalent / une usine qui tourne rond / tout en rhum / tout en sucre [For everyone knows that / ten Negroes bleeding / plus ten Negroes sweating / equal / a factory running smoothly / full of rum / full of sugar].

In the third section, introduced by "Matin grillé au sexe froid..." [Morning roasted on the cold genitals...], the poetic persona assumes a new role, one that requires a fragmentation of identity out of which human dignity may be created: "je vais à routes nouvelles qui me perdent et m'éparpillent / en promesses d'hommes [I take new roads that lose and scatter me / in manly promises]. This new experience is related in the poem to an intimate relationship between the poet and his island: "mon île / aux yeux d'oiseaux familiers / aux mains d'anciennes caresses [my island / with eyes of familiar birds / with hands of old caresses]. The poet's chosen identity, however, is not limited to his relationship with his native land. The intimacy between him and his island enables the poet to reach beyond the island and claim a plurality of lives as his own ("j'ai plus de sept vies" [I have more than seven lives]), as he asserts his identification also with the lives of revolutionary leaders in Africa, Indochina, Latin America, and the United States. This plurality of identity is inadequate and incomplete, however, without a similar (revolutionary) manifestation in the Caribbean: "et j'attends ah j'attends / cette autre qui fera pousser des étoiles / dans le ciel antillais" [and I'm waiting ah I'm waiting / for this other life that will make stars grow / in the Antillean sky]. The strength of the poet's desire and his impatience are transmitted by the repetition of "j'attends" [I'm waiting] and enhanced by the sigh of "ah." "Cette autre [vie]" [this other (life)] is thus an indispensable part of the complex trajectory, and one of the essential lives, experienced by the poet.

The new orality implied earlier in "je tutoie ton rêve d'être" [I familiarly greet your dream of being] and the undertaking of new activity suggested in "je vais à routes nouvelles" [I take new roads] converge in the fourth section, where the poet reflects on the change that has taken place in his attitude: "Plus jamais chevaucher ton silence de mauvaise foire / Plus jamais l'aiguille du jour dans le foin de la nuit" [Nevermore to sit astride your silence like on a bad binge / Nevermore the day's needle in night's hay]. These dense images dramatize one way in which the poet has attempted to express his problematical situation. "Ton" [your], as a pronoun pointing to an "other," represents an unwelcome facet of the poet's dilemma. He realizes that his past tendency toward silence, toward concealment of the voice, must be rejected. The textual inscription of falsity ("mauvaise foi") in public displays of silence ("mauvaise foire") and the figurative awareness that the strategy of finding the needle in a haystack must be changed lead to an inescapable solution to the dilemma. The transformation sought by the poet will demand a new voice, a new (non-white) method of poetic activity:

> plus jamais l'ivresse blanche des nuits
> je te retrouve visage des visages jamais connus
> aux quatre coins des mots sans mémoire
> où je passais mon temps à séparer
> mon rêve de moi-même

[nevermore the sleepless intoxication of nights / I find you again face of faces never known / at the four corners of words without memory / where I spent my time separating / my dream from myself].

Here "blanche," which connotes both "white" and "sleepless," indicates the situation that must be rejected if the poet is to recapture his authentic self. This rejection permits the poet to hear the voice of the "Négresse d'amour vacant" [Negress of vacant love] whose past words promise the reconciliation hoped for by the poet: "le Nègre sans surprise reconnaîtra le Nègre" [the Negro without surprise will recognize the Negro].

In the final section, as the poem moves toward a climax, the possessives "ma" and "mon" [my] are used insistently to enumerate the various aspects of the reality that the poet claims as his own. He is thus able to establish identification with "chaque homme opprimé" [every oppressed man]. The concept of blackness is shown to include "chaque cœur noirci du goudron de la faim" [every heart blackened with the tar of hunger], and "toutes ces terres / où noire misère devient richesse blanche" [all these lands / where black poverty becomes white wealth]. The "blackness" with which the poet identifies is no longer merely racial or cultural, but economic and social. The native land is no longer restricted to Martinique: "ma Patrie ma Patrie c'est Morne-Capot / Calcutta Fu Baï Récife Yaoundé ou Panama" [my Country my Country is Morne-Capot / Calcutta Fu Baï Récife Yaoundé or Panama]. The poet assumes a communal identity, one based not simply on color or biological connectedness but on a common experience of economic suffering and exploitation at the hands of whites.

Significantly, the poem now becomes self-referential, essentially a communal rather than an individual project, and the product of shared experience: "un jour / en lettres-soleils sur fond nocturne / des mains de terre / écriront ce merveilleux poème [one day / in sun-letters on a nocturnal background / earth hands / will write this wonderful poem]. The voice transmitted in the poem is that of all the people and countries the poetic persona has already included under the umbrella of "blackness" and the poem as poem is shown to represent the reconciliation of word and action:

> j'arrive où tu m'appelles
> comme la rime au bout du vers
> ce point-critique où la parole
> épelle l'action
> où le présent s'abolit en futur

[I come where you call me / like the rhyme at the end of the line / the critical point where speech / spells action / where present fades into future].

The cryptic call for "SILENCE" at the end of the poem demonstrates, however, how difficult it is for the poet to arrive at a clear resolution to his dilemma.

This poem attempts to articulate the way in which the conflicting temptations toward silence and speech affect the whole issue of cultural identity in a poet who is conscious of his relationship to others who have like himself suffered from exploitation at the hands of whites. It is indeed a wonderful poem, in which the poet's hesitations and uncertainty are permitted to play themselves out dramatically. The poet's mastery of his medium is evident. He displays perfect control of sound and rhythm, of repetition and enumeration. The images he uses are illuminating and forceful. It is to my mind a highly successful marriage of technical poetic skill and political commitment.

> Hier hier l'ébène l'ivoire la route des épices coupée
> en soleil de négrier
> ma vie brûlée au Minuit des voyances selon la loi
> des bâtisseurs de silence
> alors commença l'ère des vérités jésufiées la grande
> cacophonie des désirs la faim ma compagne de peur
> des journées de chicotte la sereine orchestration
> de l'oubli de moi-même
> on me voulait absence
> pensez pensez une seule race à supporter le poids
> du globe seul sang pour étancher la soif des
> vampires
> ah ma souffrance globe-trotter
> mon visage à neige jeté ma face gommée
> des trombinoscopes absence
> gibier de mauvais ciel abonné des grandes rafles
> ni été ni printemps l'hiver perpétuel
> sabotait mon présent en de futures épices
> souvenir pénible des grimaces qu'étaient rires
> pourtant je portais espoir au fin fond des paupières

et j'avais force pour nommer
les choses de moi-même
j'étais poète de moi-même
vint le premier henissement de mon sang
Makandal debout
Makandal nègre-marron amant premier
de dame liberté
calebasse dégoupillée poussée sismique des colères
indomptées
à faire gicler le sang dans l'exacte névralgie des
mémoires
et je devins le fiévreux artisan des insomnies
blanches
l'empêcheur-d'assassiner-en-rond
un vrai Nègre vous dis-je
Delgrès-Matouba coup d'arrêt à la sottise galonnée
Toussaint ah Toussaint Louverture
le vent souqué à cette fureur de chanter juste
la musique de l'homme
ma soif en typhon dans les yeux du monde
sur la bouche du monde
au cœur même du monde
comme un amour dégainé dans la douceur d'un soir
de grande fraternité
Malcolm pilote dompteur de grandes houles
ma flamme inextinguible
et Fanon
Fanon ma conscience défoncée
hissée au mât
des luttes populaires
et l'indépendance
pour créer un pays d'hommes debout
sonne le glas
du colonialisme français

☙

Yesterday yesterday ebony ivory the spice route cut
into a slave-ship sun
my life burned at the Midnight of clairvoyances
according to the law
of the silence builders
then began the era of jesufied truths the great
cacophony of desires hunger my companion in fear
of days of lashes the serene orchestration
of forgetfulness of myself
they wanted me to be absence
think think one race to bear the weight
of the globe one blood to quench the thirst of the
vampires
ah my globe-trotting suffering
snow thrown in my face my picture erased
from the registers absence
ill-omened prey subscriber of the great raids
neither summer nor spring perpetual winter
sabotaged my present into future spices
painful memory of the grimaces that laughs were
however I carried hope deep behind my eyelids
and I had strength to name
the things of myself
I was a poet of myself
came the first neighing of my blood
Makandal standing up
Makandal a maroon negro first lover
of lady liberty
calabash with its pin pulled out seismic thrust of
untamed angers
to make blood spurt in the precise neuralgia of
memories

and I became the feverish craftsman of white
insomnias
the preventer-of-killing-in a circle
a real Negro I tell you
Delgrès-Matouba putting the brake on braided
stupidity
Toussaint ah Toussaint Louverture
pulling hard against the wind in this rage to sing
man's music right
my thirst like a typhoon in the eyes of the world
on the mouth of the world
in the very heart of the world
like a love unsheathed in the sweetness of an
evening
of great fraternity
Malcolm the pilot tamer of great swells
my inextinguishable flame
and Fanon
Fanon my smashed down conscience
hoisted to the mast
of popular struggles
and independence
to create a country of men standing up
tolls the knell
of French colonialism

In "Hier hier l'ébène ..." [Yesterday yesterday ebony] (29), the lived
experience of blacks and the poet's concern with personal issues,
evident in the repetition of "moi-même" [myself], provide the
foundation on which the poem is constructed. The poet's voice,
through which his real self finds expression, emerges as a counter
to the forces that threaten to impose silence. As the poem opens, the
poet's existence ("ma vie" [my life]) is linked to a past ("Hier"
[Yesterday]) in which the Europeans' search for a route to trade in
the spices of the Indies was to produce both slavery and the

subsequent exploitation of African resources: "Hier hier l'ébène l'ivoire la route des épices coupée / en soleil de négrier [Yesterday yesterday ebony ivory the spice route cut / into a slave-ship sun]. The term "bois d'ébène" [ebony wood] was used to refer to ships' cargo of Africans who became slaves. Here, the juxtaposition of "ébène" [ebony] and "ivoire" [ivory], both typically associated with ("black") Africa, and often used as similes of blackness and whiteness, strikes an ironic note and serves to accentuate the ambiguities of signification and of cultural differentiation.

The image of the "bâtisseurs de silence" [silence builders] evokes both the stereotypical European pride in architecture as an indication of "civilization" and memories of the traditional silence imposed by Europeans on African cultures. The poet also places his personal (and communal) experience in an historical context that was characterized by religious repression and deliberate cultural alienation:

> alors commença l'ère des vérités jésufiées la grande
> cacophonie des désirs la faim ma compagne de peur
> des journées de chicotte la sereine orchestration
> de l'oubli de moi-même
> on me voulait absence

> [then began the era of jesufied truths the great /
> cacophony of desires hunger my companion in fear
> / of days of lashes the serene orchestration / of
> forgetfulness of myself / they wanted me to be
> absence].

The "silence" of European history is linked to the silencing of the truth of use of organized Christianity in the process of enslavement and colonization, which resulted in "oubli" and "absence," both metaphors of silence. This silence is contrasted with the "cacophonie" [cacophony] that the poem produces.

The painful experience of cultural dispersion caused by the systematic attempt on the part of Europeans to deny and erase the cultural identity of Africans is presented as another aspect of the dilemma faced by the (black) poet: "ah ma souffrance globe-trotter / mon visage à neige jeté ma face gommée / des trombinoscopes absence [ah my globe-trotting suffering / snow thrown in my face my picture erased / from the registers absence]. The poet, however, assuming subjectivity as the imperishable, enduring voice of his people, is able to give an account of, and celebrate, the survival both of an awareness of self and of the creative capacity to voice this awareness: "pourtant je portais espoir au fin fond des paupières / et j'avais force pour nommer / les choses de moi-même / j'étais poète de moi-même [however I carried hope deep behind my eyelids / and I had strength to name / the things of myself / I was a poet of myself]. These lines reflect one of the insights the poet has gained from the experience of his people: poetic practice is a profoundly creative means of expressing and affirming the authentic self.

Consequently, the poetic "je" [I] celebrates the exploits of Caribbean heroes who form part of his lineage ("mon sang" [my blood]): Makandal ("nègre-marron amant premier / de dame liberté" [a maroon nigger first lover / of lady liberty]), the leader of a slave revolt in Haiti; the Martinican-born Louis Delgrès, defender of the liberty of blacks, who played his violin in defiance of the French army at Matouba in Guadeloupe and chose suicide rather than servitude;[4] the Haitian general Toussaint Louverture, who defied Napoleon Bonaparte and tried to established Haiti as an independent black republic; Malcolm X, the American Nation of Islam ("Black Muslim") revolutionary in the U.S.; and the Martinican psychiatrist, Frantz Fanon, who became a revolutionary fighter in Algeria. The examination of the significance of the exploits of these heroes leads to an inescapable conclusion for the poet: the achievement of an authentic cultural identity is inseparable from the political necessity of independence from France. And it is the poem that both proclaims and illustrates this truth.

This poem, like "Dessus ma peur...," is technically more complex than the poems of *Bonheur de poche*. The poet invests the poem with a strong impression of orality by such devices as the use of "ah," the lack of punctuation, enumeration, run-ons from line to line between, for example, adjective and noun or subject and verb, vernacular expressions (such as "vous dis-je" [I tell you]), and variations in rhythm. The poem traces a trajectory from past to present and extends it into the future. It serves as a means of perceiving and expressing truth by extracting the significant convergences between personal experience and that of the community. In this way, the poem helps to cut through the obscurities of history and provide clarification on questions about the meaning of the poet's life and of that of his country. The poem thereby affirms the need for political and cultural independence.

> Il y a ceux qui se créent afro-ceci
> Afro-cela
> Ceux qui se disent
> pas entièrement nègre
> pas tout à fait blanc
> Il y a les ça-ne-fait-pas-bien-de parler
> créole-devant-les-Blancs
> il y a ceux qui se disent
> noir-européen comme on dit noir-américain
> ceux qui mettent la France
> à la droite du père
> ceux qui écoutent Wagner
> et lisent la page financière du journal
> ceux qui changent de trottoir
> pour ne pas croiser
> un balayeur congolais
> ceux dont les Blancs disent
> « Ce sont des types bien »
> il y a ceux qui font sérieux
> et ceux qui font suer
> il y ceux qui dissertent
> et ceux qui divaguent
> ceux qui font sciences-éco

comme on fait la vaisselle
il y a ceux qu'on décore
ceux qui ont le cœur à droite
et la tête bleu-blanc-rouge
il y a les fils à papa
ceux qui sont vieux à quinze ans
ceux qui se savent de l'instruction
il y a ceux qui lutherkinisent
à qui mieux mieux
sur tous les boulevards de France
il y a tous ceux-là
ceux à qui nous disons
merde

ॐ

There are those who claim to be afro-this
Afro-that
Those who say they are
not entirely black
not completely white
There are the it's-not-nice-to-speak
creole-in-front-of-Whites
there are those who say they are
European-black like you say American-black
those who put France
on the right side of the father
those who listen to Wagner
and read the financial pages of the newspaper
those who change sidewalks
so as not to pass
a Congolese street-sweeper
those about whom Whites say
"They are nice guys"
there are those who pretend to be serious

and those who are a pain in the neck
there are those who hold forth
and those who ramble on
those who do econ
like you do the dishes
there are those who are decorated
those with their hearts on the right
and their heads red-white-and-blue
there are the daddy's boys
those who are old at fifteen
those who know they're educated
there are those who try to outdo one another
lutherkingizing
on every boulevard in France
there are all those

those to whom we say
shit

The spoken word is the motive force behind the poem, "Il y a ceux qui ..." [They are those who...](34-35). The importance of orality is evidenced by such linguistic devices as the preponderance of verbs of saying ("se créent" [claim to be], "disent," "disons" [say], "dissertent" [hold forth], "divaguent" [ramble on]), the use of hyphenated expressions representing often repeated statements, and the transposition of a statement in direct speech (using inverted commas). This orality reaches its climax at the end of the poem in the familiar expression of disgust and contempt, "merde" [shit].

This poem presents the most direct and dramatic statement in this collection of the poet's attitude toward blacks who have, in the poet's opinion, responded inappropriately to their situation in relation to European culture, by choosing form of accommodation and assimilation. These responses are enumerated in a succession of oratorical clauses, introduced by "Il y a ceux qui..." [There are those who...], that indicate the poet's awareness of being different from those whom he is describing who are victims of the alienation that the poet himself resists. Cultural affiliation is shown to be reflected in differences of linguistic practices that are rejected by the poet, whose political choice can be conjectured only by default. This choice is not stated directly in the poem. All the poem provides are the alternatives that the poet rejects.

The poet distances himself from various forms of self-definition practiced by some blacks through which the choice of identity is transmitted. The terms the poet hears used, however, ("afro-ceci" [Afro-this], "Afro-cela" [Afro-that], "pas entièrement nègre" [not entirely black], "pas tout à fait blanc" [not completely white], "noir-européen" [European-black], "noir-Américain" [American-black]) are problematical. What these terms have in common, and the factor that the poet finds objectionable, is an implicit lack of "definition" and an element of compromise and complicity that amounts to a dilution of self. The poet takes issue also with certain behaviors, often considered by blacks as stereotypically "white," and which are interpreted as representing alienation from an authentic "black" identity. The degree of such alienation is, as the poet indicates, signaled by the approval and acceptance accorded by whites. Indeed, the expression of approval presented in the poem ("Ce sont des types bien" [They are nice guys]) is ironically considered by many blacks as profoundly insulting. The poet's rejection develops in the poem to include any form of accommodation in behavior or attitude. Thus, the neologism "lutherkinisent" conveys his rejection of even the non-violent stance associated with Martin Luther King as an ineffective solution for the situation of blacks within the French context. . ·

This poem is thus an expression of disdain for the solutions other blacks arrive at in attempting to resolve the problem of their relationship to the white world. The poetic voice here is bitter, angry, and contemptuous. In its negativity, however, it further exemplifies how complex the issue is for the poet, since the poet is refusing to support some black people who are enmeshed in the same sociocultural problematic. At the same time the textual subjectivity assumed by the poet is plural ("nous disons" [we say]). He projects himself as the voice of a group of unalienated blacks.

Polius is a representative of the generation of "younger" French Caribbean writers, growing up and writing in the shadow of Aimé Césaire, Frantz Fanon, and Edouard Glissant. In these three, Polius had recent models of activism in politics and writing as a response to the difficult sociocultural and political situation of the French Caribbean vis-à-vis metropolitan France. It is hardly surprising, therefore, that Polius continues the tradition of French Caribbean poets who combine political and literary activism. Few fundamental changes took place, or could have taken place, in the sociocultural situation of the French Caribbean in the period between the late 1930s, when Césaire began publicly to explore issues of cultural identity through the *Cahier d'un retour au pays natal*, and the late 1960s, when Polius published his first collection of poetry. Changes did take place in the political status of the French Caribbean territories vis-à-vis metropolitan France, in that Martinique, Guadeloupe, and Guyane became officially no longer colonies but Overseas Departments. Césaire's new political party, the Parti Progressisiste Martiniquais, consistently dominated the mayoral elections in Fort-de-France since 1956. None of the Overseas Departments, however, has embraced the idea of political or psychological independence from the metropolis, which would have represented a fundamental change. Against this background, it is interesting to observe how Polius, a representative of a newer generation, exploits poetry in response to his sociopolitical situation.

Social and political awareness is the force that stimulates Polius's poetic activity. His poetry reveals a poetic persona who has a close emotional commitment to a native Madiana-Martinique, an island whose sense of self, like that of all the ex-colonies in the Caribbean, has been damaged by the historical impact of slavery, colonization, and assimilation. The emotional and cultural contradictions that these experiences have engendered find reflections in the form and the language of Polius's poems. Indeed, the poet is evidently conscious of a sense of inadequacy in relation to his poetic language. His poetry tends at times to become self-referential, as the poet searches for a literary solution to what he conceives of as a political problem. His over-riding political interest, however, maintains a balance between referentiality and self-referentiality in his poetry. He definitely belongs to the "tribe" of poets, referred to by Chidi Amuta, "who use their talents to challenge the ruling class and thus champion the cause of those who bear the burden of oppression" (Amuta 1989:177). Polius resembles Amuta's picture of the bourgeois poet in Africa:

> Because the art (all art) which he practices stands in eternal opposition to the dehumanization which tyranny and private property constitute, the poet tends to turn his back on his ruling and propertied colleagues and instead pitches his tent with the people in their struggle for justice and humane existence. (177)

Polius describes himself as driven by the "emancipatory dynamics and humanistic and therefore revolutionary dimension" of three forms of consciousness: racial consciousness, national consciousness, and class consciousness. He states further: "my life is a constant rejection of injustice, an intractable struggle for the dignity of man, an unshakeable support of the oppressed."[5]

Polius's poetry is the arena in which he attempts to elaborate a combined political and poetic solution. This solution is to use the poem to call for the political independence of Martinique; in other words, to become effectively the poetic voice of political militancy. We know that his empathy for the youth of his country was expressed not just in words but in direct political action, as is attested by his formation of a political youth group in his home town of Lamentin. Polius's own commentary on his work (quoted on the back cover of *Martinique debout*) expresses the essence of his poetic philosophy:

Je veux que ma poésie reste engagée dans la vie quotidienne, qu'elle tente d'être l'une des expressions du vécu collectif de mon peuple, un véhicule de son cri.

La poésie doit garder comme une exigence vitale l'intégration de toutes les luttes du peuple; mettre en mots les actes réalisés par les hommes qui dès aujourd'hui préparent la Martinique de demain.

[I want my poetry to remain involved in daily life. I want it to try to be one of the expressions of the collective life of my people, a vehicle for their cry.

Poetry must keep as a vital necessity the integration of all the struggles of the people; it must put into words the acts accomplished by the men who from this day on are preparing the Martinique of tomorrow.]

Notes

[1] Stated in private correspondence to the author.

[2] Joseph Polius, *Bonheur de poche* (Paris: Oswald, 1968). The page citations that follow refer to this edition.

[3] Joseph Polius, *Martinique debout* (Paris: L'Harmattan, 1977). Subsequent page citations in this chapter refer to this edition.

[4] Aimé Césaire paid homage to the heroism of Delgrès in a poem, "Mémorial de Louis Delgrès." See Césaire1960: 66-71.

[5] Stated in private correspondence to the author, 12 January 1994.

9

Gilette BAZILE,
Marcelle ARCHELON-PÉPIN, and
Michèle BILAVARN

F or a variety of reasons, there have been many more publications of male poets than of female poets, particularly up to the 1970s. Since then, quite a few women have published collections of poetry. While, however, women novelists like Maryse Condé and Simone Schwarz-Bart have made their presence felt and have earned international reputations, women poets from the Caribbean are still to receive intensive attention from critics. Because women's voices have been generally under-represented, I have decided to devote this chapter to a few women poets whose work I came across by chance in bookstores in the French Caribbean. The poems I have chosen represent a range of poetic expression and should complement the predominantly male voices we have discussed so far.

Virtually no biographical information is available on these three poets. Gilette Bazile from Guadeloupe is the author of three collections of poetry, *Fleur sauvage* (Paris: Barré-Dayez, 1976), *Ma vérité* (Nîmes: Bené, 1979), and *Clins d'œil* (Nîmes: Bené, 1988). Marcelle Archelon-Pépin (Guadeloupe) has so far published one slim volume of poetry, *Ciselures sur nuits d'écume* (Paris: Silex, 1987). Michèle Bilavarn from Martinique has so far published one collection, *Les ombres du soleil* (Saint-Estève: IMF, 1984).

COMPLAINTE NOIRE

Pleure mon île jolie, pleure.
Tes pleurs du fond des âges
Ont perlé sur tes beaux atours
au vert impérissable
Enchanteresse tu demeures
du regard et du cœur.

Pleure mon île jolie, pleure.
tes plages d'or volées
Ne comptent plus dans tes atours:
L'inquisiteur est maître
et les vêt à l'américaine
du papier des dollars.

Pleure mon île jolie, pleure.
Ton tam-tam oublié
ne chante plus tes beaux atours
Tes contes délaissés
chevrotent dans la nuit des vieux
quand résonne le disco.

Espère mon île jolie,
espère en tes fils fiers
éperdus de passé, d'histoire.

O nostalgique ébène,
ta route embrase de pardons
et ton cœur est de chair.

Danse mon île jolie, danse.
Tes jupons blancs s'apprêtent
à s'étourdir, tes hanches-hâle
à chevaucher le siècle !
Etonnante terre de jade
en mal d'identité !

❦

BLACK LAMENT

Weep my pretty island, weep
Your tears from the depths of time
Have formed drops of pearls on your lovely attire
of imperishable green
An enchantress you still are
in look and in heart.

Weep, my pretty island, weep.
your stolen beaches of gold
are no longer part of your attire
The inquisitor is in control
and dresses them up American-style
in paper dollars.

Weep, my pretty island, weep.
Your forsaken tom-tom
no longer sings about your lovely attire
Your neglected tales
quaver in the old folks' night

when the disco booms.

> Have hope, my pretty island,
> have hope in your proud sons
> distraught with past, with history.
> O nostalgic ebony,
> your path is aglow with pardons
> and your heart is of flesh.

> Dance, my pretty island, dance.
> Your white petticoats are preparing
> to get giddy, your tanned hips
> to straddle the century !
> Amazing land of jade
> in a crisis of identity !

One part of the title of this poem, "Complainte" [Lament] (Bazile 1988:80),[1] connects it to a well-established function of poetry, that of expressing negative emotions derived from the contrast between external reality and internal malaise. Within the metropolitan French tradition, this vein was popularized particularly by Jules Laforgue in a collection entitled *Les Complaintes*, published in 1885. The other part of the title, "noire" [black], links it to a specific cultural experience: the negative emotions are not those of an individual responding to a general situation, but rather those of a member of a particular group, expressing the responses of that group to a situation that is not at all generalized. In other words, the title implicitly insists on the difference of the black experience, and this blackness, inscribed in the title, extends its influence over the rest of the poem. The contrast of the title is reflected also in the form of the poem. The traditional fixed form is manifested in the division of the poem into five verses of six lines each, while the abandonment of rhyme and the variation in length of line indicate a departure from that same convention.

The dominant emotion suggested in the title and explored in the poem is that of sadness. This emotion is stressed in the first line of the poem, "Pleure, mon île jolie, pleure" [Weep, my pretty island, weep], and repeated at the beginning of the next two verses. The displacement of the adjective "jolie" from its expected position in front of the noun is related, it would seem, more to considerations of euphony (to avoid the awkwardness of "ma jolie île") than to any desire to place emphasis on "jolie" [pretty]. The repetition of the phrase that identifies the addressee, "mon île jolie" [my pretty island], in every verse emphasizes the intimacy of the communication between poet and island. Suffering is shown by the poet to be an historical characteristic ("du fond des âges" [from the depths of time]) of the condition of her native island. The island is depicted here as a woman of great external beauty, remarkable particularly, as the repeated references indicate, because of her attire ("atours"), typified here by the green color ("vert") associated with the Caribbean waters, whose white beads of foam are used by the poet to symbolize the island's tears ("pleurs"). The image that is projected of the island as an enchantress retains this ambivalence and combines the island's power to seduce as well as its deceptively beautiful exterior that conceals an inner sadness.

The poem becomes more explicitly social commentary in the second verse, when the poetic persona begins to outline the reasons for island's tears. The first reasons given relate to socioeconomic losses. The appearance of "volées" [stolen] at the end of the second line comes as a shock, breaking the mood of sad beauty created up to this point. Now this past participle presents the island as a victim robbed of some of her natural wealth (implicit in "d'or" [of gold]). L'inquisiteur" [The inquisitor] of the fourth verse signifies a foreign authority which now controls the island's resources. This control is conveyed through the verb "vêt" [dresses], which maintains continuity of the same image used to typify the island as woman in the first stanza. The magnitude of the loss experienced by the island is expressed by the difference between the original "or" [gold] and the present "papier" [paper] in which the beaches are clothed. The poet's opposition to this change is clear. This verse refers explicitly (through "à l'américaine" [American-style] and "dollars") to France's promotion of the tourism industry in Guadeloupe and Martinique by erecting large American-style hotels along the best beaches, the effect of which has been that it is now more difficult for locals to have access to beaches which were formerly open to everyone.

The following stanza continues the outline of losses that give reason for tears. The emphasis in this stanza is on cultural losses. The "tam-tam oublié" [forsaken tom-tom] is a metaphor for the decline of the African cultural element, while the "contes délaissés" [neglected tales] refer to the abandonment of an oral tradition of story-telling in favor of the popular "disco" entertainment. The poem does not, however, remain at the stage of bewailing losses. The poet proceeds in the final two verses to express encouragement to the island. The formula set in the first three stanzas, "Pleure mon île jolie, pleure" [Weep, my pretty island, weep], gives way to "Espère mon île jolie" [Have hope, my pretty island] and to "Danse mon île jolie, danse" [Dance, my pretty island, dance] for the final two stanzas. The poet suggests that the interest displayed by some young people in re-examining the past and in rewriting their history ('éperdus de passé, d'histoire" [distraught with past, with history] is a sign of hope. The apostrophe, "O nostalgique ébène" [O nostalgic ebony] is itself an historical allusion, recalling the term "bois d'ébène" [ebony wood] used by slavers to refer to their cargo of African slaves. This apostrophe establishes an indissoluble link between the island constantly addressed by the poet and the population of descendants of African slaves. The hope expressed by the poet extends to the possibility of amends ["pardons"] for the slave trade, while "chair" [flesh] introduces a more human element to the depiction of the island. The progression from weeping to hoping to dancing may be read as a reaction typical of the Caribbean, where even tragedy is transformed into the substance of Carnival. It is in this light that the qualifier "étonnante" [amazing] proves to be appropriate. The final line of the poem gives a neat summary of the problem that island is both confronting and surmounting: the crisis of cultural identity. It is here that the "black" lament of the title reaches its full significance.

This poem declares itself as the production of a self-conscious black poet. Language and emotion, form and focus, are all determined by the poet's racial experience. Bazile shows herself no less conscious than any of her male counterparts of her racial identity and of the threat of cultural annihilation that is a consequence of the political relationship between the Caribbean territories and metropolitan France. She is equally impelled by love of country and evidences a similar geographical and social attachment. The poem serves, therefore, as the vehicle for defining her personal and cultural space. In this way, Bazile aligns herself with the mainstream of the French Caribbean literary tradition such as it has evolved in the twentieth century and as illustrated in the works of the other poets we have presented.

FEMME

Femme, fugitive en des siècles passés, barbares et
dompteurs,
Houle dans le temps et l'alcôve déserte ou chaude,
          [dans le rêve de l'homme antique
          et nouveau,
Je te salue, ô multiple et multipliée, omniprésente
          [dans la vie où rien ne te fut servi,
          [où tout a soif et faim de toi, où tout t'est
          revenu.
L'homme s'est meurtri de ta Beauté.

ಇ

WOMAN

Woman, a fugitive in past centuries of barbarity and domination,
At one time a sea swell and a warm or deserted alcove,

> [in the dreams of men ancient and new,

I salute you, O multiple and multiplied, omnipresent

> [in life in which nothing was served to you,

[in which everything thirsts and hungers for you, in which everything has come

> back to you,

Man has bruised himself on your Beauty.

This short poem, "Femme" (*Clins d'œil*, 115), is a meditation on the significance of woman in her various life contexts through the ages. The issue of race plays no part here. The issue of gender is central. The contexts are introduced by the prepositions "en" or "dans" in expressions of time or location. The adjectives ("barbares et dompteurs" [barbaric and dominating]) used to describe the first temporal context, "en des siècles passés" [in past centuries], allude to past patriarchal societies driven by desires of conquest. In this context, woman's survival, the poem suggests, depended on her being a "fugitive" [fugitive], that is to say, on her ability to escape man's persistent attempts at dehumanizing control. The second temporal phrase, "dans le temps" [at one time], refers to a past more recent than that of "en des siècles passés" [in past centuries]. Thus in just these two lines the pattern of the role played by women throughout history is traced. The metaphor of a "houle" [sea swell] signifies the undulatory movement of the sea without crests being formed. This image conveys a general impression of apparent placidity and contained power while also hinting at a movement associated with sexual activity. In similar vein, the metaphorical representation of woman as "l'alcôve" [alcove] subtly recalls her role within the male imagination as the physical site of intimacy, dependent on the male presence to be either "déserte ou chaude" [deserted or warm].

The first two of the three descriptors used in the apostrophe, "ô multiple et multipliée, omniprésente" [multiple and multiplied, omnipresent] share a common etymological root whose repetition places emphasis on both quantity and variety. While "multiple" [multiple] conveys the notion of being composed of several parts or existing in several models, "multipliée" [multiplied] transmits a stronger sense of self-reproduction and an increase in numbers. The third term, "omniprésente" [omnipresent] extends the notion of multiplicity to the dimensions of time and space, establishing woman as a constant presence. The poem moves now to reflect on woman's general role in life, within a temporal context that bridges the past and the present. This bridge is created by the use of various verb tenses: the form of the past anterior in "rien ne te fut servi" [nothing was served you] signifies a past situation that is no longer true; the present in "tout a soif et faim de toi" [everything is thirsty and hungry for you], referring to a condition that is valid for the present; and the perfect (compound past) in "tout t'est revenu" [everything has come back to you], relates to a situation that had its origin in the past but is true in the present.

The final line of the poem sums up the relationship between man and woman through the ages. The capitalization of "Beauté" [Beauty] marks this, not without irony, as woman's prime characteristic. However, this line carries the implication that the perception of this beauty is different for men and for women. The line implies that for the woman poet woman's beauty is related to all the qualities and roles outlined in the poem whereas for the man it is perceived as external. What is also suggested here is that since the internal is the protective quality by means of which woman has survived and triumphed, it is here that man has consistently but unknowingly met his match: "L'homme s'est meurtri de ta Beauté" [Man bruised himself on your Beauty].

Bazile introduces a thematic orientation that has been undeveloped within the evolving tradition of French Caribbean poetry. The possibility of a conflictual relationship between Caribbean women and men has hitherto, to my knowledge, not even been hinted at in poetry, although the issue has been treated in short stories written particularly by Marie-Magdeleine and Claude Carbet (see particularly Claude et Marie-Magdeleine Carbet [1936], *Féfé et Doudou, Martiniquaises*). Bazile's richly dense poem moves beyond considerations of race and problems of cultural identity to explore courageously the issue of gender and to give a (Caribbean) woman's perspective on a topic that Caribbean male poets have traditionally ignored. In his way, she makes a valuable contribution in extending the range of creative options available to French Caribbean poets, both female and male.

CHANTER

Cette eau de cristal
lente, douce
accouche de mon corps
Mes larmes se mêlent
à ce fleuve qui m'emporte.
Je voudrais
être cette voix,
seule à l'envolée
pour chanter vos déchirures.
Je n'ai que ma plume à vous offrir.

❦

TO SING

This crystal water
slow, fresh
is born from my body
My tears mingle
with this river that carries me away.
I wish
I were this voice,
the only one in flight of inspiration
to sing of your lacerations.
All I have to offer you is my pen.

Guadeloupean Marcelle Archelon-Pépin's *Ciselures sur nuits d'écume* is filled with poetic gems. Archelon-Pépin is a poet's poet, who exploits with consummate skill the magical potential of words and images to produce poetry of indescribable beauty. The title of this poem, "Chanter" [To Sing] (Archelon-Pépin 1987:21)[2] is a reminder of one of the traditional functions of poetry - the lyrical - and the relation of poetry to orality and to music. An immediate impression of euphony is created by the alliteration of the sibilants in "cette," "cristal," and "douce," of the liquids "cristal," and "lente" (continued in "larmes" and "mêlent"), and of the plosives "accouche" and "corps." This impression is enhanced by the assonance of "douce" and "accouche." The break produced by a comma between two ordinarily banal adjectives, "lente, douce" [slow, fresh], invests each epithet with new and significant value. The verb "accouche," normally used to indicate the action of a woman delivering a baby, both establishes the gender of the poetic persona who is speaking and points to the part of the woman's body always involved in the birth process. The qualities of the water that issues from the poet's body, "de cristal" [crystal], "lente" [slow], and "douce" [fresh], are associated with purity, innocence, and gentleness. These qualities spill over on to "Mes larmes" [my tears] which are linked metonymically to "eau" [water]. This link suggests that the tears referred to here are tears as much of pleasure as of sadness, emotions related to the third metonym of water in the poem, "ce fleuve" [this river]. Three nouns are obviously joined by the accompanying demonstrative pronoun: "Cette eau" [This water], "ce fleuve" [this river], and "cette voix" [this voice]. This syntactical connection adds to the associative potential of "fleuve" [river], which may be read, beyond its most transparent reference to an experience in physical reality (an actual river), as both sexual passion and the excitement of creative inspiration, implicit in "m'emporte" [carries me away" and "à l'envolée" [in flight of inspiration]. Similarly the sadness normally associated with "larmes" [tears] finds its expression in the poem through the poet's regret: "Je voudrais / être" [I wish I were]. The poet's emotional ambivalence (the experience of both joy and sadness) meets a parallel in "vos déchirures" which may refer to the lacerations [your lacerations] produced in the person to whom the poem is addressed as well as to those caused by that person in the poet [the lacerations you caused]. The flight that was already evoked in "m'emporte" and "à l'envolée" becomes focused in the final line in the image of the poet's pen, "ma plume," which is also literally a feather. The poem thus becomes self-referential, translating the dilemma of a poet who is aware that singing ("chanter") is the traditional function of the poet, but who finds herself now confronted with the inadequacy of poetry. Her regret is related to the fact that she considers writing, represented as "ma plume" [my pen], an unsatisfactory substitute for orality ("voix" [voice]. The written poem becomes the visible sign of its limitations.

> Hier
> je t'ai aimé
> pour les reflets de ton ombre.
> Aujourd'hui, je t'aime
> pour la transparence de tes yeux.
> Etranger

Vais-je t'aimer demain ?

❦

Yesterday
I loved you
for the reflections of your shadow
Today, I love you
for the transparency of your eyes.
Stranger
Am I going to love you tomorrow?

In just three sentences this poem *(Ciselures...,* 25) captures the drama of a love affair through the mind of one participant, the poet. The poem is thus a meditation on love and provides a poignantly lucid analysis of the poet's motivations. The analysis is conducted with reference to three logical periods, the past ("Hier" [Yesterday]), the present ("Aujourd'hui" [Today]), and the future ("demain" [tomorrow]). The loved one's masculinity is indicated grammatically in the past participle "aimé" [loved] which adopts the masculine gender of its preceding direct object, "t'" [you]. The reasons given for the poet's love appear to be literally superficial, inauthentic, insubstantial, since "ombre" [shadow] denotes something that is difficult to see because of a lack of light, an image that is in any case not the real object. This sense of illusion is reinforced by the use of "reflets" [reflections] which implies a further level of unreality, heightened even more by the paradox of a term that is normally used with light being used here with darkness. The impression that emerges from this combination of antithetical images is that the foundation of the poet's love in the past was profoundly questionable.

The explanation given for the poet's love in the present is equally superficial. The quality of "transparence" [transparency] forms an ironic contrast with both "reflets" [reflections] and "ombre" [shadow], since it indicates the capacity for all light to penetrate while also connoting a lack of intellectual profundity. Furthermore, the quality of transparency is related not even to the person but merely to the eyes, which makes the attraction seem even less defensible and the loved one less real.

The final question confirms the picture of the lover given in the preceding two affirmative sentences. From the perspective of the poet he can only be an "Etranger" [Stranger], someone hitherto unknown, not part of the community with which the poet is familiar, absent as a real presence even from the poem. The question is rhetorical, emphasizing the tragedy of the poet's situation, confronted as she is with the prospect of a love that is ultimately impossible.

MESSAGE

Dans vos yeux
mon essence de femme
s'est évaporée.
Vous avez voulu de vos mains
la tenir en berceau.
Entre vos doigts, elle est passée
Comme vous passez

❦

MESSAGE

In your eyes
my woman's essence
evaporated.
You wanted with your hands
to keep it cradled.
Between your fingers it passed
As you are passing

This poem ("Message," *Ciselures...*, 27) is built on a more developed ternary structure than "Hier...." It similarly comprises just three sentences, but each of these sentences may further be divided into three rhythmic and syntactic parts. The regularity thus produced lends harmony to the poem. It is indeed, as the title indicates, a "message," a communication or signal addressed to a lover. This self-referential message-poem is an announcement of the end of a relationship, of the inevitable end of an impossible love. The poet's reasons are stated in compressed form. The first reason given is: "Dans vos yeux / mon essence de femme / s'est évaporée" [In your eyes / my woman's essence / evaporated]. The poet presents herself generically as a "femme" [woman]; it is as a woman that she speaks; it is her womanness that is at issue in the relationship. The term "essence" signifies the permanent reality and the concentrated constituent element as well as the perfume that so often serves as a referent for woman. It is to the last two senses that the verb "s'est évaporée" [evaporated] is linked. The first reason therefore amounts to this: the failure of the man to see her as a woman; his perception of her denies her womanness.

The second reason, "Vous avez voulu de vos mains / la tenir en berceau" [You wanted with your hands to keep it cradled], points, particularly in "en berceau" [cradled], to the poet's rejection of the male's desire to infantilize the woman. The physical impossibility for "mains" [hands] to contain an "essence" emphasizes the futility of the man's desire. The final sentence continues the image, describing the inevitable result: "Entre vos doigts, elle est passée" [Between your fingers it passed]. The message becomes clear only in the final line: the comparison underlines the fact that the relationship is as doomed to failure as the man's attempts to repress the nature of woman.

These poems by Archelon-Pépin are examples of a movement away from poetry that is transparently politically motivated towards writing that seeks to exploit the figurative potential in language, in order to express flashes of insight and sentiment. It would be misleading, however, to suggest that commitment to the native land is lacking. In this collection Archelon-Pépin's link to Guadeloupe is seen most clearly in the fact that she has titled three poems "Mon île." It would be true to say, however, that her poetry does not appear to have its source in problems of cultural identity or in a desire to contribute to political change. Archelon-Pépin thus represents a new direction in French Caribbean poetry.

FEMMES

Il est des jours de pluie
où l'âme de son cœur
pleure
comme il pleut
à l'intérieur.

Il est des jours de pluie
où tout s'arrête de vivre
vie
vigne
croissance

Je crois à l'intérieur de moi
mon âme
solidifie
pure
sa délicatesse
mais
il reste encore
un morceau de ce lac
à apaiser enfin...
Les vagues de cette âme...
douloureuse,
blessantes

souffrance à l'intérieur
les vagues de cette âme
           à calmer
      caresser
              là
           tranquilles
           lasses
           assoupies
                  enfin.

J'aime Femme que tu sois
           toi
grande belle
j'aime Femme que tu te débarrasses
           de ta carapace
                  d'enfant
face à l'homme
te sens-tu vulnérable?
           instable?

Face à l'homme
c'est si difficile
de résister à l'homme...
D'imposer ta présence de Femme
           Pluie
           Fleur
           Finesse

           Odeur du corps
                  terre
                  Mer
                  Océan
           loin de tous
           entre en toi

Laisse tomber la peau
la marque de fabrique
et sors nue,
Pure
toi
Femme
Ame
Cœur
Espoir...

❦

WOMEN

There are rainy days
when her heart's soul
weeps
like it rains
inside.

There are rainy days
when everything stops living
life
vines
growth

I am growing inside myself
my pure
soul
is solidifying
its delicacy
but
there still is
a piece of this lake
left to be calmed...

The hurtful
  waves of this soul...
      in distress,
  anguish inside
the waves of this soul
    to be soothed
    caressed
          there
          quiet
          weary
          dozing
          at last.

I like you Woman to be
          you
tall beautiful
I like you Woman to get rid of
      your childish
          shell
in front of man
do you feel vulnerable?
      insecure?

In front of man
it's so difficult
to stand up to man...
To establish your presence as Woman
      Rain
      Flower
      Grace

      Scent of body
      land
      Sea

> Ocean
> far from everybody
> enters into you
> Shed your skin
> your brand name
> and come out naked,
> Pure
> you
> Woman
> Soul
> Heart
> Hope...

Most of the forty-three poems in Michèle Bilavarn's *Les ombres du soleil* (1984)[3] are internal responses to and meditations on external manifestations of nature. A significantly high number of these poems focus explicitly on woman and translate impressions and emotions related to the situation of women. These include "La mère," "Une femme d'ombre," "Mouvement de femme," "Nina," "Femme," and "Petite fille d'amour," as well as "Femmes." "Femmes" (13-14) is a visually striking poem, whose elongated and sinuous arrangement on the page transmits an impression of sensuality that is enhanced by the rhythms of the poem. Any poem written in French that uses the combined images of "pluie" [rain], "pleurs" [tears], and "cœur" [heart] would inevitably awaken echoes of Verlaine's "Il pleure dans mon cœur." Bilavarn similarly exploits the potential for musical harmony through rhyme ("cœur"/"pleure"/"intérieur") and alliteration ("pluie"/"pleure"/"pleut") in the first stanza and through alliteration and assonance in the second ("vivre"/"vie"/"vigne"). The title of this poem, however, establishes an entirely new context for the mood evoked in the poem. The plural "Femmes" [Women] directs the focus of the poem away from a general human condition to the specific experience of women and it is this specificity that is conveyed by the possessive pronoun "son" [her] of the second line.

The use of this third person possessive establishes a distance between the poetic persona and the woman being discussed and gives the declaration the force of an objective truth. The poem is attempting to penetrate beneath the surface and describe what is really happening emotionally on the inside. The phrase "l'âme de son cœur" [her heart's soul], in which "l'âme" [soul] represents the essential, internal part of a "cœur" [heart] that is itself an interior, emphasizes the contrast between interior and exterior that is developed in the poem. The internal weeping of women is conveyed by the simile of rain occurring indoors ("à l'intérieur"), an image that speaks to conditions of adversity and neglect characterizing woman's soul, which is compared indirectly to a house with an inadequate roof.

The mood of depression introduced in the first stanza is continued in the second through the repetition of the opening phrase ("Il est des jours de pluie / où" [There are rainy days / when]). The mood is intensified, however, with the statement that "tout s'arrête de vivre" [everything stops living]. The three nouns used in apposition to "tout" [everything] are all linked in a complex relationship of sound and sense. The concrete "vigne" [vine] contrasts with the abstract "vie" [life] and "croissance" [growth] but at the same time serves as a metaphor for both abstractions.

The exploitation of the verb/noun connection by a shift from the infinitive "vivre" [to live] to the noun "vie" [life] is repeated in a reverse movement that provides a transition between the second and third stanzas: the noun "croissance" [growth] paves the way for the verb "je croîs" [I am growing]. This third stanza introduces a dramatic change in the poem with the assumption of subjectivity ("Je" [I]) by the poet. The poem thus leaves the realm of philosophical generalization to become personal testimony. The link to the previous statements is maintained, however, by the repetition of "à l'intérieur" [inside], which draws attention to the contrast already alluded to between exteriors and interiors. The liquidity ("pleure" [weeps] and "pleut" [rains]) associated with the woman's "âme" [soul] of the first stanza is partly contradicted by the verb "solidifie" [is solidifying], which suggests some difference between the poet and the women referred to at the beginning of the poem. The assertion, "je crois à l'intérieur de moi" [I am growing inside myself], may be read as an expression of the poet's pride in her progress. But this pride does not elevate her above other women. This apparent difference serves as a reminder of what connects her to other women. Her progress is shown to be only partial: "il reste encore / un morceau de ce lac / à apaiser enfin..." [there still is / a piece of this lake / to be calmed...]. The suspension points used here and in three other places in the poem impose a pause in the rhythm and signify a continuation without end of the state evoked.

The liquid lake ("lac") with all its waves ("les vagues de cette âme" [the waves of this soul]) is going to be used from this point as the principal metaphor of woman's soul. The allusion here is to the biblical incident of the miraculous calming of the waves of a tempestuous lake by Jesus reported in the Gospels (see Luke 8: 22-24 and Matthew 8: 23-26). This image is fused with the evocation, in the last single-word lines of the poem, of the gentle stroking of a restless child. The syntactical arrangement becomes more complex, with adjectives becoming more or less separated from the noun it qualifies: "Les vagues / ... / blessantes" [The hurtful / waves]; "cette âme ... / douloureuse" [this soul... / in distress]. The accumulation of "douloureuse" [in distress], "blessantes" [hurtful], and "souffrance" [anguish] emphasize how much the poet associates suffering with the situation of women. The poem adopts the voice of a comforting mother and its rhythm and spatial arrangement convey the slow fall into peaceful sleep: "caresser / là / tranquilles / lasses / assoupies / enfin " [caressed / there / quiet / weary / dozing / at last].

In the second half of the poem the poet turns from the indirect third-person stance of the opening stanzas and from the self-directed expression of the third to address her comments directly to a single person, referred to in the final three stanzas as

"Femme" [Woman], the capitalization of which invests its referent
with dignity and importance. The intimacy of the connection
between the poet and this person is reflected in the use of the
familiar "tu" [you]. The repetition of "J'aime Femme" [I like
Woman] and of consonant and vowel sounds in "tu sois"/ "toi,"
"débarrasses" / "carapace" / "face," "enfant" / "sens-tu," and
"vulnérable" / "instable" adds to the musical harmony of the poem.
The poet's desire for Woman is total ("que tu sois / toi" [you to be
you]), which requires the assumption of full maturity. This new
state is represented metaphorically by the removal of the protective
"carapace / d'enfant" [childish shell]. That the responsibility is the
woman's is indicated by the pronominal verb "tu te débarrasses"
[you get rid of]. The attitude of the poet, however, is one of
empathy, as the questions posed at the end of the stanza imply: "face
à l'homme / te sens-tu vulnérable? / instable?" [in front of man / do
you feel vulnerable? / insecure?].

The poet's empathy is conveyed further by the unambiguous
language used to articulate the problem: "Face à l'homme / c'est si
difficile / de résister à l'homme...) [In front of man / it's so difficult
/ to stand up to man]. The language becomes highly figurative in
order to represent Woman: "Pluie / Fleur / Finesse" [Rain / Flower
/ Grace]. The first of these terms reproduces the image with which
the poem opens; the second is in metonymic relationship to the
growth alluded to between the second and third stanzas; while the
third term is a new quality. The capitals used for these terms and
for others in the final stanza help to underline the importance and
dignity of these womanly attributes.

In the first part of the final stanza, the language becomes
more ambiguous: syntactical relationships are unclear. Is, for
instance, "Odeur du corps" [Scent of body] the subject of the verb
"entre" [enters]? Are "Mer" [Sea] and "Océan" [Ocean] in
apposition to "Odeur" [Scent]? Since "terre" [land] is not
capitalized, is it linked elliptically to "corps" [body]? To what is
"loin" [far] attached? There are no obvious answers to any of these

questions, although it would be logical to consider "Mer" [Sea] and "Océan" [Ocean] as metaphors of woman. The exhortation with which the poem ends is more explicit: "Laisse tomber la peau / la marque de fabrique / et sors nue" [Shed your skin / your brand name / and come out naked]. The action called for here is more radical than that suggested earlier: removal of the skin rather than just the shell. The position of "la marque de fabrique" [brand name] makes it an alternative designation for the noun it immediately follows ("la peau" [skin]). The advice to abandon the external distinguishing sign is the only hint in the poem that the poet is recommending a gender loyalty that transcends race. The purity that the poet had earlier claimed (third stanza) as a characteristic of her own soul is now projected as the essential characteristic of her ideal woman. In similar vein, the two attributes associated with woman presented in the second line of the poem are now re-established and invested with greater significance by the use of the initial capital: "Âme / Cœur" [Soul / Heart], while the optimism of the final term, "Espoir..." [Hope], projects itself with the help of suspension points into an unending future. The poem thus becomes a powerful message of encouragement and faith.

This poem, like many of those of Bazile and Archelon-Pépin, demonstrates a high level of technical, linguistic, competence as well as an interest in giving voice to the perceptions and preoccupations of women and engaging in a communication among women. These poets demonstrate that French Caribbean poetry is not and should not be limited to the exploration of themes related to racial or cultural malaise. The fact that social and political ideology does not dominate and frequently is not directly inscribed in the poetic productions of these women writers suggests a less conflictual relationship with French culture and politics, a greater acceptance of their sociopolitical situation as French and Antillean, a change in the conception of the focus and function of literary activity, as well as a greater awareness of themselves as women. These women illustrate the diversity and dynamism that indicate the profoundly evolutionary nature of French Caribbean literature and society.

Notes

[1] All page citations for Bazile's poems refer to this edition.

[2] All page citations for Archelon-Pépin's poems refer to this edition.

[3] Page citations that follow refer to this edition.

10

Conclusion

My visit with the works of these poets has left me with a feeling of inadequacy at the prospect of providing an insightful synthesis and of trying to draw general conclusions that would be valid for all or for the majority of the writers. In fact, what has in some ways been most striking is the degree of diversity among them. Each of them seems curiously to stand alone. Their differences are as marked as their similarities. For my own convenience, I have asked myself the following questions: What is the significance of "race" in relation to the poetic productions of these writers? What, in general terms, can we learn from these poets about what it means to be black, to be a French West Indian of color? What does it mean to be a poet in the French Caribbean? What is the poet's role? What is the function of poetry? What links or differences exist between these poets and poets from other parts of the Caribbean?

The question of racial identification and consciousness is a sensitive and difficult one and "race" provides a clear line of divergence among French Caribbean writers. It would be ingenuous to preclude the impact of race from any discourse in twentieth century American and Caribbean societies. It exists even when unmentioned. It underpins every aspect of American society. It may be disguised, muted, ignored. It may be said that the Caribbean exists along a historical fault line (in the geographical sense). The consciousness of a historical fault affects every aspect of human relationships across racial lines in the U.S. and the Caribbean. Although all the poets have some African ancestry, not all of them identify themselves explicitly as "black" either in or through their poetry. Carbet's attitude to race, as expressed in her poetry, is radically different from that of many of the male writers, particularly Damas, Césaire, Tirolien, and Polius. Although I know from private conversations with Anna (as Carbet is known within her family) and some of her relatives that she was deeply conscious of herself as "black," yet her poetry rarely presents itself explicitly as the voice of a black person. The creative point from which she writes is not her blackness but the passionate sensitivity of a human being to the beauty of life, as manifested in relationships with family and friends as well as in nature. Clearly, Carbet was ardently attached to the culture of her native land. Her respect for its folklore is reflected in her poetry as well as in her short stories. It would seem that she accepted this culture as being Caribbean and non-French without attempting to relate its underpinnings to Africa, which remained for her a sympathetic but foreign culture. It is this attitude to Africa and things African that separate her from Damas and Césaire, all of whom started publishing within a few years of one another and may be considered as virtual contemporaries, and even from Glissant who took pains to trace the cultural connection. The debate on "*métissage*" or racial mixing reflects the search for a means of coping with or explaining away this fault. Damas is able to demonstrate from his own experience that "*métissage*" is a producer of pain rather than a solution in the present state of society.

For Damas, Césaire, Tirolien, Padoly, and Polius, the awareness of being black provides at least an initial impetus as well as a framework for the poetic enterprise. Their race consciousness invests their poetry with a political function. Poetic expression is frequently inseparable from ideology. Polius stands out among this group, however, because for him race is subordinated to the anticolonialist and anti-imperialist agenda for political independence for his country. Glissant has steadfastly resisted using racial consciousness as a stimulus for creative expression, but his poetry does recreate the voices of hitherto unheard Africans that he regards as cultural ancestors. The social consciousness of Bazile and Bilavarn is directed more toward gender than toward race, toward their situation as women rather than as blacks. Bilavarn distinguishes herself sharply from all the others in that her poetry does not reveal any explicit signs of a concern for social issues.

These poets differ too in their conception of the role of the poet and in the function of poetry. Each poet conceives of the role and function of the poet in a different way. Most of these poets refuse or reject what they would consider as the presumptuous role, assumed most notably by Césaire, of the poet as the chosen spokesperson for a people. Césaire often presents himself as the voice, the chosen spokesperson, the leader with the vision of the future not yet shared by the people he leads. Césaire's poetic persona establishes a distance between him and his people. The poet is ahead and above, the possessor of a special gift of communication and of vision, chosen to speak and to lead. Glissant's poetic persona makes no such claims but his poetic vision is equally compelling and his hermeticism and aestheticism create an aura of poetic isolation that links him to Césaire. Glissant evidently equally writes for a future audience. He is well aware that his vision of Antilleanity and particularly of the Relation will not be easily understood. His opacity is a desired position. But Glissant and Césaire come together, despite their differing conceptions of themselves in relation to their people, in the power of their imagery and in the power of their language, which is difficult with respect to vocabulary, unusual associations, and general erudition. Tirolien, Padoly, Polius, Archelon-Pépin, Bazile, and Bilavarn resist the notion of the poet as leader, isolated in superiority above the madding crowd. On the other hand, both Polius and Tirolien show evidence of using the poem for the express purpose of political and cultural liberation. There is no indication that Archelon-Pépin's poetic persona considers herself a poet-Magus, but her tendency toward aestheticism binds her to the élite lineage of specially gifted poetic communicators.

The differences among these French Caribbean poets do not outweigh the factors that bind them together and attach them to a larger Caribbean community. What all these writers share, no matter what their individual Caribbean territory of origin, is a patent love of country and of the Caribbean region. This love reveals itself not merely in the choice of local features (geography, climate, folklore, flora, and fauna) as objects of admiration or affection but also in privileging the local natural landscape as a source of images. The whole of the Caribbean shares a legacy of dislocation, in relation to geography, culture, history, and orality. The literature of this region is therefore a literature of relocation. Barbara Webb (1992) has already explored convergences across language in the Caribbean in relation to myth and history in the novels of Glissant from Martinique, Wilson Harris from Guyana, and the Cuban Alejo Carpentier. Josaphat Kubayanda (1990) examined the parallels in relation to "Africanness" in the poetry of Aimé Césaire and the Cuban poet, Nicolás Guillén. Glissant himself has expressed a close link to Barbadian Kamau Brathwaite and St. Lucian Derek Walcott within the context of his conception of the Relation and the impact of the Plantation in the Americas (*Poétique de la Relation*, 86). Brathwaite acknowledges links to both Césaire and Glissant: like Césaire it is through the acknowledgement of his African heritage that his poetic activity develops; like Glissant he is deeply conscious of the ways in which the historical context of slavery and plantation life has affected the Caribbean and has given an epic account of the emergence of the Caribbean people from Africa to the Americas.

Brathwaite and Glissant go further than most writers from the English, French, or Spanish-speaking Caribbean, in challenging European literary assumptions and practices.

All writing is in a way a commentary on the social matrix that produces it. And this is part of the essential diversity of the Caribbean. The convergences in attitude, vision, and language practice among these writers are real. It is true that these writers intersect across barriers of language and across the different political status of their respective countries of origin. While the difference in the sociopolitical context out of which these writers emerge cannot be underestimated, it is remarkable that the majority of Caribbean writers tend to manifest a high degree of creative independence unrelated to the political status of their respective countries.

For the French Caribbean poets whose work we have examined poetry seems to represent access to a world of beauty and of privilege that has been denied them, as a result of historical experiences. Thus, there is a concern with defining this world and appropriating it. It is here that they rejoin writers from throughout the Caribbean. All Caribbean people suffer from a tenuous sense of property, with no historical or racial memory of having owned the space they now occupy or even their self. Writing is one cultural activity for making up for this deficit. Writing is, as we have intimated earlier, the means of supplementing the break of orality occasioned by the circumstance of forced separation from communities in Africa, the silence of slave ships, and the equally forced adaptation to new speech habits on plantations, complicated by denial of access to the superior world of writing. The suppression of black speech on slave ships and plantations has produced a compensatory tendency towards defiance in utterance and towards the demonstration of linguistic mastery, often taking the form of self-conscious preciosity, as in Glissant and Walcott. All of these writers, despite superficial differences in the relative "simplicity" of their productions, manifest sophistication in their use of language. Language use often represents a subversion of the linguistic and cultural system. This subversion is related to the transgressive nature of all Caribbean literature, which exists in defiance of the forces, present and past, that militate against its existence and survival. Thus, all Caribbean writing forms part of an evolutionary struggle to appropriate a creative space for the Caribbean.

It is difficult to find a way of concluding this dialogue with so many poetic voices of the Caribbean. I hope I have demonstrated that, in these days when five-second sound bites and ten-second commercials appear to represent the highest form of creative expression in the minds of many, there is an evolving literature in the French Caribbean that is worth not merely being talked or written about but actually attentive reading. I have been moved by my exposure to these poets who are all seekers after beauty, seekers after the best in themselves and in humanity, beyond the limitations placed on their lives as people trying to recover from the ravages of recent enslavement and colonization. These poets serve as reminders that poetry still represents one of the most profoundly useful, inspiring, and hopeful activities in which we as human beings can participate, whether as writers or as readers. They remind us that poetry is itself an affirmation of creativity and of life, no matter how depressing the material environment in which it is produced. These studies demonstrate that the French Caribbean, whatever its handicaps in terms of size, economic viability, or geopolitical importance, provides through its poetry light by which we may all see ourselves in a different way and grow to a newer and more beautiful life.

Bibliography

A. *PRIMARY POETIC TEXTS*

Archelon-Pépin, Marcelle. *Ciselures sur nuits d'écume*. Paris: Silex, 1987.

Bazile, Gilette. *Clins d'œil*. Nîmes: Bené, 1988.

Bilavarn, Michèle. *Les ombres du soleil*. Saint-Estève: Imprimerie Michel Fricker, 1984.

Carbet, Marie-Magdeleine. *Point d'orgue*. Paris: La Productrice, 1958.

———. *Rose de ta grâce*. Paris: Le Cerf Volant, 1970.

Césaire, Aimé. *Cadastre*. Paris: Seuil, 1961.

Damas, L.-G. *Pigments*. Paris: Présence Africaine, 1962.

———. *Névralgies*. Paris: Présence Africaine, 1966.

Glissant, Édouard. *Poèmes complets*. Paris: Gallimard, 1994.

Padoly, Yves. *Le missel noir*. Monaco: Poètes de notre temps, 1965.

Polius, Joseph. *Bonheur de poche*. Paris: Oswald, 1968.

———. *Martinique debout*. Paris: L'Harmattan, 1977.

Tirolien, Guy. *Balles d'or*. Paris: Présence Africaine, 1961.

B.   *SELECTED BIBLIOGRAPHY*

Affergan, Francis. "Je est-il un autre ou l'identité déplacée." *Les Temps Modernes* 441-42 (avril-mai 1983): 2038-42.

Alante-Lima, Willy. "Tendances actuelles de la poésie en Guadeloupe. *Lettre et Cultures de Langue Française* VII 3 (1985): 31-43.

Almeida, Lilian Pestre de. "Ariettes retrouvées, contes recréés. Quelques aspects de la création chez Césaire dans ses rapports avec l'oralité." *Etudes créoles* 8.1-2(1985): 103-26.

Almeida, Lilian Pestre de, and Maria Bernadette Velloso Porto. "Lecture symbolique d'un poème d'Aimé Césaire, 'Débris.'" *Présence Francophone* 17 (automne 1978): 133-50.

Amuta, Chidi. *The Theory of African Literature: Implications for Practical Criticism*. London: Zed, 1989.

André, Jacques. "L'Identité ou le retour du même." *Les Temps Modernes* 441-42 (avril-mai 1983): 2026-37.

Armet, Auguste. "Aimé Césaire, homme politique." *Etudes Littéraires* 6.1 (avril 1973): 81-96.

Arnaud, Jacqueline. "Littérature maghrébine et littérature afro-antillaise d'expression française." *Notre Librairie* 65 (July - September 1982): 47-56.

Arnold, A. James. Introduction. *Lyric and Dramatic Poetry 1946-82: Aimé Césaire*. Trans. Clayton Eshleman and Annette Smith. Charlottesville: Univ. Press of Virginia, 1990.

——. *Modernism and Negritude: The Poetry and Poetics of Aimé Césaire*. Cambridge, Mass.: Harvard University Press, 1981.

Bader, Wolfgang. "Poétique antillaise, poétique de la relation: Interview avec Edouard   G l i s s a n t ." *Komparatistische Hefte* 9-10 (1984): 83-100.

Baker, Houston A., Jr. *Afro-American Poetics — Revisions of Harlem and the Black Aesthetic.* Wisconsin: Univ. of Wisconsin Press, 1988.

Battestini, M. et S., and Mercier, R. *Aimé Césaire.* Ecrivain martiniquais. Paris: Nathan, 1967.

Baudelaire, Charles. *Les Fleurs du mal et poésie diverses.* Paris: Larousse, 1927.

———. *Œuvres complètes.* Vol.1. Paris: Gallimard, 1975.

Baudot, Alain. "De l'autre à l'un. Aliénation et révolte dans les littératures d'expression française." *Etudes française* 7.4 (novembre 1971): 331-58.

———. "D'un pays (re)possédé." *Etudes françaises* 10.4 (novembre 1974): 359-73.

———. "Edouard Glissant: A Selected bibliography." *World Literature Today* 63.4 (Autumn 1989): 567-77.

———. "Les écrivains antillais et l'Afrique." *Notre Librairie* 73 (1984): 31-45.

Baudot, Alain, and Marianne R. Holder. "Edouard Glissant: A Poet in Search of His Landscape ('For What the Tree Tells')." *World Literature Today* 63.4 (Autumn 1989): 583-88.

Bazile, Gilette. *Fleur sauvage.* Paris: Barré-Dayez, 1976.

———. *Ma vérité.* Nîmes: Bené, 1979.

Beckles, Hilary McD. *A History of Barbados: From Amerindian Settlement to Nation-State.* Cambridge, New York: Cambridge Univ. Press, 1990.

Benamou, Michel. "Literature and Cultural Connotations." *Teaching Language through Literature* 12.2: 6-12.

———. "The Testament of Negritude: 'Dit d'errance' by Aimé Césaire." *Teaching Language through Literature* 14.1: 1-11.

Bernabé, Jean. "De la négritude à la créolité: éléments pour une approche comparée." *Etudes françaises* 28.2-3 (1992-1993): 23-38.

Bernabé, Jean, Patrick Chamoiseau, and Raphaël Confiant. "In Praise of Creoleness." *Callaloo* 13.4 (Fall 1990): 886-909.

Berrian, Brenda F. "Francophone Caribbean Literature." *Callaloo* 9.4 (Fall 1986): 646-60.

Bouckson, Germain, and Édouard Bertrand. Les Antilles en question. *Fort-de-France: Imprimerie Antillaise, 1972.*

Breton, André. Preface. *Cahier d'un retour au pays natal.* By Aimé Césaire. Paris: Présence Africaine, 1971.

Bubrowska-Skrodzka, H. "Aimé Césaire, Chantre de la Grandeur de l'Afrique." *Présence Africaine* 59 (3ème trimestre 1966): 34-56.

Burton, Richard D.E. "Comment peut-on être martiniquais? The Recent Work of Edouard Glissant." *Modern Language Review* 79.2 (April 1984): 301-12.

Cailler, Bernadette. *Proposition poétique: une lecture de l'œuvre d'Aimé Césaire.* Québec: Sherbrooke, 1976.

———. "Césaire ou la fidélité." *Soleil éclaté.* Ed. Jacqueline Leiner. Tübingen: Narr, 1984. 61-68.

———. "Edouard Glissant: A Creative Critic." *World Literature Today* 63.4 (Autumn 1989): 589-92.

———. "Mycéa ou le tracé des maux (réflexions sur quelques poèmes d'Edouard Glissant)." *Revue Francophone de Louisiane* 3.1 (Spring 1988): 33-37.

———. "Saint-John Perse devant la critique antillaise." *Stanford French Review* 2.2 (Autumn 1978): 285-99.

———. "Un itinéraire poétique: Édouard Glissant et l'anti-Anabase." *Présence Francophone* 19 (Autumn 1979): 107-32.

Carbet, Marie-Magdeleine. "Aux Antilles." *Culture française* (Hiver 1973): 21-25.

———. "Les écrivains antillais et les difficultés de la diffusion." *Culture française* (Hiver 1975): 69-76.

———. "La poésie en Martinique." *Lettre et Cultures de Langue Française* VII 3 (1985): 61-71.

———. *Point d'orgue.* Paris: La Productrice, 1958.

———. *Rose de ta grâce.* Paris: Le Cerf Volant, 1970.

Cartey, Wilfred. "Léon Damas: Exile and Return." In *Critical Perspectives on Léon-Gontran Damas.* Ed. Keith Q. Warner. Washington, D.C.: Three Continents Press, 1988. 67-85.

Case, Frederick Ivor. "Aimé Césaire et l'occident chrétien." *L'Esprit Créateur* 10.3 (Fall 1970): 242- 56.

———. "Edouard Glissant and the Poetics of Cultural Marginalization." *World Literature Today* 3.4(Autumn 1989): 593-98.

Césaire, Aimé. *Cahier d'un retour au pays natal.* Paris: Présence Africaine, 1971.

———. *Discours sur le colonialisme.* Paris: Présence Africaine, 1955.

———. *Et les chiens se taisaient.* Paris: Présence Africaine, 1956.

———. *Ferrements.* Paris: Seuil, 1960.

———. "Charles Péguy." *Tropiques* 1 (avril 1941a): 39-40.

———. "Culture et colonisation." (Discours prononcé au premier congrès international des écrivains et artistes noirs.) *Présence Africaine* (nouvelle série) 8-10 (juin- novembre, 1956).

———. "En guise de manifeste littéraire." *Tropiques* 5 (avril 1942a): 7-12.

———. "En rupture de mer morte. (Postface)." *Tropiques* 3 (octobre 1941b): 74-76.

———. "Introduction à la poésie nègre américaine." *Tropiques* 2 (juillet 1941c): 37-42.

———. "Introduction au folklore martiniquais." *Tropiques* 4 (janvier 1942b): 7-11.

———. "L'Homme de culture et ses responsabilités." (Discours prononcé au deuxième congrès international des écrivains et artistes noirs.) *Présence Africaine* 24-25 (juin 1959).

———. "Liminaire." *Présence Africaine* 57 (1966): 3.

———. "Maintenir la poésie." *Tropiques* 8-9 (octobre 1943): 7-8.

———. "Panorama." *Tropiques* 10 (février 1944): 7-10.

———. "Poésie et connaissance." *Tropiques* 12 (janvier, 1945): 157-70.

———. "Présentation." *Tropiques* 1 (avril 1941d): 5-6.

———. "Réponse à Depestre poète haïtien (Eléments d'un art poétique)." *Présence Africaine* (nouvelle série) 1-2 (avril - juillet 1955): 113-15.

———. "Société et littérature dans les Antilles." *Etudes littéraires* 6.1 (1973): 9-20.

———. "Sur la poésie nationale." *Présence Africaine* 4 (octobre - novembre, 1955): 39-41.

———. "Vues sur Mallarmé." *Tropiques* 5 (avril 1942c): 53-61.

Césaire, Ina, and Jodelle Laurent. *Contes de mort et de vie aux Antilles.* Paris: Nubia, 1976.

Césaire, Suzanne. "1943: Le surréalisme et nous." *Tropiques* 8-9 (octobre 1943): 14-18.

Chamoiseau, Patrick, and Raphaël Confiant. *Lettres créoles: Tracées antillaises et continentales de la littérature - Haïti, Guadeloupe, Martinique, Guyane 1635-1975.* Paris: Hatier, 1991.

Charpier, Jacques, and Pierre Séghers. *L'art poétique.* Paris: Séghers, 1956.

Chemain, Arlette. "Damas et la littérature: création esthétique et décor mythique. Deux régimes de l'image en tension dans la poésie de Damas." In *Léon Gontran Damas: Actes du colloque Léon-Gontran Damas, Paris, décembre 1988.* Ed. Michel Tétu. Paris: ACCT/Présence Africaine, 1989. 174-81.

Chevrier, Jacques. *Littérature nègre: Afrique, Antilles, Madagascar.* Paris: Armand Colin, 1974.

Chassagne, Raymond. "Edouard Glissant: homme de rupture et témoin Caraïbéen." *Conjonction* 148 (July 1980): 63-77.

———. "Seuils de rupture en littérature antillaise." *Conjonction* 155 (Dec. 1982): 57-68.

Christian, Barbara. "But What Do We Think We're Doing Anyway: The State of Black Feminist Criticism(s) or My Version of a Little Bit of History." In *Changing Our Own Words. Essays on Criticism, Theory, and Writing by Black Women*. Ed. Cheryl A. Wall. New Brunswick, NJ: Rutgers Univ. Press, 1989. 58-74.

Clark, Beatrice Stith. "IME Revisited: Lectures by Edouard Glissant on Sociocultural Realities in the Francophone Antilles." *World Literature Today* 63.4 (Autumn 1989): 599-605.

Clark, Vèvè A. "Studies in Caribbean and South American Literature: An Annual Annotated bibliography. 1986. Francophone Caribbean Literature." *Callaloo* 10.4 (Fall 1987): 705-732.

Clark, Vèvè A., Ruth-Ellen B. Joeres, & Madelon Sprengnether, Eds. *Revising the Word and the World: Essays in Feminist Literary Criticism*. Chicago and London: Univ. of Chicago Press, 1993.

Condé, Maryse. "Cahier d'un retour au pays natal." *Césaire. Analyse critique*. Paris: Hatier, 1978.

——, ed. *L'Héritage de Caliban*. Pointe-A-Pitre: Editions Jasor, 1992.

——. *La poésie antillaise*. Paris: Nathan, 1977.

——. "Autour d'une littérature antillaise." *Présence Africaine* 81 (1er trimestre 1972): 170-176.

——. "Négritude césairienne, négritude senghorienne." *Revue de littérature comparée* 48: 409-19.

Condé, Maryse, and Alain Rutil, eds. *Bouquet de voix pour Guy Tirolien*. Pointe-à-Pitre: Jasor, 1990, p. 59.

Corzani, Jack. *La littérature des Antilles et Guyane françaises*. 6 vols. Fort-de-France: Désormeaux, 1978.

——. "A propos d'un archipel 'inachevé': l'Antillanité, rêve et réalité dans la littérature des Antilles françaises." *Ethiopiques* 1.3-4 (1983): 25-35.

——. "Césaire et la Caraïbe oubliée...". *Soleil éclaté.* Ed.
Jacqueline Leiner. Tübingen: Narr, 198, 89-99.
——. "Problèmes méthodologiques d'une 'histoire littéraire' des
Caraïbes." *Komparatistiche Hefte* 11 (1985): 49-67.
Coulthard, G.R. *Race and Colour in Caribbean Literature.*
London: Oxford Univ. Press, 1962.
Creque-Harris, Leah. "Literature of the Diaspora by Women of
Color." *SAGE* 3.2 (Fall 1986): 61-64.
Crosta, Suzanne. "La réception critique d'Edouard Glissant."
Présence Francophone 30 (1987): 59-79.
Cutler, Maxine G. "Aimé Césaire's 'Barbare': Title, Key Word and
Source of the Text." *Teaching Language through
Literature* 21.2 (Dec. 1981): 3-13.
Damas, L.-G. *Pigments.* Paris: Présence Africaine, 1962.
——. *Névralgies.* Paris: Présence Africaine, 1966.
Damato, Diva Barbaro, L.C. Darin, and L.C. Menezes de Souza.
"The Poetics of the Dispossessed." *World Literature Today*
63.4 (Autumn 1989): 606-08.
Danaho, Raoul-Philippe. "Regards sur la poésie guyanaise." *Lettre
et Cultures de Langue Française* VII 3 (1985): 46-60.
Dash, J. Michael. *Edouard Glissant.* New York: Cambridge Univ.
Press, 1995.
——. Introduction and trans. *Caribbean Discourse. Selected
Essays. By Edouard Glissant.* Charlottesville: UP of
Virginia, 1989.
——. "Le cri du morne: la poétique du paysage césairien et la
littérature antillaise." *Soleil éclaté.* Ed. Jacqueline Leiner.
Tübingen: Narr, 1984. 101-10.
——. "Towards a West Indian Literary Aesthetic: The Example of
Aimé Césaire." *Black Images* 3.1 (1974): 21-28.
——. "The World and the Word: French Caribbean Writing in the
Twentieth Century." *Callaloo* 11.1 (1988): 112-30.
——. "Writing the Body: Edouard Glissant's Poetics of
Re-membering." *World Literature Today* 63.4 (Autumn
1989): 609-12.

Dathorne, O.R. *Dark Ancestor: The Literature of the Black Man in the Caribbean*. Baton Rouge: Louisiana State UP, 1981.

Dayan, Joan. "The Figure of Negation: Some Thoughts on a Landscape by Césaire." *The French Review* 56.3 (Feb. 1983): 411-23.

Davis, Carole Boyce, and Elaine Savory Fido. eds. *Out of the Kumbla: Caribbean Women and Literature*. Trenton, New Jersey: Africa World Press, 1990.

Davis, Gregson. *Non-vicious Circle. Twenty Poems of Aimé Césaire*. Stanford: Stanford UP, 1984.

Degras, Priska, and Bernard Magnier. "Edouard Glissant, préfacier d'une littérature future: Entretien avec Edouard Glissant." *Notre Librairie* 74 (1984): 14-20.

Depestre, René. "Réponse à Aimé Césaire. (Introduction à un art poétique haïtien)." *Présence Africaine* 4 (oct.-nov. 1955): 42-62.

Desportes, G. "Points de vue sur la poésie nationale." *Présence Africaine* 11 n.s. (déc.1956-janv. 1957): 88-99.

Devonish, Hubert. *Language and Liberation: Creole Language Politics in the Caribbean*. London: Karia Press, 1986.

Diop, David. "Suite du débat autour des conditions d'une poésie nationale chez les peuples noirs.Contribution au débat sur la poésie nationale." *Présence Africaine* 6 n.s. (févr.-mars 1956): 113-15.

Du Bois, W.E.B. *The Souls of Black Folk*. New York: Bantam, 1989.

Ducornet, Guy. "Edouard Glissant and the Problem of Time: Prolegomena to a Study of His Poetry." *Black Images* 2.3-4 (Autumn-Winter 1973): 13-16, 46.

Fanon, Frantz. *Peau noire masques blancs*. Paris: Seuil, 1952.

Fayolle, Roger. "Quelle critique africaine?" *Présence Africaine* 123 (1982): 103-10.

Fonseca, Maureen. *Conflict and Conquest in the Poetry of Aimé Césaire: Political Limitations and Poetic Universality.* Diss., Fordham University. 1986. Ann Arbor: University Microfilms International, 1986. 8615724.

Frutkin, Susan. *Aimé Césaire: Black Between Worlds.* Florida: Coral Gables, 1973.

Garrett, Naomi M. *The Renaissance of Haitian Poetry.* Paris: Présence Africaine, 1963.

Gates, Henry Louis Jr., ed. *Black Literature and Literary Theory.* New York: Methuen, 1984.

——, ed. *"Race," Writing, and Difference.* Chicago and London: University of Chicago Press, 1985, 1986.

——. "Canon-formation, Literary History, and The Afro-American Tradition: From the Seen to the Told." In *Afro-American Literary Study in the 1990s.* Ed. Houston A. Baker, Jr. and Patricia Redmond. Chicago and London: U of Chicago P, 1989. 14-50.

Gérard, Albert S. ed. *European-Language Writing in Sub-Saharan Africa.* Budapest: Akadémiai Kiado, 1986.

Gleason, Judith. "An Introduction to the Poetry of Aimé Césaire." *Negro Digest* 19.3: 12-19, 64-65.

Glissant, Edouard. *Le sel noir.* Paris: Seuil, 1960.

——. *L'intention poétique.* Paris: Seuil, 1969.

——. *Le discours antillais.* Paris: Seuil, 1981.

——. *Poétique de la relation.* Paris: Gallimard, 1990.

——. *Caribbean Discourse.* Trans. J. Michael Dash. Charlottesville: UP of Virginia, 1989.

——. "Le chaos-monde, l'oral et l'écrit." In *Ecrire la parole de nuit: La nouvelle littérature antillaise.* Ed. Ralph Ludwig. Paris: Gallimard, 1994. 111-129.

——. "Césaire et la découverte du monde." *Les Lettres Nouvelles* 4.1 (1956): 44-54.

Gratiant, Gilbert. *Credo des sang-mêlé ou Je veux chanter la France.* Fort-de-France: Courrier des Antilles, 1948.

———. "D'une poésie martiniquaise dite nationale." *Présence Africaine* 5 (déc. 1955-janv. 1956): 84-89.

———. *Fab' compè Zicaque.* Fort-de-France: Courrier des Antilles, 1950.

———. *Poèmes en vers faux.* Paris: La Caravelle, 1931.

Guberina, Petar. "Structure de la poésie noire d'expression française." *Présence Africaine* 5 (déc. 1955-janv. 1956): 52-78.

Guyanneau, Christine. "Francophone Women Writers from Sub-Saharan Africa and its Diaspora." *Callaloo* 8.3 (Fall 1985): 612-15.

Hale, Thomas A. "Structural Dynamics in a Third World Classic: Aimé Césaire's Cahier d'un retour au pays natal." *Yale French Studies* 53 (1976): 163-74.

Herdeck, Donald E., ed. *Caribbean Writers: A Bio-Bibliographical-Critical Encyclopedia.* Washington: Three Continents Press, 1979.

Higginbotham, Evelyn Brooks. "African-American Women's History and the Metalanguage of Race." In *Revising the Word and the World: Essays in Feminist Literary Criticism.* Vèvè A. Clark, Ruth-ellen B. Joeres, & Madelon Sprengnether eds. Chicago and London: University of Chicago Press, 1993. 91-114.

Hodge, Merle. "Beyond Négritude: The Love Poems." *Critical Perspectives on Léon-Gontran Damas,* ed. Keith Q. Warner, Washington, D.C.: Three Continents Press, 1988, 119-145.

Hourbette, Patrice. "Propos sur l'Antillanité." *Französische Heute* 18.4 (Dec. 1987): 346-50.

Hurley, E.A. "Commitment and Communication in Césaire's Poetry." *Black Images* 2.1 (1973): 7-12, 43.

———. "In Search of an Attitude." In *Bouquet de voix pour Guy Tirolien.* Eds. Maryse Condé and Alain Rutil. Pointe-A-Pitre: Jasor, 1990. 119-130.

——. "Link and Lance: Aspects of Poetic Function in Césaire's Cadastre -- An Analysis of Five Poems," *L'Esprit Crèateur* 32.1 (Spring 1992a): 54-68.

——. "Pigments: A Dialoque With Self." In *Critical Perspectives on Léon-Gontran Damas.* Ed.Keith Q. Warner. Washington, D.C.: Three Continents Press, 1988. 99-110.

——. "Refusing Conformity: Marie-Magdeleine Carbet's Poetic Choices in Point d'orgue," *Degré Second: Studies in French Literature* 13 (December 1992b): 65-72.

——. "The Temptation of Cliché in the Poetry of Polius." *Black Images* 4.3-4 (1975): 56-63.

——. "A Woman's Voice: Perspectives on Marie-Magdeleine Carbet," *Callaloo* 15.1 (1992c): 90-97.

Irele, Abiola. *The African Experience in Literature and Ideology.* London: Heinemann, 1981.

——, ed. *Aimé Césaire: Cahier d'un retour au pays natal.* Ibadan: New Horn Press, 1994.

Ivask, Ivor., ed. "Edouard Glissant: The New Discourse of the Caribbean." (Entire Issue) *World Literature Today* 63.4 (Autumn 1989).

Izevbaye, D.S. "Shifting Bases: The Present Practice of African Criticism." *Research in African Literatures* 21.1 (Spring 1990): 127-36.

Jackman, Annie. "The Symbolism of 'Woman' in the Poetry of Some French Caribbean Poets." *Bim* 18.72 (Dec. 1989): 14-23.

Jahn, Janheinz. *Neo-African Literature: A History of Black Writing.* Trans. Oliver Coburn and Ursula Lehrburger. New York: Grove Press, 1968.

Jakobson, Roman. *Essais de linguistique générale.* Trans. Nicolas Ruwet. Paris: Minuit, 1963.

——. *Huit questions de poétique.* Paris: Seuil, 1977.

Jean-Louis, [Maître]. "Introduction to a Study on Creole Art and Literature." *La Revue du Monde Noir.* (Oct. 1931): 8 ff.)

Jeanne, Max. "French West Indian Literature." *Présence Africaine* 121-122 (1982): 135-39.

Jeyifo, Biodun. "The Nature of Things: Arrested Decolonization and Critical Theory, " *Research in African Literatures* 21.1 (Spring 1990): 33-48.

Jiménez, Marilyn. "The Hesitations of Theory: Edouard Glissant's Theory of 'La Relation'." *Critical Exchange* 21 (Spring 1986): 109-13.

Jobin, Bruno. "Cadastre, lecture transcendante." *Etudes littéraires* 6 (1973): 74-80.

Jones, Edward A. "Aimé Césaire, Bard of Martinique." *French Review* 22.6 (May 1949): 443-47.

Joubert, Jean-Louis. "Aimé Césaire et la poétique du mot." *Soleil éclaté.* Ed. Jacqueline Leiner. Tubingen: Narr, 1984. 239-48.

Joyau, Auguste. *Panorama de la littérature à la Martinique: XIXe siècle.* Fort-de-France: Horizons Caraïbes, 1977.

Juin, Hubert. *Aimé Césaire. Poète noir.* Préface de Claude Roy. Paris: Présence Africaine, 1956.

Kennedy, Ellen Conroy. *The Negritude Poets.* New York: Thunder Mouth Press, 1975.

Kesteloot, Lilyan. *Aimé Césaire.* Paris: Séghers, 1962.

——. *Anthologie négro-africaine: panorama critique des prosateurs, poètes et dramaturges noirs du XXe siècle.* Belgique: Marabout, 1987.

——. *Les écrivains noirs de langue française. Naissance d'une littérature.* Bruxelles: Université Libre de Bruxelles, 1963.

——. "Première lecture d'un poème de Césaire, 'Batouque'." *Etudes littéraires* 6.1 (1973): 49-71.

Kesteloot, Lilyan, and Barthélemy Kotchy. *L Aimé Césaire'Homme et l'Œuvre.* Paris: Présence Africaine, 1973.

Kimoni, Iyay. *Destin de la littérature négro-africaine ou problématique d'une culture.* Kinshasa: Presses Universitaires du Zaïre, Ottawa: Editions Naaman, 1975.

Kristeva, Julia. *La révolution du langage poétique*. Paris: Seuil, 1974.

Kubayanda, Josaphat B. *The Poet's Africa: Africanness in the Poetry of Nicolás Guillén and Aimé Césaire*. Westport, Conn.: Greenwood, 1990.

Lecuyer, Maurice A. "Rythme, révolte et rhétorique, ou Aimer Césaire." *Rice University Studies* 63.1 (1977): 87-111.

Leiner, Jacqueline. "Césaire et les problèmes du langage chez un écrivain francophone." *L'Esprit Créateur* 17.2 (Summer 1977): 133-42.

———. "Etude comparative des structures de l'imaginaire d'Aimé Césaire et de Léopold Sédar Senghor." *Cahiers de l'Association internationale des études françaises* 30 (mai 1978): 209-24.

———. *Imaginaire - Langage. Identité culturelle - Négritude: Afrique-France-Guyane-Haïti-Maghreb-Martinique*. Tübingen: Narr, 1980.

———, ed. *Soleil éclaté*. Tübingen: Narr, 1984.

———, ed. *Aimé Césaire ou l'athanor d'un alchimiste*. Paris: Editions Caribéennes, 1987.

Levilain, Guy Viet. "The Francophone Antilles and the Caribbean Struggle for Liberation." *Process of Unity in Caribbean Society: Ideologies and Literature*. Ed. and intro. Ileana Rodriguez, Marc Zimmerman, and Lisa Davis. Minneapolis: Inst. for Study of Ideologies and Literature, 1983. 157-68.

Lirus, Julie. *Identité antillaise*. Paris: Editions Caribéennes, 1979.

Ludwig, Ralph, ed. *Ecrire la parole de nuit: La nouvelle littérature antillaise*. Paris: Gallimard, 1994. Maran, René. Batouala. Paris: Albin Michel, 1921.

———. "Préface." *Batouala*. Paris: Albin Michel, 1938.

Marteau, Pierre. "A propos de Cadastre d'Aimé Césaire." *Présence Africaine* 37 (2ème trimestre 1961): 125-35.

———. "La mort de l'impossible et le mot du printemps." *Présence Africaine* 30 (février-mars 1960): 82-95.

Maugée, Aristide. "Aimé Césaire poète." *Tropiques* 5 (avril 1942): 13-20.

———. "Poésie et obscurité." *Tropiques* 2 (juillet 1941): 7-12.

Mbom, Clément. "Aimé Césaire, poète du renouveau nègre." *Mélanges Africains.* Yaoundé: Editions Pédagogiques Afrique-Contact, 1973.

Ménil, René. "Laissez passer la poésie." *Tropiques* 5 (avril 1942): 21-28.

———. "Naissance de notre art." *Tropiques* 1 (avril 1941): 54-64.

———. "Orientation de la poésie." *Tropiques* 2 (juillet 1941): 13-21.

Mouralis, Bernard. "Césaire et la poésie française." *Revue des sciences humaines* 176.3 (1979): 125-52.

Nadeau, Maurice. "Aimé Césaire Surréaliste." *La Revue internationale* 10 (nov. 1946): 289-94.

Nantet, Jacques. *Panorama de la littérature noire d'expression française.* Paris: Fayard, 1972.

Nardal, Jeanne. "Ce que nous voulons faire." *La Revue du Monde Noir*, April 6 1932: i.

Nardal, Paulette. "Eveil de la Conscience de Race/Awakening of Race Consciousness." *La Revue du Monde Noir* 6 (Avril 1932): 25-31.

Nenekhaly-Camara, Condotto. "Conscience nationale et poésie négro-africaine d'expression française." *La Pensée* 103 (mai-juin 1962): 7-17.

Ngal, Georges. "L'image et l'enracinement chez Aimé Césaire." *Présence Francophone* 6 (1973): 5-28.

Ngal, M. a M. *Aimé Césaire: un homme à la recherche d'une patrie.* Dakar: Les Nouvelles Editions Africaines, 1975.

Ngaté, Jonathan. "'Mauvais Sang' de Rimbaud et Cahier d'un retour au pays natal de Césaire: la poésie au service de la révolution." *Cahiers césairiens* 3 (Spring 1977): 25-32.

N'Goala, Aline. "Moi,laminaire, cette halte sur une route de soif tenace." *Présence Africaine* 126 (1983): 27-33.

Ntonfo, André. "Jalons pour une autonomie de la littérature antillaise." *Présence Francophone* 22 (Spring 1981) 141-56.

Okam, Hilary. "Aspects of Imagery and Symbolism in the Poetry of Aimé Césaire." *Yale French Studies* 53 (1976): 175-96.

Ormond, Jacqueline. "Héros de l'impossible et de l'absolu." *Les Temps Modernes* 23.259 (déc.1967): 1049-73.

Padoly, Yves. *Poèmes pour adultes*. Paris: La Pensée universelle, 1971.

———. *L'art d'emmerder (et autres pièces optimistes de jeunesse*. Fort-de-France: Désormeaux, 1994.

Patri, Aimé. "Deux poètes noirs de langue française: A. Césaire et L.S. Senghor." *Présence Africaine* 3 (1er trimestre, 1948): 378-87.

Pigeon, Gérard Georges. "Le rôle des termes médicaux, du bestiaire et de la flore dans l'imagerie césairienne." *Cahiers Césairiens* 3 (Spring 1977): 7-24.

Pizarro, Ana. "Reflections on the Historiography of Caribbean Literature." *Callaloo* 11.1(1988): 173-85.

Prudent, Lambert Félix. "L'émergence d'une littérature créole aux Antilles et en Guyane." *Présence Africaine* 121-122 (1982): 109-29.

Racine, Daniel. "The Antilleanity of Edouard Glissant." *World Literature Today* 63.4 (Autumn 1989): 620-25.

———. "Léon Gontran Damas and Africa." *Critical Perspectives on Léon-Gontran Damas*. Ed. Keith Warner. Washington, D.C.: Three Continents Press, 1988. 49-62.

Ramraj, Victor J. "The West Indies." *Journal of Commonwealth Literature* 21.2 (1986): 137-47.

Rancourt, Jacques. *Poètes et poèmes. Approches de la poésie de langue française en Afrique noire, île Maurice, Antilles frінçaises et Haïti depuis 1950*. Paris: ACCT/Eds. Saint-Germain-des-Prés, 1981.

Robinson, Ella. "Myth and Regeneration in Aimé Césaire's Poetry." *Journal of Black Studies* 18.2 (December 1987): 162-69.

Rodriguez, Ileana. "The Literature of the Caribbean: Initial Perspectives." *Process of Unity in Caribbean Society: Ideologies and Literature.* Eds. Rodriguez, and Marc Zimmerman. Minneapolis: Inst. for the Study of Ideologies and Literature, 1983.

Rodriguez, Ileana, and Marc Zimmerman. eds. *Process of Unity in Caribbean Society: Ideologies and Literature.* Minneapolis: Inst. for the Study of Ideologies and Literature, 1983.

Roget, Wilbert J. *Edouard Glissant and "Antillanité".* Diss. Pittsburg University. 1975. Ann Arbor: University Microfilms International, 1975. 7600369.

——. "The Image of Africa in the Writings of Edouard Glissant." *CLA Journal* 21.3 (March 1978): 390-99.

——. "Land and Myth in the Writings of Edouard Glissant." *World Literature Today* 63.4 (Autumn 1989): 626-31.

——. "Littérature, conscience nationale, écriture aux Antilles: Entretien avec Edouard Glissant." *CLA Journal* 24.3 (March 1981): 304-20.

Rosello, Mireille. *Littérature et identité aux Antilles.* Paris: Karthala, 1992.

Rouch, A., and G. Clavreuil. *Littératures nationales d'écriture française: Afrique noire, Caraïbes, Océan Indien. Histoire littéraire et Anthologie.* Paris: Bordas, 1987.

Rowell, Charles H. "C'est par le poème que nous affrontons la solitude: Une interview avec Aimé Césaire." *Callaloo* 12.1 (Winter 1989): 48-67.

Roy, Claude. Préface. *Aimé Césaire. Poète noir.* By Hubert Juin. Paris: Présence Africaine, 1956.

Royer, Jean. "À la découverte de l'antillanité." *Ecrivains contemporains* 3. Québec: L'Hexagone, 1985. 95-104.

Sartre, Jean-Paul. "Orphée noir." Preface. *Anthologie de la nouvelle poésie nègre et malgache de langue française.* By L.S. Senghor. Paris: Presses Universitaires de France, 1948.

Sautreau, Serge, and André Velter. "Aimé Césaire: à l'échancrure du poème." *Les Temps Modernes* 231 (août 1965): 367-70.

Scarboro, Ann Armstrong. "Aimé Césaire, René Depestre and Jocelyn Valverde: Three Generations of Caribbean Salt Thieves." *Concerning Poetry* 17.2 (Fall 1984): 121-34.

Scharfman, Ronnie Leah. *"Engagement" and the Language of the Subject in the Poetry of Aimé Césaire.* Gainesville: University of Florida Press, 1980.

———. "'Corps Perdu' Moi-nègre retrouvé." *Soleil éclaté.* ed. Jacqueline Leiner. Tübingen: Narr, 1984. 375-87.

———. "Repetition and Absence: The Discourse of Deracination in Aimé Césaire's 'Nocturne d'une nostalgie'." *The French Review* 56.4 (1983): 572-578.

Sellin, Eric. "Aimé Césaire and the legacy of Surrealism." *Kentucky Foreign Language Quarterly* 13 (1968, Supplement for 1967): 71-79.

———. "Negritude: Status or Dynamics?" *L'Esprit Créateur* 10.3 (Fall 1970): 163-81.

———. "Soleil cou coupé." *Romance Notes* 14.1 (Autumn 1972): 13-16.

Senghor, L.S. *Anthologie de la nouvelle poésie nègre et malgache de langue française.* Paris: PUF, 1948.

———. "Suite du débat autour des conditions d'une poésie nationale chez les peuples noirs. Réponse." *Présence Africaine* 5 n.s. (déc. 1955-janv. 1956): 79-83.

Sieger, Jacqueline. "Entretien avec Aimé Césaire." *Afrique* 5 (October 1961): 64-67.

Smith, Valerie. "Black Feminist Theory and the Representation of the 'Other'." In *Changing Our Own Words. Essays on Criticism, Theory, and Writing by Black Women.* Ed. Cheryl A. Wall. New Brunswick, NJ: Rutgers University Press, 1989. 38-57.

Snyder, Emile. "The Problem of Negritude in Modern French Poetry." *Comparative Literature Studies* (Special Advance Number, 1963): 101-14.

———. "A Reading of Aimé Césaire's Return to My Native Land." *L'Esprit Créateur* 10.3 (Fall 1970): 197-212.

Songolo, Aliko. *Aimé Césaire: une poétique de la découverte.* Paris: L'Harmattan, 1985.

———. "Cadastre et Ferrements de Césaire: une nouvelle poétique pour une nouvelle politique." *L'Esprit Créateur* 17.2 (1977): 143-58.

———. "Surrealism and Black Literatures in French." *French Review* 50.6 (1982): 724-32.

Spackey, G.M. "Surrealism and Negritude in Césaire's Return to My Native Land." *East African Journal of Literature and Society* 1.2 (1973): 45-63.

Spivak, Gayatri Chakravorty. In *Other Words: Essays in Cultural Politics.* New York: Routledge, 1988.

Steins, Martin. "Black Migrants in Paris." In *European-Language Writing in Sub- Saharan Africa.* Ed. Albert S. Gérard. Budapest: Akadémia Kiado, 1986. I: 374-75.

Tétu, Michel. ed. Léon Gontran Damas: *Actes du colloque Léon-Gontran Damas, Paris, décembre 1988.* Paris: ACCT/Présence Africaine, 1989.

Tirolien, Guy. *Feuilles vivantes au matin.* Paris: Présence Africaine, 1977.

Toumson, Roger. *La transgression des couleurs. Littérature et langage des Antilles XVIIIe, XIXe, XXe siècles.* Paris: Editions Caribéennes, 1989.

———. "Les écrivains afro-antillais et la réécriture." *Europe* 58.612 (April 1980): 115-27.

———. "La littérature antillaise d'expression française: problèmes et perspectives." *Présence Africaine* 121-122 (1982): 130-34.

———. "The Question of Identity in Caribbean Literature." *Journal of Caribbean Studies* 5.3 (Fall 1986): 131-44.

Towa, Marcien. "Aimé Césaire, prophète de la révolution des peuples noirs." *Abbia* 21 (1969): 49-57.

———. "Les pur-sang (Négritude césairienne et Surréalisme)." *Abbia* 23 (1969): 71-82.

Vaillant, Janet G. *Black, French, and African: A Life of Léopold Sédar Senghor.* Cambridge, Mass.: Harvard UP, 1990.

Wade, Amadou Moustapha. "Débat autour des conditions d'une poésie nationale chez les peuples noirs: Autour d'une poésie nationale." *Présence Africaine* 11 n.s. (déc. 1956-janv. 1957): 84-87.

Walker, Keith Louis. *La cohésion poétique de l'œuvre césairienne.* Tübingen: Narr, 1979.

———. "Le rire chez Damas." In *Léon Gontran Damas: Actes du colloque Léon-Gontran Damas, Paris, décembre 1988.* Ed. Michel Tétu. Paris: ACCT/Présence Africaine, 1989. 142-51.

Wall, Cheryl W., ed. *Changing Our Own Words: Essays on Criticism, Theory, and Writing by Black Women.* New Brunswick, NJ: Rutgers UP, 1989.

Wanjala, Chris L. "Césaire's Responsibilities as a Poet." *Thought and Practice* 1.1 (1974): 59-72.

Warner, Keith Q., ed. *Critical Perspectives on Léon-Gontran Damas.* Washington, D.C.:Three Continents Press, 1988a.

———. "New Perspectives on Léon-Gontran Damas." In *Critical Perspectives on Léon-Gontran Damas,* ed. Keith Q. Warner. Washington, D.C.:Three Continents Press, 1988b: 87-98.

Winter, Sylvia. "Beyond the Word of Man: Glissant and the New Discourse of the Antilles." *World Literature Today* 63.4 (Autumn 1989): 637-47.

Zimmerman, Marc. "The Unity of the Caribbean and its Literatures." *Process of Unity in Caribbean Society: Ideologies and Literature.* Eds. Ileana Rodriguez and Zimmerman. Minneapolis: Institute for the Study of Ideologies and Literatures, 1983. 28-56.

Zimra, Clarisse. "Negritude in the Feminine Mode." *Journal of Ethnic Studies* 12.1 (Spring 1984): 53-77.

———. "Patterns of Liberation in Contemporary Women Writers." *L'Esprit Créateur* 17.2 (Summer 1977): 103-14.

Index